EMPIRE'S

# Empire's Law

## The American Imperial Project and the 'War to Remake the World'

Edited by

AMY BARTHOLOMEW

Pluto Press
LONDON • ANN ARBOR, MI
and
Between the Lines
TORONTO

First published 2006 by Pluto Press
345 Archway Road, London N6 5AA
and 839 Greene Street, Ann Arbor, MI 48106
www.plutobooks.com

and

Between the Lines
720 Bathurst Street, Suite 404, Toronto, Ontario M5S 2R4, Canada
www.btlbooks.com

British Library Cataloguing in Publication Data
A catalogue record for this book is available from the British Library

ISBN 0–7453–2370–7 hardback
ISBN 0–7453–2369–3 paperback
ISBN 1–897071–09–4 paperback (Between the Lines)

Library of Congress Cataloging in Publication Data applied for

Library and Archives Canada Cataloguing in Publication
    Empire's law : the American imperial project and the 'war to remake the world' /
Amy Bartholomew, editor.
    Includes bibliographical references and index.
    ISBN 1–897071–09–4
    1. United States—Foreign relations—21st century. 2. United States—History,
Military—21st century. 3. Iraq War, 2003–. 4. United Nations—History—
21st century. 5. International law.
    I. Bartholomew, Amy, 1955–.

JZ1480.E46 2006    327.73'009'0511              C2005-906591-5

Between the Lines gratefully acknowledges support for our publishing programme from
the Canada Council for the Arts, the Ontario Arts Council, the Government of Ontario
through the Ontario Book Publishers Tax Credit program and through the Ontario Book
Initiative, and the Government of Canada.

10 9 8 7 6 5 4 3  2 1

Designed and produced for Pluto Press by
Chase Publishing Services, Fortescue, Sidmouth, EX10 9QG, England
Typeset from disk by Newgen Imaging System (P) Ltd, Chennai, India
Printed and bound in Canada by Transcontinental Printing

*To my mother, Gerry Bartholomew.*
*And, to those who resist empire's law.*

# Contents

# Acknowledgements

In addition to the authors in this volume, I wish to thank all of the participants in the Anti-War Roundtables held at Carleton University, Ottawa, Canada, in the winter and spring of 2002–03. I also want to thank the organizers of, and participants in, the World Tribunal on Iraq (WTI), the most serious political interrogation of empire's law I have witnessed. The WTI included hearings across the world with a culminating session in Istanbul, in June 2005. Those involved in the BRussells Tribunal (intentionally spelled with a capital 'R' and an extra 'l' to make the connection to the Russell Tribunal on the Vietnam war of the 1960s), whose hearings were held April 2004 in Brussels, have been particularly important to me, especially Dirk Adriaensens, Samir Amin, Abduhl Ilah Al Bayaty, Hana Al Bayaty, Jean Bricmont, Lieven De Cauter, François Houtart and Haifa Zangana. I must also thank two former international civil servants who have repeatedly displayed the courage of their convictions and who have allowed me to publish the important testimony they gave at the Istanbul session of the WTI: Denis Halliday and Hans von Sponeck. Special thanks must go to Leo Panitch, Trevor Purvis and Peter Swan, with whom I have discussed these issues, and especially to Leo who also acted as editor for my chapter. Peter Fitzpatrick, Sundhya Pahuja and Costas Douzinas welcomed me to their excellent workshop on Imperialism and International Law at Birkbeck College School of Law, University of London, in May 2004. Thanks to them and to the participants there, who showed the liveliest intellectual interest in the subject that one could hope for. Thanks also to Dianne George, my colleague in the Department of Law and to my students for making life there interesting. The latter include the following graduate students with whom I have been lucky to work over the past few years: Jennifer Breakspear, Susan Brophy, Christina Doonan, Karen Lu, Kalapi Roy, Philip Steiner, Steve Tasson and Kevin Young. Special thanks must go to Chris Whitehead, another graduate student in Legal Studies at Carleton University and my research assistant for this volume, for his excellent research assistance. Thanks as well to my friend of many years, a progressive lawyer (and novelist) who fights the tentacles of empire's law in Canadian immigration matters, Ron Poulton. Finally, thanks to the editors at Pluto as well as to the anonymous reviewers of the original proposal and to the journal *Constellations* and Blackwell Publishing for permission to publish the following articles: Jürgen Habermas, 'Interpreting the Fall of a Monument', *Constellations* 10:3 (2003): 364–70; and Ulrich K. Preuss, 'The Iraq War: Critical Reflections from "Old Europe"', *Constellations* 10:3 (2003): 339–51.

This book is dedicated to my mother, Gerry Bartholomew. Living all of her life in Ohio, in the heart of the beast, she may not resist American Empire (quite to the contrary), but her care and respect for me has enabled me to do so. That is a mother's love and I love her for it very much. It is also dedicated to those who resist empire's law, including lawyers and legal groups, among whom must be counted in the first rank the Center for Constitutional Rights in New York, the American Civil Liberties Union, Lawyers Against the War, Peacerights and Public Interest Lawyers, and independent journalists like Robert Fisk, Seymour Hersh and Dahr Jamail.

# Introduction

*Amy Bartholomew*

On 27 June 2005 the Jury of Conscience presiding at the culminating session of the World Tribunal on Iraq, held in Istanbul, issued its Preliminary Declaration on the invasion and occupation of Iraq by the United States and its greatly diminished 'coalition of the willing'. It established that the invasion was an illegal war of aggression and that the occupation itself was also illegal, while both have been (and are) devastating to human security and the very fabric of Iraqi society. Importantly, it also found against the UN Security Council for, among other things, failing to intervene against the illegal war and against the war crimes and crimes against humanity committed by the US and for 'allowing the United States to dominate the United Nations'. It also ruled against the 'coalition of the willing' and other supporting governments, private corporations and the corporate media for complicity in their respective roles in this 'war to remake the world'.[1] Perhaps most tellingly, it declared:

> In pursuit of their agenda of empire, the Bush and Blair [Administrations] blatantly ignored the massive opposition to the war expressed by millions of people around the world. They embarked upon one of the most unjust, immoral, and cowardly wars in history.[2]

This indictment of the United States, its 'coalition of the willing' and its allies in the global 'war on terror' – both state and 'private' allies – publicizes the role the US is now playing in the world with the imbrication of the Bush Doctrine in American foreign policy. This may be contrasted in some important respects with the position it adopted in the immediate post-World War II era.

The United States has long played a pre-eminent role in the spread of legal forms across the world, nationally, internationally and globally. One means of its spread has been through the emulation of American legal forms, ranging from its esteemed constitution and civil rights cases to its private law, forms now widely practised in both common and civil law countries. Since World War II, the dominant stature of the US has also been reflected in its key role in the Nuremberg Tribunal, the language and content of the Universal Declaration of Human Rights, the structure of the United Nations and institutions like the World Bank, as well as many other international initiatives. In fact, the US was initially behind the innovations found in the International Criminal Court, the Landmines Treaty and the Kyoto Protocol. And, of course, it was the predominant actor in the constitutionalization projects of postwar Germany and Japan. It also influenced the development of legal structures and legal culture through its funding agencies, such as USAID, and its participation in legal reform movements, with private organizations, like the American Bar Association, taking a leading role in legal reform projects throughout the world. So much has this been the case that we can speak of the global expansion of 'law's empire', to adopt Ronald Dworkin's felicitous phrase[3] for another context, as largely having taken place under American example, leadership, direction, tutelage and domination. In the international context, the idea of 'law's empire' gains even more relevance when one traces it back to the Martens Clause in international humanitarian law (originally drafted by a delegate to the Hague conferences of 1898 and 1907), which states that

> [u]ntil a more complete code of the laws of war is issued, the high contracting Parties think it right to declare that in cases not included in the Regulations adopted by them, populations and belligerents remain under the protection and empire of the principles of international law.[4]

It is important to recognize that the spread of an international law's empire has long been under the imprimatur of American power and self-interest, as is evidenced by the leading role the US played in creating the United Nations and the lasting impact this has had on its flawed structures and capacities. Still, if we appreciate the idea of law's empire as spreading an empire of law that is, at least in principle, internally legitimate in terms of its principle of impartiality, and not an empire 'of men', the Bush Doctrine and its violent expression in the war against Iraq bring into sharp relief the extent to which efforts that are currently under way aim to transform law's empire into another kind of project – one that is far more menacing: the project of 'empire's law'. If one demands a further element of legitimacy for law, democratic legitimacy, one can see that the Bush

Doctrine also attacks the limited but principled commitment of international legality to equal sovereignty, a commitment that reigned, in principle, in the post-World War II era.

With the end of the Cold War and the absolute rise of the US as the sole superpower, the deepening and extension of law's empire internationally has been thrown radically into question. NATO's intervention in Kosovo marked a significant shift in global politics, making human rights protection the object of military humanism threatening to ride roughshod over the principle of the sovereign equality of states. The legitimacy of that intervention has been deeply contested, spawning a legacy of reflections on the legality and legitimacy of 'humanitarian intervention'. But, as Fuyuki Kurasawa argues in his chapter in this volume, so too has the *failure* to intervene branded this period with painful moral and legal dilemmas. The US's most recent war against Iraq and the associated Bush Doctrine raise related issues, but even more clearly reveal the nature of the American imperial project. Here, human rights have been instrumentalized as a justification for war, as they were as well at least on some accounts in Kosovo, but now they are more closely associated with the discourses and practices of 'security' and 'regime change' while international law's prohibitions on the unilateral use of force have been rejected in favour of unilaterally declared and pursued preventive war to secure the American 'homeland' and to achieve an even broader reach of American power in the world. Presented for public consumption as securing the conditions for human rights, freedom and democracy, both at home and abroad, these very values have instead been put at egregious risk across the globe, along with the legal institutions with which they are associated, by the global 'war on terror' in general, and the war against Iraq in particular.

Functioning as an informal empire, as Leo Panitch and Sam Gindin argue in their chapter, which opens this volume, is not particularly new for the US. It is not a merely conjunctural feature of the world post-September 11. In fact, to understand what is at stake in the post-September 11 era, we require a serious theorization of American Empire which traces its conditions of possibility and its historical path and locates it within a theory of the 'internationalization of the state' and an analysis of the *American* state functioning as global capitalism's missing 'global state', as Panitch and Gindin provide. While American Empire is characterized by the penetration and incorporation of other capitalist states within its embrace, it also undertakes the 'imperial policing' of and military interventions in so-called 'rogue' and 'problem' states which have not yet been sufficiently incorporated into neoliberal global capitalism. Panitch and Gindin argue that this role of American Empire, which claims a '"sovereign" right to reject international rules and norms when necessary', is what marks it *as* imperialist. But September 11, the rise of the Bush Doctrine and the 'preventive' and 'humanitarian' war on and 'for' Iraq, located within the broader context of the global 'war on terror', mark something new in the annals of American Empire: it marks the threatening rise of empire's law. What that something new is appears, in fact, to be best captured by the explicit proclamation of empire's law, with all that implies when this proclamation comes not at the end of the nineteenth century but at the beginning of the twenty-first.

Perhaps the most succinct description of the Bush Doctrine was provided by Jonathan Schell, whose description is worth quoting at length:

> Its aim, which many have properly called imperial, is to establish lasting American *hegemony* over the entire globe, and its ultimate means is to overthrow regimes of which the United States disapproves, *pre-emptively* if necessary. The Bush Doctrine indeed represents more than a revolution in American policy; if successful, it would amount to an overturn of the existing international order. In the new, imperial order, the *United States would be first among nations*, and *force would be first among its means of domination*. Other, weaker nations would be invited to take their place in shifting coalitions to support goals of America's choosing. The United States would be so strong, the President has suggested, that other countries would simply drop out of the business of military competition, 'thereby making the destabilizing arms races of other eras pointless, and limiting rivalries to trade and other pursuits of peace.' Much as in the early modern period, when nation-states were being born, absolutist kings, the masters of overwhelming military force within their countries, in effect said, 'There is now a new thing called a nation; a nation must be orderly; we kings, we sovereigns, will assert a monopoly over the use of force, and thus supply that order,' so now the United States seemed to be saying, 'here now is a thing called globalization; the global sphere must be orderly; we, the sole superpower, will monopolize force throughout the globe, and thus supply international order.'[5]

The progeny of the Bush Doctrine has included the global 'war on terror', which strikes both externally and internally, with an imperial president who, heading the international state, relies on his 'commander-in-chief' powers to 'rule by executive fiat', claiming 'the unilateral authority to arrest virtually anyone ... if he deemed them an enemy combatant'.[6] It also includes the illegal war against Iraq, 'shock and awe', as the initial assault on Baghdad was called, as well as widespread, sustained, insistent reports of torture and imprisonment without trial. One report maintains 17,000 'security detainees' – persons detained without trial – in Iraq in spring 2005,[7] while another claims 70,000 detainees held by the US outside of its territory.[8] Imperial policing includes the proliferation of 'ghost prisoners', 'extraordinary renditions'[9] and a world-wide system of incarceration developed by the US, which has been described by Amnesty International as an 'archipelago of prisons' around the world.[10] In this context too, torture is not just practised now by the imperial state and its subordinates, *but is parsed and virtually justified* by the Bush Administration and many of its allies in the global 'war on terror', thus threatening to move torture from the despicable, sub-terranean, illegal action to which a state responding to crises might illegitimately resort, to one that has legal standing with terrible implications for the rule of law not to mention human rights.[11]

This is also an era in which the increasingly widespread judgment that the 'coalition' attack on Fallujah in November 2004 represents the twenty-first century's (first) Guernica, an act of collective punishment involving 'remorseless bombing and bombardment', in which 'large swathes of Fallujah have been literally pulverised, ground to powder by the kind of destructive machine that Hermann Goering could hardly imagine'.[12] The use of incendiary weapons, which amount to modern forms of napalm[13] by the 'coalition of the willing', in addition to the deployment of other indiscriminate weapons, like depleted uranium and cluster bombs, which target civilians and those who resist an invasion and occupation in the interest of self-determination just as surely as they do 'terrorists', must also be taken into account.[14] Furthermore, this 'coalition' attacks hospitals and medical personnel.[15] All of these are glaring violations of international humanitarian law to accompany the violation of international law extant in a war of aggression that the Nuremberg Tribunal called the 'supreme international crime'. This raises the question (and provides the answer to): Who is the pre-eminent 'problem' and 'rogue state' according to the US's own definition?

And yet it is not for reasons like these that Michael Ledeen, holder of the 'Freedom Chair' at the American Enterprise Institute and a prominent neo-conservative close to the Bush Administration, called the Iraq war an 'epochal war' which may turn out to be the 'war to remake the world'.[16] He is, after all, also credited with saying: 'Every ten years or so, the United States needs to pick up some small crappy little country and throw it against the wall, just to show the world we mean business.'[17] What Ledeen meant when he said, in 2003, that this may be a 'war to remake the world' is that the US might be 'obliged' to start a 'regional war' in the Middle East in order to 'dominate evil'.[18] And this it certainly might still attempt to do, obliged to or not, as more recent incarnations of the Bush Doctrine suggest with its stated commitment to 'end tyranny' and 'spread freedom'. But what is more properly the hallmark of the war against Iraq as a 'war to remake the world' is the degree to which it and the Bush Doctrine, its global 'war on terror' and fight against 'tyranny', all threaten and enact draconian domination and violence on those it seeks to 'police' – and this includes nearly all of humanity. The self-evident violations of both domestic law and anything that could be considered an 'international rule of law', as Trevor Purvis argues in his chapter in this volume, are what is truly remarkable about this 'war to remake the world'. This is not just about lawlessness. This war is not just another evasion of legality; it is not just another attempt to get one's way internationally. All of that we have seen often enough in the past. Nor is it just another 'intervention' – humanitarian or otherwise. Rather, the Bush Doctrine, brought to fruition with the illegal war against Iraq, represents a fundamental departure from, and a series of attempts to reconstitute, the norms that were accepted, at least formally, during the reign of law's empire.

What Jonathan Schell does not emphasize enough in his otherwise excellent description of the Bush Doctrine is that at its doctrinal heart lies what Jürgen Habermas calls in his chapter in this volume the 'revolutionary' challenge to the project of international law. Habermas maintains that 'the neo-conservatives make a revolutionary claim: if the regime of international law fails, then the hegemonic imposition of a global liberal order is justified, even by means that are hostile to international law'. Drawing on his analysis of the contribution that the legal medium makes to the regulation of social relations, global as much as domestic, Habermas argues that 'egalitarian universalism' requires the protection and further development of that legal medium. Ulrich K. Preuss similarly conceives of this as an 'international constitutional moment' in which the American Empire is attempting to establish a new world order based on 'absolute security', thereby fundamentally challenging the international legal order. The Bush Doctrine is, according to Preuss's analysis, an attempt to establish an order 'whose law is not yet visible'. That this may be a turning point in international politics *and* legal relations is made clear, as well, in the normally staid *American Journal of International Law* where, in the introduction to its 'Agora: Future Implications of the Iraq Conflict', the editors note: 'The military action against Iraq in spring 2003 is one of the few events of the UN Charter period holding the potential for fundamental transformation, or possibly even destruction.'[19]

Current challenges by the American imperium – as it polices and attempts to refashion the world in accordance with its conception of the requirements of global capitalism – to fundamental commitments of (liberal) legality, human rights and the rule of law range from attacks on and subversions of such ancient legal principles as *habeas corpus* to the principle of innocent until proved guilty, as well as challenges to the *jus cogens* norms against the unilateral use of force and torture – norms that have long been flouted in practice, of course, by many states. All of this is wedded to the doctrine of preventive war, again explicitly justified by the Bush Administration, a doctrine that marks a fundamental break, in principle, with the international system of governance that has reigned since World War II with its explicit prohibition on war. And this marks a potential shift in the US's relations of rule internally and externally such that now it justifies extraordinary, exceptional measures as a *right of Empire*, measures that are denied to others, thereby evincing a fundamental repudiation of the underlying commitment to equality of parties within legitimate law.

So much is this the case that Amnesty International, a normally circumspect liberal human rights organization often criticized by the Left for its failure to confront the US, has taken the US to task for its apparent breaches of the Geneva Conventions, calling for investigations into the possibility of prosecuting leading officials of the Bush Administration for war crimes, and calling the prison at Guantánamo Bay 'the gulag of our time'. Amnesty has this to say about American Empire:

> The USA, as the unrivalled political, military and economic hyper-power, sets the tone for governmental behaviour worldwide. When the most powerful country in the world thumbs its nose at the rule of law and human

rights, it grants a license to others to commit abuse with impunity and audacity. From Israel to Uzbekistan, Egypt to Nepal, governments have openly defied human rights and international humanitarian law in the name of national security and 'counter-terrorism'.[20]

While such example-setting is relevant, Amnesty's criticism of the US for its failure to act as a 'benevolent hegemon' thereby licensing the misdeeds of others, misses some of the real import of American Empire. The emphasis on the US as a recalcitrant 'leader', or a dissolute father who has now gone significantly to pot, one that threatens to provide a poor example for others thus loosening the reins on their own brutal temptations, misses much that is now at stake. It fails to recognize that the threats we face are not just, nor even primarily, the threat of the US *repudiating* its role as a 'benevolent hegemon' (as Habermas has called it) thus giving others scope to act badly too – a contagion conception of global rule. Rather, the significance of American Empire, as Panitch and Gindin show, is how it rules through other states, directing, demanding, threatening, cajoling and bribing them to participate as junior partners in the global 'war on terror', thus spreading its paranoid style of politics[21] much more forcefully than even Amnesty seems to recognize. From the UK, as junior partner in the American Empire post-9/11, to Pakistan, as an important acolyte valuable only in so far as it carries out the Bush Administration's demands, the US does indeed rule through other states and polices 'the Gap' through the constitution of a world-wide system of imperial policing of, and military intervention in, states which have not (yet) 'been incorporated into the neoliberal capitalist order'. It is this, rather than poor example-setting, that is the primary meaning, and the primary threat, of American Empire.

The extraordinarily important testimonies delivered at the Istanbul session of the World Tribunal on Iraq by Hans von Sponeck and Denis Halliday open the second part of this volume. Their testimonies address the relationship between American power and the United Nations and the failures of the Security Council, the General Assembly and the UN civil service itself to demand that the illegal invasion and occupation of Iraq cease or to hold the US accountable in any way. Both Halliday and Sponeck were long-term, high-level international civil servants in the United Nations. Both held the post of Assistant Secretary General of the UN and each served as UN Humanitarian Coordinator for Iraq as well as head of the oil-for-food programme. Most remarkably, first Denis Halliday and then

Hans von Sponeck resigned from the United Nations, publicly denouncing the crimes that the UN, under pressure from the US, engaged in through policies like the genocidal sanctions programme imposed on Iraq after the first Gulf War. Not only do Halliday's and Sponeck's testimonies movingly address the crumbling edifice of law's empire at the hands not only of the US (and UK) but also through the United Nations, but their actions display the continuing relevance of exercising conscience in the face of empire. They give hope to those of us who are sometimes dispirited by its power.

Chapters in this volume by Doris Buss, Trevor Purvis, Peter Swan and Amy Bartholomew all seek to extend these reflections by focusing on the challenges that American Empire, the Bush Doctrine and the invasion of Iraq pose for international law, the emergent global legal order of the post-World War II era, human rights and international relations in the age of empire's law.

Doris Buss examines one type of response to the challenge posed by 9/11: that by international law scholars writing in the prestigious *American Journal of International Law* who, in large part, view the challenge as one of strengthening and expanding international law's avenues for the legal use of force, arguing for a new, more 'muscular' international law. Buss interrogates this impulse, asking especially what the assumptions behind it are and, on the basis of feminist analysis, reveals the limited conception of threats to human security it represents, such that terrorism and 'rogue states' are deemed threatening but water-borne parasites and other contributors to human insecurity and global social injustice are not. She further argues that such appeals situate international law as the 'moral' and responsible father figure.

Trevor Purvis takes a rather different tack by seeking to evaluate the possibilities of an international rule of law under current conditions where the Bush Doctrine so radically attempts to rupture it. He does so by analysing both the conceptual contours of the contested concept of the rule of law and tracing its variable post-World War II meanings and manipulations. He shows how the Bush Administration has both instrumentalized it in its justifications for imperial war and domination and profoundly threatened it in its precarious international incarnation and its national ones as well. Following in the footsteps of Edward Thompson's celebrated analysis of the rule of law, Purvis indicates why and how the Left should realistically assess the damage done to an emerging international rule of law under the Bush Doctrine and the war against Iraq. In doing so he also begins to reveal the connection between the neo-liberal version of the rule of law, which, in the case of the invasion of Iraq, takes the form of what Herbert Docena has called 'the most ambitious, most radical, and most violent project to reconstruct an economy along neo-liberal lines in recent history', in which 'shock therapy' was delivered through 'shock and awe',[22] and the Bush Administration's challenge to the international rule of law.

Peter Swan considers whether the US's posture of 'legal exception-alism' may be addressed by turning to Alexandre Kojève's work. Kojève envisaged an alternative form of empire which he proposed as a 'counterweight' to hegemonic power and as an alternative to the nation-state as the primary container for democratic politics, thus foreshadowing many of the European debates today. Swan argues that his work on the juridification of empires may give us reason to hope for a contest between *'empires' laws'* offering some optimism in the face of the challenges posed by a unilaterally inclined hegemon.

My chapter attempts to conceptualize empire's law in relation to law's empire and argues that, rather than drawing on cosmopolitan morality in the absence of attention to legality, a progressive politics must seek to retrieve and enrich the resources that can be found in law's empire as resources to contest the American imperial power's attempts to install an exceptional empire's law.

One of the fundamental contradictions of empire's law is its attempt to impose democracy through 'fire and sword'.[23] In the case of Iraq, war has been succeeded by an occupation in which the 'soft power' of empire is harnessed to its prodigious 'hard power' in its attempt to mould Iraq under the auspices of 'regime change'. As the authors in the third part of the volume make clear, the painful con-sequences of this endeavour are borne most directly by the Iraqis whom the US claims to be liberating. Nehal Bhuta emphasizes the fact that this is one of the very few expressly belligerent occupations of the post-World War II period, importantly arguing against grant-ing legal imprimatur to the emerging conception of 'transformative occupation', a concept that threatens to instantiate empire's law even more deeply and broadly. Andrew Arato shows that the people American Empire claims to be liberating are treated not as partners in democratization and constitution-building projects, but rather merely as empire's territory; here, too, is found a difference between the post-World War II project of law's empire and that which now obtains. Arato argues that the contemporary era is marked by a struggle between international law and imperial hegemony, but with the war against Iraq we enter a new period where international law no longer appears to be the main framework for projects of democratization. For Arato, 'Iraq is a clear sign of something new' in terms of the challenge that the Bush Doctrine poses to human rights, democracy and civil society while justifying its actions precisely in these terms. And yet, as he also shows, imperial power is caught in a performative contradiction when it attempts imperial democratization, a contradiction that may hold possibilities for a dialogue between 'our' liberal democracy and Iraq's struggle for autonomous democracy against the aims of those who seek to impose imperial democracy.

Finally, Haifa Zangana, a survivor of Saddam's prisons, traces the role of occupiers with a friendly face, those who are associated with the institutions of civil society, thereby supporting Arato's attention to civil society in Iraq. Zangana focuses on NGOs, missionaries and women's organizations who are beholden to the US/UK and are bent on remaking Iraq in America's image – an imperial project that, as she shows, is one that Frantz Fanon would have no difficulty identifying as a colonial project but which may be even better understood today as part of 'informal imperialism'.

All of these dimensions of empire's law, which, it must be stressed, as overwhelming as they are, remain just one small sliver of the rule of American Empire, must be assessed further in terms of what resources may be available to marshal against the aggressive undermining of law's empire and the continuation of an American Empire. Whether it is ruling through the newly emerging, highly coercive and profoundly undemocratic relations of empire's law or whether it returns to a paradigm of law's empire – a paradigm of human rights and the rule of international law rather than militarism, brute force and unilateralism, much to be preferred but *still* likely to be ruled and led by empire – American Empire must be challenged and resisted through ethical, political and legal projects.

Reg Whitaker's contribution opens the fourth and final part of this volume and provides the only case study outside of Iraq in this collection. His analysis addresses the degree of relative autonomy the Canadian state has been able to negotiate in relation to American Empire, particularly in relation to the invasion of Iraq in which Canada's decision to stay out of the war indicated that 'something had changed on America's northern border'. Similarly, Canada's rejection of the US's ballistic missile defence shield and border security proposals, the latter of which threatened a 'Fortress North America', reveal Canada's ability to negotiate a political space that has been surprisingly robust, producing a case of 'selective' autonomy which indicates that 'American Empire is fraying just a little on the northern edges of the homeland'. Whitaker's study is extremely important because, as the US's closest ally and neighbour, sharing the longest border with the US and a long history of close relations, it shows there is, even here, room for manoeuvre, a possible relative autonomy from the American Empire, and even in respect to matters bearing on security. If Canada can, in some respects, carve out this space, it may raise our hope that others can as well.

Other strategies of resistance are dependent on recuperating the resources of humanitarianism that dwell within commitments to humanitarian intervention and just war theory, positions that have been sorely tested by the US Administration's instrumentalization of human rights, freedom, liberty, humanitarianism and just war, instrumentalizations that have been accepted with a vengeance by Tony Blair's Labour government. In analyses that assess the pitfalls but also the possibilities of humanitarian intervention and just war theory after the invasion of Iraq and the broader 'global war on terror', David Coates and Fuyuki Kurasawa find ways in which to refuse to 'throw the baby out with the bathwater' – a knee-jerk reaction that must be avoided if we are to recuperate a project of law's empire that respects both human rights commitments and the demands of self-determination and equal sovereignty. Both argue, absolutely correctly in my opinion, that an 'anti-imperialist absolutism that is skeptical of the discourse of human right as such' (Kurasawa) must be avoided as much as the undifferentiated humanitarian embrace which marks the position of the 'human rights hawks' (Bartholomew) as well as the Bush and Blair governments (Coates). Coates argues that the Iraq war was not a just war; nor was it a war with just outcomes. In part, this is because the means by which regime change was effected weakened the institutions of international law that alone, in the long run, can 'sustain a morally just global order'. Kurasawa argues that we can distinguish between a 'strong' and a 'weak' interventionism, with the latter providing the conceptual framework that will allow the Left to reject the instrumentalization of human rights in the service of imposition while also fulfilling the duty to protect persons from crimes against humanity. He argues that humanitarian intervention should be viewed as a 'mode of socio-political practice' (rather than as a norm), which must be sensitive to the publicity generated in civil society and dependent on far-reaching structural transformations of the institutions of global governance including enforceable international law.

Finally, Jayan Nayar and Samir Amin provide analyses of the possibilities for, respectively, developing a peoples' law perspective capable of fundamentally challenging empire's law by rejecting American Empire's self-proclaimed right to rule the globe and thinking critically about the sorts of structural reforms that would be required to make the United Nations a space of polycentric contention, that is, contention based on a 'principle of negotiation between states aimed, in part, at protecting their political, economic and cultural autonomy'. Nayar focuses on the World Tribunal on Iraq, a peoples' tribunal in the tradition of the Bertrand Russell Tribunal during the Vietnam War, providing an analysis of the contribution (and the difficulties that it has encountered) that such a civil society-initiated project might make to challenging empire's law.

Amin's concluding chapter takes us back in some important respects to the opening chapter by Panitch and Gindin. He suggests that global capitalism has now entered a barbaric stage, spreading 'apartheid on a global scale' which involves, in particular, permanent war against the peoples of Asia and Africa, and which, in the absence of a world state (which is impossible anyway) is entrusted primarily to the American state (and the Triad). It attempts to manage the crisis of contemporary capitalism, to fulfil the barbaric plan, through neoliberal capitalist globalization and its coercive and militarist enforcement. An alternative to this, Amin argues, lies in 'socialization through democracy', a long-term project that requires the defeat of the American imperial project and in which he identifies a transformed United Nations and international and cosmopolitan law as central to it. With the aim of advancing such a progressive project, Amin outlines important proposals for the renaissance of the UN, international law and cosmopolitan law.

Amin's analysis is remarkable on the Marxist Left for viewing the United Nations as designed to promote polycentric globalization – that is, globalization that respects the equal sovereignty of nation-states and an associated principle of negotiation among states aimed at protecting key features of political, cultural and economic autonomy – and for treating it as an important site of contention, not merely an 'instrument' of empire. In this regard, he furthers Sponeck's suggestion that we need to begin analysing the United Nations through a more subtle lens than that of instrumentalism. On the other hand, arguing against thinking that meaningful reform of the UN is possible in the short term through hastily con-cocted utopian schemes, Amin importantly argues for the relevance of mobilizing behind projects of reform and transformation over the long term with a careful eye on the ever-present possibility that they could be 'incorporated into the dominant imperialist strategies'. For this reason, he argues against pressuring governments immediately for UN reform and working, instead, through the public sphere and civil society, particularly through the Social Forums. Once that fight for transforming public opinion is well on its way, global campaigns may begin to press for such fundamental transformations.

The United Nations and international and cosmopolitan law, at once invested with the hopes of much of the post-World War II generation, key figures in the American-led project of law's empire after that war and now deeply threatened by the American imper-ial project that aims to impose empire's law actualized in the global 'war on terror' and the war against Iraq, remain important ful-crums on which projects of recuperating and transforming human rights and international law into venues for polycentric negotia-tion and the protection of human rights might turn. And this might proceed alongside projects of alternative building in order to transform this crucial 'international constitutional moment' (Preuss) by contesting empire in all its varieties and delegitimizing it. This reveals the importance of further theoretical work on the United Nations and international (and cosmopolitan) law, which aims at clarifying the character of their institutional materiality in order better to be able to analyse their receptivity to reform, reveal their weak spots and unearth their potential. But it is also clear from nearly all the essays in this volume that progressive politics today requires strategies that seek not just to constrain or contain American Empire – as important as those aims are – but to *under-mine* it. It is here also that we need to locate the importance of the Iraqi resistance as a resistance against the imperial project of American Empire. It is a struggle against the 'war to remake the world', and it may remake it in quite different ways from the way intended by the leaders and supporters of American Empire. But, that is for another book.

# NOTES

1 The idea that the Iraq war is a 'war to remake the world' is Michael Ledeen's (of the American Enterprise Institute), quoted in William Pfaff, 'Americans on Their Own Now, Lone Rangers, Riding toward the Sunset', *International Herald Tribune* (28 March 2003), available at *Common Dreams*, http://www.commondreams.org/cgi-bin/print.cgi?file=/views03/0328-04.htm.

2 Preliminary Declaration of the Jury of Conscience, World Tribunal on Iraq, Istanbul, 23–27 June 2005. The jury included among its members François Houtart, David Krieger, Chandra Muzzafar, Arundhati Roy and Eve Ensler. http://www.worldtribunal.org/main/?b=1.

3 Ronald Dworkin, *Law's Empire* (Cambridge, MA: Belknap Press, 1986).

4 Quoted in Michael Byers, 'The Laws of War, US-Style', *London Review of Books*, 25, no. 4 (20 February 2003), http://www.lrb.co.uk/v25/n04/byer01_.html.

5 Jonathan Schell, 'The Empire Backfires', Znet. www.zmag.org/content/showarticle.cfm?SectionID=11&ItemID=5129.

6 Michael Ratner and Ellen Ray, *Guantanamo: What the World Should Know* (White River Junction, VT: Chelsea Green Publishing, 2004), 15 and 25.

7 Jonathan Steel, 'Don't be Fooled by the Spin on Iraq', *Guardian* (13 April 2005).

8 Amnesty International, 'USA: "War on Terror" Detentions – Frequently Asked Questions', http://web.amnesty.org/web/web.nsf/print/C33CEAD 19EB7F8B78025701F0055FC3B.

9 See, for example, Craig Whitlock, 'New Swedish Documents Illuminate CIA Action', *Washington Post* (21 May 2005), at http://www.washington-post.com/wp-dyn/content/article/2005/05/20/AR2005052001605.html. Matthew Rothschild quotes the *New York Times* (6 March 2005), as saying that ' "a still classified directive signed by President Bush within days of the September 11 attacks" gave the CIA broad authority to transfer suspected terrorists to foreign countries for interrogations.' 'Stripping Rumsfeld and Bush of Impunity', *The Progressive* (July 2005), http://www.progressive.org/?q=mag_impunity.

10 Amnesty International USA Executive Director, William Schultz, 'Guantanamo Bay: A "Gulag of Our Times" or a "Model Facility"? A Debate on the U.S. Prison & Amnesty International', *Democracy Now* (1 June 2005), hosted by Amy Goodman. Transcript available at http://www.democracynow.org/article.pl?sid=05/06/01/1441204.

11 See Amnesty International for one report among many others. Amnesty says:

> the US government has gone to great lengths to restrict the application of the Geneva Conventions and to 're-define' torture. It has sought to justify the use of coercive interrogation techniques, the practice of holding 'ghost detainees' (people in unacknowledged incommunicado detention) and the 'rendering' or handing over of prisoners to third countries known to practice torture. The detention facility at Guantanamo Bay has become the gulag of our times, entrenching the practice of arbitrary and indefinite detention in violation of international law. Trials by military commissions have made mockery of justice and due process.

'Foreword, Report 2005', Amnesty International, http://web.amnesty.
org/report2005/message-eng. Also see the paper by the liberal legal theorist,
Jeremy Waldron, 'Torture and Positive Law: Jurisprudence for the White
House', Public Lecture, Victoria University of Wellington, New Zealand,
19 August 2004, revised version for Boalt Hall, GALA Workshop,
30 September 2004. Waldron makes the important point about the distinction between torture as a practice of states and torture as a legal policy. The efforts that are made in the various torture memos in
Washington are efforts, in Waldron's words, to 'see whether something
like torture can be accommodated within the very legal framework that
purports to prohibit torture. An effort is being made to see whether
the law can be stretched or deformed to actually permit and authorize
this sort of thing'. At 58–9.

12  Ken Coates, 'Fallujah: Shock and Awe', *Common Dreams* (19 November
2004), http://www.commondreams.org/views04/1119-32.htm.

13  See Dahr Jamail, 'Unusual Weapons Used in Fallujah' (26 November
2004), http://www.countercurrents.org/iraq-jamail301104.htm; Ben
Cubby, 'New, Improved and More Lethal: Son of Napalm', *Sydney
Morning Herald* (8 August 2003); Ben Cubby, 'Napalm by Any Other
Name: Pentagon Denial Goes up in Flames', *Sydney Morning Herald* (9
August 2003), available at http://globalresearch.ca/articles/308A.html;
James W. Crawley, 'Officials Confirm Dropping Firebombs on Iraqi
Troops', *San Diego Union-Tribune* (5 August 2003), available at *Common
Dreams*, http://www.commondreams.org/headlines03/0805-01.htm; Iraq
Analysis Group, 'Fire Bombs in Iraq: Napalm by Any Other Name'
(March 2005), www.iraqanalysis.org; and Ken Sanders, 'Fallujah:
Dresden in Iraq', www.politicsofdissent.blogspot.com.

Mike Lewis, a spokesman for the Iraq Analysis Group, told the
*Independent* that the 'US has used internationally reviled weapons that
the UK refuses to use, and has then apparently lied to UK officials, showing how little weight the UK carries in influencing American policy'.
Quoted in Colin Brown, 'US Lied to Britain over Use of Napalm in Iraq
War' (17 June 2005), http://news.independent.co.uk/uk/politics/story.
jsp?story=647397.

14  On depleted uranium, see Karen Parker, 'The Illegality of DU Weaponry'
(24 April 2004), International Committee to Ban Uranium Weapons,
http://www.bandepleteduranium.org/modules.php?name=News&file=
article&sid=123. Juan Cole suggests that 'In order to kill approximately
two thousand die-hard proponents of jihad, and to capture 1400, the US
reduced the formerly bustling desert port and truck stop to a ghost town.
Hundreds of civilians appear to be among the dead'. 'The Reelection of
Bush and the Fate of Iraq', *Constellations* 12, no. 2 (2005): 164–172, 169.
Martin Shaw argues that the 'direct killing of civilians by Western forces
has been a normal feature of recent campaigns'. 'Risk Transfer Militarism
and the Legitimacy of War after Iraq', *Foreign Policy in Focus*, 30 June
2004, at 3, www.fpif.org.

15  See Dahr Jamail's important report 'Iraqi Hospitals Reeling under
Occupation' (21 June 2005), http://www.brusselstribunal.org/Dahr
ReportSummary.htm.

16 Quoted in Pfaff, 'Americans on Their Own Now'.

17 Quoted in 'Crappy Little Countries', *Left Business Observer* 104 (April 2003), http://www.leftbusinessobserver.com/Crappy.html.

18 Michael Ledeen, 'Evil Within', *National Review Online* (19 July 2005), http://www.nationalreview.com/ledeen/ledeen.asp.

19 Lori Fisler Damrosch and Bernard H. Oxman, 'Agora: Future Implication of the Iraq Conflict: Editors' Introduction', *American Journal of International Law*, 97 (2004): 553.

20 Amnesty International Press Release, 'Report 2005, A Dangerous New Agenda', 25 May 2005 http://web.amnesty.org/library/index/engPOL 100062005?open&of=eng-200.

21 See David Harvey, *The New Imperialism* (Oxford: Oxford University Press, 2003), 49.

22 Herbert Docena, ' "Shock and Awe" Therapy: How the United States is Attempting to Control Iraq's Oil and Pry Open its Economy', testimony delivered at the World Tribunal on Iraq, Istanbul, 24 June 2005, http://www.focusweb.org/pdf/Shock%20and%20Awe%20Therapy% 20Final.pdf, 1; Naomi Klein, 'The Rise of Disaster Capitalism', *The Nation* (2 May 2005), http://www.thenation.com/doc.mhtml?i=20050502&s= klein; and Harvey, *The New Imperialism*.

23 This is an early translation of Habermas's essay which is more evocative in this regard than the subsequent one found in 'Interpreting the Fall of a Monument', in this volume. See 'What Does the Felling of the Monument Mean?' http://slash.autonomedia.org/analysis/03/05/12/1342259.shtml.

# I

# The American Imperial Project and the 'War to Remake the World'

# 1

# Theorizing American Empire

*Leo Panitch and Sam Gindin*

The exposure of the face of American Empire, so clearly revealed in the unilateral nature of America's most recent war against Iraq, reinforces the long-standing need for a new theorization of imperialism. This must go beyond merely drawing an analogy between the American Empire of the twenty-first century and the Roman Empire – as has become so commonplace today. But it must also resist recycling the longstanding Marxist thesis of inter-imperial rivalry, on the one hand, or embracing the postmodernist conception of empire as without a centre, on the other. None of these allows us to apprehend the form of imperialism, uniquely embodied in the American state, which has emerged in the contemporary era. It is characterized above all by economic penetration and informal incorporation of other capitalist states, but at the same time it both permits and requires imperial policing and military intervention in 'rogue states' which have not been incorporated into the neoliberal capitalist order. These two forms of American imperial statecraft – penetration and incorporation on the one hand, policing and intervention on the other – are intimately related. What brought us to the Iraq war, and its consequences, cannot be understood in the absence of either.

America's informal empire is not new. In the Western Hemisphere, as we shall see, its roots go back to the foundation of the republic and evolved through the articulation of the Monroe Doctrine with capitalist development in the nineteenth century, reaching its apogee with the presidencies of Theodore Roosevelt and Woodrow Wilson. But despite the latter's ambitions to extend this new form of informal imperialism at the end of World War I to the global level, it was only through the crucible of the Great Depression, the New Deal and World War II that the American state developed sufficient capacity to globalize its imperial reach. In this context the *internationalization of the state* came to be a critical element in capitalism's preservation and extension. This entailed capitalist states explicitly accepting responsibility for coordinating their management of the domestic capitalist order so as to contribute to managing the international capitalist order. For the American state, under whose aegis this coordination took place, this had a very special meaning: it defined the American national interest in terms of the reproduction and spread of global capitalism. The tensions this produced – in so far as this state still represented the array of social forces specific to the American social formation – were allayed by the increasingly global accumulation strategies of the dominant sections of the US capitalist class. Since World War II, the American state has not only been the state of the world's dominant social formation, but has been filling in for global capitalism's absent 'global state'.

By 1948, the Canadian historian Harold Innis could already astutely observe that 'American imperialism ... has been made plausible and attractive in part by the insistence that it is not imperialistic'.[1] What made this new no-name imperialism plausible and attractive in the second half of the twentieth century had very much to do with the legitimacy that its liberal democratic ideas and institutions lent to the American state worldwide. The reproduction and eventual 'globalization' of capitalism in the second half of the twentieth century relied on the extended legitimation of the American state's role in policing global order, including remaking the world's states in the image of the US as the leading capitalist state. The liberal democratic nature of that state lent credibility to the claim that even American military interventions were all about human rights, democracy and freedom. The reproducibility beyond the republic of its distinctive administrative, legal and constitutional forms and the ideological force of their cultural, political and juridical features were also important to this.

The role of the American state in policing global capitalism had already been fully encapsulated in National Security Council document NSC-68 of 1950. It articulated most clearly the goal of constructing a 'world environment in which the American system can survive and flourish ... Even if there were no Soviet Union we would face the great problem ... [that] the absence of order among nations is becoming less and less tolerable'.[2] The wording employed 50 years later in President George W. Bush's *National Security Strategy* of 2002 (written by the Republican intellectuals who founded the Project for a New American Century in the 1990s with the goal of making imperial statecraft the explicit guiding principle of American policy in the wake of the collapse of the Soviet Union) was not very different.[3] What was different about the new conjuncture, however, was that the imperial quality of the American state was so obvious that it could scarcely be concealed. Now, another Canadian intellectual, Michael Ignatieff, was given the front page of the *New York Times Sunday Magazine* from which to proclaim: 'what word but "empire" describes the awesome thing that America is becoming? ... Being an imperial power ... means enforcing such order as there is in the world and doing so in the American interest.'[4] But despite Ignatieff's entreaties, in this context, the liberal democratic form of the American state no longer has the global cachet it once did.

In terms of accounting for this passage from concealed to unconcealed empire, the much discussed contrast between the unilateralism of the Bush Administration and the multilateralism of previous administrations (which primarily involved the latter being more inclined to seek and take the counsel of the other rich capitalist states) only touches the surface of what needs to be explained. At a more profound level, what has made 'empire' manifest is that the neoliberal mode of imperial penetration and social rule, as it has evolved over the past three decades, has not only meant increased inequality around the world, but has also revealed a greater need to create 'effective states' through which this form of global capitalism can be managed. This is seen in the constitutional effect that international trade agreements have on the states that sign them in terms of the protections they afford to the rights of capital. But it is also seen in the increase in American military bases and in the power of intelligence and police apparatuses of *all* the states of the empire (coordinated by its imperial centre). When these mechanisms have been inadequate or failed to work quickly enough, the US has been increasingly tempted to turn to military intervention. But, the claim that the US's standing as the world's foremost democracy confers upon it the right to deploy its unparalleled means of violence around the world is increasingly seen as dubious, both because its own democratic standing has been questioned and because its global deployment of force does not necessarily lead to the spread of human rights and liberal democracy. The declining legitimation capacity of America's informal empire has myriad unpredictable ramifications.

A new theorization of imperialism today must account for both the plausibility of the American Empire's claim not to be imperialistic for much of the twentieth century *and* for the implausibility of this posture – and the growing unattractiveness of the empire – at the beginning of the twenty-first century. As we suggested at the outset, most of what passes for serious analysis in justifying the use of the term 'empire' in relation to the US today is really just an analogy, implicit or explicit, with imperial Rome. This was well captured in Zbigniew Brzezinski's 1997 book, *The Grand Chessboard: American Primacy and Its Geostrategic Imperatives*: 'the three great imperatives of geo-political strategy are to prevent collusion and maintain security dependence amongst the vassals, to keep tributaries pliant, and to keep the barbarians from coming together'.[5] On the face of it, this analogy is by no means absurd since 'Roman supremacy was based on a masterful combination of violence and psychological persuasion – the harshest punishment for those who challenged it, the perception that their power knew no limits and that rewards were given to those who conformed'.[6] But an analogy is not a theory. The neglect of any serious political economy or pattern of historical determination that would explain the emergence and reproduction of today's American Empire, and the dimensions of structural oppression and exploitation pertaining to it, are striking.

This serves as a poignant reminder of why it was Marxism that led the running in theorizing imperialism for most of the twentieth century. Yet there were severe analytical problems in the Marxist theory of imperialism, as was increasingly obvious by the beginning of the 1970s – the last time the concept of imperialism had much currency – amidst complaints that the Marxist treatment of imperialism 'as an undifferentiated global product of a monopoly stage of capitalism' reflected its lack of 'any serious historical or sociological dimensions'.[7] As Giovanni Arrighi noted in 1978, 'by the end of the 60s, what had once been the *pride* of Marxism – the theory of imperialism – had become a tower of Babel, in which not even Marxists knew any longer how to find their way'.[8] Indeed, it is notable that those who clung to the concept of inter-imperial rivalry inherited from the classical Marxist theorists at the beginning of the twentieth century soon joined in the superficial view that American 'hegemony' was in decline in the face of regional economic competition.

It was perhaps not surprising in this context that, as Bruce Cumings noted at the time of the first Gulf War at the beginning of the 1990s, one still needed 'an electron microscope to find "imperialism" used to describe the U.S. role in the world'.[9] And this remained the case even as the Clinton Administration unleashed military power to suppress resistance to 'an open and integrated international order based on the principles of democratic capitalism'.[10] But this continuing avoidance of the term 'imperialism' as a descriptor for the US role in the world could hardly last when, in 1998, Clinton's Secretary of State, Madeline Albright, justified the war against Yugoslavia in the following terms: 'if we have to use force it is because we are America. We are the indispensable nation'; or when, in 2000, Richard Haas, soon to be the State Department's Director of Policy Planning in the incoming Bush Administration, called on Americans to reconceive their state's 'global role from one of traditional nation state to imperial power'.[11] Such statements only serve to reveal that the popularity of Hardt and Negri's tome *Empire* reflected the new discursive conjuncture, even as their deployment of postmodernism's and contemporary globalization theory's superficial conceptions of decentred power in a borderless world rendered their primary claim that '*the United States does not, and indeed no nation state can today, form the centre of an imperialist project*' bizarrely out of step with the times.[12]

What is needed is a new theorization of imperialism capable of accounting for the central role that the American state has come to play in the global capitalist order. In the face of the superficial and misleading discursive and theoretical counterposition of state and markets in our era, such a theory needs to begin with the recognition of the key role played by states in the constitution of the capitalist world. The rise of capitalism and the realization of its structural tendency to globalization are inconceivable without the role that European states played in establishing the legal and infrastructural frameworks for property, contract, currency, competition and wage-labour within their own borders, while also generating a process of uneven development (and the attendant construction of race) in the modern world. Nor is imperialism reducible to an economic explanation, even if economic forces are always a large part of it. We need, in this respect, to keep imperialism and capitalism as two distinct concepts. Competition among capitalists in the international arena, unequal exchange and uneven development are all aspects of capitalism itself, and their relationship to imperialism can only be understood through a theorization of the state. When states pave the way for their national capitals' expansion abroad, or even when they follow and manage that expansion, this can only be understood in terms of these states' relatively autonomous role in maintaining social order and securing the conditions of capital accumulation; and we must therefore factor state capacities as well as class, cultural and military determinations into the explanation of the imperial aspect of this role. Capitalist imperialism needs to be understood through an extension of the theory of the capitalist state, rather than derived directly from the theory of economic stages or crises.

The British state's transition to the modern capitalist form of imperialism (the first state that 'created a form of imperialism driven by the logic of capitalism'[13]) involved the articulation of a mercantile formal empire with a new informal empire spawned in the mid nineteenth century during the era of 'free trade' (India and Argentina representing the archetypical examples of formal and informal linkage to the British Empire at the time). The main factor that determined the emergence of inter-imperial rivalries, and a new wave of colonization after the 1880s, was not the inadequacy of Britain's relationship with its own informal empire, nor the emergence of the stage of monopoly or finance capital, but rather Britain's inability to incorporate the newly emerging capitalist powers of Germany, the US and Japan into 'free trade imperialism'. In this context, the international institutional apparatuses of diplomacy and alliances, British naval supremacy and the Gold Standard were too fragile even to guarantee equal treatment of foreign capital with national capital within each state (the key prerequisite of capitalist globalization), let alone to mediate the conflicts and manage the contradictions associated with the development of global capitalism by the late nineteenth century. No adequate means of overall global capitalist coordination existed, leaving the international economy and its patterns of accumulation increasingly fragmented, and thus fuelling the inter-imperial rivalry that led to World War I.

The classical theorists of imperialism, from Hobson to Lenin, were often perspicacious in their analysis of the economic dynamics underlying this inter-imperial rivalry. But their treatment of the state was largely reductionist and instrumental.[14] Nor could they clearly see (although Kautsky glimpsed it) how the process of capitalist globalization that had developed in the nineteenth century might be revived under the aegis of American policy-makers who, given developments inside the American social formation and state as well as internationally between the two world wars, came to believe that 'only the US had the power to grab hold of history and make it conform'.[15]

The role the United States came to play in world capitalism was not inevitable, but nor was it merely accidental: it was not a matter of teleology but of capitalist history. The capacity it developed to 'conjugate' its '*particular* power with the *general* task of coordination' reflected 'the particular matrix of its own social history', as Perry Anderson has recently put it. This was founded on 'the attractive power of US models of production and culture ... increasingly unified in the sphere of consumption'. Coming together here were, on the one hand, the invention in the US of the modern corporate form, 'scientific management' of the labour process and assembly-line mass production; and, on the other, Hollywood-style 'narrative and visual schemas stripped to their most abstract', appealing to and aggregating waves of immigrants through 'dramatic simplification and repetition'.[16] The dynamism of American capitalism and its worldwide appeal combined with the universalistic language of American liberal democratic ideology to underpin a capacity for informal empire far beyond that of nineteenth-century Britain's.

Yet it was not only the economic and cultural formation of American capitalism, but also the formation of the American state that facilitated a new informal empire. Against Anderson's impression that the American state's constitutional structures lack the 'carrying power' of its economic and cultural ones (by virtue of being 'moored to eighteenth-century arrangements')[17] stands Thomas Jefferson's observation in 1809 that 'no constitution was ever before as well-calculated for extensive empire and self-government'.[18] The famous Madisonian 'checks and balances' in the American Constitution did not anticipate the sort of amorphous power that Hardt and Negri imagine characterized the US historically and that they imagine characterizes their decentred 'Empire' today. On the contrary, the constitutional framework of the new American state gave great powers to the central government, above all to expand trade and make war.

When, as early as 1783, George Washington spoke ambitiously of the new state as 'a rising empire',[19] he was obviously thinking in terms of the mercantile empires of the eighteenth century. But the state that emerged out of the ambitions of the 'expansionist colonial elite' of Northern merchants and Southern planters evinced from its beginnings a different trajectory, one that led to capitalist development and informal empire.[20] The initial form this took was through territorial expansion westward, largely through the extermination of the native population, and blatant exploitation not only of the black slave population but also debt-ridden subsistence farmers and, from at least the 1820s on, an emerging industrial working class. Yet the new American state could still conceive of itself as embodying republican liberty, and be widely admired for it, largely due to the link between 'extensive empire and self-government' embedded in the federal constitution. 'The American empire would not be mercantilist but in still another respect something new under the sun: the West was not to be colonies but states.'[21]

And 'state rights' were no mirage: they reflected the two different types of social relations – slave and free – that eventually led to civil war, the defeat of the plantocracy and the abolition of slavery. The outcome of the civil war allowed for a reconstruction of the relationship between financial and industrial capital and the federal state, inclining state administrative capacities and policies away from mercantilism and towards extended capitalist reproduction.[22] What American capitalism became most distinctively known for – 'unencumbered property rights, untrammelled litigation, the invention of the corporation' – rested, as Anderson discerns, on 'a juridical system disembedding the market as far as possible from ties of custom, tradition or solidarity, whose very abstraction from them later proved – American firms like American films – exportable and reproducible across the world, in a way that no other competitor could quite match'.[23]

The expansionist tendencies of American capitalism beyond its own borders in the latter decades of the nineteenth century primarily involved the state undertaking literally thousands of naval 'ports of call' to protect American commercial interests in Latin America, very much along the lines of British informal imperialism in the region.[24] US military interventions became commonplace by the turn of the century, but the establishment of colonies in Puerto Rico and the Philippines and the annexation of Hawaii were 'a deviation ... from the typical economic, political and ideological forms of domination already characteristic of American imperialism'.[25] Rather, it was through American foreign direct investment and the modern corporate form that the American informal empire soon took shape in a manner quite distinct from the British one. The articulation of the new informal American Empire with sporadic military interventions was expressed by Theodore Roosevelt in 1904 (in language now familiar again) in terms of the exercise of 'international police power'. In the absence of other means of international control, the US would intervene to establish regimes that know 'how to act with reasonable efficiency and decency in social and political matters' and to ensure that each such regime 'keeps order and pays its obligations.' This was all part of America's 'general world duty ... A great free people owes to itself and to all mankind not to sink into helplessness before the powers of evil.'[26]

The American genius for presenting its informal empire in terms of the framework of universal rights reached its apogee under Woodrow Wilson, who explained the military interventions of his first Administration as follows: 'I am going to teach the South American Republics to elect good men.'[27] It also reached under Wilson the apogee of hypocrisy, especially at the Paris Peace Conference, where John Maynard Keynes concluded that Wilson was 'the greatest fraud on earth'.[28] Indeed, it was not only the US Congress's isolationist tendencies, but the incapacity of the American presidential, treasury and military apparatuses that explained the failure of the United States to take responsibility for leading European reconstruction after World War I. It was only during the New Deal that the US state really began to develop the modern planning capacities that would, once they were redeployed in World War II, transform and vastly extend America's informal imperialism. As Brian Waddell aptly put it, there was a shift of 'U.S. state capacities towards realising internationally-interventionist goals versus domestically-interventionist ones'.[29]

This proved crucial to the revival of capitalism's globalizing tendencies which had been so badly interrupted during World War I and the Great Depression. Amidst the radical postwar reconstruction of all the states at the core of the old inter-imperial rivalry, the most important new dimension of the relationship between capitalism and imperialism was that *the densest imperial networks and institutional linkages, which had earlier run north–south between imperial states and their formal or informal colonies, now came to run between the US and the other major capitalist states.* The processes binding these states to the American Empire were institutionalized, beginning with Bretton Woods, through the IMF and World Bank (whose headquarters were established at American insistence in Washington, DC) as well as through the institutions of NATO, operating alongside the hub-and-spokes networks binding each of the other leading capitalist states to the intelligence and security apparatuses of the US as part of the strategy of containment of communism during the Cold War.

But much more than the containment of communism was going on. American economic penetration shifted towards the other advanced capitalist countries, so that between 1950 and 1970 Latin

America's share of total American Foreign Direct Investment (FDI) fell from 40 per cent to under 20 per cent, while Western Europe's more than doubled to match the Canadian share of over 30 per cent.[30] It was hardly surprising that acute observers began to discern in Europe a tendential 'Canadianization' as the model form of integration into the American Empire.[31] Capital as an effective social force within any given state now tended to include both foreign capital and domestic capital with international linkages and ambitions. Their interpenetration made the notion of distinct national bourgeoisies – let alone rivalries between them in any sense analogous to those that led to World War I – increasingly anachronistic.

None of this meant, of course, that the north–south dimension of imperialism became unimportant. But it did mean that the other core capitalist countries' relationships with the Third World, including their ex-colonies, were imbricated with American informal imperial rule. The core capitalist countries might continue to benefit from the north–south divide, but any interventions had to be either American-initiated or at least have American approval (as Suez proved). Only the American state could arrogate to itself the right to intervene against the sovereignty of other states (which it repeatedly did around the world) and only the American state reserved for itself the 'sovereign' right to reject international rules and norms when necessary. It is in this sense that only the American state was actively 'imperialist'.

The particular 'Keynesian' pattern of capitalist 'reconstruction' established at Bretton Woods was inherently transitional. The very internationalization of trade and US direct foreign investment that Bretton Woods promoted contributed to the gradual restoration of global financial markets, the corresponding erosion of capital controls and the vulnerability of fixed exchange rates.[32] But in spite of new tensions between the US, Europe and Japan which had already become visible by the 1960s once their rebuilt economies became internationally competitive, the past was not replayed. American dominance, never fundamentally challenged, would come to be reorganized on a neoliberal basis, and international integration was not rolled back but intensified. In the context of the economic crisis of the 1970s, there was a further important internationalization of the state.[33] During the course of the protracted and often confused renegotiations of the terms that had, since the end of World War II, bound Europe and Japan to the American Empire, all the nation-states involved came to accept a further responsibility for creating the necessary *internal* conditions for sustained *international* accumulation, such as stable prices, constraints on labour militancy, national treatment of foreign investment and no restrictions on capital outflows.

The resolution of the crisis of the 1970s, however, depended ultimately on what the American state finally did itself. The critical turning point came in 1979 with the 'Volcker Shock', the American state's self-imposed structural adjustment programme. The Federal Reserve's determination to establish internal economic discipline by allowing interest rates to rise to historically unprecedented levels led to the vital restructuring of labour and industry and brought (bought?) the confidence that the money markets and central bankers were looking for. Under the umbrella of the more general neoliberal policies for 'competitiveness', which evolved into a relatively coherent capitalist policy paradigm through the 1980s, the new state-reinforced strength of financial capital accelerated the drive to a seamless world of capital accumulation, and set the stage for what came to be popularly known as 'globalization' in the last decades of the twentieth century.

The mechanisms of neoliberalism (the expansion and deepening of markets and competitive pressures) may be economic, but neoliberalism was essentially a *political* response to the democratic gains that had been previously achieved by subordinate classes and which had become, in a new context and from capital's perspective, barriers to accumulation. Neoliberalism involved not just reversing those gains, but weakening their institutional foundations – including a shift in the hierarchy of state apparatuses in the US towards the Treasury and Federal Reserve at the expense of the old New Deal agencies. The US was, of course, not the only country to introduce neoliberal policies, but once the American state itself moved in this direction, it had a new status: capitalism now operated under 'a new form of social rule' that promised, and largely delivered, (a) the revival of the productive base for American dominance; (b) a universal model for restoring the conditions for profits in other developed countries; and (c) the juridical as well as economic conditions for integrating global capitalism.[34] 'Empire's law' in this context involved what Stephen Gill called the 'constitutionalization of neoliberalism' as international economic treaties required the free mobility of capital and the equal treatment of foreign and domestic capital. What Saskia Sassen termed 'the Americanization of commercial law' developed alongside this, as US legal practices in business were diffused throughout the world.[35]

The reconstitution of the American Empire in this remarkably successful fashion through the last decades of the twentieth century did not mean that global capitalism had reached a new plateau of stability. Indeed, it may be said that dynamic instability and contingency are systematically incorporated into the reconstituted form of empire, in good part because the intensified competition characteristic of neoliberalism and the hyper-mobility of financial liberalization aggravate the uneven development and extreme volatility inherent in the global order. Moreover, this instability is dramatically amplified by the fact that the American state can only rule this order through other states, and turning them all into what the World Bank calls 'effective states' is no easy matter. It is the attempt by the American state to address these problems, especially vis-à-vis what it calls 'rogue states', that leads American imperialism today to present itself in an increasingly unconcealed manner.

What is clear, however, or at least should be, is that we cannot understand US imperialism today in terms of economic crises giving rise to inter-imperial rivalry. First of all, the advanced capitalist states have exhibited a common interest in limiting the duration, depth and contagion of crises – and working together, under the aegis of the American imperial state, they have, to date, demonstrated a remarkable ability to do this. Beyond this, the term 'rivalry' inflates economic competition between states far beyond what it signifies in the real world. The distinctive meaning the concept had in the pre-World War I context, when economic competition among European states was indeed imbricated with comparable military capacities and Lenin could assert that 'imperialist wars are absolutely inevitable', is clearly lacking in the contemporary context of overwhelming American military dominance. The meaning it had in the past is also contradicted by the distinctive economic as well as military *integration* that exists between the leading capitalist powers today. In this context, the extent of the theoretically unselfconscious use of the term 'rivalry' to label the economic competition between the EU, Japan/East Asia and the United States is remarkable.

The evolution of the European Union does not itself, as many seem to think, make the theory of inter-imperial rivalry relevant for our time. Encouraged at its origins by the American state, its recent development through economic and monetary union, up to and including the launching of the Euro and the European Central Bank, has never been opposed by American capital within Europe, or by the American state. What it has accomplished in terms of free trade and capital mobility within its own region has fitted, rather than challenged, the American-led 'new form of social rule' that neo-liberalism represents. And what it has accomplished in terms of the integration of European capital markets has not only involved the greater penetration of American investment banking and its principle of 'shareholder value' inside Europe, but has been 'based on the deregulation and internationalisation of the US financial system'.[36] Despite the halting steps towards an independent European military posture, pragmatic European politicians have never entertained any illusions about what this really amounts to. As Joschka Fischer, Germany's ex-Foreign Minister, put it: 'The transatlantic relationship is indispensable. The power of the United States is a decisive factor for peace and stability in the world. I don't believe Europe will ever be strong enough to look after its security alone.'[37]

As for East Asia, where Japan's highly centralized state once seemed to give it the imperial potential that the relatively loose-knit EU lacks, it has shown even less capacity for regional, let alone global, leadership independent of the US. Its ability to penetrate East Asia economically, moreover, has been and remains mediated by the American imperial relationship.[38] This was rudely underlined by the actions of the American Treasury in the East Asian crisis of 1997–98, when it dictated a harsh conditionality right in Japan's backyard. Those who interpreted Japan's trade penetration of American markets and its massive direct foreign investments in the US through the 1980s in terms of inter-imperial rivalry betrayed a misleadingly short-term and economistic perspective. And while China may eventually emerge as a pole of inter-imperial power, it will obviously be very far from reaching such a status for a good many decades. The fact that certain elements in the American state are concerned to ensure that its 'unipolar' power today is used to prevent the possible emergence of imperial rivals tomorrow can hardly be used as evidence that such rivals already exist.

None of this means, of course, that state and economic structures have become homogeneous or that there is no divergence in many policy areas, or that contradiction and conflict are absent from the imperial order. But these contradictions and conflicts are located not so much in the relationships between the advanced capitalist states, as *within* these states, as they try to manage their internal processes of accumulation, legitimation and class struggle. To the extent that there is a crisis of American imperialism internationally today, it arises in relation to the states outside the capitalist core. Where these states are – as in much of the Third World and the former Soviet Bloc – relatively less developed capitalist states, yet increasingly located within the orbit of global capital, the international financial institutions, as well as the core capitalist states acting either in concert or on their own, have intervened to impose neoliberal structural 'reforms'. All too often these interventions have aggravated rather than solved the problem because of the abstract universalism of the remedy. Whatever neoliberalism's alleged successes in relation to strengthening an already developed capitalist economy, it increasingly appears as a misguided strategy for capitalist development itself.

As for so-called 'rogue states' – those that are not within the orbit of global capitalism so that neither penetrating external economic forces nor international institutions can effectively restructure them – direct unilateral intervention on the part of the American state became increasingly tempting after the end of the Cold War. It is this that has brought the term 'empire' back into mainstream currency. In this context, the collapse of the communist world that stood outside the sphere of American Empire and global capitalism for so much of the postwar era has become particularly important. On the one hand, there was a rapid penetration and integration by global capital and the institutions of informal American Empire (such as NATO) of so much of what had been the Soviet Bloc, and a no less rapid opening of China and Vietnam to foreign capital and their integration in world markets (even if under the aegis of communist elites). This also largely removed the danger that direct US intervention in states outside the American hemisphere would lead to World War III and nuclear Armageddon. The fact that even liberal human rights advocates and institutions through the 1990s repeatedly called for the US to act as an international police power reflected the new conjuncture. But, on the other hand, both the hubris and the sense of burden that came with the now evident unique power of the American state led it to question whether even the limited compromises it had to make in operating through multilateral institutions were unnecessarily constraining its strategic options.

The 'loneliness of power' was increasingly involved here. The perceived burden of ultimate responsibility (and since 9/11 the much greater sensitivity to US vulnerability as a target of terrorism at home as well as abroad) promotes the desire to retain full 'sovereignty' to act as needed. This is what underlies the increasingly unconcealed nature of American imperialism. The problem it now faces in terms of 'conjugating its particular power with the general task of coordination' (to recall Anderson's incisive phrase) can clearly be seen not only in relation to the economic contradictions of neoliberalism discussed above, but also in the growing contradictions between nature and capitalism. These issues are multiplied all the more by the role the American imperial state now has come to play (and often is expected to play) in maintaining order around the whole globe. Just as neoliberalism at home did not mean a smaller or weaker state, but rather one in which coercive apparatuses flourished (as welfare offices emptied out, the prisons filled up), so has neoliberalism led to the enhancement of the type of coercive apparatus the imperial state needs to police social order around the world.[39]

All this was already apparent in the responses to 'rogue states' under the Bush I and Clinton Administrations. The remarkable staying power, and even apparently the continuing plausibility and attractiveness, of America's informal imperialism seemed to be confirmed by the imprimatur it drew from the UN for the first Gulf War at the beginning of the 1990s (and for the sanctions that followed), and by America's ability to get every NATO state to sign up to the war on Yugoslavia over Kosovo at the end of the decade. To be sure, the US did have to work hard at the time of the 1990–91 Gulf War, as it 'either persuaded or coerced everybody else', as the Canadian Ambassador to the UN put it at the time, to support the way it played 'fast and loose with the provisions of the UN Charter'. This especially unnerved 'a lot of developing countries, which were privately outraged by what was going on but felt utterly impotent to do anything – a demonstration of the enormous US power and influence when it is unleashed'.[40] Yet at the very same time, it also made American strategists aware just how little they could rely on the UN if they had to go to such trouble to get their way. The UN, by its very nature as a quasi-parliamentary and diplomatic body made up of all the world's states, could not be as easily restructured as were the IMF and World Bank in the turn to neoliberalism after the crisis of the 1970s. This, as evidenced in the repeated use of the American veto in the Security Council, was a constant irritant. And while NATO could be relied on as a far more reliable vehicle for the American war on the former Yugoslavia over Kosovo (with the added benefit of making clear to the Europeans exactly who would continue to wield international police power in their own backyard), even here the effort entailed in having to keep each and every NATO member onside was visibly resented within the American state itself.

George W. Bush's isolationist rhetoric in the 2000 election campaign, questioning the need for American troops to get involved in remote corners of the globe, was bound to be reformulated once he was actually burdened with (and appropriately socialized in) the office of a presidency that is now as inevitably imperial as it is domestic in nature. For this, the explicitly imperial statecraft that the geopolitical strategists close to the Republican Party had already fashioned was ready and waiting. September 11 alone did not determine their ascendancy in the state, but it certainly enhanced their status. Their response has revealed all the tensions in the American state's combination of its imperial function of general coordination with the use of its power to protect and advance its national interests. Defining the security interests of global capitalism in a way that also serves the needs of the American social formation and state becomes especially tricky once the security interests involved are so manifestly revealed as primarily American. This means that while threats to the US are still seen by it as an attack on global capitalism in general, the American state is increasingly impatient with making any compromises that get in the way of its acting on its own specific definition of the global capitalist interest and the untrammelled use of its particular state power to cope with such threats.

The unconcealed imperial face that the American state is now prepared to show to the world above all pertains to the increasing difficulties of managing a truly global informal empire – a problem that goes well beyond any change from administration to administration. The need to try to refashion all the states of the world so that they become at least minimally adequate for the administration of global order is now the central problem for the American state. This could turn out to be a challenge as great as that once faced by formal empires with their colonial state apparatuses. The immense difficulty of constructing outside the core anything like the dense networks that the new American imperialism succeeded in forging with the other leading capitalist states is clear from the halting progress that has been made in extending the G7 even to the G8, let alone the G20. This explains not only the extension of US military bases and the closer integration of intelligence and police apparatuses of all the states in the empire in the wake of September 11, but the harkening back to the founding moment of the post-1945 American Empire in the military occupations of Japan and Germany as providing the model for restructuring Iraq within the framework of American Empire. The logic of this posture points well beyond Iraq to all states 'disconnected from globalization', as a US Naval War College professor advising the US Secretary of Defense put it. In this 'Gap', constituting what he called 'a strategic threat environment', were to be found Haiti, Colombia, Brazil and Argentina, former Yugoslavia, Congo and Rwanda/Burundi, Angola, South Africa, Israel-Palestine, Saudi Arabia, Iraq, Somalia, Iran, Afghanistan, Pakistan, North Korea and Indonesia – to which China, Russia and India were added, for good measure, 'as new/integrating members of the core [that] may be lost in coming years'.[41]

The trouble for the American Empire as it inclines in this strategic direction is that very few of these states, given their economic and political structures and internal social forces, are going to be able to be reconstructed along the lines of postwar Japan and Germany, even if (indeed especially if) they are occupied by the US military, and even if they are penetrated rather than marginalized by globalization. What is more, an American imperialism that is so blatantly imperialistic risks forgoing the advantages of not appearing imperialist – that appearance which historically made it plausible and attractive. The disagreements over the war on Iraq between France, Germany and even Canada, on the one hand, and the American state, on the other, need to be seen in this light. These tensions pertain very little to economic rivalries. Indeed, their bourgeoisies – visibly troubled by not being on the same page as the Americans – are even less inclined to challenge American hegemony than they were in the 1970s. The tensions pertain rather more to an inclination on the part of these states themselves (in good part reflective of their relatively weak autonomous military capacity) to prefer the use of multilateral institutions given their subordinate status in the American Empire.

The US's inability to secure UN support in the run-up to the second Bush war on Iraq was certainly a significant indicator of the problems of legitimacy to which its explicit imperial posture increasingly gives rise. But if the UN's initial position suggested that US power and influence at the UN was becoming more tenuous, this was contradicted when the Security Council voted in the spring of 2004 and again in the fall of 2005 to endorse the American occupation. Moreover, the war on terrorism the US declared after 9/11 had effects far beyond Afghanistan and Iraq. It served to legitimate and sustain other states' repression of separatist groups along with other dissident domestic ones. Less well known than the free hand given to the Russians in Chechnya was the free hand given to the Chinese communist-capitalist elite to act against Muslim separatists in their westernmost province without fear that this will be used by the Americans against them in their ongoing negotiations over the terms of integration into the capitalist world economy. Consistency need not be a principle of imperial strategy, and this was never more evident than in the stunningly quick about-face the US made after the war on Yugoslavia, when the justification for that war was the right of self-determination in the old Communist world for every ethno-nationalist group that demanded it.

Moreover, the larger implication of the post-9/11 'you-are-with-us-or-with-the-terrorists' stance of the Bush Administration was to require that the other capitalist states restructure their coercive apparatus to fit America's strategic concerns. This would seem to reinforce the earlier requirement set by the imperium that they restructure their economic apparatus to fit with an American-led neoliberal globalization of capitalism. The USA PATRIOT Act greatly enhanced the power and resources of the coercive and security apparatus in the imperial centre with broad implications in terms of repressing dissent and protest. There was at the same time considerable pressure from Washington that other states should adopt similar anti-terrorist measures. The United Kingdom immediately derogated itself from Article 5 of the European Human Rights Convention to pass its Anti-Terrorism, Crime and Security Act 2001. But the December 2001 Framework Decision on Combating Terrorism, issued by the Council of the European Union, was itself remarkably broad in its coercive implications for political dissent of a non-terrorist kind. However much such legislation was presented in terms of their own 'national security', the explicit justification offered by other states for such measures – in terms of the need for coordination among states to deal with 'international terrorism' – suggested that the more accurate designation would have been 'imperial security'.

That said, it is also true that the adoption of these measures was also fuelled internally, as the forces which were already arraigned against anti-globalization protests and immigrants' rights rushed into the post-9/11 mix. In the wake of the Genoa protest in July 2001, the European Police Office had been given licence to create an EU-wide database on 'suspected' protesters and develop an action plan to place them under surveillance. After 9/11, the main focus of such data-sharing, formalized by two formal agreements signed with the US, was related to enhancing

> the cooperation between the EU Member States – acting through Europol – and the USA in preventing, detecting, suppressing and investigating serious forms of international crimes [which] include not only terrorism … .[This] establishes a new level of intensive cooperation between Europol and American law enforcement agencies … and will allow for an unprecedented dimension of data exchange both in terms of quantity as well as in terms of sensitivity of data.[42]

The real problem for American imperialism today lies not with the European and Japanese states' own imperialist inclinations. On the contrary, it is the danger posed to these states' legitimacy once they are located in a framework of American imperialism that is so visibly and coercively imperialistic. The American state's occupation of Iraq, precisely because it is so flagrantly imperial and so openly connected to a doctrine that expresses the broader purposes of establishing neoliberal capitalist order on a global scale, has evoked an unprecedented popular revulsion against American imperialism, including within the capitalist core states. This is especially significant because, since the American Empire can only rule through other states, the greatest danger to it is that the states and ruling classes within its orbit will be rendered illegitimate by virtue of their articulation to the imperium. But such is their degree of integration with the imperium that they are unable to break with it.

The American Empire remains hegemonic vis-à-vis these states, their capitalist classes and their various elite establishments, but it has never entailed, for all of the American economic and cultural penetration of their societies, a transfer of direct popular loyalty to the American state itself. Indeed, the American form of rule – founded on the constitutional principle of 'extensive empire and self-government' – has never demanded this. The economic and cultural emulation of the American way of life by so many ordinary people abroad may perhaps properly be spoken of as hegemony in Gramsci's terms. But however close the relationship between the American state and capitalist classes and their counterparts in the informal empire, this did not extend to anything like a sense of patriotic attachment to the American state among the citizenry of the other states. Nor did the American state ever take responsibility for the incorporation, in the Gramscian sense of hegemony, of the needs of the subordinate classes of other states within its own construction of informal imperial rule. Their active consent to its informal imperial rule was always mediated by the legitimacy that each state could retain for itself and muster on behalf of any particular American state project – and this has often been difficult to achieve in the case of American coercive interventions around the globe over the past 50 years. A good many of these states thus distanced themselves from repeated US interventions in Latin America and the Caribbean since 1945, and indeed since 1975, not to mention America's subversion of governments elsewhere, or the Vietnam War.

In this sense the unpopularity of American military intervention – and even its lack of endorsement by other advanced capitalist states – is not new. This dimension of the imperial order is proving to have particularly important consequences in the current conjuncture. To be sure, even in France and Germany where the opposition was greatest, many more people today attribute 'the problem with the US' as due to 'mostly Bush' rather than to the 'US in general'. This suggests that the possibility of a 'benign imperium' is still widely thought to exist even in the other advanced capitalist countries.[43] But in so far as the conditions making for American military intervention clearly transcend a given administration, and in so far as a benign imperium can hardly prove to be more than an illusion in today's world, this is a currency that could be less stable than the American dollar. The ideological space may be opening up for the kind of mobilization from below, combining the domestic concerns of subordinate classes and other oppressed social forces with the anti-globalization and anti-war movements, that can eventually lead to a fundamental change in the domestic balance of social forces, and the transformation of the nature and role of those states can bring about their disarticulation from the empire.

It is the fear of this that fuels, on the one hand, the pleas of those who entreat the imperium to be more benign and to present itself in a more multilateralist fashion, at least symbolically; and, on the other hand, the actions of those who are using the fear of terrorism to close the space for public dissent within each state. This is especially so within the US itself. The old question posed by those who, at the founding of the American state, questioned whether an extended empire could be consistent with republican liberty – posed again and again over the subsequent two centuries by those at home who stood up against American imperialism – is back on the agenda. The need to sustain intervention abroad by mobilizing support and limiting opposition through instilling fear and repression at home raises the prospect that the American state may become more authoritarian internally as part of it becoming more blatantly aggressive externally. But the unattractiveness of an empire that is no longer concealed in its coercive nature at home as well as abroad suggests that anti-imperialist struggles – even in the rich capitalist states at the heart of the empire as well as in the poor ones at its extremities – will have growing mass appeal and force.

## NOTES

1  Harold Innis, 'Great Britain, The United States and Canada', Twenty-First Cust Foundation Lecture, University of Nottingham, 21 May 1948, in Harold Innis, *Essays in Canadian Economic History* (Toronto: University of Toronto Press, 1956), 407.

2  Quoted in William Appleman Williams, *Empire as a Way of Life* (New York: Oxford University Press, 1980), 189.

3  See 'Rebuilding America's Defenses: Strategy, Forces and Resources For a New Century', A Report of the Project for the New American Century, http://www.newamericancentury.org/publicationsreports.htm; and *The National Security Strategy of the United States of America* (Falls Village, CT: Winterhouse, 2002).

4  Michael Ignatieff, 'The Burden', *New York Times Magazine*, 5 January 2003.

5  Zbigniew Brzezinski, *The Grand Chessboard: American Primacy and Its Geostrategic Imperative* (New York: Basic Books, 1997), 40.

6  Antonio Santosuosso, *Storming the Heavens: Soldiers, Emperor, and Civilians in the Roman Empire* (Boulder, CO: Westview Press, 2001), 151–2.

7  Gareth Stedman Jones, 'The Specificity of US Imperialism', *New Left Review* 60 (first series, March/April 1970): 1.

8  Giovanni Arrighi, *The Geometry of Imperialism* (London: New Left Books, 1978), 17.

9  Bruce Cumings, 'Global Realm with No Limit, Global Realm with No Name', *Radical History Review* 57 (1993): 47–8.

10  Andrew L. Bacevich, *American Empire: The Realities and Consequences of U.S. Diplomacy* (Cambridge, MA: Harvard University Press, 2002), 3.

11  Quoted in ibid., 1, 219.

12  Michael Hardt and Antonio Negri, *Empire* (Cambridge, MA: Harvard University Press, 2000), xiv, emphasis in text. See our review essay, 'Gems and Baubles in Empire', *Historical Materialism* 10 (2002): 17–43.

13  Ellen Meiksins Wood, *Empire of Capital* (London: Verso, 2003), 72.

14  See John Willoughby, *Capitalist Imperialism: Crisis and the State* (New York: Harwood Academic Publishers, 1986), esp. 7–8; and Harry

Magdoff, *The Age of Imperialism* (New York: Monthly Review Press, 1969), esp. 13.

15 Williams, *Empire as a Way of Life*, 185, quoting a biographer of Dean Acheson.

16 Perry Anderson, 'Force and Consent', *New Left Review* 17 (September/October 2002): 24.

17 Ibid., 25. See also Daniel Lazare, *The Frozen Republic* (New York: Harcourt Brace, 1996).

18 Quoted in Williams, *Empire as a Way of Life*, 61. Jefferson had already come to accept Madison's 'expansionist' perspective that republican liberty was not incompatible with an extended state, or with a strong federal government.

19 Quoted in Williams, *Empire as a Way of Life*, 43.

20 See Marc Engel, *A Mighty Empire: The Origins of the American Revolution* (Ithaca, NY: Cornell University Press, 1988).

21 Bernard DeVoto, *The Course of Empire* (1952) (Lincoln, NE: University of Nebraska Press, 1983), 275.

22 See the first two chapters of Gabriel Kolko's *Main Currents in Modern American History* (New York: Harper & Row, 1976); see also Charles C. Bright, 'The State in the United States During the Nineteenth Century', in Charles Bright and Susan Harding (eds.), *Statemaking and Social Movements* (Ann Arbor, MI: University of Michigan Press, 1984).

23 Anderson, 'Force and Consent', 25.

24 Williams, *Empire as a Way of Life*, 122.

25 Stedman Jones, 'The Specificity', 63.

26 Quoted in Gilbert Achcar, *The Clash of Barbarisms* (New York: Monthly Review Press, 2002), 96.

27 Quoted in Margaret Macmillan, *Paris 1919* (New York: Random House 2003), 9. See also Neil Smith, *The Endgame of Globalization* (New York: Routledge, 2004), esp. Chapter 2.

28 Letter to Duncan Grant, quoted in Nicholas Fraser, 'More than Economist', *Harper's Magazine* (November 2001), 80. The issue here, of course, was the American state's refusal to forgive Allied war debts, with all the consequences this entailed for the imposition of heavy German reparations payments. See Michael Hudson's *Super Imperialism: The Economic Strategy of American Empire* (New York: Holt, Rinehart and Winston, 1971).

29 Brian Waddell, 'Corporate Influence and World War II: Resolving the New Deal Political Stalemate', *Journal of Political History* 11:3 (1999): 2.

30 Michael Barratt Brown, *The Economics of Imperialism* (Harmondsworth: Penguin, 1974), 208–9.

31 See Raymond Aron, *The Imperial Republic: The United States and the World 1945–1973* (Cambridge, MA: Winthrop, 1974), esp. 168 and 217; and Nicos Poulantzas, *Classes in Contemporary Capitalism* (London: New Left Books, 1974), esp. 39 and 57.

32 On the relationship between the collapse of the gold standard, capital mobility and the development of democratic pressures, see Barry Eichengreen, *Globalizing Capital: A History of the International Monetary System* (Princeton, NJ: Princeton University Press, 1996), Chapters 2–3.

On the developments within US finance itself in the 1970s, and their impact abroad, see Michael Moran, *The Politics of the Financial Services Revolution* (London: Macmillan, 1991).

33  See Poulantzas, *Classes in Contemporary Capitalism*, esp. 81; and Robert Cox, *Production Power and World Order* (New York: Columbia University Press, 1987), 253–67.

34  See Greg Albo, 'Contesting the New Capitalism', and Leo Panitch and Sam Gindin, 'Euro-Capitalism and American Empire', both in David Coates (ed.), *Varieties of Capitalism, Varieties of Approaches* (New York: Palgrave Macmillan, 2005).

35  See Saskia Sassen, *Losing Control? Sovereignty in an Age of Globalization* (New York: Columbia University Press, 1996). See also Stephen Gill, *Power and Resistance in the New World Order* (New York: Palgrave Macmillan, 2003).

36  John Grahl, 'Globalized Finance: The Challenge to the Euro', *New Left Review* 8 (March/April 2001): 44. On the increasing adoption of American management practices in Europe, see Mick Carpenter and Steve Jefferys, *Management, Work and Welfare in Western Europe* (London: Edward Elgar, 2000).

37  *Economist* (27 May 2003).

38  See Dan Bousfield, 'Export-Led Development and Imperialism: A Response to Burkett and Hart-Landsberg', *Historical Materialism* 11:1 (2003): 147–60. The counter-argument, in terms of Japan's 'leadership from behind', is best set out in Giovanni Arrighi and Beverly Silver (eds.), *Chaos and Governance in the World System* (Minneapolis, MN: University of Minnesota Press, 1999).

39  See Paul Rogers, 'The US Military Posture: A Uniquely Benign Imperialism', in Leo Panitch and Colin Leys (eds.), *The New Imperial Challenge: The Socialist Register 2004* (London: Merlin, 2003), 146–65.

40  'The United Nations after the Gulf War: A Promise Betrayed', Stephen Lewis interviewed by Jim Wurst, *World Policy Journal* (Summer 1991): 539–49.

41  Thomas P. M. Barnett, 'The Pentagon's New Map: It Explains Why We're Going to War and Why We'll Keep Going to War', *Esquire* (March 2003).

42  Nicholas Lavranos, 'Europol and the Fight Against Terrorism', *European Foreign Affairs Review* 8 (2003): 264–5.

43  See the report on the Pew Global Attitudes Survey in the *Financial Times* (4 June 2003).

# 2
# Interpreting the Fall of a Monument

*Jürgen Habermas*

Translated by Max Pensky

On 9 April 2004, the entire world watched as American troops threw a noose around the neck of the dictator and, surrounded by a jubilant throng of Iraqis, pulled him off his pedestal. The apparently unshakeable monument tottered, and then finally fell. But before it crashed satisfyingly to the ground, there was a momentary pause before the force of gravity could overcome the statue's grotesquely unnatural, horizontal posture. Bobbing gently up and down, the massive figure clung, for one last moment, to its horror.

Just as an optical illusion, looked at long enough, will 'flip' into a new form, so the public perception of the war in Iraq seemed to perform an about-face at this one scene. The morally obscene – the 'shock and awe' inflicted on a helpless and mercilessly bombed population – morphed into the image of joyful citizens freed from terror and oppression in the Shi'ite district of Baghdad. Both images contain a grain of truth, even as they evoke contradictory moral feelings and attitudes. Must ambivalent feelings lead to contradictory judgments?

The matter is simple enough at first glance. A war in violation of international law remains illegal, even if it leads to normatively desirable outcomes. But is this the whole story? Bad consequences can discredit good intentions. Can't good consequences generate their own justifying force after the fact? The mass graves, the underground dungeons and the testimony of the tortured all leave no doubt about the criminal nature of the regime. The liberation of a brutalized population from a barbaric regime is a great good; among political goods it is the greatest of all. In this regard, the Iraqis themselves, whether they are currently celebrating, looting, demonstrating against their occupiers or simply apathetic, contribute to the judgment on the moral nature of the war. But in Germany, two reactions stand out in the political public sphere.

On one side, pragmatic minds affirm the normative force of the factual. They rely on the powers of practical judgment and a healthy sense of the political limits of morality, which let them appreciate the consequences of victory. In their eyes, protracted arguments over the justification for war are simply *fruitless*. The war is now an historical fact. Others simply *capitulate* to the force of the factual, whether out of conviction or opportunism. They brush aside what they now see as the dogmatism of international law, reasoning that just this dogmatism, held captive by a sort of post-heroic squeamishness over the risks and costs of military force, has become blind to the true value of political freedom.

Both of these responses are inadequate. They both succumb to an emotional response to the supposed abstractions of a 'bloodless moralism' without having grasped just what the neo-conservatives in Washington have actually offered up as their alternative to the domestication of state power through international law. Their alternative is neither political realism nor the pathos of freedom. Instead, the neo-conservatives make a revolutionary claim: if the regime of international law fails, then the hegemonic imposition of a global liberal order is justified, even by means that are hostile to international law.

Wolfowitz is not Kissinger. He is a revolutionary, not a cynical technician of political power. To be sure, the American superpower reserves the right to take unilateral action, pre-emptive if necessary, and to employ all available military means to secure its hegemonic status against all possible rivals. But global power is not an end in itself for the new ideologues. What distinguishes the neo-conservatives from the 'realist' school of international relations is the vision of an American global political order that has definitively broken with the reformist programme of UN human rights policies. While not betraying liberal goals, this vision is shattering the civil limits that the UN Charter – with good reason – had placed on their realization.

At present, the United Nations is certainly not yet in any position to compel a non-compliant member state to guarantee democracy and the rule of law to its own citizens. And the highly selective enforcement of the UN's human rights policy is itself the product of political realities: equipped with veto power, Russia need not fear any armed intervention in Chechnya. Saddam Hussein's use of nerve gas against the Iraqi Kurdish population is only one of many chapters in the disgraceful chronicle of failures of a world organization that has averted its gaze even from genocide. In the aftermath of World War II, the core mission of the UN – enforcing the prohibition on wars of aggression – eliminated the *jus ad bellum* and placed the sovereignty of individual states under new limits, thus taking a first decisive step on the path towards a cosmopolitan legal order. That core mission is now more crucial than ever.

For half a century the United States could be counted as the pace-maker for progress on this cosmopolitan path. With the war in Iraq, it has not only abandoned this role, it has also given up its role as guarantor of international rights. And its violation of international law sets a disastrous precedent for the superpowers of the future. Let us have no illusions: the normative authority of the US lies in ruins. Neither of the two conditions for a legally permissible use of military force was fulfilled: the war was not a case of self-defence against an actual attack or the immediate threat of one, nor was it authorized by a decision of the Security Council according to Chapter VII of the UN Charter. Neither Resolution 1441 nor any of the 17 previous (and 'spent') resolutions on Iraq can count as a sufficient authorization. The 'coalition of the willing' confirmed this failure performatively as it initially sought a 'second' resolution, but in the end refused to bring the motion to a vote because it could not even rely on the 'moral' majority of the Security Council not to veto. The whole procedure turned into farce as the President of the United States repeatedly declared his intention of acting without the mandate of the UN if necessary. From the very beginning the Bush Doctrine made it impossible to understand the military deployment in the Gulf region as a mere threat, for this would presuppose that somehow the threatened sanctions could have been averted.

Nor does a comparison with the intervention in Kosovo offer an excuse. Of course, in the case of Kosovo too, there was no authorization by the Security Council. But three circumstances of the intervention there offered legitimation after the fact. First, the intervention aimed at the prevention of ethnic cleansing, which was known at the time of the intervention to be taking place. Second, it was tasked with fulfilling the provision of international law for emergency aid, addressed to all nations. And finally, we can refer to the undisputed democratic and rule-of-law character of all the members of the acting military coalition. Today, normative dissent has divided the West itself.

Already at that time, in April 1999, a remarkable difference had emerged between the continental European and the Anglo-American powers over strategies for justifying military action. The Europeans had drawn the lesson from the disaster at Srebrenica: they understood armed intervention as a way of closing the gap between efficiency and legitimacy that had been opened by earlier peacekeeping operations, and thus saw it as a means for making progress towards fully institutionalized civil rights. Britain and America, conversely, satisfied themselves with the normative goal of promulgating their own liberal order internationally, through violence if necessary. At the time of the intervention in Kosovo, I had attributed this difference to contrasting traditions of legal thought – Immanuel Kant's cosmopolitanism on the one side, John Stuart Mill's liberal nationalism on the other. But in light of the hegemonic unilateralism that the leading thinkers of the Bush Doctrine have pursued since 1991 (see the documentation by Stefan Frölich in *Frankfurter Allgemeine*, 10 April 2003), one suspects in hindsight that the American delegation had already led the negotiations at Rambouillet from just this peculiar viewpoint. Be that as it may, George W. Bush's decision to consult the Security Council certainly did not arise from any wish for legitimation through international law, which had long since been regarded, at least internally, as superfluous. Rather, this rear guard action was desired only in so far as it broadened the basis for a 'coalition of the willing', and soothed a worried population.

All this notwithstanding, we should not interpret the neo-conservative doctrine as the expression of a normative cynicism. Geostrategic objectives such as securing spheres of influence or access to essential resources, which the doctrine must also meet, may well invite analysis in terms of a critique of ideology. But such conventional explanations trivialize what, until 18 months ago, was still an unimaginable break with norms that the US had been committed to. We would do well, in other words, not to guess at motives, but to take the doctrine at face value. For otherwise we fail to recognize the truly revolutionary character of a political reorientation; a transformation that finds its sources in the historical experiences of the previous century.

Hobsbawm rightly named the twentieth century the 'American century'. Neo-conservatives can see themselves as 'victors' and can take undisputed successes – the reordering of Europe and the Pacific after the surrender of Germany and Japan, as well as the reshaping of Eastern and Central Europe after the collapse of the Soviet Union – as the model for a new world order, all carried out under the leadership of the United States. From the liberal perspective of a *post-histoire*, *à la* Fukuyama, this model has the advantage of making laborious and awkward discussions of normative goals pointless: what could possibly be better for people than the world-wide spread of liberal states and the globalization of free markets? Moreover, the road there is clearly marked: Germany, Japan and Russia were forced to their knees by war and the arms race. In today's era of asymmetric warfare, military might is now more attractive than ever, since the victor is determined *a priori* and can purchase victory with relatively few victims. Wars that make the world better need no *further* justification. From this point of view, at the minor cost of some collateral damage, they remove undisputed evils that would survive under the aegis of a powerless community of nations. Saddam Hussein pulled from his pedestal *is* a sufficient argument for justification.

This doctrine was developed long before the terror attack on the twin towers. The cleverly manipulated mass psychology of the all too understandable shock of September 11 certainly helped to create the initial climate in which the new doctrine could find widespread support – now in a rather different, more potent version, intensified by the addition of a 'war against terrorism'. This intensification of the Bush Doctrine depends on defining an essentially new phenomenon in the terms of conventional warfare. In the case of the Taliban regime, there was a causal connection between an elusive terrorism and a 'rogue state' – an enemy that could be attacked and seized. This provided a model for understanding interstate warfare as a weapon against an insidious threat emerging from highly diffuse and globalized networks.

As opposed to the doctrine's original version, this connection between hegemonic unilateralism and doing battle against a creeping threat introduces the argument for self-defence. But this also imposes new burdens of proof. The American government had to try to convince a global public sphere of contacts between Saddam Hussein and al-Qaeda. At least at home, the disinformation campaign was so successful that, according to the most recent polls, 60 per cent of Americans welcomed the defeat of Saddam as 'payback' for the terror attacks of September 11. Apart from the difficulty of the lack of evidence, the Bush Doctrine doesn't even offer a plausible explanation for the *preventive* use of military force. The violence of the new kind of global terrorism – 'war in peacetime' – escapes the categories of state warfare. It cannot justify the necessity of revising and loosening the strict clause that regulates states' self-defence in international law, and by no means in favour of permitting an anticipated *military* self-defence.

In the face of enemies who are globally networked, decentralized and invisible, the only effective kinds of prevention will be on *other* operative levels. Neither bombs nor rockets, neither fighter jets nor tanks will be of any help. What *will* help is the international networking of flows of information among intelligence services and prosecutorial authorities, the control of flows of money and the rooting out of logistical supplies. The corresponding 'security programmes' in pursuit of these goals are relevant for civil rights within a state, not international law. Other dangers which arise from failures of negligence in non-proliferation policies (concerning nuclear, chemical and biological weapons) are at any rate better handled through stubborn negotiation and inspection than with wars of disarmament, as the subdued reaction to North Korea illustrates.

The addition of a war on terrorism to the original doctrine therefore offers no new legitimacy for the pursuit of a hegemonic world order. Saddam toppled from his pedestal remains the argument: a symbol for a new liberal order for an entire region. The war in Iraq is a link in the chain bringing about a new world order, justifying itself with the claim that it replaces the futile human rights politics of an exhausted world organization. What speaks against it? Moral feelings lead us astray because they attach to individual scenes and particular images. There is no way to avoid the question of how to justify the war as a whole. The crucial issue of dissent is whether justification through international law can, and should, be replaced by the unilateral, world-ordering politics of a self-appointed hegemon.

*Empirical* objections to the possibility of realizing the American vision converge in the thesis that global society has become far too complex; the world is no longer accessible to centralized control, through politics backed up by military power. In the technologically supreme and heavily armed superpower's fear of terrorism, one can sense a 'Cartesian anxiety' – the fear of a subject trying to objectify both itself and the world around it, trying to bring everything under control. Politics loses its primacy over the horizontally networked media of both markets and communication once it attempts to regress to the original, Hobbesian form of a hierarchical security system. A state that sees all its options reduced to the stupid alternatives of war or peace quickly runs up against the limits of its own organizational capacities and resources. It also steers the process of political and cultural negotiation down a false track, and drives the costs of coordination to dizzying heights.

But even if the design for a politics of hegemonic unilateralism could be implemented, it would generate side-effects that are undesirable according to its own normative criteria. The more that political power (understood in its role as a global civilizing force) is exercised in the dimensions of the military, secret security services and the police, the more it comes into conflict with its own purposes, endangering the mission of improving the world according to the liberal vision. In the US itself, the administration of a perpetual 'wartime president' is already undermining the foundations of the rule of law. Quite apart from methods of torture that are practised or tolerated outside the nation's borders, the wartime regime has not only robbed the prisoners in Guantánamo of the rights they are entitled to according to the Geneva Convention; it has expanded the powers of law enforcement and security officials to the point of infringing on the constitutional rights of America's own citizens. And wouldn't the Bush Doctrine demand normatively counterproductive measures in the (not improbable) scenario that the citizens of Iraq, Syria, Jordan, Kuwait, etc. made a less than friendly use of the very democratic freedoms that the American government wants to give them? The Americans liberated Kuwait in 1991; they didn't democratize it.

Above all, however, the American superpower's self-proclaimed role of trustee runs up against the objections of its own allies, who remain unconvinced *on good normative grounds* of its paternalistic claim to unilateral leadership. There was a time when liberal nationalism saw itself justified in promulgating the universal values of its own liberal order, with military force if necessary, throughout the entire world. This arrogance doesn't become any more tolerable when it is transferred from nation-states to a single hegemonic state. It is precisely the universalistic core of democracy and human rights that forbids their unilateral realization at gunpoint. The universal validity claim that commits the West to its 'basic political values', that is, to the procedure of democratic self-determination and the vocabulary of human rights, must not be confused with the imperialist claim that the political form of life and the culture of a particular democracy – even the oldest one – is exemplary for all societies.

The 'universalism' of the old empires was of this sort, perceiving the world beyond the distant horizon of its borders only from the centralizing perspective of its own worldview. Modern self-understanding, by contrast, has been shaped by an egalitarian universalism that requires a decentralization of one's own perspective. It demands that one relativize one's own views to the interpretive perspectives of equally situated and equally entitled others. It was precisely the insight of American pragmatism that reciprocal perspective-taking paves the way for grasping what is in each case equally good for all parties. The 'reason' of modern rational law does not consist of universal 'values' that one can own like goods, and distribute and export throughout the world. 'Values' – including those that have a chance of winning global recognition – don't come from thin air. They gain their binding force only within normative orders and practices of particular forms of cultural life. If thousands of Shi'ites in Nasiriya demonstrate in equal measure against both Saddam and the American occupation, they express the truth that non-Western cultures must appropriate the universalistic content of human rights from their own resources and in their own interpretation, one that will construct a convincing connection to local experiences and interests.

And this is why multilateral will-formation in interstate relations is not simply one option among others. From its self-chosen isolation, even the good hegemon, having appointed itself the trustee of general interests, cannot *know* whether what it maintains is in the interest of others to do is, in fact, *equally* good for all. There is no sensible alternative to the ongoing development of international law into a cosmopolitan order that offers an equal and reciprocal hearing for the voices of all those affected. The world organization of the United Nations has so far not suffered truly significant damage. In so far as the 'small' member states on the Security Council refused to buckle under pressure from the larger states, it has even gained in prestige and influence. The reputation of the world organization can suffer only self-inflicted damage: if it were to try, through compromises, to 'redeem' the irredeemable.

# 3

# The Iraq War: Critical Reflections from 'Old Europe'

*Ulrich K. Preuss*

Translated by Christiane Wilke

On 24 August 1814, English troops occupied Washington, the capital of the newly founded and still fragile United States of America. The troops, led by General Robert Ross and Admiral Sir George Cockburn, deliberately burned down all public buildings, including the Capitol and the White House. General Ross personally supervised the soldiers, who piled up the furniture from the White House and then set it on fire. The well-disciplined troops were ordered to leave private property untouched. Among the public buildings, only the Patent Office was spared. The wily director of the office had convinced Ross that the patents stored there were the private property of their inventors.

President Madison and his administration were forced to flee to neighbouring Virginia. Madison never recovered from this humiliation. More importantly, the event remained engraved in the nation's collective memory. Washington in flames became the tangible and material evidence that even the blessings of the geographical distance from Europe, with its multiple quarrels and wars, could not fully protect the American Republic. Staying away from Europe was a fundamental political principle of the young republic. 'Why,' George Washington asked in his Farewell Address on 17 September 1796, 'by interweaving our destiny with that of any part of Europe, entangle our peace and prosperity in the toils of European ambition, rivalry, interest, humor or caprice?' He promptly answered his rhetorical question: 'It is our true policy to steer clear of permanent alliances with any portion of the foreign world.' Being a realist, he added that this stance applies only in so far 'as we are now at liberty to do it'.

This doctrine marks the core of a powerful and sometimes dominant current of American foreign policy. In a study of the history of American foreign policy published towards the end of the twentieth century, James Chace and Caleb Carr characterized this foreign policy tenor as 'the quest for absolute security'.[1] Absolute security means independence from any power or alliance, friendly or not, in matters of national security. The exemplary counter-concept was the widely criticized European model of relative security. This balance-of-power model had emerged from the logic of the Westphalian Order. The external security of states was made dependent on the mutual balance of power, on shifting alliances and skilful manoeuvring, diplomatic finesse, cunning intrigues, treachery, and cold-blooded interest calculations by different actors in a game full of plotting and scheming. However repugnant and cynical this system may seem to us, it contained an early form of collective security in so far as national security is thought to be possible only in relation to and in cooperation with other states.

Given this history, it should not surprise us that the American proponents of the concept of absolute security have seen – and probably continue to see – the contrast with the European model not only as a political and strategic difference, but also in terms of a moral contrast. America was the embodiment of the universal republic, founded on reason, self-evident truths and inalienable rights. In contrast, the Europe of dynasties, with their courtly etiquette, intrigues and diplomatic hair-splitting, represented the dark and backward past from which the Pilgrim Fathers and many other upright, honest men and women had fled. The geographical distance between the United States and Europe corresponded to a superiority vis-à-vis the old continent. This sense of superiority was ultimately based on the deep religious conviction of being a chosen people.

At first glance, it is startling that, in spite of this geographically and historically grounded philosophy of foreign policy self-sufficiency, the United States was drawn into foreign conflicts in Europe and other distant corners of the earth. We certainly need to take into account not only the general doctrine, but also Washington's caveat that there will always be geopolitical situations in which the US cannot afford to abstain from close political alliances with other nations. The Cold War – between the end of World War II and the fall of the Berlin Wall – was certainly a period in which pure isolation was not tenable. Nevertheless, a closer examination reveals that US global intervention did not occur in spite of this doctrine, but because of it. Absolute security demands nothing less than the control of all forces that could potentially endanger the territorial integrity or political independence of the nation. In an increasingly interdependent world, such dangers might be posed by states far removed from the United States. The insistence on complete independence forecloses the option of making national security dependent on relationships of trust or even friendship with other states. The quest for absolute security therefore tends, according to Chace and Carr, to support military responses to perceived threats. For this reason, Americans have never shied away from using unilateral force as a means of protecting national security in regions they perceived as a vital threat. The intervention in Afghanistan is only the most recent instance of a refusal to put national security interests into the hands of an alliance.

Such unilateralism is the flipside of the genuinely American principle of relying on one's own strength to solve problems. But the imperative of absolute security has the disquieting attribute of being internally unbounded. Whoever strives for invulnerability based on his own power must extend the realm of his control indefinitely and yet will never feel completely safe. Absolute security will come only when everything has ceased to change and we are at the End of History. This might be the reason why Francis Fukuyama's *End of History* became so popular in the United States. The promise of the book's title might just as well have been 'Absolute Security'.

It is not a coincidence that Fukuyama's thesis was premised on the final victory of liberal democracy over all competing systems of government. In fact, the world might be made significantly safer if elementary forms of self-determination, the rule of law and the protection of human rights existed in all states. But the world is not perfect. Whoever demands perfect security in an imperfect world invariably faces enigmas. Most importantly, whoever demands perfect security in an imperfect world is a problem for others. A nation claiming the privilege of absolute security for itself will tend to see despotic regimes as threats to its national security and will insist on its right to rid the world of them by military means. The United States can do this without embarrassment since – unlike Europe – it does not see any contradiction between state sovereignty and human rights. Did not the founding fathers declare the right to political self-determination a fundamental human right? How can liberating a people – if necessary by military means – be construed as a violation of sovereignty? Accordingly, the national security rationale for intervention is reinforced by a universalistic legal and moral principle.

Robert Kagan has rightly claimed that Americans and Europeans have different perspectives on international politics. The phrase 'old Europe', brought up by the US Secretary of Defense, Donald Rumsfeld, is only the polemical dramatization of a quintessentially correct analysis. Contemporary Europe's visions of international security are in fact a continuation of the old dynastic system of balancing power among equally sovereign states – adapted to the democratic age, to be sure, but the principle is the same. The international law framework of the United Nations is the appropriate current form of this old principle. It is a system of collective security that incorporates potential aggressors into a network of common obligations, institutions and procedures, thereby creating trust and transforming the international state of nature into an international legal condition. The philosophical origins of this concept lie in Immanuel Kant's 'federation of free republics', but, paradoxically, the political institutionalization of this concept was initiated by Woodrow Wilson. In the United States, Wilson does not enjoy a particularly good reputation. His idea of the League of Nations was never popular in the United States. It is one of the great ironies of history that the president who created the League of Nations could not convince his nation to become a member. Yet this is not a break with US foreign policy traditions. The reason why the US never joined the League of Nations is that the Senate refused to ratify the Treaty of Versailles – the first 26 articles of the treaty were simultaneously the statute of the League of Nations. George Washington posthumously won against Woodrow Wilson.

The differences between American and European views about the order of world politics are thus deeply rooted in the history of international relations. It should come as no surprise that these differences resurfaced during the Iraq crisis. In this situation, the two concepts of security clashed directly: the concept of relative security with the UN model of collective security on the one hand, and the concept of absolute security based on the unilateral protection of national security on the other. During the intervention in Afghanistan that followed 11 September 2001, these two approaches could still be brought into convergence. The Europeans gained the reassurance of two UN Security Council resolutions that authorized the military actions as an exercise of the right to self-defence pursuant to Article 51 of the UN Charter. The Americans, in contrast, assumed the existence of a situation triggering the duties of assistance among NATO partners according to Article 5 of the NATO Treaty. Once their troops were on the ground, however, they politely but firmly refused any assistance offered by NATO partners, with the justification that their own military capacity permitted them to go it alone. Both sides had good reasons for claiming that they were remaining true to their respective principles while in full agreement with the other side.

The dissonances between the United States and 'old' Europe that were already apparent during the Afghanistan crisis have deepened tremendously during the Iraq crisis. The issue was not, as it seemed to the casual observer, the choice between war and peace. The actual stakes of this trans-Atlantic dispute can be seen only once we acknowledge the real point of disagreement: war according to the criteria of the US, or war according to the legality of the UN. How is this choice to be understood?

Military measures can only be in accordance with the UN Charter if they are 'military sanctions' authorized by the UN Security Council in cases where non-military means of conflict resolution have failed – setting aside for the moment the right to self-defence under Article 51, which cannot justify intervention in Iraq. These military sanctions are coercive measures that the international legal community can take against member states that breach or threaten international peace or security. Since the UN does not have its own troops, member states acting on the basis of a Security Council authorization execute these coercive measures. The external appearance of these 'measures' exhibits all the characteristics of war: the blind destructive force of military might certainly does not fail to register in such cases. Yet there is a good reason why the UN Charter avoids the terminology of war in this context. The 'military measures' are, strictly speaking, no longer wars in the classical sense. The classic notion of war is that of an exercise of force between states that, due to the lack of a common law and a common judge, settle their disputes over legal claims or legally protected interests through the exercise of military might.

According to these criteria, military measures on the basis of Security Council resolutions are not wars because the UN Charter is a legal order binding on all nations and thus capable of providing legally ordered procedures for conflict resolution. The most extreme of these legal measures for resolving disputes are the 'military sanctions' mentioned above; they represent an embryonic form of police measures taken by a community against those members derelict in their duties. This type of force is aimed at the re-establishment of a damaged legal order. This conception might explain why many people do not view 'military measures' authorized by the Security Council as moral catastrophes on a par with 'real wars'. At the least, as we saw in the case of Iraq, military sanctions trigger significantly less resistance than pure wars among states. If the suffering of the victims was the yardstick, such a differentiation would not be very convincing. Even though measures authorized by the Security Council fulfil a police function, their use of force is essentially a military one. The purpose of the use of force in police operations is strictly limited to warding off dangers, with the permissible means restricted accordingly. The aim of police operations is to incapacitate individuals threatening public safety. Military operations, in contrast, are aimed against an entire country and its inhabitants. Even if international law declares only military objects to be legitimate targets, this restriction is not very effective, given the current complex interconnections between civilian and military infrastructure. The so-called collateral damage to civilians and civilian infrastructure can easily exceed the damage to military targets, as we saw in the war in Kosovo.

In the case of Iraq, the mix of police functions and military attributes which characterizes the UN-sanctioned 'military measures', leads to complicated self-contradictions.

Iraq was ruled by a hideous regime headed by a brutal autocrat. It was pressured to destroy weapons of mass destruction which experts had good reason to believe existed within its boundaries. Severe measures, including military sanctions, were used as threats in the event of non-compliance. However, there is no definitive knowledge as to whether the regime possessed such weapons, or how many. Even if it had been known with certainty that the regime possessed such weapons, military measures would not have been advisable. In that case, military measures would only have provoked the use of the weapons of mass destruction by a regime that was virtually unsurpassed in unscrupulousness. At the very least, a ground invasion would have been ruled out. This was the rationale for the – not implausible – argument of those who asserted that the US was preparing for war against Iraq, despite the fact that the existence of weapons of mass destruction there remained uncertain, while at the same time it was negotiating with North Korea, another regime belonging to the 'axis of evil' and certainly in possession of such weapons. On the other hand, military measures against Iraq could also have been ruled out if one had known with certainty that the regime did *not* possess such weapons. In this case, it would have been likely that the regime could not have used weapons of mass destruction or passed them on to terrorist groups. In order to eliminate this uncertainty, UN inspectors worked to scrutinize the country's facilities. If the inspectors had never found such weapons, there would have been no *casus belli*. If they failed to locate such weapons, there would have been strong arguments against the war as well, since the danger could have been most effectively removed by forcing the country to destroy them – or taking their own steps to destroy them. Military enforcement of disarmament would only be warranted if the country violently resisted the destruction of any weapons found. But this situation never arose.

The only remaining possible justification for military action within the UN framework would be the use of military measures in order to force the Iraqi regime to disclose its arsenals so that the world might finally have full certainty about its weapons of mass destruction. In fact, domestic regulations of police conduct usually provide for the authorized use of force where grave danger is suspected. For example, if there is uncertainty about whether all animals in a herd of cattle are infected with BSE, the authorities may cull all the animals in order to protect the life and health of consumers. But is it possible to wage a war without the certainty that there is a *casus belli*? Is a 'war grounded on a reasonable suspicion' imaginable?

In this situation riddled with uncertainties, the conduct of some governments raises further questions. Even after the EU members agreed on a common position on 17 February 2003, the German government – more precisely, the Chancellor and, in a more roundabout way, the Foreign Minister – rejected the use of force in Iraq, irrespective of the outcome of the UN weapons inspections. At the same time, the Chancellor and the Foreign Minister supported the US threat of military force as a means of buttressing the work of the inspectors. So far, however, neither of them has explained the feasibility of a strategy that pressures a regime to cooperate by military threats while simultaneously issuing assurances that the threat of force will under no circumstances – not even in the case of persistent non-cooperation – be transformed into actual use of force. On the other hand, there is the question why the US fiercely insisted on proving the existence of weapons of mass destruction in Iraq and tried to force Saddam Hussein to admit their existence, while at the same time it became apparent that war against Iraq would be waged irrespective of the results of the UN inspections. Given these circumstances, what incentives for cooperating with the US could Saddam possibly have had in a situation in which he seemed unable to prevent his own downfall?

Quite obviously, a war aimed at the disarmament of a state merely suspected of having weapons – it is even less certain whether the weapons, which were last sighted five years ago, are still functional – cannot be justified. War is despicable even to people who are not commited pacifists. War is, as the preamble to the UN Charter expresses rightly and with pathos, 'a scourge, which ... has brought untold sorrow to mankind'. War is a rupture of civilization; war embodies the negation of basic principles of well-ordered societies. The logic of war implies the indiscriminate killing of persons, and the destruction of the natural environment, infrastructure, foodstuffs and cultural artefacts. War implements the principle of collective responsibility that the modern world in its legal-moral development has long overcome. The legal recognition of war is restricted to its elementary form: the right to self-defence against an armed aggressor. Under no circumstances may war be conducted as 'the continuation of politics by other means', as Karl von Clausewitz naively defined it at the beginning of the nineteenth century.

Even those motivated by justified anger or benign calculations who seek to employ military force for the destruction of an abhorrent regime will inevitably be entangled in the moral contradiction that war – in its indiscriminate character effectively indistinguishable from collective punishment – will invariably kill and injure the innocent. Given the empirical evidence, war will, in all likelihood, harm more innocent people than guilty ones. Which moral reasons could justify the death of so many innocent people as the price to be paid for the punishment and dethronement of a few culprits?

To pose the reverse question: was it morally justified to exclude the sanction of war against Iraq under all circumstances, irrespective of the results of the neutral inspectors' inspection of the destructive capabilities of the regime? After all, there might have been a chance that the Iraqi regime, which could be relied on to be unscrupulous, would have tried to hold the entire Gulf region, including Israel, hostage in order to force its will on the world. In such a situation, how much should America risk, and how much should Europe risk? Is North Korea not enough of a warning? In contrast to Iraq, in the case of this sinister regime, which is driving its own population to the brink of starvation, we need not rely on speculation. Obviously, even a regime of UN inspections could not prevent North Korea from gaining nuclear weapons and from threatening South Korea, Japan and even the United States. Even though neither Iraq nor North Korea possesses systems capable of delivering nuclear warheads beyond their respective regions, how can we be certain that networks of suicide bombers that exist in different parts of the globe could not be converted into human carriers or mobile launching sites for nuclear bombs? After September 11, is this still merely *science fiction*?

A war started without due consideration of the good reasons cautioning against it is morally unjustified. But peace without due consideration of the good reasons cautioning against it is also morally unjustified.

The only issue we could and should have argued about is this: which risks was the world willing to take in the face of an Iraqi regime threatening to use weapons of mass destruction and thereby forcing its will on the international legal community? We need to demand the calm sobriety of a world police capable of weighing up the risks and dangers. The greater the potential damage from weapons of mass destruction in the hands of the Iraqi regime, the smaller we needed to keep the likelihood of the occurrence of this scenario. As such calculations remind us, war harbours risks, but so does peace. The risks of a war are: the destruction of a country, its infrastructure and its oil wells; harm to hundreds of thousands of civilians; and in addition the possibility of a political explosion in a region already wrought with crises, where Israel still faces neighbours threatening its extinction. The risks of peace are: attacks still more devastating than those of September 11; the persistent threat posed by further attacks possibly more intense in their malicious destructive force; the continuing threat of the death of thousands of people due to the now readily available 'small' weapons of mass destruction; and the increasing vulnerability to blackmail by criminal regimes and their terrorist support squads.

Accordingly, the justification of a war of disarmament against Iraq did not require a 'smoking gun', the piece of evidence in criminal law that would prove the existence of functional weapons of mass destruction in the hands of the Iraqi regime 'beyond reasonable doubt'. On the other hand, a merely abstract danger that the regime could possess such weapons, use them or pass them on to terrorist groups was not a sufficient justification for an act as grave and far-reaching as war.

Since we need to rely on complex calculations of risk and the balance of interests, we need to examine the stakes more carefully. What are the implications of the simple fact that the price for liberating a people from brutal dictatorship is the death of many innocent civilians? If a people liberates itself from illegitimate rule through a rebellion or revolution, it is proper to say that the people are taking their fate in their own hands; they take responsibility for the sacrifices necessary to achieve their goal. This case is different from the scenario in which these liberties are introduced from abroad through military intervention by more or less altruistic third parties. John Stuart Mill, like many nineteenth-century liberals, argued that a people needs to fight for its own freedom. Freedom cannot be imposed or granted from abroad.[2] Given the experiences of totalitarian conditions, this position might seem too demanding or even frivolous, since such regimes have superior means of force over the human body and soul. The implication would be that a people living under such circumstances might need to wait for many generations until it is liberated.

Moreover, a people living under totalitarian rule cannot express its opinion on whether it would like to be liberated or not, and what price it would be willing to pay. Without doing violence to the facts on the ground, one can assume that no people, including the Iraqi people bent and brutalized by 40 years of one-party rule, will voluntarily renounce basic human rights guarantees – however problematic the use of the term 'voluntary' might be. On the other hand, among the masses of the people the desire for liberation is never so strong and absolute that any price for liberty would be acceptable. Thus, the brightly shining moral reasons for ousting the criminal regime are dulled by considerations about the price of the liberation. These considerations are all the more important since it is not the liberated but the liberator that unilaterally dictates the price that is overwhelmingly to be paid by the to-be-liberated. This dilemma demonstrates the full range of moral ambiguities surrounding the issue of liberating a people from the rule of a wicked and illegitimate regime through military force.

Given these considerations, it is not surprising that the permissibility of humanitarian intervention is hotly contested among international lawyers and practitioners of international politics. Even those who generally recognize the protection of basic human rights and minimum standards of civilizational achievements as grounds for a legal military intervention are careful to formulate a number of restrictive conditions. Among these conditions is that military intervention must be strictly necessary: military interventions are permissible only as a last resort after all other available means for ending mass human rights violations are exhausted.[3] The cause of human rights, though a morally unambiguous good, needs to demonstrate its feasibility in real life. Paradoxically, the cause of human rights fares best in these tests when the implementation of human rights seems the lesser evil in real-world circumstances. It is only this realism that prevents the highflying or even arrogant idealism of human rights from losing touch with the real existing people and their needs.

Another part of the feasibility test that human rights claims for intervention have to face is the consideration of the consequences of humanitarian intervention on the international political order. Such intervention is an encroachment on state sovereignty as protected by international law, so there is additional warrant for a cautious approach. The sovereignty of states should not be seen as an absolute, even if only because it is too often a shield that ruthless dictators like Saddam Hussein use to protect themselves from international scrutiny and secure impunity for malicious crimes. On the other hand, the equal sovereignty of all states, be they small, poor and powerless or big, wealthy and powerful, is an important step in the direction of civilizing international affairs. In the absence of an international community of equal and sovereign states, the world would relapse into a state of nature where the natural right of the strongest is supreme. In the democratic age, the respect for state sovereignty also entails the respect for the right to self-determination of the people organized in the state. Still, according to international law, non-democratic states also have a claim to the recognition of their sovereignty. In these cases, international law faces a tension between the promotion of human rights and the recognition of equal state sovereignty. Our moral intuitions would lead us to resolve this tension in favour of human rights. However, in the world of states there is no court standing above all states that could lend validity to the moral and legal principles recognized by all. In order to secure a minimum of order and predictability in international affairs, we must accordingly continue to affirm the morally neutral principle of state sovereignty as the basic ordering principle of international politics. State sovereignty protects democratic and non-democratic states equally from interventions and is thus unsatisfactory from a moral point of view. Were this principle to hold sway completely, the world would be forced to stand aside passively while rulers deny people their liberty and their modest share in the achievements of human civilization.

In order to avoid these consequences, the international legal community increasingly favours a cautious restriction of state sovereignty in order to protect fundamental human rights. Still, the same additional restrictions apply here that we discussed in the context of liberating humanitarian interventions: the sacrifices that are typically to be made by the liberated need to be taken into account, and we need to apply the standard of strict necessity. Only when there is a reasonable chance that the long-term benefits of an encroachment on state sovereignty will be higher than the damage to the international order, and if it can be assumed that the intervention will improve the human rights situation in the long run, is humanitarian intervention justified.

Taking these considerations as a yardstick, it is highly questionable whether the US intervention in Iraq met the requirements for a justified intervention. Here we must disregard the knowledge we gained from the war and after the war: it is the situation of uncertainty before the war that is decisive. We have many indications that economic and political pressure on the regime aiming at improving fundamental human rights was by no means exhausted. One could even say that options in this direction were barely explored, since all non-military pressures on the regime were aimed at controlling the stockpiling of weapons of mass destruction. As a consequence, the situation was not one in which the military intervention was the *ultima ratio* for the protection of human rights.

Irrespective of such considerations about balancing uncertainty and risk, the Americans were determined to go to war, while the Germans were determined to oppose it. We may thus assume that these inconsistencies reveal motivations that follow a different logic from that of the function of a world police warding off dangers to the international community. Since the German position will not influence the course of history, let us focus on the determination of the Americans to go to war against Iraq. Why didn't the Americans want to acknowledge that the world would be in a more civilized state if the United States had committed its superior military capacities to the service of the UN and, like a world police, took military measures only in accordance with the Security Council's assessment of the risks and dangers?

The answer to this question is as simple as it is painful to the Europeans: the US military is being used unilaterally because the US military and the resources that US society designated for its use are primarily, if not solely, dedicated to the goal of protecting national security; and because the Americans, as we have seen, traditionally do not make their national security dependent on the decisions of other states, and will certainly not put it in the hands of international institutions.

The hyper-power of the United States, lacking a serious geopolitical rival, does not act as the trustee of the international community, nor is it motivated by the vision of restoring the integrity of the international legal order jeopardized by the lawless Iraqi regime. Rather, the US perceives the establishment of a new world order to be the primary challenge. According to this view, the events of September 11 clearly and brutally demonstrated the necessity of a new world order. This day became an 'international constitutional moment' for the world, but especially for America, as an American lawyer recently stated: a rapid, sudden, extraordinary and dramatic overthrow of the old order. On the rubble of this old order, something new must be built. We are only just starting to understand the character of this new order.

Without much sentimentality, the US faces the fact that now, for the first time since the humiliating 24 August 1814 when Washington went up in flames, it cannot provide reliable security to its people within its territory. This recognition comes in an historical period that marks the peak of US military might, unrivalled by any other power. (To give just one example: the air force second in size to the US Air Force is that of the US Navy.) More systematically and consistently than ever before, the US government is pursuing the goal of achieving security at home through the exercise of power in many faraway regions around the globe, while these efforts are simultaneously met with deep hatred in many parts of the world. America sees itself as forced into the role of an order-creating world power that is ultimately responsible for international security in a global civilization crippled by fragmentation, state disintegration and global terrorism.

It is no coincidence that more thoughtful American discourse increasingly discusses whether the US is becoming an empire – a globally dominant power in possession of a rule spanning nations, bearing all the corresponding burdens and responsibilities. If one follows this perspective for a moment, one needs to add that at least the US is becoming an empire against its will, driven instead by the internal logic of an expansive and insatiable drive for absolute security, incapable of investing trust in others. Louis Begley writes that he is especially proud of one quality of the American Empire, which is that it, in contradistinction to the now collapsed Soviet Empire, rests on states that want to be allies and parts of the empire. While Begley's distinction between the American and Soviet empires seems unobjectionable, it poses the question whether an 'empire of allies' is not an impossible constellation. Allies are in relationships of equal rights and equal footing, mutual respect, voluntary cooperation and, most of all, mutual trust. How can such a concept be reconciled with the unilateral and hierarchical power of an empire over satellite states?

Once we view the United States as an empire, we can plausibly solve the puzzle of why the Americans were seemingly determined to go to war regardless of the results of the weapons inspections. Thus, it is not the cowboy mentality that Europeans like to ascribe to Americans, nor an unresolved father–son relationship in the Bush family, nor the interest in oil – the favourite topic of all geopolitical strategists posing as realists – that would explain US insistence on going to war, but the US resolution to establish a new world order. This world order will not be the international legal community of the United Nations armed with police-like authorities. Rather, this is the order of a strange and unique empire. This empire connects the universal ideals of human rights and democracy to the very particular religious notion of the chosen American people and its historic mission of bringing democracy to the world. It might have been precisely this sense of being the chosen people that gave the generation of the American founders the best reasons for protecting national security like a sanctuary even from the co-determination of democratic allies.

Accordingly, the American Empire is an almost inescapable consequence of American unilateralism, and of the diffuse feeling of the historic mission of the American people. For the last half-century, Europeans have lived quite comfortably in the enjoyment of liberties that were fought for and guaranteed by America. For Europeans, the empire was a friendly one. Empires, however, have their unique political logic. They are not, as Begley assumes, alliances among equals. According to the laws of empire, it is entirely legitimate to force regime change in a country falling within the empire's sphere of interest and influence. In the UN Charter, such action is categorically ruled out. The logic of empire accordingly implies that the UN requirements of legality do not hold a special place in the considerations of the United States. Michael Ignatieff, who is certainly no proponent of the current Bush Administration's policies, expresses a widespread mood when he writes that America feels like Gulliver: an imperial giant whom European dwarves in their legalistic fervour try to bind with the thin threads of law in order to prevent it from achieving its mission.

This view has its own logic, which is the logic of Thomas Hobbes: in order for law to exist, there needs to be an order that provides law with social validity. America's war against Iraq would then be a war for the creation of a new world order whose law is not yet visible. This logic also implies that the new order, like any order based exclusively on power, tends not to be constrained by law. Law creates trust, predictability, security; law enables. The power that rejects law as a source for its validity in order to rely on violence alone will rob itself of an extension of its potential opportunities through reciprocity. Hannah Arendt, who first distinguished between communicative power and violence, could, in an analysis sharpened by an intimate knowledge of European catastrophes, teach her compatriots that the unilateral power of the lone ruler will in the end consist of nothing more than the non-communicative violence of the military. Accordingly, American vulnerability within its state borders at the peak of its international power might not be as paradoxical as Americans tend to think. Their mute power might in fact prevent them from understanding the world around them.

Power is not only a blessing. When power turns into hyper-power, it can become dangerous even to its wielder. The American political scientist Karl Deutsch coined the now famous aphorism that power is 'the ability to afford not to learn'. Power can be such a dangerous gift in our world. Prudent power-holders thus constrain their power and accordingly force themselves to react to the onslaught of new challenges with intelligence, creativity, perseverance and other 'civil' attributes. Any order that does not force itself to learn gambles with its future. This is the lesson that both the Americans and the Europeans learned at the end of the eighteenth century when they took the step from the principle of the ever-present controlling power of a hegemonic-absolutist ruler to the democratic constitutional state. It is only this change that enabled intellectual and political dispute as well as peaceful social conflict – the basis of the Euro-Atlantic model of civilization. It hardly renounces the use of power and coercion, but it tames them and makes them instruments of law.

When we think of empires, we cannot help but recall the cause of the decline of virtually all empires in world history: the overextension of their rule. Rousseau put it in words that are still valid today: 'The strongest is never strong enough to be master all the time, unless he transforms force into right and obedience into duty.'[4] There are many indications that Rousseau will continue to prevail against Hobbes. The 'old' Europe that has become wise should not become tired of showing this insight to its American friends.

## NOTES

1   James Chace and Caleb Carr, *America Invulnerable: The Quest for Absolute Security from 1812 to Star Wars* (New York: Summit, 1988).
2   John Stuart Mill, 'A Few Words on Non-Intervention', in J. S. Mill (ed.), *Dissertations and Discussions*, Vol. III (New York: Haskell House, 1873), 238ff.
3   See Peter Malanczuk, *Akehurst's Modern Introduction to International Law*, 7th edition (London: Routledge, 1997), 27ff.
4   Jean-Jacques Rousseau, *The Social Contract*, trans. Maurice Cranston (New York: Penguin, 1968), bk. 1, ch. 3.

# II

# Empire's Law: War, Human Rights and International Law

# 4

# The Conduct of the UN before and after the 2003 Invasion

*Hans von Sponeck*

Testimony given to the World Tribunal on Iraq
Istanbul, 24 June 2005

In discussing UN involvement before and after the 2003 invasion by the US, UK and other coalition forces of Iraq, a clear distinction has to be made between the policy-makers and the civil servants expected to carry out the policies, i.e. between member governments in the UN Security Council and the UN Secretariat.

If this is done, it quickly becomes clear that primary responsibility for the human catastrophe in Iraq lies with the political UN, with those member governments in the UN Security Council who had the power to make a difference. The failure of the Security Council to make a humanitarian, ethical and legal difference is much more monumental than is commonly recognized. There is not only the betrayal of the Iraqi people, but also the betrayal of the UN Charter as well as the betrayal of international conscience.

Why is this?

World leaders were hiding behind the veil of the UN Security Council to premeditate their betrayal before and after the illegal war of 2003. There can be no more doubts, the facts are present, that the US and UK governments were actively pursuing regime change by force at a time when the world was led to believe that international law, peaceful solutions to the conflict and the protection of the Iraqi people were part of the US and UK governments' approach. They were not. Once the asymmetrical war was 'over', it also became clear to the international public that those who waged this war had reached even greater heights of irresponsibility by fighting this war without a strategy for peace.

The objective was to maintain a stranglehold on Iraq. Means of 'disarray' and 'deception' were deployed to justify the end of 'domination'. Iraq's armed forces were sent home. Civil servants were retired without any evidence of wrongdoing, simply because they had been members of the Ba'ath Party. New laws, contained in the Transitional Administrative Law (TAL), were introduced by decree. These laws tried to recolonize Iraq economically and institutionally and create dependence even in such areas as agriculture by banning local seed stocks in favour of genetically modified seeds to be imported from the United States. The ensuing Iraqi opposition and chaos left the occupying powers stymied and bewildered.

How did the UN Security Council and the UN Secretariat react to these bilateral aberrations?

Over a decade, the UN Security Council condoned what two permanent members, the US and the UK, were doing to pursue, first, their Iraq containment policy and later their regime change agenda. This amounted to nothing less than the *de facto* bilateralization of the Security Council. The rhetoric of the Iraq debates in the Security Council showed that there was abundant awareness of the evolving humanitarian crisis in Iraq. At the same time, there was a severe shortage of political will to take timely steps to redress this situation.

It was known to all members of the Security Council that the link between disarmament and comprehensive economic sanctions meant that the people of Iraq were forced to pay a heavy price in terms of life and destitution for acts committed by their government. It was known to all members of the Security Council that the inadequacy of its allocations for the oil-for-food programme and the bureaucracy with which this humanitarian exemption was implemented worsened the chances of survival of many Iraqis. It was known to all members of the Security Council that its refusal to allow the transfer of cash to Iraq's central bank needed to run the nation, to pay for training, installation of equipment and institution-building, encouraged the government of Iraq to increase illegal means to obtain cash.

It was known to all members of the Security Council that the establishment of the two no-fly zones within Iraq had little to do with the protection of ethnic and religious groups, and a lot to do with destabilization. All members of the Security Council were aware that, following 'Operation Desert Fox' in December 1998, the US and the UK governments, giving their pilots additional rules of engagement, used Iraqi air space as a training ground, in preparation for an eventual war. The Security Council had access to air strike reports when such reports were prepared by the UN in Baghdad and therefore all members of the Security Council knew of the destruction of civilian life and property. Yet, the Security Council did not once debate the legality of the no-fly zones or challenge two of its members that they were maintaining these zones without a UN mandate.

All this was known.

With rare exceptions, members of the Security Council allowed the Council to become a convenient tool for the pursuit of bilateral policies. There was ample experience in the Council of the danger of misuse of consensus resolutions as demonstrated by the handling of Resolutions 687 (1991) and 1284 (1999) by the US and the UK governments. This did not deter members of the Security Council from going along with yet another consensus resolution – 1441 (2002). The likelihood of misuse by individual members of the Security Council of provisions such as 'material breaches' and 'serious consequences' to justify military invasion should have prevented the adoption of such a resolution.

For its part, the UN Secretariat acquiesced when the US and UK, two founding members of the UN, insisted in the Security Council on an economic sanctions regime that created a human tragedy. The UN Secretariat remained mute when these same governments dropped out of the international community to mount an illegal invasion of Iraq unilaterally. The UN Secretariat did not react even at this critical time when the very foundation of the institution was threatened. Dr Hans Blix, chief UN arms inspector, had reported progress in verifying Iraq's lack of weapons of mass destruction and was pleading for more time to complete the inspection process. The UN Secretariat should have used this to confront the two governments about their war plans, but chose not to do so. Rather, without protest, the UN Secretariat withdrew the UN arms inspectors in March 2003.

The UN Secretariat could not have prevented the long-planned decision to go to war. But the sheer seriousness of the violation of international law by two member countries and the sidelining of a world body created to prevent wars represented a challenge for the UN civil service to show that, ultimately, conscience is superior to obedience. It failed to do so.

Since the illegal invasion of Iraq, there has not been a single debate in the Security Council about the fundamental disregard by the coalition forces of existing conventions created to ensure that the occupation armies act in accordance with the Hague and Geneva Conventions to which they are parties. Looting and burning of the national museum and the national library, the damaging of archeological sites and the humiliating treatment of civilians by the US armed forces provoked no protest in the Security Council.

The Security Council watched impotently when the soul and ethos of Iraq was attacked. The detention of political figures for indefinite periods and the unimaginable brutality and sadism with which detainees were treated not just in Abu Ghraib and Camp Bucca but also in other prisons were not the subject of Security Council concern. Carpet bombing of towns such as Fallujah, Tal Afar and Al Qaim did not ruffle the Security Council or lead to emergency meetings. There were no protests in the Security Council that CPA Administrator Paul Bremer and other CPA officials represented an allegedly liberated and sovereign Iraq at major international meetings such as the World Economic Forum in Amman and the WTO in Geneva. The Security Council took no note that the assignment of a human rights rapporteur for Iraq was abruptly terminated by the UN Human Rights Commission in Geneva following the illegal war. The Security Council agreed in 2003 to the continuation of payments by the UN Compensation Commission even though it had earlier agreed to discontinue the entertainment of claims.

The Security Council did play an important role in the preparations for an interim Iraqi administration and elections, but ultimately succumbed to US heavy-handedness in deciding the details of the process.

In the history books of the United Nations the handling of the Iraq conflict by the Security Council will be recorded as a massive failure of oversight responsibility.

The history books should also record that the people replaced the UN Security Council as the voice of international conscience. This voice must not relent in its demands that the US and UK governments, bilaterally as national administrations, and multilaterally as permanent members of the UN Security Council, are accountable to their people and to the world community for their wrongdoing against Iraq, before, during and after the illegal war.

It is a crime in many countries to leave the scene of an accident without offering to help the victims. This also applies to the responsibility of the international community to help Iraqi victims. Conscience, compassion and a sense of responsibility are powerful reasons to stay involved. There must be involvement at two levels: Iraq and UN reforms.

Political leaders urge that we should look forward. This we must. However, looking forward receives legitimacy only when it is linked to accountability for the past. This applies to nations, communities, individuals – to everyone, particularly to those in power. The forthcoming trial of Iraq's former president, Saddam Hussein, acknowledges his accountability for past crimes against his people. The same applies to crimes against humanity committed by those who maintained economic sanctions with total disregard for the human costs, who fought a silent war in the no-fly zones, who invaded Iraq, who abused, maimed, tortured and killed its people. The dock of the courtroom for Iraq has to have more than one chair! Law and justice, need it be stressed, are not only for the losers.

There are thousands of unnamed Iraqi men, women and children who are victims of the failure to prevent war and destruction in Iraq. Let them be the stark reminders of our responsibility to keep the debate alive, at least until the terms of accountability are met.

In summary, Iraq remains 'unfinished business' for the international peace movement and responsible citizens everywhere. The challenge ahead is to address three major issues:

1. The United Nations has failed in preventing unjust economic sanctions, an illegal war and carnage under occupation.

    This means that, in the short term, the peace movement must persevere in its demands that those responsible be brought to justice. It must not be forgotten that what was done in the name of 'freedom', 'democracy' and 'human rights' represents a travesty of the meaning of 'freedom', 'democracy' and 'human rights'.

    In the medium term, the peace movement must forcefully contribute to the debate on UN reforms to create a structure which is protected against misuse. This involves much more than the enlargement of the Security Council.

2. The international peace movement, too, has failed in preventing unjust economic sanctions and an illegal war.

    In the short term, the peace movement should take this as an important opportunity to carry out a self-critical review of why this failure occurred and what factors contributed to this failure.

    The dangers looming on the political and socio-economic horizon are horrific. The reaction of the peace movement, in the medium term, must be to leave turf battles and institutional or personal ambitions behind to facilitate significantly better organized responses to international crises. Only combined commitment and a joint strategy offer a chance to make a difference.

3. As individuals who understand and cherish the ethos of the UN Charter, who believe in peace and justice for all, who are appalled by what has happened in Iraq before, during and after the illegal war, we must first and foremost work on ourselves to become equipped for the tasks ahead. Beyond this obligation, we have to remain, conscious of the reality of evil and of the need for life to be conducted with decency, as Dag Hammarskjöld, the UN's second Secretary General, reminded us.

# 5

# The UN and its Conduct during the Invasion and Occupation of Iraq

*Denis Halliday*

Testimony given to the World Tribunal on Iraq
Istanbul, 25 June 2005

## INTRODUCTION AND BACKGROUND

Since 1990, the people of Iraq have been the victims of continuous US/UK-driven UN Security Council aggression. Triggered by the Iraq takeover of Kuwait, this aggression against the Iraqi people cannot be justified. I say that while in no way defending the Iraqi invasion of Kuwait, for there can be no justification for such aggression. Instead, this view reflects the US rejection of peaceful withdrawal offers by Iraq. This was due to the determination of Washington to destroy Iraq's potential and violently overthrow a no longer useful former friend and ally in Baghdad.

The resulting 1991 UN-endorsed Gulf War, and the war crimes committed in the name of the UN by US armed forces during that war, set a pattern of militaristic aggression against the people of Iraq which continues today. The result has been massive loss of civilian life, some through both political and military negligence, and some intentional as meets one essential element in the definition of genocide. This primitive response by the UN to this founding member state via deadly UN sanctions through 2002 is now sadly sustained following the illegal invasion in 2003 and military and ideological occupation by the troops of George W. Bush and Tony Blair.

Since 1945, manipulated and corrupted by the five permanent members, the UN Security Council has often been brutally employed to serve the narrow interests of the powerful. This is as intended by the 'victors' of World War II if one reads between the lines in the Council's terms of reference as set out in the UN Charter.

As a result, the UN was structured to fail the people of Iraq and continues to do so in all respects. I refer to the so-called UN coalition – US-led – of the 1991 Gulf War which destroyed civilian lives and infrastructure in violation of the Geneva Conventions and Protocols, which massacred thousands and buried alive in mass graves hundreds more Iraqi troops. The US leadership deployed that new nuclear weapon of choice, namely hundreds of tons of depleted uranium missiles and shells with horrific carcinogenic consequences which are still being revealed today.

In addition, the UN silently accepted the completely illegal no-fly zone bombing by the US/UK of Iraq, culminating in 'softening-up attacks' preliminary to the unlawful invasion of 2003. More than twelve years of genocidal UN sanctions constitute a massive breach of the UN Charter itself – Articles 1 and 2 in particular – and underline the incompatibilities of these actions with international law.

By these various means, the UN has itself destroyed the basic human rights of the Iraqi people through the wilful neglect of Articles 22–28 of the Universal Declaration of Human Rights. The UN failed to protect and safeguard the children and people before and after the 2003 invasion. And, as rare but honest news coverage demonstrates, the UN continues to fail Iraq and its people as this World Tribunal sits in Istanbul.

## US/UK INVASION, MARCH 2003

With US invasion intentions announced, where were the UN voices of morality, legality and integrity? Where was the outrage? Where was the intervention of the Secretary General as is his obligation under UN Charter Article 99? Where were the many member states committed to protecting the UN Charter and the tenets of international law? Given the forum of the General Assembly (GA) and the power of the majority, where were the states prepared to stop the oil/military strategic aggression blatantly being pursued by Bush and Blair? The answer is: they were nowhere to be found or heard.

Respect for human rights and international law, including the UN Charter itself, was undermined by the polluted and murky world of self-interest among UN member states that favour the sweaty embraces of the Bush regime. The world watched Bush threaten the heads of state present in the GA of September 2002 and then saw Bush and Blair deceive all who seemed willing to be misled, a deception culminating in General Colin Powell misleading the Security

Council in early 2003 about weapons of mass destruction and the 'danger' Iraq presented!

We were asked to believe that the spirit of Article 51 of the UN Charter dealing with national self-defence somehow justified the US invasion of Iraq as in the case of the invasion of Afghanistan. Blair informed us that Baghdad could launch a surprise attack on London in 45 minutes with terrible and illegal weapons. He referred to chemical and biological weapons that were sold to Iraq by the UK itself, or by European and American friends when earlier Baghdad took on Iran largely due to the urging and active support of Washington and London.

To argue that the Security Council in early 2003 was courageous in refusing to endorse the intended US/UK invasion is a nice idea, but nothing more. The UN was not enhanced by its action, or lack thereof, to protect the sovereign state of Iraq from raw US/UK military aggression. This was perhaps the lowest point reached yet by the UN in its short history. Even the tyranny of the 'veto' did not save UN credibility, which might have been the case had the three remaining veto powers used that dictatorial device. They did not. And the failure of the remaining member states to walk out, resign or stand up and be counted was and remains simply disgusting. When 20 months later the Secretary General remembered his duty to speak up as Article 99 requires, he mumbled off the record, but was sadly much too late.

Without the authority that resides in Article 42 of the Charter, and a Security Council resolution authorizing the specific use of force, the Bush/Blair invasion of Iraq is in complete violation of international law. The war crimes committed in that blatant military aggression – the most serious of international crimes – must be charged to Bush as the Commander-in-Chief, and to Blair as the prime minister who abused war powers. Bush should be charged with the use of state terrorism for the opening salvo of 'shock and awe' bombing strikes on Baghdad which were designed to terrorize by physically and mentally attacking the civilian population. This is the kind of state terrorism that provides a tragic reminder of the US nuclear crime of bombing Hiroshima and Nagasaki. It is the kind of state terrorism besides which small-scale 'terrorist' resistance pales in comparison. However, both forms of terrorism are internationally unlawful and unacceptable.

The UN member states listened mutely and swallowed, some of them painfully, the false arguments of Iraq's capacity to threaten its neighbours, none of whom appeared to share this fear, and of the physical threats to the UK and US! The world tried desperately to believe the nonsense of massive stockpiles of weapons of mass destruction in Iraq. And to top off the US/UK lies was the charge of a close Iraqi linkage to 'al-Qaeda' and the attack on the Twin Towers, so symbolic of western capitalistic greed, in New York City on 11 September 2001. To those who understood the secular nature of the Baghdad government and Ba'athist philosophy, this supposed lineage broke the last straw of credibility. And the UN stood by mutely. Even to this day, the Security Council is unwilling to define terrorism for fear that state terrorism employed by its permanent five member states would thereby be constrained.

Thus, the March 2003 invasion took place in breach of all known international laws, executed with the application of terrorism and the commission of war crimes, including further and massive use of depleted uranium. The UN, its member states and its Secretary General failed to employ all possible means to protect the people of Iraq. What is worse, the UN was generally seen around the world to be acquiescent and collaborative. Ironically, at the same time, Americans were outraged that the UN had failed to support US foreign policy and their self-serving military aggression on Iraq.

## UN COLLABORATION WITH US/UK OCCUPATION

Whereas the invasion was in breach of international law, although eased by the acquiescence of the UN, and was globally condemned, the occupation was, on the other hand, more readily accepted as a new, if unlawful, reality. The occupation was supported by member states and donor agencies, and then actively supported by the UN. That support and active involvement constitutes collaboration. And UN collaboration with the occupying enemy was, and is, a tragic mistake. Collaboration of this kind is an unacceptable role for the UN. We are all familiar with the rights of Iraqi self-defence and resistance to foreign military occupation as set out in Article 51 of the UN Charter. We are equally familiar with the often murderous consequences of collaboration, which the French Resistance made famous and even bizarrely glorious under German occupation in the 1940s. There is nothing glorious about killing, be it of the enemy or of one's own countrymen and women who decide, for whatever reason, to collaborate.

There was, and is, nothing glorious about UN collaboration in Iraq, and nothing glorious about the consequence – the deadly truck-bombing of the UN office building in Baghdad on 19 August 2003 when some 20 UN staff died. The Security Council and particularly the Secretary General, responsible for the welfare of staff members, appear to have failed to understand that the UN was, even before collaboration, the most hated organization in Iraq. Why? Why not? After twelve years of deadly UN sanctions which cost Iraq over one million lives, mostly children, followed by conspicuous collaboration with the common Iraqi enemy, that is, the American and British occupying enemy, after twelve years of humiliation and loss of dignity under UNSCOM's intrusive search for weapons of mass destruction, why was anyone surprised?

The UN Secretary General and his staff were obliged to remain apart from the illegal occupation, at best on standby. Unless invited by a legitimate Iraqi government to assist, and there was none remaining in Iraq after the unlawful overthrow of the Baghdad government, the UN had no role in the country. The UN had no mandate to be in Iraq. A demand from Washington and/or London does not constitute a legitimate invitation. And puppet regimes cannot be recognized by the UN, even if set up by two permanent member states of the Security Council. Airlifting of long-expatriated Iraqis together with their armed thugs and mercenaries, and setting them up as an interim regime, does not create a representative, or legal, government which the UN can legitimately serve.

However, it is considered that occupation, even unlawful occupation, comes with obligations under international law. Such obligations included the rule of domestic law, the protection of state and private property and, perhaps most importantly, the protection and well-being of the civilian population as required by international law. The occupying US and UK forces blatantly failed to meet these obligations. Instead, they allowed, even facilitated, a complete breakdown in law and order. They stood back as looting and destruction in the cities and towns of Iraq took place. As days became weeks and months, they neglected to meet the basic needs of the people, including food, housing, water, electricity, health care, education and employment. Tragically, the gutless UN stood by silently as the Americans and British created anarchy. The UN remained silent as the occupiers disbanded Iraqi defence forces, including border guards, thereby opening the country up to incursion and looting by thousands intent on chaos. In addition to the cost of Iraqi civilian well-being and lives, the intruders also came to attack the occupying common enemy of the region – the intrusive and hated American armed forces, the fearsome crusaders of Bush fundamentalism. Again, the UN failed to protect the sovereign rights of Iraq; the Security Council and the Secretary General were gagged.

Before the Iraqi economy could even begin the process of recovery from UN sanctions and military invasion, the American occupiers abolished the oil-for-food programme. Even after the invasion, this programme remained the prime source of food and other essentials for over 85 per cent of the population of some 24 million. With unemployment at over 70 per cent, plus thousands of newly disbanded defence personnel, invasion war-damage and increased homelessness, the social and economic plight of the Iraqi people had deteriorated further.

Ignorant and grossly irresponsible, Washington now looked to the modest private sector of Iraq to sell food, medicines and other essentials to a population of largely unemployed and impoverished Iraqis in the face of growing inflation. In a matter of weeks an economy that had been centralized and public sector-driven under UN sanctions was disbanded, with very painful results. Under the US/UK occupation, for example, child mortality rates have increased and malnutrition has risen. Where was the UN voice to protect basic civilian interests and demand that occupation obligations be fully met by the US and the UK?

The breakdown of personal security, social services, health care, education and basic needs has been almost total. In other words, the occupying military forces have failed in all aspects of meeting their responsibilities under international law. And the UN has been silent.

The UN has also been silent as the US set about building some 14 military bases for their own long-term strategic military requirements in the region. These are strategies relating to regional military presence, natural gas and oil reserves and control of them. However, in regard to reconstruction and new investment in infrastructure destroyed by the Gulf War of 1990, constrained by UN sanctions and weakened further by the Bush/Blair invasion, little has been done. Instead, the presence of US/UK forces has created chaos and armed resistance to their military occupation. They have alienated most of the population – not unexpectedly – but in addition, they have split this secular country into religious and ethnic divides that had been long submerged under an Iraqi national identity. Has the UN spoken up?

For the first time in many years, the dreadful possibility of civil war has been created by foreign occupation that, like an old colonial regime, has discovered the benefits of divide and rule, with disastrous results. Where is the UN demand to an end to military occupation and the belated return of Iraq to the people of Iraq?

Under initial occupation, the UN transferred some US$8 billion to a Provisional Authority headed by an American. And this was not UN money; this was Iraq government oil revenue obtained under oil-for-food programme oil sales. Worse, it is now revealed that the UN did not monitor or audit the expenditure of this $8 billion, and it appears much was mishandled and is unaccounted for by the US authorities. Some $4 billion was handed without benefit of competitive bidding to the American corporation Halliburton, connected to the White House through Dick Cheney, the vice-president. Hundreds of millions were disbursed in cash to the 'new' ministries set up with and by the Americans, staffed and managed by the Americans, without accounting. These billions, improperly handed over by the UN, were the property of the Iraqi people. Again, the UN has failed egregiously in its responsibility.

As a diversion from its own disastrous occupation, costs and loss of life, Washington has attacked the oil-for-food programme within which it appears there has been some UN mismanagement, poor contracting, weak accounting of Iraqi monies and maybe even some theft, amounting to as much as $150,000. Nevertheless, this unique and largely successful US$65 billion programme fed and provided basic human needs from 1997 to 2002 for some 24 million Iraqi people. The scandal is not UN mismanagement; it is Washington-approved billion-dollar oil sales by Baghdad outside the constraints of oil-for-food, it is the granting of 30 per cent of Iraqi oil revenue under UN oil-for-food arrangements to Kuwait, while Iraqi children die for lack of financial investment in electric power and potable water supplies. It is the genocide that the UN perpetrated in respect of the Iraqi people over some twelve years of strangulation under uniquely comprehensive sanctions.

## CONCLUSION

We find in Iraq today almost total political and social chaos. Foreign military occupation has influenced interim arrangements that are not representative and do not have the confidence of many Iraqis. We find chaos and misery for the Iraqi people, made homeless by brutal US/UK military action in civilian areas and towns such as is seen in the neighbourhoods of Baghdad and Fallujah with horrific civilian casualties. For the survivors, homelessness, unemployment and few means to survive have resulted. Health care and education are in disarray as families are afraid to send their children to clinics and schools for fear of bombing and kidnapping. Child mortality and malnutrition are on the increase. Personal security does not exist. University students stay away from class because they are in fear. The breakdown in policing since the occupation has led to a level of murder and killing unknown in a free Iraq before occupation. Many essentially experienced civil servants, intellectuals, doctors and educators have been murdered. The UN is largely silent.

Despite the courage of many Iraqis to vote under these near-impossible conditions and work towards a replacement system of government, the national institutions remain in very bad shape. Financial and human capital are both in short supply. The much-needed constitution, being drafted under American supervision and interference, is likely to have a long and hard road to acceptance. It will undoubtedly need much rewriting once the country has an elected and representative government when free of foreign occupation. It is expected that Iraq will reject many American pressures, including privatization to foreign corporations of public sector essentials such as water, oil and power. It is feared that IMF interference will lead to structural adjustment devices that will destroy the remaining strengths of the welfare system which so many Iraqis have learned to depend upon over many years.

Due to corruption of the Security Council and abuse of the UN Charter by the five permanent members, in particular, the unlawful invasion and occupation of Iraq and the many tragic consequences thereof, have not led to UN Security Council condemnation. Outrageously, the US and UK, continuing to enjoy the benefits of member states in good standing, retain their veto powers and permanent seats on the Security Council. They have not been obliged to terminate illegal military action within the sovereign state of Iraq. They have not been forced to withdraw occupying military forces. They have failed to meet their occupation obligations under international law. They have stolen and abused limited Iraqi financial resources and have under-spent their own funds that they obligated very publicly for reconstruction and development.

The UN has watched the loss of life in Iraq. The UN has watched the war crimes of US/UK forces, including the negligent bombing of civilians and use of depleted uranium devices yet again without comment. The UN has witnessed massive loss of innocent civilian life – over 100,000 has been estimated so far. US occupation forces do not bother to count the civilians they kill or maim. The UN has watched the employment of some 80,000 hired guns who serve the US authorities under no known law. The UN has watched in silence American human rights abuses, and the torture and killing of Iraqi prisoners who have been arrested and jailed without respect for their human rights or explanation to their families.

Having tragically weakened Iraq and its people during twelve years of sanctions, the UN has taken no action to stop, condemn or punish the blatant US/UK transgressions of the UN Charter, human rights and other provisions of international law.

The world has witnessed in Iraq the most serious of international crimes – the crime of military aggression on a sovereign member state by US and UK forces. The world waits for the people of Iraq to be given an opportunity to make their own decisions and resolve their own differences as they can only hope to do without foreign occupation and interference. The world waits for the UN to act in keeping with the provisions of international law, including the application of International Criminal Court provisions to Bush, Blair and their henchmen and women who have violated the core tenets of the UN Charter, the Universal Declaration of Human Rights and the Geneva Conventions and Protocols.

In the meantime, the World Tribunal on Iraq, sitting in Istanbul, has an opportunity, an obligation, to demand full international prosecution of US/UK war leaders and war criminals involved in the destruction of Iraq, the lives of its people and their human rights and well-being, through unlawful and unjustifiable armed invasion and military occupation.

# 6

# Keeping its Promise: Use of Force and the New Man of International Law

*Doris E. Buss*[1]

It may well be that under international law as presently constituted, a regime can systematically brutalize and oppress its people and there is nothing anyone can do ... unless it comes within the definition of a humanitarian catastrophe ... This may be the law, but should it be? (British Prime Minister, Tony Blair, 2004)[2]

If international law is so abject, so thoroughly receptive to power, and if, as its history richly reveals, it has been particularly accommodating of *imperium*, why should the assertion of American empire ever go beyond or be contrary to international law? Then it could be asked whether it might be that there is 'in' law, in international law, a life that in some identifiable way counters and resists *imperium*? (Peter Fitzpatrick, 2003)[3]

What, then, is the proper role for the lawyer? Surely, it is to stand tall for the rule of law. (Thomas M. Franck)[4]

Each of the above three quotes highlights, in a quite different way, the current tensions and preoccupations with international legality in 'an age of empire'. The first quote, by Tony Blair reflects the ongoing debate, within academy and policy circles, about the future of an international law that is seemingly out of date. The questions of when, how and if the international community should intervene in desperate human rights crises has preoccupied legal and policy commentators for much of the 1990s and into the twenty-first century. The concern that international law might be out of step with a changing international order is a mantra recently taken up by the administration of President George W. Bush,[5] as it runs foul of international and domestic laws concerning the treatment of prisoners. If international law is out of date, what is to be done? If international law is a product of a bygone era, does it serve any continuing purpose?

The second quote, by the legal theorist Peter Fitzpatrick, speaks to a debate that has become more recently acute. What is international law's role in a global order dominated by a hegemonic, in some accounts imperialistic, United States? With a regime willing and able to undertake unilateral and legally questionable military engagement, can we speak of an autonomous international law? Or is international law completely subservient to the power politics of the hegemon? Is there, in effect, any law in international law? And, indeed, in a unipolar global order, is there any international in international law?

The third quote, a *cri de coeur* from deep inside the international legal academy, reflects the ethically and legally difficult position international lawyers find themselves in, particularly within the United States. For Thomas Franck, international lawyers are facing an embattled time, and international law, with the apparent blessing of the Bush Administration, hovers on the brink of extinction. In the face of this challenge, the answer for Franck, and others, is to insist on, even globalize, the rule of law.

In this chapter, I am interested in the perceptions and characterizations of international law that emerge in the current preoccupation with international legality. While seemingly contradictory images of international law can be found – as embattled and in need of protection, as out of date, or as frayed at the edges but with a strong core – the recurring theme in much of the policy and academic debate is of an international law that needs to be returned to its initial promise. It is a law that is under siege but must prevail, or a law that is weak but good, or a law on the brink of extinction. The task becomes to strengthen law, to breathe in new life or add on new limbs. The shared assumption is that international law is unquestioningly a force of good. The rule of law stands in opposition to tyranny and empire. It provides the means to a new global order defined by a shared cosmopolitan ethic rather than the unilateral interests of the hegemon.

The debates on international law and its reform can be read as reflecting larger concerns and imaginings of self, community and authority at a time of perceived global change. In the following discussion, I focus on one aspect of the use of force/Iraq invasion debate as it appeared in the flagship *American Journal of International Law* (AJIL). In July 2003, the AJIL hosted a debate among selected scholars and government lawyers – chosen to represent a 'marketplace' or '*Agora*' of viewpoints – on the 'Future Implications of the

Iraq Conflict'.[6] The journal sees the *Agora* as part of its tradition of providing a space for US government legal advisers and academics to outline and exchange views on the legal and policy aspects of US international conduct. To this end, the AJIL issue on the Iraq conflict contained three submissions from current and past government lawyers and advisers, and six from academic writers.

My reading of the *Agora* focuses on two aspects: how the submissions reflect a shared narrative first about the 'crisis' facing international law, and second, the solution to that crisis through the strengthening – the remasculinization – of law. The crisis that emerges in the *Agora* submissions, I argue, is a very partial and somewhat distorting picture of international law and community. Drawing on feminist theoretical accounts of international law and relations, I consider how the *Agora* accounts of international law's crisis can be read in terms of the production and affirmation of identities of self, particularly the self of internationally-minded scholars. I develop this further by looking at masculinities and international law. Here, my interest is in how the *Agora* portrayal of law's crisis and its resolution echoes anxieties about a crisis in masculinity brought about by a changing gender order. In drawing parallels between the *Agora* 'use of force' debate and the 1990s US-based Promise Keepers movement, I consider the anxieties and desires that appear to shape the claims made about international law's authoritative promise. What image of authority do we find – hope to find – in a reinvigorated international law?

## *AGORA*

For the editors of the AJIL *Agora* on the 'Future Implications of the Iraq Conflict', the US military action in the Middle East holds the potential for one of two stark outcomes: international law will undergo either 'fundamental transformation, or ... destruction'.[7] The *Agora* starts from the premise that the US military action in Iraq may be illegal (as an unjustified use of force by one state against another), and, if so, the US has acted wilfully in disregard of law. The *Agora* presents the US war in Iraq as *potentially* posing a threat to the very future of international law. In a unipolar world, the argument goes, if the hegemon (in this case the US) persists in acting in disregard of international law, then surely international law can no longer be said to exist. The problem posed by the US invasion of Iraq is even more extreme when viewed in light of the Bush

Administration's *National Security Strategy*, which argues for a 'new strategic doctrine of preemptive use of force in respect of weapons of mass destruction and terrorism'.[8] That is, the US may be going even further in its breach of international law to institute, as a matter of policy, a doctrine of 'pre-emptive use of force', more accurately 'threat pre-emption',[9] which has even less claim to international legality. The future of international law looks bleak.

The editors suggest there might be some 'wiggle room' in the above, stark scenario. Perhaps the Iraq military action might be justified, not in terms of pure self-defence but on 'alternative and narrower' legal bases;[10] the resolutions of the Security Council, for example. And, perhaps, the Iraq conflict is not sounding the death knell of international law, but is merely an early warning signal. Perhaps Iraq exposes a problem in international law, but a problem that might be addressed by international lawyers and policy-makers working together. What if a future international law can be imagined, one that accommodates a changing international security situation by allowing military response to terrorist threats, for example, and which, therefore, might obviate the need for the 'pre-emption' envisaged in the National Security Strategy? If both, or either, of these developments are/is possible, international law might be restored to its strong footing; pulled back from its precarious position on the brink of US unilateralism.

Against this backdrop, the nine submissions composing this first part of the *Agora*, chosen to represent 'a range of viewpoints illustrative of the spectrum of opinion within the U.S. legal community',[11] are categorized by the editors into two broad groups. The first group of four authors (in three submissions) argue that the US invasion of Iraq is legal. They also find that the doctrine of preemption envisaged in the *National Security Strategy* is legal, or, if not strictly legal, has some policy merit. The second group rejects out of hand the doctrine of pre-emptive self-defence found in the *National Security Strategy*. Further, the Iraq invasion itself is illegal, or if not absolutely illegal, politically difficult. For this group, the question of international law's future in light of the Bush Administration is fraught and, individually, they advance a number of options for how international law might be reformed. The first group, perhaps not surprisingly, includes submissions from three authors I categorize as 'government lawyers',[12] and one academic, Ruth Wedgwood.[13] The second group, all academics, contains a submission by Richard N. Gardner,[14] a law professor who was, and writes from his experiences as, Deputy Assistant Secretary of State for international organization in the Kennedy Administration during the Cuban missile crisis.

Each of the submissions contains a section analysing the legality of the Iraq invasion, and the primary focus is the role of the Security Council resolutions starting from the 1991 Gulf War, in potentially authorizing the war, on 'alternative and narrower' legal bases. The legal arguments advanced on this issue do not concern me here.[15] Rather, it is the second question, on the reforms and futures of international law, that I turn to now.

The question of reforming international law on the right of a state to use force in self-defence is touched on by all the contributors, with only Richard Falk and Thomas Franck rejecting the premise that now may be a reformatory moment in international law. For Franck, the very existence of international law is under attack by the Bush Administration and the spectre of reform is an illusion: 'this is not a time for optimistic speculation about how to make the United Nations more responsive to new challenges. Rather, reformers need first to understand that the system stands in mortal jeopardy of being destroyed altogether.'[16] Falk takes an explicitly constructivist approach, allowing that there may be some scope to 'stretch' international law, but the premise that the Charter system is in disarray is flawed. The question of reform relies on a faulty characterization of the Charter system as a 'legal prison that presents states with the dilemma of adherence (and defeat) and violation or disregard (and victory). Rather, adherence is the best policy, if understood against a jurisprudential background that is neither slavishly legalistic nor cynically nihilistic'.[17]

The remaining contributors accept the starting position that reform of international law is necessary. The extent and direction of that reform varies depending on the authors' view on legality, and the extent to which the international security scenario has fundamentally altered the need for and direction of international response. Very broadly, I divide the *Agora* submissions into two camps. The first are the reformers pure and simple who see international law as either a neutral force or a potentially powerful one, with reform needed to keep it effective and on the strait and narrow. The second group is comprised of the more explicit rescuers of international law. For them, international law is either on the brink of destruction or the brink of irrelevance, though perhaps these two are one and the same.

In the first camp, Taft, Buchwald, Yoo, Gardner and Shapiro outline variations of possible reforms to international rules governing
use of force. For Taft and Buchwald, who see both the US military
action in Iraq and the Bush pre-emptive self-defence doctrine as
legal, the question of reform is not particularly pressing. But it is
Gardner who, in navigating a path between 'Bush' (as expansive
international law) and the 'Jurisprudes' (as narrow international
law), offers caution in the reform agenda. For Gardner, international
law is a resilient force and the task of reform is to 'punch a hole in
traditional legal restraints on the use of force', provided the hole is
kept 'as small as possible'.[18] International law, according to Gardner,
is potentially dangerous. An expansive right of pre-emption could
be a ' "loaded weapon" that can be used against the United States
and against the general interest in a stable world order'.[19]

The rescuers, in contrast, see a vulnerable international law. This
is an international law that is weak and potentially at grave risk of
annihilation. The risk comes from two sources: a malevolent Bush
Administration and its supporters, bent on undermining the 'fragile
normative structure' of international law,[20] and/or irrelevance
caused by international law's own failure – through the Security
Council's lack of 'collective spine',[21] for example – to offer a strong
rule of law able to address the changing realities of an international
order populated by rogue states, weapons of mass destruction, and
ne'er-do-wells. In the rescue camp, I place Yoo,[22] Wedgwood, Franck,
Farer and Stromseth.

Of the rescuers, Ruth Wedgwood[23] offers the most passionate
argument for resisting the path of irrelevance for international law,
and her sentiment, if not prescription, is clearly shared by others in
this group.[24] Wedgwood suggests a 'teleological' approach to the use
of force, identifying the roots of the existing Charter system of international law in the post-World War II 'never again' orientation:

> [W]e should never forget that the United Nations Charter system was born
> to a generation chastened by the consequences of collective passivity – the
> failure to counter the Fascist rearmament ... The United Nations Charter is
> appropriately read, even now, as an attempt to overcome the failures
> of ... [the] League of Nations and its covenant of inaction.[25]

The spectre of Rwanda and Bosnia is offered as a parallel to Iraq and
what might happen if the United Nations continues on a path of
'collective passivity'. The result of continuing inaction in the

context of Iraq might not be, Wedgwood suggests, the permanent irrelevance of the UN, but it reveals the ongoing tension between 'legitimacy and legality'. A strict legality will translate into passivity and failure to act. This in turn will undermine the legitimacy – the respect and authority – of international law.

The *Agora* can be read, on one level, as a fairly routine debate about legal doctrine and the challenges posed by legal contravention. But it can also be read, on another level, as a particular performance of the shared assumptions and expectations about what international law is, where it can be found and how it ought to develop. Read in this way, the *Agora* reveals a set of gendered assumptions about the authoritative promise and limits of international law and, I suggest, liberal legalism more generally. In the following analysis, I explore the images of international law found in the *Agora* submissions that emerge around the language of international law's crisis (emasculation) and its future (strong and responsible). I begin by looking more closely at 'the crisis' said to threaten the very future of international law.

## CRISIS? WHAT CRISIS?

As a 'marketplace' of ideas this special issue of the *American Journal of International Law* reveals itself to have rather uniform stock. To begin, this first part of the *Agora* is confined to just contributions from the United States. Thus, the *Agora* suggests less a 'marketplace' and more a 'Walmart' of ideas.[26] The range of items on the shelves diminishes further when we look at the substance of the contributions, the vast majority of which share a set of assumptions about what is at issue in the US invasion of Iraq.

All the contributors, with the possible exception of Falk, Taft and Buchwald, agree that US unilateralism, and the use of force to protect the US's perceived security interests, threaten or signal an uncertain future for international law. And they go further to suggest that the changing international security situation poses particular difficulties for international law. All the contributors, save Falk, see new threats emerging in the wake of the Twin Towers bombings of 11 September. These threats – 'catastrophic terrorism',[27] the 'proliferation of weapons of mass destruction in the hands of dangerous regimes'[28] and the 'brave new world of non-state terror networks'[29] – require 'a revitalized normative and institutional framework governing the use of force'.[30]

A shared picture emerges in the *Agora* of a dark and dangerous world on the one hand, and the need for a stronger coercive apparatus of law on the other. Tom Farer's contribution is particularly evocative: 'the world is ... a dangerous, unruly, far too lightly managed and policed place. The Bush Administration is not fighting phantoms. The continued development and spread of weapons of mass destruction ... is a huge threat to humanity.'[31] There is broad agreement among the *Agora* submissions that the Bush Administration, and the war in Iraq, notwithstanding its legal status, are a revelatory moment for international scholars: 'the fig leaf of legal justification' for use of force has been 'all but discarded'.[32] The majority[33] sees the Bush Administration, even while acting illegally, as exposing a significant problem. There *are* changing global security issues, and those issues reveal a 'gap'[34] in existing international law. That gap may have been caused by an overzealous Bush Administration or perhaps opened gradually over time, but either way, it is undermining international law. And the solution, for the majority of the contributors, is to expand the legal avenues for use of force – to close the gap – in response to the global threats outlined above.

Some degree of uniformity in the *Agora* submissions can be expected given the mandate set by the editors specifically encouraging consideration of 'the future international law of the use of force'.[35] But read as a whole, the *Agora* is remarkable for the broad agreement about fundamental assumptions, two in particular: that international law is currently in crisis, and that the answer to the crisis is a strengthened, muscular international law.

But *is* there a crisis in international law? Are there new, post-9/11 dangers that require a rethinking of the UN Charter and international law? And if there are, and if 9/11 has signalled such a transformational moment in international law and relations, why is the focus on use of force as the locus of reform? In a so-called 'marketplace' of ideas, why are these questions not being asked? What questions, in turn, are raised by such broad agreement on the nature of international law's crisis and the means of its resolution?

Hilary Charlesworth[36] argues that international law is a 'discipline of crises' in which scholars and practitioners focus on crises as the 'bread and butter and the engine of progressive development of international law'.[37] The *Agora* is no exception. But, as Charlesworth goes on to argue, the disciplinary focus on crises leads to a thin analysis; a concentration 'on a single event or series of events', missing in turn 'the larger picture',[38] and the 'structural issues of global justice'.[39]

What is missing from the *Agora*'s understanding of international law's crisis? There are three key assumptions underlying the *Agora* portrayal of international law's crisis that warrant further examination. The first is the assumption about the *source* of international law's crisis. The *Agora* participants are broadly in agreement that the Iraq war (and US extra-legal actions) crystallized the moment of international law's crisis. Certainly, this war, given its widespread opposition, human rights abuses and seemingly impossible resolution, is indeed a challenge to the international community. What is curious about the *Agora* contributions, however, is the assumption that this particular breach has threatened the foundations of international law when other extreme breaches – global poverty, the global division of labour, systemic discrimination against women, the HIV/AIDS pandemic – have *not*. While the eradication of poverty and sex discrimination and the entrenchment of self-determination are all arguably central to the Charter system of law,[40] it is the presumed *limitations* on legally sanctioned force that constitute international law's crisis.

Feminist analyses of international law[41] and relations[42] would suggest that this focus on use of force, rather than poverty, as central to the international order is not merely an oversight or a question of emphasis. Feminist scholars have demonstrated the ways in which the very definition of 'international' – as matters between states – reflects a narrow worldview and one that structures the very matters deemed central to the disciplines and practice of international law and relations. The lives of women, the poor and disenfranchised are written out of a disciplinary focus defined in terms of the heady world of inter-state politics (and law), rather than a sociology of the everyday. This is not simply a question of inclusion and exclusion of the marginal into the mainstream of international law and relations. The very categories of 'knowledge about the world'[43] presume a state-centric international order, which in turn shapes the various knowledge claims made about matters of 'international' importance; the meaning of security, peace, war and order. In the context of the *Agora*, the assumption that international law is in crisis reinforces an understanding of international law narrowly focused on the use of force and restraint of 'rogue' state behaviour. This depiction of crisis entails two other, related assumptions about what is central and significant to international law; that *new* international security threats have emerged, and that use of force is needed to counter-balance the violence of rogue states and human rights abuses.

For the *Agora* participants, the threat to international security is defined quite narrowly: rogue regimes, terrorist networks with 'catastrophic' potential and weapons of mass destruction. While these are all serious issues, for the majority of the world's population they do not constitute an international security threat greater than, for example, water-borne parasites.[44] Issues of terrorism and weapons of mass destruction may, and indeed likely are, of central importance to the government of the *United States*, and hence may inform its approach to international law. But, in the context of the *Agora* there is little mention, except through Falk's more circumspect analysis, that the very construction of the current security threats is artificially narrow. Rather, the majority of the contributions take as self-evident that these are indeed the pressing global security issues and thus constitute new developments which international law is currently ill-suited, in their analysis, to address.

If terrorism, rogue states and weapons of mass destruction are the key international security threats, then the answer – and the third assumption underpinning the *Agora* – is the need for greater use of armed intervention. That is, military intervention will stop human rights abuses (or the misuse of weapons of mass destruction). Tragically, the evidence of military interventions – even 'humanitarian' ones – in the twentieth and twenty-first centuries suggests the opposite is true. Indeed, as I write this in the spring of 2005, Iraq remains an unstable country where basic services are intermittent and uncertain,[45] and the US torture of Iraqis in, for example, Abu Ghraib,[46] underscores the insecurities caused by 'use of force'.

Yet, few in the *Agora* question the assumption that international law's crisis is caused by the limited options for legal use of force. The framework of analysis shared by almost all the submissions is that international law must be rethought against the threats posed by a 'dark and unruly' world of rogue states and weapons of mass destruction. Missing from this analysis, and as predicted in Hilary Charlesworth's analysis, is any account of the structural relations of inequality through which security and peace are compromised for the majority of the world's population in ways not accounted for by the *Agora*. How is it that this 'marketplace' of ideas offers such little choice and range of views?

International law scholar Anne Orford[47] traces a similar compression of views in the international law literature on humanitarian intervention. She argues that the debates on 'humanitarian' intervention produce a particular 'truth' about intervention; that it is fundamentally humane, necessary and, by definition, military. In her reading of the stories of intervention told in the international legal literature, but found also in the 'everyday language [of] ... media reports and political sound bites', intervention narratives create 'a powerful sense of self for those who identify with the hero of the story'.[48] The production of the heroic, in Orford's account, draws on racialized masculine and feminine stereotypes in which the international community emerges as the embodiment of human rights and democracy against the racialized threats of 'rogue states, ruthless dictators and ethnic tensions'.[49] In the intervention narratives around Kosovo, for example, the international community is joined by NATO, the Security Council and the US as 'knights in white armour',[50] the 'masculine, active hero', who intervenes to rescue the feminized and racialized victims.[51]

Orford's analysis applies also to the *Agora* submissions with their focus on the world 'as a dark and unruly place' and in which international law – through sanctioning greater use of force – might protect against the world's 'bad men'. Orford's approach usefully turns the spotlight on the international legal literature itself and the community of internationally-minded scholars to highlight the importance of gender and racial stereotypes in producing 'the desire for military intervention'.[52] We, the readers of humanitarian intervention narratives, and the viewers of the masculine, active hero, 'experience a pleasurable sense of expanded freedom to be and act in the world'.[53] There is, in other words, a tremendous pull to be part of the humanitarian intervention narratives, which, in their turn, create a sense of 'us'.[54] The stories of international law and its crises thus are also stories about our – internationally-minded scholars' – desires and fantasies[55] about community, self and the potential for the heroic.

If, following from Orford, we consider international legal literature – in this case the *Agora* – as a site for the performance and production of identity, how might we see the 'desires and fantasies' written into our analysis? One of the key mechanisms by which this happens, argues Orford, is through the positioning of options in terms of strict binaries in which one half of the binary is the dominant, powerful and preferred option. For Orford, the humanitarian intervention narratives are underpinned by a central binary between action and inaction.[56] The *Agora* participants similarly narrate their version of international law's crisis through a number of binaries. For Richard Gardner the 'problem' facing international law is best evidenced through the juxtaposition of 'Bush' and the 'Jurisprudes'.[57] These oppositional entities, for Gardner, equate to a 'narrow interpretation of the Charter by those "jurisprudes" who would permit the use of armed force only' in limited cases,[58] and the Bush Doctrine 'expanding ... the right of preventive war against *potentially* dangerous adversaries'.[59] Thus, international law has been placed in crisis by a Bush Administration pulling too far in one direction, and the 'jurisprudes' who, historically, have anchored international law firmly in an opposite place.

If the problem of international law is the pull of two extremes, the solution is equally stark. Either the international legal apparatus is expanded to allow the use of force in some pre-emptive situations, or the future of international law is uncertain. '[T]he normative rules and the enforcement mechanisms of the UN Charter system must be brought better in sync ... if the law and institutions governing the use of force established in the Charter are to play a significant role in the difficult, dangerous years ahead.'[60]

The use of binaries, as in the above two examples, functions to limit the range of analysis. The binaries reinforce the *Agora*'s central theme of international law's crisis: international law has become moribund, and must be revitalized; international law has become narrow, and must be expanded; international law has become weak, and must be made strong. In the following section, I focus on the binary of law's weakness and strength that emerges in the *Agora* contributions. This particular binary, I suggest, reveals anxieties about international law's authoritative promise in a changing order in which the Bush Administration appears to position itself as *the* global authority. These anxieties have striking parallels with those around masculinity in a changing gender order. For the *Agora* participants, these anxieties reveal themselves in the construction of international law's masculinity – as the New Man – in contradistinction to the cowboy masculinity of the Bush Administration. The result, I argue, is that international law emerges in the *Agora* as a Promise Keeper: sensitive and concerned by his own limitations, but willing, if allowed, to live up to his promises and resume his authoritative place as head of the household.

## INTERNATIONAL MASCULINITY

The gender of international law and politics has been the subject of extensive feminist analysis, too complex to revisit here. For my purposes, feminist scholars of both international relations and law have exposed the connections between gender, identity and the practice and scholarship of 'the international'. Much of the feminist literature has explored the doctrinal and performative renderings of gender through the operation of heavily weighted binaries between the heady world of diplomatic and international intrigue as against the small, contained parochial world of the national/domestic realm. My interests here are in the feminist accounts of the masculinities of the international;[61] the ways in which the international is constituted as, and in turn reinforces, masculine archetypes.[62]

Scholars of masculinity[63] have begun to examine how ideal expressions of masculinity – which vary in 'a given place or time'[64] – are hegemonic in a Gramscian sense. That is, hegemonic masculinity is one mechanism by which inequalities are reproduced and naturalized.[65] Hegemonic masculinity is defined not just against femininity/ies but other, non-dominant masculinities. And law is one arena in which hegemonic masculinities are imagined, positioned and reinforced.

At the international level, assertions of masculinity arise on a number of levels. Not only are the knowledge claims and disciplinary boundaries of international law and relations clearly gendered in their constitution and effect, but 'manliness' itself is important. The international has historically been and still is a place of almost hyper-masculinity. The periods of European empire, for example, were a time of great masculine striding,[66] where European powers set out to dominate and subjugate. Colonized peoples were infantilized and feminized,[67] and ultimately brought to kneel at the feet of paternal colonial power. In addition to these masculine archetypes, there is also an imposing embodied masculine presence in the practice of international relations where the power politics of warfare continue to be dominated by (the almost always) male heads of state, ministers of foreign affairs and the men of the military.

In *Manly States*, the international relations scholar Charlotte Hooper explores 'the media representations of glamorized masculinities in an international context'.[68] In her study of *The Economist* magazine, Hooper traces the ways in which the cultural reaffirmation of 'international adventure and masculinity' provides a 'source of imaginative inspiration that informs the meaning'[69] of international practice. There is, for Hooper, a connection between the different masculinities found in media representations of the international – whether it be 'the legend of Lawrence of Arabia', 'the myth of the French Foreign legion' or more current portrayals of diplomacy, spying, globalization or international business – and the self-identity and expectation of international practitioners.[70]

Hooper's analysis draws on the growing field of masculinity studies to emphasize the multiple masculinities that converge and diverge in the construction of hegemonic masculinity.[71] She identifies several evolving masculine archetypes underpinning different approaches in IR: the 'male warrior'; the imperial adventurer who evolves into the patriarch of the era of Christian conversion,[72] giving way ultimately to the bourgeois-rationalist New Man; and, more recently, the emergence of a new 'rock-and-roll sci-fi masculinity'.[73] Hooper's analysis is instructive about the ways in which international claims and postures echo competing masculine archetypes. The male warrior, for example, is most closely linked to realist approaches to international relations with their emphasis on a statecraft exemplified by 'elite white men' securing territorial borders against the dangerous Hobbesian state of nature. The male warrior reaches his apogee in the Cold War era of 'masculinity of tough-talking presidents and of John Wayne and James Bond'.[74] Liberalism's new man may be kinder and gentler than the male warrior, but he serves to reinforce the 'rational-actor' model of international relations with its assumptions about 'personal autonomy, instrumental rationality, and goal orientation'.[75] The New Man of IR remains, even in his softened guise, a patriarch whose gaze is limited to a public sphere defined by autonomous, individual states. And finally, while the *enfants terribles* of IR – the post-positivists and, less so, poststructuralists – claim to have destabilized the category 'man', Hooper suggests they too are acting out their own masculine fantasies as the 'rebels without a cause' of IR theory.[76]

## THE NEW MAN OF INTERNATIONAL LAW

The international masculinities outlined in Hooper's analysis resonate with the images of masculinity in the *Agora* contributions. The dominant conception of 'the problem' in the *Agora* is of an international law that has lost its way or has become deficient in the context of a changing international order. The pressing problem facing the international realm is a continuation of the 1990s debate over humanitarian intervention: when and how can the international community use (military) force against international 'bad men' who abuse their own citizens, and/or harbour terrorists or weapons of mass destruction? Implicit in the definition of the problem are two assumptions: that the old order has ended and that the new order has revealed a weakened international law.

Claims about the 'newness' of the current international order abound. Leading the way has been work such as Mary Kaldor's which emphasizes the newness of modern war and the paradigmatic shift it occasions. Her 'new wars' thesis has been critiqued as offering a simplified and distorting approach in which international conflict is understood narrowly as the product of racialized extremists who wage diabolical ethnic war.[77] In a similar way, I argue that the second assumption – about international law's weakened state – functions artificially to delimit an understanding of law's role in the current order as problematically constrained by its presumed emasculation. If the problem is law's passive inertia, the solution must be a strengthened, yet responsible, rule of law.

Take, for example, Ruth Wedgwood's *Agora* submission. Wedgwood's analysis sets up a tension between two possible futures. In the first, and hopefully rejected, option, international law is passive; it takes no action, and offers a strict legality out of touch with the real world of harsh security threats. In the other, international law is responsible and committed. It 'faces its responsibilities'[78] and, in turn, is 'strengthened by commitments to human rights and democracy'.[79] For Wedgwood the stakes are clear: either the Security Council acts decisively – it 'must rise to the occasion' to 'retain its authority'[80] – or it continues in its 'enormously weakened' state of 'ineffectual' responses to the scourge and ravages[81] of the international 'bad men' in the form of Slobodan Milosevic, Charles Taylor and Saddam Hussein.[82]

Wedgwood's choice of language is full of gendered and sexualized imagery and evocative of a particular masculinity. Her portrayal of law suggests that international law must be more muscular, somewhat akin to the warrior hero of the Cold War era, but this needs to be combined with the sense of responsibility and moral authority of the New Man. This is a masculine hero with a conscience: sensitive, modern and responsible. In situating international law at a crossroads, Wedgwood's analysis rests on two key assumptions: that international law is currently passive and irresponsible; and that this passivity, and international law's future, entail an element of choice. Somewhere and somehow – Wedgwood doesn't make this clear – international law has turned its back on its responsibilities. The task now is to make it 'face its responsibilities' by recommitting to 'human rights and democracy'.[83]

While others in the *Agora* might be less specifically gendered in their language than Wedgwood, there is a general sense in the contributions that a new, strengthened international law must emerge in an international order dominated by another, illegitimate authority figure. That is, international law is positioned as an alternative to the authority – and masculinity – of George W. Bush. Under the Bush Administration, the US and its unilateralist, 'dead or alive' approach has clear and very intentional references to what Hooper might refer to as 'John Wayne' international masculinity. The Bush Administration's pretence to the western film and novel genre is a subject in its own right and not one I can cover here. However, I argue that this Bush western-style, gun-slinging authority figure lurks in the backdrop to the *Agora* depiction of how international law must adapt itself to a 'dark and unruly' international order. It is the Bush Administration that has removed 'the fig leaf of legal justification'[84] from use of force,[85] and now strides about with its masculine pretensions on display. The question of international law's future is thus the question of who is the legitimate authority figure: 'the Iraqi crisis was not primarily about what to do but, rather, who decides'.[86]

The *Agora* portrayal of a weakened and irresponsible international law that must adapt to regain its authority has a curious parallel in the language used by the US-based Christian Right 'Men's Movement':[87] the Promise Keepers.[88] This movement came to prominence in the 1990s arguing for a strengthened conception of modern manhood. The broad orientation of this movement has been described in scholarly accounts as follows:

> there is a moral crisis in society, and . . . men play a decisive role in this crisis as being both its cause and solution. Men therefore need to come together and end their sinful lives, and take back their god-given responsibility – in the family, in the church and in society.[89]

The Promise Keepers comes out of a long tradition of Christian Right responses to feminist activism. Michael Messner, for example, writes of a 'Muscular Christianity' movement that swept the US at the turn of the twentieth century in 'response to a crisis of masculinity brought on by feminism, modernization, and wide-spread fears that boys and men were becoming "feminized" '.[90]

In its current formation, the Promise Keepers, like other aspects of the Men's Movement, aims to 'reconcile recent social change with a distinct conception of manhood',[91] in particular, a rejuvenated – vigorous – masculinity.[92] The key feature of this renewed masculinity, and which is definitive of the movement, is 'men's responsibility to retake their natural positions of leadership in their communities'.[93] The resulting masculinity combines 'strength and sensitivity'.[94] In the language of the Promise Keepers, with its emphasis on responsibility, relieving women of their burden and the resumption of a kind but firm head-of-household role, 'hegemonic masculinity becomes domesticated'.[95]

The parallels with the image of the New Man offered by the Promise Keepers and the New International Law offered by Wedgwood and others in the *Agora* are striking. Both operate from a premise that there has been a significant, transformative shift in political and social relations. As a consequence of, and contributing to, that shift has been a law/father who abdicates his responsibilities, remains in the background, fails to offer moral/spiritual guidance and often fails to contribute to day-to-day survival; a dead-beat dad. The Promise Keepers' solution is for men to reassert their authoritative place in the family; to reclaim fatherhood, share the burden with their wives and, most importantly, resume their role as spiritual and moral leader in the family. In very similar terms, the *Agora* contributors offer a vision in which law lives up to its responsibilities by providing the moral and legal framework missing from an international politics dominated by a unilateral-minded hegemon. Importantly, and like the patriarchal father of the Promise Keepers, law must combine its role as moral guide with the strength necessary to protect against the bad men, including the hegemon, who threaten international stability.

What is the significance of this parallel between New International Law and the New Man of the Promise Keepers? Both identify a crisis in authority: the authority figure of the patriarch in an age of feminism, the authoritative capacity of law in an age of empire. And both speak to a solution in which the authority figure is made muscular; a return to virility upon resumption of his proper place. For both, muscularity is a force of good; a paternal and beneficial authority. I am not suggesting that the contributors to the *Agora* are in any way advancing the agenda of the Promise Keepers. But the parallels are important because they speak to a set of assumptions about what international law is, what it can/should do and what our role as international-minded scholars might be.

The construction of international law as Promise Keeper and New Man figure positions law as beneficial, or at least benign. But this, of course, fails to address the concerns that many, including many women, might have with an international law as patriarchal authority figure, even in his sensitive, responsible guise.[96] As feminist analysis of the public/private divide in Western, liberal societies has shown, assumptions about the safety and security of the private world of the home have operated to obscure the ways in which the domestic realm, with its seemingly benign patriarch, is often a place of danger for women.[97] Similarly, recent international law scholarship has drawn attention to the colonial legacy in international law.[98] International law historically is implicated in the process of colonialism, to an extent not always fully explored in the international legal literature. While current international law and scholarship, with its cosmopolitan ethic, have moved a long way from this history, the replaying and reworking of colonial fantasies, argument and archetypes can be found in international legal debate on humanitarian intervention,[99] minority rights,[100] peacekeeping,[101] self-determination,[102] and so on. To what extent does the call to law's masculinity, with its language of responsibility and its presumption of protection, also serve to replay and rehearse colonial and masculine fantasies? What violence do we enable when 'the crisis of law' is imagined in terms of a legal lack; when more law is offered as the solution to imperialism?

## CONCLUSION

The invasion of Afghanistan by the United States, followed by the US-led invasion of Iraq, has generated a broad-based, critical and pressing examination of the meaning and future of international law and community. The recurrent theme, and the one I focus on here, is the anxiety about international law reflected in these debates. Whether its strengthening international law by updating it[103] or adding to it,[104] or in proving (reassuring ourselves) that international law is not reducible to the mere instrumentality of a realist sense of power,[105] the objective seems to be to *restore* international law.

Understanding the desires and fantasies that underpin current preoccupations with international legality is important in focusing attention on the narratives of 'northern goodness and heroism'[106] reflected in international interventions. My analysis in this chapter focuses on the special issue of the *American Journal of International Law* not because it is a definitive account of what 'the international legal academy' thinks, but because it is one particular site at which truths about 'us' are proclaimed. My analysis in this respect is influenced by Sherene Razack, who urges an examination of legal narratives 'for the ways in which they organize how we come to know ourselves'. Investigating these narratives is part of the process of dismantling 'those deeply internalized myths about our civilizing mission'.[107]

In focusing on the current preoccupations with international legality, I want to challenge the assumed goodness of international law. My argument is not that international law cannot be a force of good or an important part of a move to a fairer and more just world order. My point is that international law is not necessarily, or exclusively, either of these. It can be both, and more. The call to international law must be accompanied by a greater understanding of the complex operation of law, and its relation to gendered and racialized orders. To this end, the questions that are unstated are important. Why is it that in the international soul-searching conducted in the face of US unilateralism, we are prepared to question the authoritative claims made in the name of sovereignty but not those made in the name of international law?

## NOTES

1   Many thanks to Amy Bartholomew, Didi Herman and Diana Majury, who read and provided very helpful comments on earlier drafts of this chapter.

2   Speech by Prime Minister Tony Blair in his Sedgefield constituency (reported in full in the *Guardian*, 5 March 2004), quoted in Wade Mansell, 'Goodbye to All That? The Rule of Law, International Law, the United States, and the Use of Force', *Journal of Law and Society* 31 (2004): 433–56, 436 (fn 11).

3   Peter Fitzpatrick, '"Gods Would be Needed ...": American Empire and the Rule of (International) Law', *Leiden Journal of International Law* 16 (2003): 429–66, 457–8.

4   Thomas M. Franck, 'What Happens Now? The United Nations after Iraq', *American Journal of International Law* 97 (2003): 607–20, 620.

5   For example, at his confirmation hearings, US Attorney General nominee Alberto Gonzales is reported to have described the Geneva Convention

provisions relating to prisoners as 'obsolete' and 'quaint'. See Gary Younge, 'Bring Back the Lash', *Guardian* (10 January 2005), http://www. guardian.co.uk, accessed 7 February 2005.

6   *American Journal of International Law* 97:3 (July 2003): 553–642. A second part of the *Agora*, with which I do not engage, continued in 97:4 (October 2003): 803–72 on the issue of military tribunals.

7   Lori Fisler Damrosch and Bernard H. Oxman, 'Editors' Introduction', *American Journal of International Law* 97:3 (July 2003): 553–7.

8   Ibid., 554.

9   See Jutta Brunnée and Stephen J. Toope, 'Slouching Towards New "Just" Wars: The Hegemon After September 11th', *International Relations* 18:4 (2004): 405–23.

10  Damrosch and Oxman, 'Editors' Introduction', 554.

11  Ibid., 554.

12  These include William H. Taft IV and Todd F. Buchwald, 'Preemption, Iraq, and International Law', *American Journal of International Law* 97:3 (July 2003): 557–63. The authors' brief biographies at the end of their submission (563) refer to them respectively as the Legal Adviser of the United States Department of State and the Assistant Legal Adviser for Political-Military Affairs of the United States Department of State. John Yoo, author of the second submission, 'International Law and the War in Iraq', *American Journal of International Law* 97:3 (July 2003): 563–76, is described at 576 as 'Visiting Fellow, American Enterprise Institute; Professor of Law, University of California at Berkeley (Boalt Hall) School of Law, Deputy Assistant Attorney General, Office of Legal Counsel, U.S. Department of Justice, 2001–2003'.

13  Ruth Wedgwood, 'The Fall of Saddam Hussein: Security Council Mandates and Preemptive Self-Defense', *American Journal of International Law* 97:3 (July 2003): 576–85.

14  Richard N. Gardner, 'Neither Bush nor the "Jurisprudes"', *American Journal of International Law* 97:3 (July 2003): 585–90.

15  For an alternative, more sceptical analysis of the legal argumentation on the Security Council resolutions, see Vaughan Lowe, 'The Iraq Crisis: What Now?' in *International and Comparative Law Quarterly* 52 (October 2003): 859–71.

16  Franck, 'What Happens Now?', 616–17.

17  Richard A. Falk, 'What Future for the UN Charter System of War Prevention?', *American Journal of International Law* 97:3 (July 2003): 590–8, 598. For a similar analysis which rejects the portrayal of an acute reformatory moment in international law, arguing instead for a tweaking of existing law, see Jutta Brunnée and Stephen J. Toope, 'The Use of Force: International Law After Iraq', *International and Comparative Law Quarterly* 53 (2004): 785–806, 793.

18  Gardner, 'Neither Bush nor the "Jurisprudes"', 588. See also Miriam Shapiro, 'Iraq: The Shifting Sands of Preemptive Self-Defense', *American Journal of International Law* 97:3 (July 2003): 599–607, who argues at 603 that 'it is difficult – and dangerous – to stretch' international law too far in reinterpreting 'defensive action in the face of an imminent threat'.

19  Gardner, 'Neither Bush nor the "Jurisprudes" ', 588.

20 Franck, 'What Happens Now?', 608.

21 Jane E. Stromseth, 'Law and Force after Iraq: A Transitional Moment', *American Journal of International Law* 97:3 (July 2003): 628–42, 636.

22 Yoo, 'International Law and the War in Iraq'.

23 Wedgwood, 'The Fall of Saddam Hussein'.

24 Specifically, Yoo and Stromseth.

25 Wedgwood, 'The Fall of Saddam Hussein', 584.

26 My thanks to Diana Majury for making this connection.

27 Gardner, 'Neither Bush nor the "Jurisprudes" ', 590.

28 Stromseth, 'Law and Force after Iraq', 642.

29 Wedgwood, 'The Fall of Saddam Hussein', 582.

30 Stromseth, 'Law and Force after Iraq', 642.

31 Tom J. Farer, 'The Prospect for International Law and Order in the Wake of Iraq', *American Journal of International Law* 97:3 (2003): 621–8, 627.

32 Franck, 'What Happens Now?', 608.

33 Again, I would distinguish Falk from this view as well as Franck, who may be in broad agreement with the need to reform international law but specifically rejects *now* as the time to do it.

34 Many of the contributors refer to the 'gap' in international law by which they refer to various versions of the difference between state conduct and normative rules. Franck, for example, refers to the 'yawing gap between what states always do in their ambitious pursuit of power and what they are permitted to do by the fragile normative structure' (608). Shapiro considers 'what, if anything, can be done to reduce the gap between a security posture that is problematic and one that is not' (599), while Falk explicitly addresses the 'legitimacy/legality gap' (591).

35 Damrosch and Oxman, 'Editors' Introduction', 554.

36 Hilary Charlesworth, 'International Law: A Discipline of Crises', *Modern Law Review* 65 (2002): 377–92.

37 Ibid., 391.

38 Ibid., 384.

39 Ibid., 382.

40 See, in particular, Article 1(2) and (3) of The United Nations Charter, 1945, which respectively define the purposes of the UN as also including self-determination of peoples and 'solving international problems of an economic, social, cultural, or humanitarian character'. Wedgwood does recognize that strengthening 'commitments to human rights and democracy' may be necessary under a 'teleological understanding of the Charter', but, in her analysis, human rights protection is required in the service of countering 'unpredictable violence of state and nonstate actors.' (Wedgwood, 'The Fall of Saddam Hussein', 584.)

41 See, for example, Doris Buss and Ambreena Manji (eds.), *International Law: Modern Feminist Approaches* (Oxford: Hart, 2005); Hilary Charlesworth and Christine Chinkin, *The Boundaries of International Law: A Feminist Analysis* (Manchester: University of Manchester Press, 2000).

42 See, for example, Cynthia Enloe, *Bananas, Beaches and Bases: Making Feminist Sense of International Politics* (Berkeley: University of California Press, 2000); Christine Sylvester, *Feminist International Relations: An Unfinished Journey* (Cambridge: Cambridge University Press, 2002);

J. Ann Tickner, *Gendering World Politics: Issues and Approaches in the Post-Cold War Era* (New York: Columbia University Press, 2001); Sandra Whitworth, *Men, Militarism and UN Peacekeeping: A Gendered Analysis* (Boulder, CO: Lynne Rienner, 2004).

43  Jill Steans, *Gender and International Relations: An Introduction* (New Brunswick, NJ: Rutgers University Press, 1998) 3.

44  The British NGO – WaterAid – estimates that every year over two million people die from diseases related to lack of safe drinking water. Six thousand children die every day from diarrhoea: http://www.wateraid.co.uk, accessed 27 April 2005.

45  See *Report of the United Nations High Commissioner for Human Rights and Follow-up to the World Conference on Human Rights: The Present Situation of Human Rights in Iraq,* 9 June 2004.

46  See Human Rights Watch, *Getting Away with Torture? Command Responsibility for the U.S. Abuse of Detainees,* April 2005, available at http://www.hrw.org, accessed 27 April 2005.

47  Anne Orford, 'Muscular Humanitarianism: Reading the Narratives of the New Interventionism', *European Journal of International Law* 10 (1999): 679–711. See also Anne Orford, *Reading Humanitarian Intervention: Human Rights and the Use of Force in International Law* (Cambridge: Cambridge University Press, 2003).

48  Orford, 'Muscular Humanitarianism', 683.

49  Ibid., 691.

50  Ibid., 692.

51  Ibid., 695–6.

52  Orford, *Reading Humanitarian Intervention,* 10.

53  Orford, 'Muscular Humanitarianism', 695.

54  Ibid., 683; Orford, *Reading Humanitarian Intervention.* See also Sherene H. Razack, *Dark Threats and White Knights: The Somalia Affair, Peacekeeping and the New Imperialism* (Toronto: University of Toronto Press, 2004).

55  David Kennedy refers to international law as 'an arena of desire and fantasy'. David Kennedy, 'Autumn Weekends: An Essay on Law and Everyday Life', in Austin Sarat and Thomas R. Kearns (eds.), *Law in Everyday Life* (Ann Arbor, MI: University of Michigan Press, 1993), 191, 231, quoted in Charlesworth 'A Discipline of Crises', 387.

56  Orford, *Reading Humanitarian Intervention,* particularly chapter 1.

57  Gardner, 'Neither Bush nor the "Jurisprudes" '.

58  Ibid., 589.

59  Ibid., 588.

60  Stromseth, 'Law and Force after Iraq', 642.

61  See generally, Razack, *Dark Threats and White Knights*; Whitworth, *Men, Militarism and UN Peacekeeping*; Marysia Zalewski and Jane Parpart, *The 'Man' Question in International Relations* (Boulder, CO: Westview Press, 1998).

62  My interest in this chapter is on two competing versions of masculinity, rather than the traditional gender binary drawn between femininity and masculinity. The production of the feminine international law is also an important topic that warrants further investigation in its own right. Just as there are multiple masculinities so too are there multiple femininities.

While there is a tendency to assume that the feminine is defined by what the masculine is not, this does not capture the complex ways in which the feminine is constructed and derided in analysis of the international. See, for example, Didi Herman, 'Globalism's Siren Song: The United Nations in Christian Right Thought and Prophecy', *Sociological Review* 49 (2001): 56–77.

63  See R. W. Connell, *Masculinities* (Berkeley: University of California Press, 1995), and Michael Thomson, 'Masculinity, Reproductivity and Law', Cardiff Centre for Ethics Law and Society, April 2004; available from http://www.ccels.cf.ac.uk, accessed: 14 June 2005.

64  Thomson, 'Masculinity, Reproductivity and Law', 5.

65  Ibid., 4.

66  See Vasuki Nesiah, 'Placing International Law: White Spaces on a Map', *Leiden Journal of International Law* 16 (2003): 1–35.

67  Anne McClintock, *Imperial Leather: Race, Gender, Sexuality in the Colonial Context* (New York: Routledge, 1995).

68  Charlotte Hooper, *Manly States: Masculinities, International Relations, and Gender Politics* (New York: Columbia University Press, 2001), 88.

69  Ibid., 88.

70  Ibid., 87.

71  Connell, *Masculinities*.

72  Hooper, *Manly States*, 97.

73  Ibid., Ch. 3. Hooper goes on to note that a new 'rock-and-roll sci-fi masculinity may be emerging as a "future orthodoxy"' (115).

74  Ibid., 103.

75  Ibid., 99.

76  Ibid., 115. The 'rock and roll' masculinity is not one I discuss in this chapter.

77  See Barrie Collins, 'New Wars and Old Wars? The Lessons of Rwanda', in David Chandler (ed.), *Rethinking Human Rights: Critical Approaches to International Politics* (Basingstoke: Palgrave Macmillan, 2002), 157–75.

78  UN Secretary General Kofi Annan, quoted in Wedgwood, 'The Fall of Saddam Hussein', 581.

79  Ibid., 584.

80  Ibid., 581.

81  Ibid., 581.

82  Ibid., 578.

83  See The International Commission on Intervention and State Sovereignty, *The Responsibility to Protect* (Ottawa: International Development Research Centre, 2001). For a critical reading of *Responsibility to Protect*, see Vasuki Nesiah, 'From Berlin to Bonn to Baghdad: A Space for Infinite Justice', *Harvard Human Rights Journal* 17 (2004): 75–98.

84  Franck, 'What Happens Now?', 608.

85  On the western genre and international law, see Ruth Buchanan and Rebecca Johnson, 'The "Unforgiven" Sources of International Law: Nation-building, Violence, and Gender in the West(ern)', in Buss and Manji (eds.), *International Law: Modern Feminist Approaches*, 131–58.

86  Franck, 'What Happens Now?', 616.

87   On the mythopoetic men's movement generally, see Michael Schwalbe, *Unlocking the Iron Cage: The Men's Movement, Gender Politics, and American Culture* (New York: Oxford University Press, 1996).

88   Brian Donovan, 'Political Consequences of Private Authority: Promise Keepers and the Transformation of Hegemonic Masculinity', *Theory and Society* 27 (1998): 817–43; Michael A. Messner, *Politics of Masculinities: Men in Movements* (Thousand Oaks, CA: Sage, 1997). The academic literature tends to treat the Promise Keepers, with its evangelic Christian orientation, as a distinct part of the Men's Movement.

89   Sara Eldén, 'Gender Politics in Conservative Men's Movements: Beyond Complexity, Ambiguity and Pragmatism', *NORA* 10 (2002): 38–48, 39.

90   Messner, *Politics of Masculinities*, 25.

91   Donovan, 'Political Consequences of Private Authority', 819.

92   Ibid., 819–20.

93   Messner, *Politics of Masculinities*, 17.

94   Donovan, 'Political Consequences of Private Authority', 826.

95   Ibid., 828.

96   For a 'Third World' critique of the *Responsibility to Protect*, see Nesiah, 'From Berlin to Bonn to Baghdad'.

97   See Susan B. Boyd (ed.), *Challenging the Public/Private Divide: Feminism, Law, and Public Policy* (Toronto: University of Toronto Press, 1997); Margaret Thornton (ed.), *Public and Private: Feminist Legal Debates* (Melbourne: Oxford University Press, 1995).

98   Antony Anghie, 'Finding the Peripheries: Sovereignty and Colonialism is Nineteenth-Century International Law', *Harvard International Law Journal* 40 (1999): 1–80; Nathaniel Berman, ' "The Appeals of the Orient": Colonized Desire and the War of the Riff', in Karen Knop (ed.), *Gender and Human Rights* (Oxford: Oxford University Press, 2004); Orford, *Reading Humanitarian Intervention*; Peter Fitzpatrick, 'Terminal Legality: Imperialism and the (De)composition of Law', in Dian Kirkby and Catharine Coleborne (eds.), *Law, History, Colonialism: The Reach of Empire* (Manchester: Manchester University Press, 2001), 9–25.

99   Orford, *Reading Humanitarian Intervention*.

100  Berman, ' "The Appeals of the Orient" '.

101  Razack, *Dark Threats and White Knights*.

102  Nesiah, 'Placing International Law: White Spaces on a Map'.

103  As in the *Agora* submissions generally.

104  Jean L. Cohen, 'Whose Sovereignty? Empire Versus International Law', *Ethic and International Affairs* 18 (2004): 1–24.

105  Fitzpatrick, ' "Gods Would be Needed" '.

106  Razack, *Dark Threats and White Knights*, 8.

107  Ibid., 8.

# 7

# Looking for Life Signs in an International Rule of Law[1]

*Trevor Purvis*

On 21 September 2004 UN Secretary General Kofi Annan opened the 55th session of the UN General Assembly with a sombre assessment of the prevailing state of international affairs. At the centre of his comments was a concern that 'the rule of law is at risk around the world'. Spurred by concerns about the apparent proliferation of human rights abuses around the globe, from Darfur to Abu Ghraib, these comments reflect an all-too-general sense that international law is being flagrantly ignored, and that the rule of law as a principle governing international relations is at risk.

Annan's speech marks just one in a burgeoning array of references to the rule of law as a principle that informs and guides international relations. Indeed, for a time, talk of the rule of law had begun to infuse much of the terrain of post-Cold War international relations discourse. The European Union had established respect for the rule of law as a principal criterion for community recognition of new states and governments in the early 1990s. The rule of law (along with its apparent corollaries, 'good governance' and 'democracy') had become a principal component of international development discourse long before the events of 9/11, with governments and international agencies highlighting its importance as an indispensable component of viable and sustainable 'progress'. But since the events of early September 2001, the rule of law seems more prominent than ever as a notion with international connotations, but one whose substantive content is less and less clear. Since that time it has become a regular feature in the foreign policy rhetoric of the Administration in Washington, not least as an apparent guiding principle of the 'war on terror' and as a centrepiece in the White House's *National Security Strategy* of September 2002.[2] In these formulations the rule of law is something the inhabitants of liberal democracies enjoy by definition, but is absent (again, by definition) in 'rogue states'. All this at the same time that any number of commentators have criticized the excesses of the 'war on terror' and the principle of preventive war at the heart of the Bush Doctrine as grave assaults on the notion of international relations governed by the rule of law. One would be forgiven for feeling a little cognitive dissonance in the face of such incommensurate claims about who represents the rule of law and what might constitute its violation. Indeed, the cacophony of competing discourses makes it particularly difficult to get one's conceptual bearings, let alone settle on what a compelling conception of the rule of law might entail at the international level. Whatever the case, if we could speak of its arrival on the international stage prior to 9/11, its vitality today is seriously in question.

This chapter explores what a meaningful concept of the rule of law in international relations might entail, and offers an assessment of its prospects in a post-9/11 world. The illegality of the war in Iraq coupled with a very clear and public disdain on the part of the US Administration for the constraints of international law suggest that a consideration of the role and vitality of the rule of law in international relations is both important and timely, particularly when that Administration seems intent on ignoring international law whenever it suits its purposes to do so.

At the centre of this discussion is a call for a much more robust concept of the rule of law in international affairs than that presented by neoliberal visions of international life. But more importantly, to the extent that we might speak of the emergence of an international rule of law over the past six decades, the Bush Doctrine and the 'war on terror' represent not simply the sort of impoverished vision of the rule of law that has underpinned neoliberal rhetoric for so long, but rather issue a fundamental challenge to anything remotely resembling a compelling concept. By 'robust' I mean to move the discussion beyond a focus on law and order or the obvious presence and proliferation of legal institutions and relations – both hallmarks of the neoliberal vision. The point is not to assert an instrumental vision of the law where legal reforms are regarded as primary vehicles for realizing social, economic and political transformation; there has been a good deal of legal instrumentalism pressed upon international affairs over the past half- century, often with dubious outcomes. But if international life is to proceed absent reliance on unaccountable violence or desperation and destitution to secure conditions of compliance, law itself cannot be widely perceived to be complicit in the reproduction of that destitution and desperation. More importantly, if such conditions persist, it seems likely that to the extent that law is genuinely complicit in their reproduction, obscures their reality or simply makes no difference to their mitigation, it will be accordingly ignored, opposed or violated. The ascendancy of neoliberalism has nurtured precisely such conditions, posing a direct challenge to the vitality of the rule of law in international affairs. The belligerent imperial vision promulgated by the Bush Doctrine goes a fatal step further, and would willingly sound its death knell. In fact, one of the particularly troubling aspects of the Bush Doctrine and the 'war on terror' has been the association of the rule of law with the project of extending and securing the conditions for US imperial domination.[3]

In so far as the rule of law marks a rhetorical component of that imperial vision, there is little of a defensible concept at play in it. While foreign policy statements emanating from the White House, Pentagon and State Department frequently refer to the need to rein in those states that habitually offend international law, that same policy does not seem to apply to American foreign policy itself. There is no international rule of law here. The rule of law seems to be dramatically limited to the establishment of juridical frameworks at the state-national level, and its only requirements would seem to be that those frameworks be America- and capital-friendly. Indeed, an international rule of law *sui generis* seems to be viewed as little more than something that will naturally fall into place when the conditions of the (neoliberal) rule of law are met *within* states. An international rule of law, then, is something to be installed in modular form from the centre of American Empire outward to the less civilized quarters of the globe. In the interim, an international rule of law will have to await the completion of the new civilizing mission of the West. The great irony is that, in practice, the Bush Doctrine and the war on terror have ushered in a full-frontal assault, not only on a nascent international rule of law, but on the rule of law at home as well.

How we understand the challenges and the stakes arising from these issues will depend, of course, on what we are referring to when discussing the rule of law. Commentators on the subject frequently note the tendency of political leaders to trot out the rule of law as a sort of mystificatory shorthand in times of crisis, and the appearance of the rule of law generously peppering the rhetoric of the US Administration would seem a classic example of precisely such a hollow appropriation. But while evincing a shallow understanding of what the rule of law connotes, this 'crisis version' of the rule of law deserves at least passing consideration, as such invocations gain their broader ideological resonance, at least in part, from a perception that some actor or group of actors has breached or threatened to breach the law; and even more rigorous concepts imply that law can indeed govern its subjects with some measure of efficacy. It suggests, that is, that law can indeed 'rule'. Unfortunately, as present circumstances attest, this 'crisis version' offers up a too-ready rhetorical smokescreen for the lawless excesses of those who would portray themselves as the rule of law's most ardent defenders.

But gross violations of the law would indeed seem to indicate a genuine challenge to the rule of law, however conceived. While the rule of law implies more than simple adherence to law, if the social relations over which it supposedly governs are characterized by rampant lawlessness, and if law cannot generally govern its intended subjects, it can hardly be said to 'rule' very effectively. A good deal is lost, however, when we reduce the rule of law to the fact of simple compliance. Compliance, and the order it engenders, can be secured in many ways, and brutal, law-bound communities may evidence quite ready compliance with legal prescriptions.

The suggestion that there is a concept of the rule of law relevant to international relations no doubt gains some additional ideological resonance from a perception of the international legal field as one of the most intense areas of legal growth of the last half-century. But if conformity with law's dictates is an inadequate foundation for a serviceable concept of the rule of law, so too is a simplistic quantitative focus that takes the amount and scope of law as evidence of a flourishing international rule of law. As Arthur Watts has pointed out, the rule of law is more than simply 'rules of law'.[4] One can have an extensive array of laws that fail, in practice, to govern social relations effectively. The existence and proliferation of legal rights and obligations on paper in no way necessarily translate into their substantive realization. And while we cannot reduce the rule of law to compliance, without compliance the rule of law is nothing but an aspiration. Thus, we must also set aside formulations that associate a proliferation or densification of the international legal field as necessarily entailing the emergence of a corresponding international rule of law. Importantly, however, such a proliferation or densification *may* offer some indication of the emergence of a general sensibility that social relations *ought* to be governed by law as opposed to other forms of authority and domination.

So what is this 'rule of law', and what, if any, is its relevance to international relations? From antiquity political philosophy has been divided by concerns over how best to resolve the problem of political order. In its classic formulation the problem is posed as 'the rule of laws vs the rule of men'.[5] Those who advocate the rule of law contend it is better to be bound by the determinacy of the laws than to be subjected to the capricious whims of circumstance and power. Law is supposed to garner compliance, at least in part, because it militates against such caprice.[6] This classic philosophical theme is brought into new focus at the end of the nineteenth century when, at the hands of England's eminent jurist A.V. Dicey, the 'rule of law' gains its first clear articulation as such. Dicey's formulation has subsequently attained the status of *locus classicus* for discussions of the rule of law in Anglo-American jurisprudence. Dicey would no doubt recoil at the expansive use to which his beloved rule of law has been put. It is worth noting, however, that the impetus driving his reflections was a concern for what he perceived to be the declining reverence for the law among British subjects. For Dicey the roots of this problem lay in the expansion of discretionary powers attending the rapidly growing administrative state of the late nineteenth century. The growing scope for apparently arbitrary criteria to enter into the processes of administrative decision-making presented a critical challenge for securing conventional English 'reverence' for the law. Arbitrariness and discretion in quasi-legal guise threatened to undermine the legitimacy of law, while simultaneously infusing social relations with an untenable indeterminacy that the rule of law would otherwise assuage. In various ways similar concerns about arbitrariness, discretion and the modern state would infuse politico-philosophical reflection on the nature of advanced capitalist states more generally, and would become a focus of attention for as diverse a range of commentators as Franz Neumann and Otto Kirchheimer, on the one hand, and Friedrich Hayek and Carl Schmitt, on the other.[7] The growth of discretion and arbitrary decision-making called into question law's capacity effectively to enable social actors to govern their behaviour in a fashion consistent with the law's dictates.

It is from this broad literature that we can distil a set of generally agreed core elements commentators list as attributes a community governed by the rule of law should possess. First, law should be able to impose limits on discretion, particularly the arbitrary use of administrative power and the use of coercive force. It should be noted, however, that while clearly in agreement on the problems associated with arbitrariness and discretion, the extent to which these are considered troubling vis-à-vis the use of force depends squarely on what are considered *a priori* appropriate objects of such coercion. Second, laws should be public, stable, general in scope and prospective in nature, and thereby knowable. These conditions express the expectation that if social subjects are to be guided in their affairs by the law, they must be capable of knowledge of that law. Third, no one is above the law. All are to be equally subject to the law's provisions, including lawmakers themselves. And finally, decisions should be amenable to independent judicial review. These elements – their presence or absence – offer important indicators of the vitality of the rule of law, but a checklist approach to identifying social arrangements governed by the rule of law is also wanting, for reasons I will return to presently.

It should be acknowledged that the discussions from which these characteristics of the rule of law have been drawn have been almost exclusively pitched at the level of the nation-state. Whether they can be thought relevant to thinking about the nature of international law is less clear. A century ago practitioners of international law and diplomacy would have largely scoffed at such a suggestion. Certainly, an extensive body of customary international law existed and was recognized by European states, as too were the faint outlines of an emerging order of multilateral treaty law part distillation of customary law and part making new law. But at the turn of the twentieth century the thought that one could ascribe the characteristics outlined above to relations between states was almost unthinkable. At least since Thomas Hobbes the model of political authority that dominated Western thought was one that concentrated power in the hands of the modern state, with the realm of pure power politics and the anarchy that attended it banished to the outside of the sovereign's realm. No law, this model suggested, could quell the raw lust for power and the avaricious proclivities that undergirded the relations between states. Surely there could be generally acknowledged and agreed-upon principles governing those relations, but absent a sovereign there seemed little hope that these relations could be bound by law in any meaningful sense. Indeed, until well into the twentieth century debate continued to rage over whether or not international law could be regarded as law at all.

A more compelling case for the emergence of a nascent international rule of law might be assembled via reflection on the sweeping legal transformations that occurred in international affairs over the second half of the twentieth century. Three principal juridifying thrusts emerged in this period, each of which implicated law as a central medium governing the social, political and economic transformations of the times. The first entailed a radical deepening and intensification of international market relations, processes mediated by a rapid proliferation of complex legal networks. Second were the related processes of decolonization that ensued throughout this period, processes which contained a strong juridical thrust dominated by themes of modernization and development. Third was the emergence of the UN system and the arrival on the international legal stage of both in1ternational organizations and individuals as legal subjects. Any assessment of the vitality of the rule of law in international affairs must be cast against these three trends. Taken together they would seem to suggest a growing commitment on the part of international actors to comport themselves in accordance with the law's dictates, and on its surface this might suggest fertile ground for the rule of law in international affairs. But the respective foci of analysis and legal development contemplated by each parallel a more general aspect of debates surrounding the rule of law as it relates to international affairs.

The dramatic postwar expansion and integration of global capital cast an indispensable role for law at both the state-national and international levels, and while not always a prominent feature of discussions, the rule of law has come increasingly to occupy a central place in the discourses of economic globalization. Throughout the Cold War extensive efforts were made laying the legal groundwork for market integration among Western states and those developing countries within the West's sphere of influence. In the past 15 years the collapse of the Soviet Bloc and China's authoritarian embrace of capital have spurred a dramatic extension and deepening of these trends as the floodgates of trade liberalization have opened.[8] With neoliberalism ascendant, the rule of law has become a centrepiece of post-Cold War global market discourse and international relations.[9] But there are two pertinent spheres of law here: domestic and international. While much of this transformation has seen the proliferation of international law aimed at soothing the growing pains of rapidly globalizing markets, the concern with the rule of law has been pitched much more squarely at the level of the state. While ushering in a burgeoning network of international legal rules, the principal institutions of international capital have seen the rule of law largely as a project to be pursued 'at home', bringing municipal law into line with the legal and practical-economic exigencies of a globalizing marketplace.[10]

Closely related to these was a second juridifying thrust involving the heightened political, economic and social integration of peripheral societies and the establishment of legal mechanisms that would effectively realize those ends. The years following World War II saw a flurry of activity in legal circles related to the dismantling of European colonial interests under the banners of modernization and development. But again, the focus here was largely on institutional and practical development at the state-national level, with the rule of law expected to play an important part in these processes, providing a framework for social and economic modernization largely modelled on the advanced capitalist states of the West. Institutional development was of particular importance to these efforts, and at the top of the list were judicial reform and an apparently prominent place for law in smoothing the transition to capitalist development. Legal and regulatory reform was regarded as crucial to the integration of newly decolonized countries into the international community. But, skewed by Cold War politics, the legacies of colonial pillage, ethnocentric bias and an overbearing practical compulsion to be capital-friendly, the high hopes captured in the early work of the Law and Development literature of the 1960s and 1970s were largely dashed on the rocks of corruption and exploitation.[11] Much of the spirit of those efforts has been revived in the post-Cold War strategic planning models of the institutions of global capital, with the likes of the World Trade Organization characterized as no less than a 'welcome extension of the rule of law to the international arena'.[12]

The juridifying thrusts associated with market integration and development/modernization have, in practice, concentrated on creating mechanisms of legal communication capable of mediating the complex divide between international and municipal spheres. In these guises the rule of law seems to have acquired a new status as one of capital's primary exports (part of a package deal, along with democracy and good governance) with the clear assumption that if markets flourish, so too will the rule of law, and vice versa. Assessment of the relative success or failure of these programmes depends on the view one takes of their respective objectives and the extent to which each has been able to secure desired transformations and general compliance on the ground. But if the fact of compliance and the presence of extensive legal rules are inadequate standards against which to assess the vitality of the rule of law, then claims that these processes have led to the realization of the rule of law in international affairs are overblown. The successful creation of conditions conducive to capital accumulation has not guaranteed conditions adequate for law itself to acquire the legitimacy and authority to govern social and economic relations absent significant, often formidable, coercion. Nor, indeed, have these processes exhibited the calculability and determinacy so often touted as the natural and necessary progenitors of the rule of law and regarded as essential to market liberalization and integration. And as neoliberalism's hegemony has become more deeply entrenched in the institutions of global financial capital, market integration and development/modernization have often come at a correspondingly higher cost.

'Freer' markets have, of course, all too frequently failed to deliver the broader socio-economic transformations promised, too often ridden roughshod over tradition and culture, and in the wreckage they have engendered, deep social antagonisms have festered.[13] Under these latter circumstances, and long before 9/11, the aspiration for 'rule of law' reforms began blurring into calls for law and order. And if globalization's marginals and outcasts could not be ignored, then they would be the subjects of harsh disciplinary measures, both economic and (if necessary) military. Here the rule of law has translated into law and order backed by strong states, while the 'goodness' of good governance is to be measured in terms of market-friendliness. In the post-Cold War world of freewheeling global capital, development and progress morphed rapidly into shock therapy logics imposed on Third World peoples whose governments looked remarkably like executive sub-committees of the global bourgeoisie. In those frequent instances in which the institutions of global capital have seen fit to impose tough performance standards and demands for their implementation on those marginal states worthy of exploitation, they have proved equally content to hand over the job of policing and enforcing those standards to heavy-handed, draconian regimes willing to capitalize on their implementation. And the latter, anxious to be seen to be getting the job done (and to reap the benefits therefrom), have too often met with resounding support from developed states of the West, or with equally resounding indifference.[14]

If 'democracy' remains a desirable aspiration, in practice it has been a too easy sacrifice on the altar of West- and market-friendly good order. Unbridled markets, it seems, will deliver the rule of law and its corollaries, and the rule of law (tautologically) will offer the ideal juridical shell for nurturing free markets. But even in relation to markets themselves it would seem that all the talk of the rule of law as central to the flourishing of global capital is misleading. Despite contentions that markets will usher in the foundations for a genuine international rule of law in some magic symbiosis, significant evidence to the contrary exists. *Pace* those who see the quantitative expansion of international economic law as a first step towards a more comprehensive international rule of law, there is compelling evidence that '[e]conomic globalisation relies overwhelmingly on ad hoc, discretionary, closed, and nontransparent legal forms fundamentally inconsistent with a minimally defensible conception of the rule of law'.[15] This is not to suggest that these relations manifest chronic *illegality* (although often enough they do), but simply that in practice the relevant actors' behaviour very frequently tends to be guided by systemic norms other than the relevant legal rules. So, if an international rule of law can be said to have emerged, it would seem we should perhaps look elsewhere.

By contrast, the third juridifying thrust has taken as its sole focus of attention relations between the subjects of international law. If a genuine international rule of law can be said to have emerged over the past half-century, it would seem that this is perhaps the backdrop against which the measure of its vitality might best be taken. This broad set of transformations has included a range of closely related developments, among the most important of which are the establishment of the UN Charter regime, the related proliferation of binding universal norms in international law, the rapid proliferation of human rights instruments and the corresponding recognition of limited international legal personality of individuals (as subjects of human rights and as potentially criminally culpable for gross violations of those rights) and intergovernmental organizations, and finally the growth of international legal institutions of which the newly minted International Criminal Court is but the latest example. The resounding sensibility that succeeding generations should be spared the scourge of war is perhaps the most distinctive development of postwar international law, with its general prohibition on the use of force and a corresponding prohibition on any state interference in the internal affairs of other states that might threaten the sovereignty of the latter. Arguably the cornerstone of the UN Charter system, the prohibition of force has attained the status of a general rule of customary international law, codified in the Charter, and widely accepted by members of the international community – including the US – as a *jus cogens* norm (a peremptory norm from which no derogation is allowed).[16]

It is difficult to overemphasize the sweeping nature of this legal sea-change. While some halting efforts to restrict the use of force as an instrument of foreign policy had preceded World War II, the devastation wrought by two world wars elicited a new-found dedication on the part of the international community to the idea that international relations should be governed by law, and not by the dictates of power and force. The sentiment underpinning this turn of events was captured poignantly by the Nuremberg Tribunal in its suggestion that: 'To initiate a war of aggression ... is not only an international crime; it is the supreme international crime differing only from other war crimes in that it contains within itself the accumulated evil of the whole.'[17] The *jus ad bellum* that only a half-century earlier had been a virtual free-for-all now left very little room, in principle, for the use of military force across borders. The *only* exceptions contemplated were severely limited by the provisions in Chapter VII of the UN Charter: a state might employ armed force against another only in the case of an armed attack, or if international force was sanctioned by the new UN Security Council itself.

While contemplating a new, dramatically more expansive role for binding norms in international law, the record of the Charter regime's ability (or perhaps inclination) actually to restrain international violence in the intervening period has, however, been dismal. Not only have state actors and non-state belligerents continued to employ force in their relations with other states, but the tensions born of the Cold War and its aftermath, coupled with the economic and political tensions wrought by the forces of economic globalization, have given significant impetus to civil strife within states and created fertile breeding grounds for gross violations of human rights behind the wall of sovereign independence. If the Charter regime was envisaged as marking the advent of a rule of law governing international affairs, its life signs would seem to be rather weak indeed. But clearly, the transformations in the international legal field have been accompanied by the expectation that these legal developments would present meaningful impediments to states in their relations with one another. The import of this is that time and again states have expressed a strong commitment to the legal principles and obligations enshrined in this order, a commitment in principle the importance of which only the rogue behaviour of the United States post-9/11 might adequately (and ironically) bring home.

To the extent that we might speak of a robust concept of international rule of law, it would seem an ideal whose time is yet to come, but whose actualization must stem from a deepening of the order implied by the third juridification thrust. Thus Secretary General Annan's suggestion that the rule of law is under assault seems somewhat out of place in so far as *it has been under assault since the advent of the UN Charter era*. These assaults, however, should be seen as the growing pains typical of any nascent legal order and represent the fragility of that order; they are not an indictment of the ideal of the rule of law itself. Indeed, the transformations of the international legal field through the past six decades do suggest developments amenable to a meaningful concept of the rule of law in international affairs consistent with the elements generally associated with that ideal, despite the deepening hegemony of the neoliberal agenda that has come to dominate the first two juridification thrusts over the past two decades.

Despite their many failings, the postwar developments sketched above suggest the existence of a general acceptance on the part of state actors of the imposition of formidable legal constraints on the arbitrary or discretionary use of force in international affairs, as well as an ostensible commitment to the protection and enhancement of human rights. And international actors have, until most recently, overwhelmingly sought to justify their apparent violations in precisely legal terms, however shallow those justifications might ultimately have been. The norms attached to this postwar international legal regime also seem largely to meet the requirement that, under the rule of law, legal norms display the qualities of generality and publicity. While the rapidity with which these norms have evolved might call into question the stability of the field overall, it is worth noting that these developments have been generally linear in character. This is particularly the case with respect to the emergence of *jus cogens* norms, which by law cannot be superseded except by subsequent norms 'of general international law having the same character'.[18]

That no one is above this legal regime is a contention that has come in for more ready challenge. But the fact that actors have routinely offended the basic principles underlying this legal order is not enough to suggest that they are not bound by the law or even that they have not viewed themselves as so bound. Rather, it speaks to profound weaknesses in the area of enforcement (undoubtedly one of the weakest areas of international law), but is neither an indictment of the law itself nor of the ideal of the rule of law more generally. By extension, there is no principled reason to suggest that all are not equally subject to this law's provisions. Such a formulation is consistent with the binding character of general norms of customary international law, and more especially vis-à-vis those norms that have attained the status of *jus cogens*. Finally, that decisions should be amenable to independent judicial review is another area of apparent weakness in the international legal order. But municipal courts have been increasingly frequent interpreters of the nature of international legal obligations, and their decisions are recognized as one of the formal sources of international law as outlined in the *Statute of the International Court of Justice*.[19] Moreover, a variety of international judicial institutions have emerged throughout this period. While most of these have been seriously circumscribed by a lack of compulsory jurisdiction, the most recent – the International Criminal Court – represents a remarkable institutional innovation in this area, operating as a court of parallel, complementary jurisdiction, on the expectation that the ideal locus for judicial inquiry into the most severe violations of human rights is in the municipal courts of the states whose nationals have been accused of atrocities, or those states whose nationals have been the victims thereof, but asserting jurisdiction where such actions cannot or have not been taken.

Thus it would seem that the elements of an international rule of law have been, at the very least, tentatively established and largely acknowledged by the majority of states. And it seems reasonable to suggest that the third juridifying thrust outlined above represents the tentative consolidation of an international or, perhaps more appropriately, global, constitutional order.[20] But while the elements have been put in place, it would be an overstatement to suggest that anything like a robust, vital rule of law had come to govern international affairs even before 9/11 and the advent of the Bush Doctrine. This raises a question too little posed in reflections on the rule of law. Is a more or less complete inventory of elements enough to offer a measure of the vitality of the rule of law?

We would do well at this juncture to revisit Edward Thompson's compelling formulation of the rule of law.[21] One of the enormous strengths of Thompson's account arises from his recognition that an adequate understanding of the rule of law must move beyond a simple focus on the identifiable presence of this or that element in a given set of circumstances. His formulation is equally unconcerned with whether law itself is able to garner total compliance (indeed, quite the opposite). Rather, Thompson steadfastly refuses to condemn the ideal in the face of gross abuses of authority and limits on the efficacy of law. Indeed, his defence of the rule of law is cast precisely against the backdrop of the savage legal excesses of one of the darkest periods of English legal history.[22] His concerns, rather, take us back to those formulations that extend to antiquity – that it is better to be ruled by laws than be subjected to the avarice of men and the caprice of circumstance. Unlike so much formalist and positivist literature on the rule of law that starts from checklists of indicia, the presence of which magically reveal the vitality of the rule of law, or those more rhetorical versions which point to manifest illegality as evidence of the absence of the rule of law, Thompson's assertion is that if actors are indeed to be guided in their affairs by law, then that law must, at least occasionally, be consistent with its own principles. As he so eloquently characterized the issue:

> Most men have a strong sense of justice, at least with regard to their own interests. If the law is evidently partial and unjust, then it will mask nothing, legitimise nothing, contribute nothing to any class's hegemony. The essential precondition for the effectiveness of law, in its function as ideology, is that it shall display an independence from gross manipulation and shall seem to be just. It cannot seem to be so without upholding its own logic and criteria of equity; indeed, on occasion, by actually being just. And furthermore it is not often the case that a ruling ideology can be dismissed as a mere hypocrisy; even rulers find a need to legitimise their power, to moralise their functions, to feel themselves to be useful and just.[23]

Perhaps because he was a Marxist historian, Thompson's account is much more sensitive to the relationship between politics and law than the majority of juristic commentators who have turned their attention to the concept over the past century. His analysis reveals a markedly more sociological concern with the capacity of the legal system to secure legitimacy adequate to the task of governing society more generally. While offering a stinging indictment of both judicial excess and corruption, Thompson mounts a vigorous defence of the rule of law against those – including other Marxists – who would toss the baby out with the bathwater, the latter abandoning the ideal of the rule of law in the light of the failures of law, its practitioners and its legislators.

It is not that Thompson denies the rule of law is to be associated with a particular (if perennially hotly contested) group of core characteristics or elements; his references to the 'logic and *criteria* of equity', independence and impartiality suggest such a core is crucial to his understanding. But so too is its association with a constellation of other concepts, such as justice, legitimacy, hegemony and the function of law as ideology. There is an inherent reflexivity in Thompson's account that nicely captures the precarious position the rule of law necessarily occupies as it straddles the divide between law and politics. And this is the point elided by, and a crucial source of weakness in, strict formalist and positivist formulations of the rule of law offered up by the liberal and neoliberal canon.

At least since Weber, there has been a tendency towards tautology in these accounts, that as modernity develops, law's legitimacy, and thereby its capacity to secure compliance outside of recourse to other modes of legitimation or violent coercion, is to be grounded in the determinacy and calculability it grants to social relations. Law is seen as legitimate precisely because it is the principal medium that enables social actors to negotiate the manifold complexities of modern life, enabling them to form reasonable and reciprocal expectations of the responses their actions should engender. The rule of law operates through formal, procedural consistency and the application of clear and general rules with a minimum of discretion.[24] The poverty of this functional tautology is brought to the fore perhaps most poignantly by Joseph Raz who, taking his inspiration from Friedrich Hayek, suggests the rule of law is:

> not to be confused with democracy, justice, equality (before the law or otherwise), human rights of any kind or respect for persons or for the dignity of man. A non-democratic legal system, based on the denial of human rights, on extensive poverty, on racial segregation, sexual inequalities, and religious persecution may, in principle, conform to the requirements of the rule of law better than any of the legal systems of the more enlightened Western democracies.[25]

Such formulations suffer from a too-ready distancing of law from the historical, economic and socio-political conditions that undergird its legitimacy. They engender a vision of the rule of law that stresses its formal attributes while ignoring whether 'laws, and not the passions of men', *actually rule*, most particularly in those spheres of human activity that, in practice, tend to stir those passions most.

A minimally defensible conception of the rule of law does require that law be consistent, transparent and equally applied to all, but in turn, *pace* Raz, does have an essential connection with basic principles of justice – a strict, formal, procedural justice. These procedural guarantees are in no way to be scoffed at, and in turn ground the most compelling dimensions of the formalist programme, offering not just calculability and determinacy to life, but drawing on constitutional principles above which no one stands. In Thompson's case this was comprised of the elements of the English Constitution; in the present case the nascent order implied by the third wave of juridification discussed above suggests the growth of an analogous set of supranational constitutional provisions above which no actor stands. As Thompson is quick to remind us, such principles *sometimes do* have the effect of granting quite meaningful protections to the oppressed (indeed must, if law is to work 'as ideology'). In so doing they help to secure a certain 'reverence for law' (to borrow Dicey's phrase) that not only enables actors to be guided by law, but instils in them a ready willingness to subject themselves to the law's prescriptions.

Those in Thompson's account who resisted 'bad law' were not offending against the rule of law (although their actions do raise questions as to the robustness of the rule of law at that time). They were, rather, protesting at the gap between justice and the prevailing order, an order of which that law was part. Likewise, through the democratic revolutions that followed on the heels of the bleak era Thompson chronicles, the legislative apparatuses of rule were compelled, in the face of protracted struggle, to respond to demands for political and social transformation. As they did so, the juridical foundations underpinning 'the rule of law and not men' shifted accordingly, thereby securing its ideological resonance with those it 'ruled'. As popular sensibilities regarding basic standards of justice shifted, so too did demands for legal guarantees that those standards would be realized. Today, the socio-economic, political and legal changes demanded by those subject to the injustices engendered by the juggernaut of modern capitalism have been spurred, not by the internal logic of the rule of law, but rather by a similar demand that the global order be a just one. Their demands are for substantive social, political and economic transformations – transformations that will affect how the law's subjects will apply their logic and criteria of equity and justice and take their measures thereof. If laws, and not the whims of the powerful, are to rule, their protections must extend to real, substantive guarantees *outside* the largely formal guarantees offered by the narrow formalist vision of the rule of law. The burgeoning array of human rights norms and institutions associated with the third wave of juridification – whatever its flaws and limitations – marks an important example of precisely such an evolution. Thus, if international law is indeed to 'rule', it will have to rule not only in response to formal procedural logics, but also in response to social demands for emancipation. Again, the point is not to suggest the rule of law must imply a steady shift towards legal instrumentalism, but rather that if law is to prove efficacious in legitimately governing the behaviour of social actors absent preponderant reliance on other modes of legitimation or recourse to violent coercion, it can do so only in a milieu that is generally perceived to be just. The internal guarantees of formalism are an important start. But Raz's formulation highlights just how limited a start it provides.

The formalist/positivist programme is one that has held particularly prominent sway over the first and second juridification thrusts discussed earlier. But so long as the rule of law could be regarded as compatible with non-democratic systems, based on the denial of human rights, on extensive poverty, racial segregation, sexual inequalities or religious persecution (*à la* Raz), it contemplated a very thin concept indeed. With the ascendancy of neoliberalism, any sense that the rule of law might bear some important relationship to genuinely substantive social, economic and political change (outside of those conducive to the imperatives of capital accumulation, of course) was largely discarded in these projects. The institutions of global capital, despite a professedly strong commitment to the rule of law, set about systematically dismantling the institutional foundations that might have offered a measure of substantive justice adequate to legitimate either the international legal order or the municipal legal orders that were thereupon set to the tasks of clearing the way for unfettered accumulation.[26] The formal guarantees of this narrow vision of the rule of law may suggest it is the ideal shell for the efficient and stable regulation of markets, as Hayek and his intellectual progeny have insisted. But the polarization between rich and poor, North and South, attests to a crisis of legitimacy of enormous proportions for this model. And if the criminal attacks of 9/11 are not a resounding affirmation of this, the cheering those horrific events engendered in the streets of Gaza, and which echoed in slums around the world, certainly is. So too is the anti-globalization movement that has taken to the streets of major cities around the world. To the extent that law is irrelevant to the lives of the marginalized and oppressed, or even more, is simply a manifestly crass instrument of that oppression, it will fail to capture the 'hearts and minds' of its intended subjects and thus fail to 'rule'. In this sense, the rule of law's role as a primary export of capital seems a dismal failure.

But if these two broad projects implicating the rule of law have become little more than instruments in the globalizing agenda of capital, the same cannot be said of the third wave of juridification. The extensive transformation of the international legal field that characterized the third wave has yielded a set of legal innovations that, however flawed it may be, reflects a growing groundswell of opposition to oppression, war, poverty, racism, sexism and myriad other forms of oppression. Moreover, it reflects a growing cosmopolitan sensibility that law must play an important role in mediating the transformation to a better world, while providing bulwarks against the illegitimate exercise of power against those least capable of defending themselves against its excesses. A genuine set of constitutional foundations to govern the global order has emerged out of these transformations, foundations whose substance marks the emergence of popular sensibilities of basic standards of global justice against which global subjects will take their ethical-political bearings. If the gap between those sensibilities and the lived reality of those subjects is pushed even wider than the excesses of global capital have pushed them, then an already fragile, nascent international rule of law is not only imperilled; it may be extinguished. The belligerence of the current US Administration promises just such a breach.

When George W. Bush came to office in January 2001, his Administration's foreign policy horizon would clearly be dominated by neoliberal imperatives which promised to deepen further the schisms between North and South, rich and poor (not unlike its domestic agenda). That agenda alone threatened to imperil further an already fragile international rule of law. The rapid moves ushered in shortly after the Administration's ascendancy to withdraw unilaterally from many international treaty instruments further signalled a general hostility towards and rejection of international legal constraints. But contrary to the perception conveyed by much of the widespread and very vocal opposition these moves engendered, these actions were generally made in accordance with the letter (even if fundamentally offending the spirit) of the relevant international laws. The events of 9/11, however, ushered in a dramatic and ominous shift in the Administration's approach to international law. Disdain has morphed into ridicule and rejection. And with the advent of the Bush Doctrine the Administration has unilaterally pronounced a death sentence on those features of international law that marked the specificity of the post-World War II international order and that had underpinned the fragile emergence of an international rule of law *sui generis*.

The Bush Doctrine represents a fundamental challenge to that postwar order. The doctrine itself can be distilled from any number of Administration policy statements, but perhaps most crucially the 2002 *National Security Strategy*. It is comprised of a core set of closely linked elements: the resolve to pursue preventive war when strategically advantageous to US interests; a similarly resolute undertaking to do so unilaterally should such action be deemed necessary; and finally, a commitment to ensure and assert *unchallengeable* military superiority around the globe. The first two of these elements strike directly at the heart of the postwar international legal order, offering the mechanisms whereby the third will, whenever necessary, be realized.[27] Through the resolve to engage in preventive war the US has arrogated to itself the right to intervene unilaterally by military force in the internal affairs of other states. While international law had throughout the post-World War II era failed with dismal frequency to rein in military adventurism, both internationally and intranationally, the extent to which most bellicose parties had, throughout this period, sought to justify their actions in terms of legalities was one of the remarkable features of the postwar period. State actors would generally go to great lengths to characterize their actions as legitimately falling within the very narrow confines left them by the new order: self-defence or coming to the aid of an ally at the latter's request.[28] With the Bush Doctrine, and its interrelated planks of unilateralism, preventive war and global military superiority, all such pretensions have been put to one side, and the illegal war against Iraq has put this doctrine into brutal effect. With the pointed reaffirmation of the core elements of the Bush Doctrine in the *National Defense Strategy* issued by Donald Rumsfeld in March 2005, the Administration's resolve has ossified into a general strategy of belligerence.[29]

The current foreign policy of the United States continues to attribute an important place to the rule of law in the extension and protection of American interests abroad and the 'spread of freedom and democracy'. Hardly a public foreign policy announcement seems to emanate from the White House, Pentagon or State Department today that is not generously peppered with references to the rule of law.[30] No doubt something of the mystificatory shorthand typical of the 'crisis version' of the rule of law mentioned earlier is at work here. And, no doubt, the Administration's appropriation of the language of the rule of law in the post-9/11 context gains significant ideological purchase in the minds of an American public barraged by daily reminders, issued by both the Administration and a variously cowed or sycophantic media, of the apparent lawlessness of the international (dis)order. But the tenor of the principal statements of American foreign policy since 9/11 suggests an Administration myopically focused on a world ordered in accordance with US interests, and undermines any assertion that its pursuit of those interests via the Bush Doctrine can be squared with a remotely defensible concept of international rule of law. For all its attendant talk of the rule of law, democracy and good governance, the present Administration has shown itself quite content to engage in egregious violations of international law and to trample on the human rights and civil liberties of its own citizens and resident 'aliens', let alone those of foreign states and their citizens.[31]

Despite the proprietary proclivities of its juristic advocates, the *vitality of the rule of law* cannot be measured solely by, or equated with, the presence or absence of particular elements. While the elements generally associated with it mark the foundations of a minimally defensible concept, the vitality of the rule of law is equally dependent on law's efficacy and the depth of its legitimacy. The rule of law can no more be equated with democracy than it can with free markets. It is irreducible to the presence of judicial review; and a full measure of its vitality cannot be taken by simple reference to the degree of judicial impartiality a legal system manifests. A lack of compliance may offer an indicator of its health, but laws will be broken (if they are not, they become redundant). But so long as the principal actors in a legal system remain dedicated to its central tenets, the rule of law seems likely to survive as an ideal that might help to guide, even corrupt, societies back to justice. But when those actors take it upon themselves not simply to break the law, but to declare themselves above it, the cornerstone of the rule of law has been shattered, and the whole edifice of legal legitimacy is condemned to collapse. In law's wreckage we seem bound to encounter Aristotle's beast, whose passions and desires would prove too much for even the best of men,[32] let alone the likes of George W. Bush and his henchmen. In so far as the rule of law in international affairs is concerned, only a concerted and relentless political counter-attack and steadfast resistance to the perversions of the Bush Doctrine will be adequate to the task of its preservation. If nothing else has taught us the importance of the rule of law, the Bush Doctrine, which represents a full-frontal assault on an international rule of law, must.

The concept of the rule of law alone is sorely inadequate to the tasks of international peace and justice – inadequate, but essential. It is inadequate precisely because its self-referential guarantees of justice offer only the protections of self-limitation the law places on its subjects – both the governing and the governed. The fragility of this self-binding under conditions of American Empire is evidenced in spades in the Bush Doctrine and the US's illegal war on Iraq. Standing at the intersection of law and politics, the rule of law is cursed with the task of having to mediate their interrelation. Law cannot rule if its dictates are ignored, and in these terms the actions of the US in Iraq suggest it is eminently reasonable to call *it* a 'rogue state'. The rule of law alone is insufficient to secure the legitimatory foundations for its own sustained 'rule'; or, put another way, is incapable of securing the conditions of substantive justice adequate to mitigate the excesses of, or provide the means to transcend, a world of global capitalism. Its legitimacy is only incompletely secured within its own terms of reference. That legitimacy might be more heartily secured from without, through the legally sanctioned use of violence, and nevertheless remain wholly consistent with the tenets of the rule of law, provided that force is not arbitrarily applied, but is, rather, invoked in conjunction with the constraints dictated by those tenets. One can, for instance, readily envisage a Hayekian world governed by liberal markets and strong repressive states as one wholly consistent with the minimal, neoliberal rule of law. But just how long such a rule of law might be able to sustain its capacity indeed to 'rule' is worthy of consideration. For history suggests that in order for law to rule it must be seen to be just. The self-referential guarantees of the classical liberal model of the rule of law can offer no such guarantees of justice.

If the shallow rhetoric of the rule of law employed in the imperial view of the world is to secure its domination, it seems likely that it will have to be bolstered by an ever-stronger network of repressive apparatuses to watch for the barbarians at the door, both abroad and at home. It is a deeply impoverished vision of the rule of law that contemplates an international ethos reminiscent of Anatole France's suggestion that 'The law, in its majestic equality, forbids rich and poor alike to sleep under bridges, beg in the streets or steal bread'. Law may well operate against a backdrop of consistency, knowability and access to judicial institutions, but its capacity to rule under such circumstances seems likely to depend on managing globalization's riff-raff with a very strong, very violent, arm. For the rule of law to operate as ideology its tenets must to some extent be brought into line with the aspirations of its subjects, or it must effectively dispel those aspirations. Law can rule quite effectively backed by threats of the most draconian sort, but history suggests it will do so only for a limited time. Such a vision has little to do with the robust concept advocated here.

While it is inadequate to the justice demands of so much of the world's population, a robust international rule of law remains essential to their realization. A framework for meaningful transformation in the institutions and practices of international life commensurate with those demands must secure the insufficient but not insignificant guarantees of formal justice implicit in the rule of law. But the rule of law, residing at the nexus of law and politics, must also play midwife to the transformations demanded of the global political economy and its institutional structures in the pursuit of more substantive forms of justice than the limited vision offered by more formalistic conceptions. That is, for an international rule of law to take hold in the long term, it must be underpinned by a dedication to addressing the political and material demands of globalization's disenfranchised. The rule of law cannot accomplish this task alone. Such transformation will come out of social and political struggle, an important feature of which will be the prohibition on arbitrary violence of the sort manifest in American imperial intrigue today.

In light of the foregoing it would seem reasonable to suggest that, to the extent we have made headway in recent years towards the establishment of something like a rule of law in international life, those advances are fragile indeed. However, acquiescence to the claims to a right of exceptional unilateralism may sound the death knell of an international rule of law altogether. The Left would do well to tread cautiously here and beware of assumptions that, because the formal elements are in place, we have somehow achieved a meaningful rule of law. Events are overtaking us, and a fragile, tentative order that might wed justice to law, and thereby foster a robust concept of the rule of law in international affairs, may well be slipping from our grasp. The compelling vision of hope held up by those concerned to foster such a robust conception must be steadfastly juxtaposed to the excesses, injustices and crude illegalities of empire and its apologists. But we are wise to eschew a romantic lament for something lost that was, at best, only very tentatively gained. The project must be to bring politics to law in international affairs. If the socio-economic and related political foundations adequate to secure law's hegemony in the preponderance of international relations are absent, the rule of law will grow increasingly irrelevant to globalization's outcasts and the casualties of imperial intrigue. It is only when justice is wed to law that law can sustain the legitimacy it requires to rule. International relations past and present have not evinced these qualities; international law has glimpsed them; the new imperialism disregards them altogether. Democracy and good governance will not be realized at gunpoint. Nor will the rule of law take hold, let alone flourish, in the crosshairs of empire.

The lawyers have only imagined a better world. The task is to change it.

## NOTES

1 Rosemary Nagy and Lorraine Lacroix offered very helpful comments on early formulations of the arguments presented here. Particular thanks to Amy Bartholomew for her patience and invaluable input.

2 The rule of law is mentioned eight times in this short document. See *National Security Strategy of the United States of America*, online at www.whitehouse.gov/nsc/nss.html.

3 It should be stressed that American imperialism pre-dates the Bush Doctrine by close to two centuries, its origins dating perhaps most evidently to the Monroe Doctrine (see Panitch and Ginden in this volume). My concern here is with the politico-juridical implications arising from the Bush Doctrine and what marks its specificity in the evolution of American Empire.

4 Sir Arthur Watts, 'The International Rule of Law', *German Yearbook of International Law* 36 (1993): 15–45.

5 See Aristotle, *The Politics* (Cambridge: Cambridge University Press, 1988), 1287b, 19–33.

6   For useful overviews of this debate, see the very different treatments offered by Norberto Bobbio, *The Future of Democracy* (Minneapolis: University of Minnesota Press, 1987), 138–56; and Terry Nardin, 'International Pluralism and the Rule of Law', *Review of International Studies* 26 (2000).

7   See Franz Neumann, *The Rule of Law: Political Theory and the Legal System in Modern Society* (Dover: Berg Publishers, 1986); William E. Scheuerman (ed.), *The Rule of Law under Siege: Selected Essays of Franz L. Neumann and Otto Kirchheimer* (Berkeley: University of California Press, 1996); Friedrich A. Hayek, *The Road to Serfdom* (Chicago: University of Chicago Press, 1944); Friedrich A. Hayek, *The Constitution of Liberty* (London: Routledge, 1960); Carl Schmitt, *Legality and Legitimacy* (Durham, NC and London: Duke University Press, 2004).

8   For an excellent survey of these processes and their juridical implications, see Bonaventura de Sousa Santos, *Toward a New Legal Common Sense: Law, Globalization, and Emancipation* (London: Butterworths, 2002), 163–311.

9   Hayek's now classic invocation of Mannheim as the backdrop for his vision for the rule of law captures nicely the flavour of this orientation: 'Recent studies ... once more confirm that the fundamental principle of formal law by which every case must be judged according to general rational precepts, which have as few exceptions as possible and are based on logical subsumptions, obtains only for the liberal competitive phase of capitalism.' Hayek, *The Road to Serfdom*, 72.

10  These processes are reminiscent of earlier *missions civilisatrices* in which variants of the rule of law have played an important role. See Antony Anghie, 'Colonialism and the Birth of International Institutions: Sovereignty, Economy, and the Mandate System of the League of Nations', *New York University Journal of International Law and Politics* 34:3 (2002): 513–633; and Maxwell O. Chibundu, 'Globalizing the Rule of Law: Some Thoughts at and on the Periphery', *Indiana Journal of Global Legal Studies* 7:1 (1999): 79–116.

11  For useful overviews and criticisms of the Law and Development movement, see Elliot M. Burg, 'Law and Development: A Review of the Literature and a Critique of "Scholars in Self-Estrangement" ', *American Journal of Comparative Law* 25 (1977): 492–530; John H. Merryman, 'Comparative Law and Social Change: On the Origins, Style, Decline & Revival of the Law and Development Movement', *American Journal of Comparative Law* 25 (1977): 457–83; David M. Trubek and Marc Galanter, 'Scholars in Self-Estrangement: Some Reflections on the Crisis in Law and Development', *Wisconsin Law Review* (1974): 1062–101. Many of these themes are picked up in more current discussion by Brian Z. Tamanaha, 'The Lessons of Law-and-Development Studies', *American Journal of International Law* 89:2 (1995): 470–86; Kevin E. Davis and Michael J. Trebilcock, 'Legal Reforms and Development', *Third World Quarterly* 22:1 (2001); and Santos, *Toward a New Legal Common Sense*, 313–52.

12  Keith Griffin, 'Economic Globalization and Institutions of Global Governance', *Development and Change* 34:5 (2003): 789. Julio Faundez (ed.), *Good Governance and Law: Legal and Institutional Reform in*

*Developing Countries* (New York: St. Martin's Press, 1997), examines both convergences and divergences between the earlier law and development literature and more recent discussions. The place of legal transformation and the rule of law in current contexts is the subject of the World Trade Organization's *Legal Institutions of the Market Economy: Rule of Law and Development*, available online at http://www1.worldbank.org/publicsector/legal/ruleoflawandevelopment.htm (2004).

13  For a stinging indictment of these processes, see Michel Chossudovsky, *The Globalization of Poverty: Impacts of IMF & World Bank Reforms* (London: Zed Books, 1997).

14  I am indebted to Amy Bartholomew for calling my attention to this connection. For further reflections on this point, see my 'Regulation, Governance and the State: Reflections on the Transformation of Regulatory Practices in Late-Modern Liberal Democracies', in Michael MacNeil et al. (eds.), *Law, Regulation, and Governance* (Don Mills: Oxford University Press, 2002), 28–53.

15  William E. Scheuerman, 'Economic Globalization and the Rule of Law', *Constellations* 6:1 (1999): 3.

16  Perhaps the most important statement of the *jus cogens* character of the prohibition on the use of force is offered in the contentious case of *Nicaragua v. US*. Ironically, while the authority of that case has been repeatedly questioned by those offended by the Court's decision to proceed following the US's failed effort to contest the Court's jurisdiction, '[t]he United States, in its Counter-Memorial on the questions of jurisdiction and admissibility, found it material to quote the views of scholars that this principle is a "universal norm", a "universal international law", a "universally recognized principle of international law", and a "principle of *jus cogens*" '. *Military and Paramilitary Activities in and against Nicaragua (Nicaragua v. United States of America)(Merits)* [1986], I.C.J. Rep 14, 101.

17  Available online at http://www.yale.edu/lawweb/avalon/imt/proc/judnazi.htm. Ironically, aggression (or 'crimes against peace', as it was originally termed) was included as one of the crimes listed in the *Nuremberg Charter*, largely at the initiative of the United States; see http://www.crimesofwar.org/onnews/news-us-icc.html. Notably, while as yet an inoperative category, aggression appears as one of the international crimes listed in the *Rome Statute of the International Criminal Court*.

18  Article 53 of the *Vienna Convention on the Law of Treaties*.

19  See specifically Article 31(d) of the *Statute of the International Court of Justice*.

20  The age-old conceptual coupling of constitutionalism and the rule of law has largely evaded discussions of an international rule of law. For a useful discussion of the conventional understanding of this relationship see C. L. Ten, 'Constitutionalism and the Rule of Law', in Robert E. Goodin and Philip Pettit (eds.), *A Companion to Contemporary Political Philosophy* (Oxford: Blackwell, 1993), 394–403. Despite a good deal of attention to 'global constitutionalism' in a wide-ranging literature, those discussions have largely not come into contact with the more limited international rule of law literature. For a tentative, but very useful,

exception, see Jean L. Cohen's insightful 'Whose Sovereignty? Empire versus International Law', *Ethics and International Affairs* 18:4 (2004): 1–24.

21  Edward P. Thompson, *Whigs and Hunters: The Origin of the Black Act* (Harmondsworth: Penguin, 1975), *passim*, especially 258–69.

22  This is an important point to be kept in mind with respect to one of Thompson's more frequently misunderstood (and maligned) formulations. One might reasonably question the characterization of anything as *an 'unqualified human good'*, as Thompson does the rule of law. But while posed against the backdrop of eighteenth-century English law, Thompson's characterization is simultaneously an indirect but powerful retort to those critics who, challenging Margaret Thatcher's Conservative regime and its 'law-and-order' orientation which systematically violated the basic tenets of the rule of law, seemed willing to abandon the ideal as *mere sham*. If an overstatement, his characterization seems less so than the abject dismissal by other critics.

23  Thompson, *Whigs and Hunters*, 263.

24  Max Weber, *Economy and Society* (Berkeley: University of California Press, 1968).

25  Joseph Raz, *The Authority of Law: Essays on Law and Morality* (Oxford: Clarendon, 1979), 211.

26  See Chossudovsky, *The Globalization of Poverty*.

27  Not only does it undermine the relevant treaty prohibitions, but it also offends against the customary international legal rules governing the use of force in 'self-defence'. The *locus classicus* for the latter is the formulation derived from the 1832 *Caroline* case in which US Secretary of State Daniel Webster laid down the foundations of the rule on this issue: viz. that force can be used in self-defence only when 'necessity of that self-defense is instant, overwhelming, and leaving no choice of means, and no moment for deliberation'; cited in Malcolm N. Shaw, *International Law*, 5th edition (Cambridge: Cambridge University Press, 2003), 1025. Arthur Schlesinger, former adviser to President J. F. Kennedy, offers a delightful analogy that nicely captures the absurdity of the Bush Administration's characterization of its doctrine of preventive war as one of 'self-defence'. 'The Bush administration hawks just know, if we do not act today, that something horrible will happen to us tomorrow. Vice President Dick Cheney and Secretary of Defense Donald Rumsfeld evidently see themselves as Steven Spielberg's "precogs" in *Minority Report*, who are psychically equipped to avert crimes that are about to be committed.' 'Unilateral Preventive War: Illegitimate and Immoral', *Los Angeles Times* (21 August 2002).

28  For a useful overview of the evolution of international legal restraints on the use of force, see Christine Gray, *International Law and the Use of Force* (Oxford: Oxford University Press, 2000).

29  United States Department of Defense, *National Defense Strategy* (March 2005).

30  In April 2005, a search for 'rule of law' on the White House website returned over 600 documents, 299 of which refer to Iraq. Similar numbers are attained through document searches at the Department of

Defense website (although there is some notable overlap in the documents). The State Department's website permits a maximum search of 100 documents, but a combined boolean search of 'Iraq' and 'rule of law' yields a solid 100 results. While a thoroughgoing textual analysis of the content of these documents is beyond the scope of this chapter, a review of the materials indicates the repeated proximity of 'rule of law' with other crucial terminological couplets, such as freedom/tyranny, democracy/dictatorship, good governance/corruption, friend/enemy and good/evil. In this respect it is perhaps most noteworthy that 'rule of law' returns no hits on a keyword search, suggesting the powerful rhetorical, common-sense implications of its deployment. Interestingly, the discursive work the 'rule of law' seems to do in these contexts is to condense the 'negative' side of each of these other binary oppositions. Other searches reveal similiar results in the documents available through Downing Street.

31  From strategies of extraordinary rendition, through deliberately pushing the envelope on definitions of acceptable measures of physical and emotional 'punishments' that seek plausible deniability of torture, to efforts to create sovereignty-free zones where the Administration will be bound not only by international law (such as the Geneva Conventions), but by the US Constitution as well, the Administration has shown its manifest disdain for the rule of law in general. Joan Dayan has recently shown how the US's treatment of prisoners in the global war on terror – and in the official justifications for it – have 'perfected' the legal decimation of personhood which began with slavery. See 'Cruel and Unusual: The End of the Eighth Amendment', *Boston Review* (2004), online at http://www.bostonreview.net/BR29.5/dayan.html. In an important respect many of these activities represent a reduction of captive 'enemies' to the forms of 'bare life' contemplated by Giorgio Agamben in *Homo Sacer: Sovereign Power and Bare Life* (Stanford, CA: Stanford University Press, 1998).

32  'And the rule of the law, it is argued, is preferable to that of any individual. On the same principle, even if it be better for certain individuals to govern, they should be made only guardians and ministers of the law ... [H]e who bids the law rule may be deemed to bid God and Reason alone rule, but he who bids man rule adds an element of the beast; for desire is a wild beast and passion perverts the minds of rulers, even when they're the best of men'. Aristotle, *The Politics*, 1287b, 19–33.

# 8

# American Empire or Empires? Alternative Juridifications of the New World Order

*Peter Swan*

The era where all of humanity together will be a political reality still remains in the distant future. The period of national political realities is over. This is the epoch of Empires, which is to say of transnational political unities, but formed by affiliated nations.[1]

During the last decade, emerging issues of politics, security and risk have brought into question institutions of governance at both the national and global levels. This has also been a period marked by efforts to reconceptualize problems of governance in social, legal and political thought in order to make sense of their broader impacts. However, in the wake of the events of 11 September 2001, the resulting global 'war on terror' and the willingness of the Bush Administration to wage 'pre-emptive wars' against what it claims are dangerous, 'rogue' regimes, there is a new sense of urgency in these discourses. Along with an increasing *angst* about security and relations between the West and the Islamic world, there is a sense that the national and international institutions that have been responsible for 60 years of relative peace may no longer be adequate to politics in an increasingly globalized world.

That there is ultimate disagreement on how to address the perception and reality of these contemporary challenges and risks is reflected in fundamental differences in attitudes towards constraints on the use of force at the international level. This is demonstrated in the disagreement between America, and its 'coalition of the willing', and 'Old Europe' over the legality of the war against Iraq. In this chapter, I will argue that this 'interpretive battle' over the legal right to use force goes beyond traditional concerns about the inviolability of the sovereignty of the nation-state and beyond questions of the contemporary status and viability of international law to raise questions about the possibility of new modes of ordering global political relations.

Following the terminology of the German legal and political theorist, Carl Schmitt, I suggest that these divisions may even point to the potential emergence of a new *nomos* or means of legally and spatially ordering relations among entities at the global level.[2] In this sense, *nomos* may refer to the project of a 'New World Order' with its associate forms of juridification. However, as I will suggest, the nature of such an order is contested and remains to be determined.

One of the main contenders within this renewed discourse on the nature of political regimes has been the resurrected concept of empire. As a term of empirical and normative analysis, empire has been appropriated by those occupying a range of positions across the political spectrum and given impetus by the popularity of the formulation by Michael Hardt and Antonio Negri. Using questions of the legality of the Iraq war as a context, I will reconsider the idea of empire by examining the character of the relationship between contemporary imperial political power and law. Following from the Schmittian conception of *nomos*, I will argue that empire must be understood in relation to varying conceptions of juridification.

I begin by briefly considering the debates over the interpretation of Security Council Resolution 1441 in the lead-up to the war against Iraq. After discussing the evolution of key aspects of American foreign policy in the 'unipolar moment' during which the United States has been described as a contemporary empire, I briefly assess the role of law in relation to contemporary imperial power. After considering how the US continues to use international law to support its hegemony, I point to the characterization of the US 'war on terror' as leading to a permanent 'state of exception', where not only decisions about war and peace but also decisions affecting the constitutional rights of individuals are made outside the framework of law. Turning to the some of the little-known writings of the Russian-French philosopher Alexandre Kojève, I advance an alternative interpretation that suggests the possibility of the emergence of regional empires in the plural that emphasizes different conceptions of justice and that may counter US hegemony. I conclude that the choice of models of empire has profound implications for understanding the possibility of non-hegemonic politics under conditions of late modernity.

## MILITARY INTERVENTION IN IRAQ AND
## AMERICAN EMPIRE

On 8 November 2002, the UN Security Council unanimously adopted Resolution 1441, which found Iraq to be in 'material breach' of previous Security Council resolutions requiring it to account for its entire arsenal of chemical, biological and nuclear weapons. Those hoping that this agreement reflected a real commitment to an international rule of law by all major powers were soon disappointed. Resolution 1441 specified that Iraq's failure to comply would constitute a further 'material breach' and that continued violations of its obligations would have 'serious consequences'. Deep differences emerged over whether the text of the resolution authorized the use of force to uphold its provisions, with the US and Britain arguing for this interpretation and major European nations, including France and Russia, arguing that there was no provision for the use of force. Failing to reach agreement on this issue, the US and Britain invaded Iraq in March 2003.

More than two years later these differences over Resolution 1441 reflect a deep crisis that threatens the future viability of the UN as an institution and more broadly the future of international peace and security law.[3] Moreover, with the growing political opposition of France and Germany to US unilateralism, the continued existence of the 'Atlantic Alliance' may be endangered.

Much of the growing tension between the US and the people of Europe and many European governments may be attributed to the policy of US predominance that guides the current Bush Administration. Arguing that this 'neo-conservative' administration has undermined many of the elements of postwar international cooperation, Stanley Hoffmann has detailed some of the US 'bullying' which provided the context for the interpretive battle around Security Council Resolution 1441.[4]

Prior to discussion of Security Council Resolution 1441, the Bush Administration had threatened to implement its policy of preventive war (the Bush Doctrine) by acting unilaterally to remove Saddam Hussein 'on the basis of much earlier UN resolutions, which demanded proof of the destruction of weapons of mass destruction'.[5] Resolution 1441 itself, adopted unanimously in November 2002 after weeks of negotiations, was deliberately ambiguous and thus left room for interpretation that allowed politics to prevail.[6] Prompted by the British, the US introduced a second resolution in March promising war, despite the reports of the UN weapons inspectors' evidence of some progress toward compliance. The US Administration then resorted to threats and inducements aimed at obtaining the nine votes needed for the resolution to pass. 'When it became clear that those votes could not be secured and the text would be vetoed by France and Russia, the US withdrew it, went to war, [and] denounced the UN as a failure ...'.[7]

On the surface, the above analysis suggests that the adoption of a strategic doctrine that gives a prominent place to pre-emptive war and the decision to go to war without the support of the Security Council are all part of a tough new policy of US predominance. This is largely a liberal view that implies that this is an aberration that must be attributed to the 'neo-con' agenda of the Bush Administration. To the extent that American foreign policy has come to be expressed in the crusading zeal and moral language of 'good' and 'evil' of fundamentalist Christianity, this view is correct. However, it may be overly simplistic to suggest that the current administration in Washington represents an aberration that will be remedied with a different government.[8]

The real point of disagreement in the trans-Atlantic dispute is 'war according to the criteria of the US, or war according to the legality of the UN?'[9] This is not surprising considering that the rules on the use of military force to ensure international peace and security are among the most highly contested and therefore politicized areas of international law. While the twentieth century witnessed an 'unprecedented regulation' of the waging of war, the US has been 'ambivalent about legal constraints on the use of force since it emerged as a major military power'.[10]

An important analysis of the history of the American government's attitude towards military intervention can be found in Carl Schmitt's evaluation of international law during the 1930s.[11] Schmitt contends that, since the proclamation of the Monroe Doctrine in 1823, the United States had not only successfully excluded the European powers from the American continent but had also justified its sole right to intervene in the affairs of other countries on the continent.[12] Of particular interest to Schmitt are the 'contracts of intervention', which acted like bilateral treaties and allowed the US to intervene in the affairs of other states in the Western Hemisphere on the pretence of aiding in the defence of the independence of weaker states.[13] The decision to intervene in such cases was to be determined by the US alone. Fast-forwarding to the Kellogg–Briand Pact of 1928, Schmitt suggests that, although the Pact was intended to 'outlaw war as a means of national politics', in fact it gave its creators, and especially the US, the sole right to determine when a war was just or unjust, while undermining the power of the League of Nations to make crucial decisions regarding world peace.[14] The Pact could thereby play a role similar to the Monroe Doctrine with respect to American power.[15]

Although there are such historical precedents for interpreting US hegemony in foreign affairs as a mode of imperial politics, over the last decade the US, as the sole remaining superpower, has pushed its challenge to traditional international legal limitations on the use of force even further.[16] Not only did the administration of George Bush Sr begin to endorse the arrival of a 'New World Order', but many of the key themes of current policy such as the emphasis on maintaining overwhelming military supremacy over all potential rivals and the option of pre-emptive war originated in the early 1990s.[17] With the decline in the risk of nuclear war in the immediate post-Cold War years, America took advantage of this unipolar moment and began to assert the unique role of its military power in policing the world and spreading its own version of democracy and free markets.

A leaked Pentagon document published in the *New York Times* in March 1992 stated that: 'Our first objective is to prevent the re-emergence of a new rival, either on the territory of the former Soviet Union or elsewhere, that poses a threat on the order of that posed by the former Soviet Union.'[18] This document further suggested that the US should attempt to deter *any* potential competitors from even aspiring to a larger regional or global military role.[19] The maintenance of global peace was to be left solely to the US, which was only too willing to exercise the role of global policeman. The expectation that America had the right to police the world and spread its particular vision of democracy has become the basis for the idea of *Pax Americana*. It has also led many political observers to revive the trope of Empire to describe US hegemonic power in the present unipolar moment.

A preoccupation with the extension of this unipolar moment is clearly reflected by the neo-conservative thinkers associated with Project for a New American Century, who, in a report entitled *Rebuilding America's Defenses*, argued, in 2000, for a restoration of higher levels of military spending to ensure that America can retain its relative advantage against any possible state challengers to its hegemony.[20] The overall thrust of the document is to enhance the security of the United States relative to potential state rivals.

However, as Chantal Mouffe, drawing on Carl Schmitt, has suggested, such strategies neglect the inherent instability associated with unipolar domination from an imperial centre. Unable to contest hegemony and perceptions of injustice through either domestic or international law, elements of political resistance shift to non-state actors, who, like the imperial centre, do not feel bound by the legal rules aimed at the maintenance of peace and security.[21] Seen in this way, terrorism becomes the other side of the coin of imperial politics.

Many of the above themes of the last decade and a half of American foreign policy have been incorporated in the Bush Administration's response to the terrorist attacks of 11 September 2001 in *The National Security Strategy of the United States of America* (NSS).[22] This document articulates the 'Bush Doctrine' of pre-emptive war within the context of the recognition of the exigencies of warfare in the twenty-first century. As a result, the NSS explicitly acknowledges that the old policy of deterrence which relied on military superiority no longer works against terrorists, 'whose most potent protection is statelessness'.[23]

At the same time, however, the global 'war on terror' is also linked to the older defensive posture towards rival states. Invoking international law and the right to self-defence, the NSS contends that states that sponsor terrorism or that attempt to develop weapons of mass destruction (WMD) become legitimate targets for pre-emptive military strikes aimed at preserving the security of the US. Therefore, the logic of deterrence is revived in another form as pre-emptive attacks on 'rogue states' that may support terrorism, thus preventing the terrorists from acquiring WMD that can be used against the US and the West.[24] The NSS thereby implies the right of the US to determine who is a potentially dangerous state and when to attack it, while avoiding the restrictions on the use of force imposed by international law. This strategy of pre-emption goes beyond the use of war as a strategy of ordinary international politics to confirm the reality of the 'imperial ambition' of the US.[25]

## AMERICAN EMPIRE AND LAW

The above analysis raises questions about the character of the politics of American Empire. It is clear that, according to the Bush Doctrine, the US may well evade international law when it determines that it is in America's security interests to do so. However, as shown by the US's attempt to garner support for its interpretation of Security Council Resolution 1441, it would be simplistic to suggest that even an imperial power can dispense with law whenever it desires. Law may be both an instrument of power and an obstacle to the exercise of that power.

As I have suggested above, the US has often had an ambivalent relationship to international law. This ambivalence has increased since it has become the world's sole hegemonic power.[26] Nico Krisch has suggested that predominant states such as the US 'oscillate between the instrumentalisation of and withdrawal from international law'.[27] Hegemonic states often use international law to constitute or reinforce the international order in conformity with its particular world-view.[28] In accordance with both aspects of the above logic, it is not surprising to find that the US has been especially proactive in the area of international trade and investment law. Here the US has pursued a neoliberal agenda to lead the way in creating trade rules that have increased the free flow of goods around the world. As the most powerful trading nation on earth, it has been one of the main beneficiaries of the legalization of trade rules. It thus is able to use these rules to maintain its dominant economic position in the world. However, this policy of enlargement of the global economy has also has been incorporated in Bush's *National Security Strategy*.[29] As well as removing recalcitrant dictators, the current Administration is also fighting for American-style capitalism as a way to guarantee its security. Thus capitalism and security are perceived to be mutually reinforcing.

During the last decade, the US also has played an initiating role in areas such as the statute establishing the International Criminal Court (ICC), the Kyoto Accord and the Ban on Landmines. However, in most of these instances, it has not ratified these treaties. With respect to the ICC in particular, the US has refused to allow members of its armed forces to face an international tribunal for war crimes. This is indicative of the development of a form of legal exceptionalism[30] for the US. While it has been willing to help create laws for other nations, it often has not been willing to apply those same laws to itself.

With the invasion and occupation of Iraq in 2003, this contempt for international law has been explicitly affirmed. According to Jean Cohen, when linked with a cynical resort to moralistic discourses of humanitarian intervention in the name of enforcing human rights, this hostility towards international law and the UN denotes a mode of 'order and orientation' that may be appropriately labelled as empire.[31]

However, this mode of exceptionalism has been interpreted in an even more radical manner by the Italian philosopher Giorgio Agamben. Drawing on the early work of Carl Schmitt and Walter Benjamin, Agamben argues that we are now entering into a permanent 'state of exception' in which most political decisions are made not in accordance with the law, but 'outside the law' as an extension of emergency powers.[32] This interpretation of the state of the exception expresses a paradox in which there is a suspension of the juridical order for the purpose of preserving that order in times of crisis and emergency.[33]

On Agamben's account, the state of exception responds to internal unrest and includes both the extension of the wartime authority of the military into the civil sphere and the suspension of the constitution. Its most notorious modern expression occurred with the seizure of emergency power and the cessation of normal processes of law under Fascist and National Socialist regimes during the twentieth century. But Agamben contends that the Bush Administration is once again creating a situation of the state of exception in which the American government can decide whether domestic or international law should be suspended in the name of security. According to Agamben, Bush's assumption of the label of 'wartime president' after the 9/11 terrorist attacks 'entails a direct reference to the state of exception' and an attempt 'to produce a situation in which the emergency becomes the rule, and the very distinction between peace and war (and between foreign and civil war) becomes impossible'.[34]

This state of exception is clearly expressed at the international level in the refusal to be bound by the ICC and in the stated policy of reserving the right to determine when military action is necessary against other sovereign nations. However, the most direct evidence of an emerging state of exception is found in President George W. Bush's issuing of the military order of November 13, 2001, which allows for the taking into custody and indefinite detention of suspect aliens and captured Taliban fighters from Afghanistan. This presidential order also allows for the possibility of trial for the violation of the laws of war and other law by a military tribunal, which may disregard the principles of law and evidence used in criminal law. In accordance with Bush's order, those who are detained lose not only their status as prisoners of war but also any legal status under American law.[35] Labelled simply as detainees and 'enemy combatants', they become non-persons, who resemble Schmitt's dehumanized 'enemies of humanity'. That they are treated as non-human has become clear not only from Guantánamo, but also with the evidence of the treatment of prisoners in Abu Ghraib prison in Iraq.[36] Empire's law is thereby expressed in the paradoxical situation of a state acting beyond its own domestic law and international law in the name of preserving the proclaimed values of civilization and humanity.

## A PLURALITY OF EMPIRES: ALEXANDRE KOJÈVE'S VISION OF GLOBAL ORDER

As I have suggested above, the Bush Administration's engagement with empire as a project that is far from complete and its attempt to establish a state of exception as the rule of global politics has been enabled, in part, by a unipolar moment in which the US exists as the sole world superpower. Using trade laws to promote its neoliberal economic vision, it is also able to rely on its military might to influence other nations to support military intervention or to shortcircuit the UN by unilaterally deciding to intervene whenever it determines that it is in America's interest to do so. America can do this because it has no rivals for imperial power. In this section, I will reveal another model of empire that was proposed as a counterweight to the growing power of the Anglo-American and Soviet power blocs in the immediate post-World War II era and which was also meant to outline the possibility of empire as an alternative to the nation-state as a contemporary political regime.

An intimation of this alternative formulation of empire can be found in the international political theory of Carl Schmitt. In an article published in 1955 as an Addendum to *The Nomos of the Earth in the International Law of the Jus Publicum Europaeum*, Schmitt argued that there were three possible choices to replace the Westphalian sovereignty order as a new *nomos* or legal-spatial orientation of the earth. These alternatives included: (1) the dualism of West and East in the Cold War would be resolved with a victory for one side or the other as the 'world's sole sovereign'; (2) a new principle of spatial ordering may emerge based on the balancing structure of the previous *nomos*, which is consistent with contemporary technical means and will lead to the domination of land, sea and air by virtue of technological advantage; and (3) the emergence of a plurality of regional great spaces which, as repositories of agonism, could balance one another while continuing to dominate lesser powers as European states had formerly dominated their less developed colonies.[37]

The third of these alternatives anticipates an interpretation of empire that contests the idea of unlimited power arising from one imperial centre. This version of empire finds its most sophisticated articulation in some of the least well-known work of the Russian-French philosopher and civil servant, Alexandre Kojève, who had grand ideas for both France and Europe.[38]

These ideas were presented to the French government in the immediate aftermath of World War II in his 'Outline of a Doctrine of French Policy'.[39] Ostensibly submitted as advice on how France could protect itself from the dangers associated with the inevitable rise of German economic and political power and from the risk of becoming involved in a third world war, Kojève's paper has far wider theoretical implications for the contemporary politics of empire.

Writing in 1945, Kojève announced the proposition that the world is 'witnessing a decisive turning point' comparable to one that occurred at the end of the Middle Ages in terms of the mode of its governance.[40] Just as feudal formations gave way to nation-states, he submitted that nation-states themselves are being superseded by transnational political formations which he designates as 'empires'.[41] On this basis Kojève proposed the creation of a Latin Empire, with France taking the leading role in order to assure a central position in the emergence of a new Europe and as a way to maintain indepen-dence from the Anglo-American and Slavo-Soviet empires.

Kojève initially suggested that one of the main reasons that con-crete historical conditions were particularly auspicious for such 'imperial formations' was that this was one of the few ways to assure an adequate base in military power.[42] However, the changing char-acter of military power is only one aspect of the 'political unreality' of the nation-state. Kojève's analysis contests both the liberal per-ception of no political entity beyond the nation-state and the socialist-internationalist view of no viable polity short of humanity.[43] While the former view fails to recognize transnational unions as an intermediary form that accurately reflects political reality, the latter simply presents humanity as an abstraction or utopian ideal that has yet to be realized. 'Before being embodied in Humanity, the Hegelian *Weltgeist*, which has abandoned the Nations, inhabits Empires.'[44]

Despite his earlier controversial contention that a universal and homogeneous state was a reality in principle,[45] in his advice to the French government Kojève maintained that 'the era where all humanity together will be a political reality still remains in the distant future'. The contemporary period was to be 'the epoch of *Empires*' or '*transnational* political unities' based on the kinship of '*affiliated* nations'.[46]

Kojève contended that such a kinship or affiliation already existed between the main Latin nations: France, Italy and Spain. This was a 'deep spiritual kinship' which was based on a shared commitment to Catholicism and a close affinity of languages that facilitates sustained contact between them. Above all their union was encouraged by the 'fundamental unity of the "Latin mentality" '.[47] He believed that this mentality has the potential to contribute something that is unique 'in the eyes of the world and of History', which cannot be provided by the Anglo-American and Soviet empires. While the strengths of these two empires is found in the realms of work and in the ability to mobilize for political struggles respectively, for Kojève, the Latin mentality is less materialistic and more oriented to the perfection of leisure and the 'organization' and 'humanization' of free time, which will be so important to the future of humanity. He also contended that the spiritual and mental kinship of Latin nations reinforces and guarantees that the values of liberty, equality and fraternity which are essential to any true democracy will remain central to their relations within their new imperial form.[48] These qualities remain critical for the development of a unique form of empire.

However, in order to secure the creation of empire, the Latin nations will also have to become both 'an *economic unity* and a *political unity*' that is capable of resisting the power and influence of the Slavo-Soviet and Anglo-American empires.[49] This must be accomplished without imitating the existing political structure of either of these already constituted imperial formations. Kojève insisted that the Latin Empire must find a unique 'imperial concept' with its own social and economic organizations capable of avoiding both the brutality of a 'liberalism' of great unregulated cartels and massive unemployment and the 'levelling and sometimes "barbaric" "statism" of the Soviet Union'.[50]

Kojève maintained that the real goal of the imperial union of Latin nations, and indeed of any imperial union, is political. Its success depends on the presence of an appropriate political ideology which must inspire its creation.[51] The motivating political ideology of Latin Empire is based on the need to create and maintain autonomy within the global community. For the idea of political will, defined as a will to power and greatness, Kojève substituted a 'will to *autonomy'*, which he believed is necessary for the realization of greatness. To establish itself as an empire, the Latin peoples must strive for as much independence as possible from foreign wills and actions.

Basing this idea of the will to autonomy in his own philosophy of struggle, Kojève was aware that the project of imperial autonomy can only be realized 'by meeting and overcoming resistance'. To do so requires the maintenance of an imperial military presence to secure its political existence. To avoid creating the perception of militarism, Kojève insisted that the imperial need not be 'imperialist'. The role of the military of the Latin Empire would be to ensure security and to create peace as both a condition for and the result of the assertion of the will to autonomy.

In addition, there are two other features of Kojève's characterization of empire that are designed to ensure its uniqueness when measured against then-contemporary concepts and practices of empire. The first is that Kojève saw the institutionalization of the Latin Empire as posing 'new problems for democratic political thought' which require creating conditions for reflecting on and overcoming the traditional ideological attachment to the nation-state in which the democratic project can only be partially realized.[52] Empire thus creates the conditions for democracy's realization in a different and more appropriate political form. It also forces the recognition that contemporary democracy begins to make sense only as transnational and postnational democracy.

Second, Kojève began to formulate a very different approach to the 'Arab Question'. In order to create the economic unity that will be the foundation for the political unity of the Latin Empire, Kojève contended that it is necessary to involve all the former colonies of France, Italy and Spain in Mediterranean Africa.[53] This consolidation of former colonies is necessary to pool economic resources and thus provide a basis for economic competition with other imperial formations. However, this proposal is presented while acknowledging the history of enmity between Catholicism and Islam. Kojève even suggested that empire may be a way to resolve this hostility which, he suggested, is bound up too much with national interests; in other words, with what he saw as the increasingly irrelevant concerns of nation-states.

As in much of the 'Doctrine of French Policy', Kojève's discussion of the relationship of the Latin and Arab elements within empire remains fairly cryptic. Yet he clearly believed that his concept of empire provides an alternative to the dominant conceptualization of the relationship between Islam and the West as a 'clash of civilizations' which can be solved only through the use of military force to impose abstract fundamentalist liberal views of democracy on recalcitrant Arab regimes.[54] It may also be prescient in its recognition of the feasibility of a Euro-Mediterranean partnership that is premised not only on a more equal economic exchange between former colonizing states and their former colonies, but also on co-operation for the promotion of mutual security. Kojève's Latin Empire can thus be regarded as a theoretical precursor to the Barcelona Process, which since 1995 has dealt with the creation of a new European Security Strategy which is in part premised on the establishment of a 'political and security partnership' between Europe and north African nations.[55]

The Latin Empire thus can be interpreted as providing a theoretical model for the consolidation of regional blocs into imperial unions that can challenge the overwhelming dominance of a single hegemonic power such as the US. Kojève expected rival empires to have different fundamental strengths that would allow them to focus on different aspects of social development. He believed that one of the important qualities of his European empire would be its ability to apply its unique mentalities to advance the cause of transnational democratic governance but recognized that this will be a long process. However, his model also envisages economic and political co-operation in a federal union or a series of unions that will allow different power blocs to act together to challenge the economic dominance of the American hegemon without relying on aggressive military power. This can be seen in the growing economic strength of the European Union.

## LAW AND THE LATIN EMPIRE

Kojève's 'Outline of a French Policy' emphasizes the political, cultural and economic dimensions of the governance of what he saw as an emergent global order. Accordingly, empire represents the logical evolution of the political aspects of governance at the transnational level with the gradual elimination of enmity and the promotion of co-operation as conflicts based on narrow nationalism begin to recede. Most observers of Kojèvian thought would see this theory as emerging from his views on the social struggle for recognition as presented in his famous lectures on Hegel's *Phenomenology of the Spirit* in the 1930s.[56] While this emphasis on the struggle for recognition is essential for understanding Kojève's thoughts on empire, it neglects an important institutional dimension that emphasizes the juridical aspects of his vision of an increasingly globalized world.

This vision is most clearly elaborated in Kojève's little-known *Outline for a Phenomenology of Right*.[57] Written in the summer of 1943 but only published posthumously in 1981, this book may be Kojève's richest work,[58] representing the most elaborate version of his political thought. It also shows the centrality of law and justice to his view of the development of global forms of governance. While he does not explicitly refer to law in his 'sketch' of the Latin Empire, in other work he contends that a polity cannot exist without *Droit*, or a system of law.[59] I therefore would like to suggest an interpretation of the juridification of empire that is consistent with his philosophical analysis of the logic of the evolution of the juridical form in contemporary society.

In his *Phenomenology of Right*, Kojève explains the nature of systems of law or right as it is experienced when an 'impartial and disinterested third' intervenes in an interaction between two parties to enforce a right or duty owed by one party to another.[60] From this basic description Kojève analyses the logic of law and suggests the historical conditions necessary for the final realization of the *Rechtsstaat*. His objective is to clarify the 'possibilities and logical necessities implicit in the definition of right itself and in its historical evolution'.[61]

In the *Phenomenology*, Kojève argues that although humanity is born in the anthropogenic opposition of Master and Slave, it is only realized in the synthesis of Mastery and Slavery within the modern form of citizenship. Mastery and Slavery as logical 'principles' never exist in a pure state and must be actualized in the historical evolution of citizenship during which one or the other of these constitutive elements of humanity may prevail in a relative sense.[62] According to Kojève, this evolutionary process describes not only the dialectic of universal history, but also his dialectic of *Droit* and the justice that informs these systems of law.[63]

While Kojève's elaboration of the dialectic of *Droit* and the ideal of justice is too complex to examine within this chapter, below I will briefly attempt to show how it suggests the possibility of different paths towards the juridical evolution of citizenship. According to Kojève, the anthropogenic struggle for recognition may be regarded as just because the participants consent as *equal* adversaries who freely agree to enter the contest for recognition.[64] This agreement expresses 'aristocratic' justice based on equality. If one of the adversaries gives up the struggle and recognizes the victor in exchange for his life, the situation may still be just because the benefit of the security of keeping one's life is *equivalent* to Mastery or *'compensates* for the burden of servitude'.[65] This is the 'bourgeois' justice of *equivalence*. Out of this engagement for recognition emerge ideals of justice, right and positive forms of legal relations.[66]

For Kojève, the evolution or actualization of law as a dialectic of *Droit*/right must take the form of a synthesis of 'aristocratic' justice expressed as formally equal status under the law and 'bourgeois' justice defined as reciprocity of economic benefits and burdens. This evolution is expressed in the synthetic justice of the citizen: *Equity*. However, Kojève is careful to point out that this synthesis as the evolutionary history of justice is carried out gradually in time.[67] All *Droit* is based on accepted ideals of justice based on syntheses that are unstable, and may be little more than compromises between *equality* and *equivalence*.[68]

Since the process is a dynamic one, it is difficult to prevent either some element of equality or equivalence from prevailing in the short run. Various 'disturbances and adjustments' result from political switches between a market-oriented political Right that is willing to allow for unequal market outcomes and a political Left that will emphasize more regulation to promote greater social-economic equality.[69] This not only confirms Kojève's views on the unstable character of the synthesis of *equality* and *equivalence*, but also suggests the possibility of different paths to the realization or actualization of *Droit* in different polities.

According to Kojève, all real *Droit* or systems of law remain as relative *Droit* as long as one empire is not realized at the end of history. Until such time there can be no ultimate realization of justice in *Droit* and, as is often the case in his writings, Kojève is careful to deny the existence of a final form of empire in the *Phenomenology*. Indeed, he suggests that this empire may never be realized because 'historical evolution proceeds by negation – that is freely or in an unforeseeable way'.[70] However, he also suggests the possible emergence of federally organized blocs of nations wherein international law between the member states of that bloc can be transformed into a form of internal or domestic law. Again, it is clear that although Kojève may be reluctant to proclaim the arrival of empire with a single actualized *Droit*, he does not hesitate to acknowledge the reality of *empires' laws* with very different ideological perspectives on the synthetic law and justice of the citizen.

Just as in his Latin Empire, Kojève is able to base the possibility of empires in different languages, cultures and mentalities, and in different attitudes towards autonomy and democracy, so in the *Phenomenology* he is willing to suggest the emergence of federations of states based on different compromises between the constituent elements of justice as equality and justice as equivalence. In the *Phenomenology* he can find the possibility for a unique attitude to justice and an appropriate realization of that justice in *Droit*. This allows for a unique imperial conception of social and economic organization of the Latin Empire and its own unique form of legality.

## A EUROPEAN ALTERNATIVE TO AMERICAN EMPIRE?

So, how is this relevant today under conditions of an American imperial project in the making? In contrast to an American imperial project that seeks to establish a state of exception at both the domestic and global levels with a wider imposition of empire's law, aspects of Kojève's analysis of the possibilities of a plurality of empires have been taken up by contemporary European theorists such as Jürgen Habermas[71] and Ulrich Beck. Below I will focus on Beck's conjunctural evaluation of what he believes to be fundamental differences between Europe and the United States to reveal some continuities with Kojève's proposal for European or Latin Empire.

In an article in the German newspaper *Die Tageszeitung*, published in May 2002, Norman Birnbaum exhorts Europe to show some self-respect by standing up to a US foreign policy driven by a moralism grounded in Protestant fundamentalism.[72] In doing so he appeals to a quality of 'Europeanness' that presents an alternative to the narrow fundamentalism that appears to guide the US.

This idea of 'Europeanness' has also become an important element in the discourse of contemporary public intellectuals in Europe. In answer to the question: 'What will make Europe more European?', Beck responds with the idea of 'a more cosmopolitan Europe'.[73] The cosmopolitan ideal that should motivate European domestic and foreign policy is what makes Europe different from the US. It is also the real basis for the difference between Europe and the US over the legality of the war in Iraq. Indeed, Beck contends that what is really at stake in the 'second Gulf War' is the structure of global politics and governance. A new 'global order is inevitable'. The fundamental division between the US and Beck's 'New Europe' is about the 'kind of order we are going to get'.[74]

Beck's cosmopolitan response to an American foreign policy dominated by aggressive militarism can be summed up in the anti-war slogan 'Make Law, Not War'.[75] The essence of the cosmopolitan ideal for Europe is an emphasis on constructing a form of cosmopolitan law that aims both to protect the weak and to provide them with rights.[76] The basis of European distinctiveness should therefore be premised on building a 'world of laws rather than of men'. Such a world of laws can only be constructed within the context of the radical reform of the United Nations, which must be reconstructed to meet contemporary needs.[77]

This opposition of a European commitment to cosmopolitan law and American imperial militarism may, however, be overdrawn because in the 'new world order' both law and military power will be necessary to address the global character of risks such as terrorism. But Beck's attempt to point out different European and American 'mentalities' and his emphasis on the European embrace of cosmopolitan law resonate with Kojève's alternative conceptualization of empire and with Europe's contemporary self-reflection on its identity as an alternative to American hegemonic power. It also provides a conceptual link to Kojève's vision of a transnational institutionalization of legality as an alternative to the current regime of international law and to an American policy of militaristic imperialism that either instrumentalizes international law or seeks to act beyond law in a state of exception that resembles the state of emergency imposed by the Nazis during the 1930s.

Kojève's articulations of empire and of law can play a role in reformulating a vision of European identity that provides an alternative to America but also an alternative to Europe as an association of individual nation-states. However, this will require considerable reflection on the implications of Kojève's thought for the nation-state. On the surface, Kojève's Latin Empire was presented as a way of consolidating economic and political power in an attempt to balance the growing influence of American power and culture in Europe. However, the real object of Kojève's critique is the nation-state itself. For Kojève, empire is more than a tool of *realpolitik*; it is his answer to Carl Schmitt's question of what should emerge as a 'new *nomos* of the earth'. It represents a new mode of governance whose basis is the realization of the rule of law at the transnational level and the consolidation of various domestic laws into an imperial federation of regional states. It would therefore require the evolution of the EU and other potential regional entities into supra-national imperial states that go beyond looser federal arrange-ments.[78] Within this vision there will be no room for a 'state of exception' beyond law, but only decisions that are made in accor-dance with the vision of justice of Kojève's disinterested Third.

## CONCLUSION

Despite Jedediah Purdy's pronouncement that the concept of empire 'has shed its pariah status',[79] the moralization that is attached to the assertion of American Empire seems to confirm Schmitt's assessment of America's tendency towards the instrumen-talization of international law. The American Constitution may indeed be the model of law that is spreading to democratize the world, but this version of the rule of law cannot simply be regarded as an 'unqualified human good'. Representing American foreign relations as a form of 'weak imperial policy'[80] cannot hide the fact that America is taking advantage of the present 'unipolar moment' and asserting its right to use military force against weaker, 'less civilized nations' both to pre-empt terrorist attacks arising from 'rogue states' and to spread its narrow fundamentalist version of democracy. It also does not hide the fact that America is all too will-ing to use both international law and domestic law in an effort to maintain and expand its hegemony.

Does Kojève's conception of empire(s), as the juridical form of the 'new world order', provide a theoretical model that can be used to create an institutional and political alternative to counter American Empire? Kojève's emphasis on a plurality of empires suggests, at the very least, the possibility of creating countervailing powers capable of preventing domination by a single imperial hegemon. The clear-est articulation of such a project today may be found in a reconfig-uration of the European Union. As an emerging empire, the EU may threaten the US and put it on the defensive. It also may have the potential to undermine the 'unipolar moment' that has made the most aggressive assertions of American unilateralism possible. In the long run this may force a modified version of the old Atlantic Alliance. A combination of European cosmopolitanism based on a different version of justice and *Droit* with American power may, as

Beck suggests, lead to the reform of the United Nations and at the same time create a mode of 'global governance' that can more effectively deal with global terrorism and the global risk society.

Yet Kojève's project of a European or a Latin Empire is far from realization. If, as Jean Cohen suggests, American Empire remains a project to be realized,[81] Kojéve's project for a Latin Empire and his ideal of a plurality of empires to prevent the emergence of unipolar moments dominated by a single hegemonic empire remains far from its actualization. At the core of his version of empires as a 'new world order' is his insistence that each empire must find a unique 'imperial concept' with its own social and economic organizations. Kojève was particularly clear that his new imperial formation should avoid the brutal excesses of capitalism as well as providing an alternative to the obstacles to social, political and economic innovation and the barbaric totalitarianism that he believed marked the communist experiment. Despite continuing to emphasize a vision of justice that stresses equality over equivalence in its more generous social policy, the European Union does not offer a form of social organization that is fundamentally different from the free market capitalism that remains at the centre of the American imperial project. In spite of suggestions that a strong and united Europe may act as a barrier to the excesses of globalization, the same free market ideology that drives the US also motivates Europe.

In addition, as is clear from the participation of Britain and many of the newest members of the EU in the war against Iraq, Europe (or at least its governments) is not united in its opposition to American military intervention in foreign countries. In both the above senses Europe remains complicit in the project of American Empire. Kojève always maintained that the institutions of law and politics would remain dynamic as long as injustice and non-recognition remained. In today's world, this political and legal dynamism is mostly confined to actors in transnational civil society. As long as the formal institutions of society maintain their distance from these struggles, his project of the actualizations of empires as a new mode of transnational governance will remain just that, a project that is far from actualization.

As I have tried to show, a second feature of Kojève's model for an emerging political regime has been his emphasis on the centrality of law and of legal relations. Kojève's emphasis on an increasing juridification of both domestic and foreign relationships within empire envisages an evolution of law that is able to maintain control of the state of exception by regulating it legally. The right to determine the state of exception would be established by law rather than by power alone. This should help to prevent excesses such as forceful detentions and torture in the name of protecting the world from terror.

My reading of Kojève has chosen to emphasize an interpretation wherein *Droit* is realized in the political form of a plurality of transnational empires which may be capable of balancing competing powers at the global level. Kojève's vision, however, is premised on a Schmittian notion of politics expressed in the friend/enemy distinction and on a Marxist conception of class struggle. Within this conceptualization, all politics will disappear with the end of enmity.

When we replace this vision with a notion of politics that emphasizes the need to maintain the contestability of the terms of social life, then politics remains a possibility within the confines of empire(s). This politics is not based on a power that is immanent within the multitude, but rather on an unending interrogation of the tension between society as instituted and the power of those who would contest the particular form of that institution. It is only the active questioning of the partial notions of justice embodied in institutions that will ensure the possibility of democracy within empire(s).

This brings us back to the Iraq war. The debate over the interpretation of Security Council Resolution 1441 reflected a clear division between the US and some of the most powerful representatives of the governments of 'old Europe' and the US went to war without the support of some of its traditional allies. In the last few years European public opinion has supported the idea of the EU becoming a military and economic superpower like the US in order to be better able to restrain an aggressive and imperialistic US militarism. This would be consistent with a more Schmittian interpretation of a plurality of empires as a way to restore the old 'Balance of Power System', which regulated the conduct of war in Europe in the century before World War I. While there are aspects of Kojève's conception of Latin Empire and empires that reflect the idea that imperial strength will create a countervailing power to the Anglo-American Empire, Kojève was careful to play down the role of the military in the Latin Empire. Its strategic role was to be defensive. More importantly he emphasized the role that empire would play in creating conditions for the realization of political autonomy and for releasing the potential for democracy that he argued was constrained by its ideological links to nationalism and the nation-state.

Perhaps Kojève was thinking about an imperial polity generating more democratic public institutions. However, he may also have recognized that these public institutions may promote democracy within the arena of an informal transnational public sphere. If the rule of law is best realized within a transnational arena that enhances conditions for recognition, why should this not also be the case for democracy?

On 17 February 2003, the *New York Times* journalist, Patrick Tyler wrote: 'the huge anti-war demonstrations around the world this weekend are reminders that there may still be two superpowers on the planet: the United States and world public opinion'.[82] Perhaps it will not be Kojève's empires that will emerge as the superpowers to challenge most effectively American imperial militarism, but rather the peaceful superpower of the will of the people that is expressed in a global social movement beyond the framework of the nation-state. This may be the power that brings about a 'real state of exception'.

## NOTES

1  Alexandre Kojève, 'Outline of a Doctrine of French Policy (27 August 1945)', *Policy Review*, 126 (August/September 2004), at http://policyreview. org/aug04/kojeve_print.html.

2  See Carl Schmitt, *The Nomos of the Earth in the International Law of the Jus Publicum Europaeum*, trans. G. L. Ulmen (New York: Telos, 2003). See also Jean L. Cohen, 'Whose Sovereignty? Empire versus International Law', *Ethics and International Affairs* 18 (2005): 1–24.

3  Michael Byers, 'Agreeing to Disagree: Security Council Resolution 1441 and Intentional Ambiguity', *Global Governance* 10:2 (2004): 165–86, 165.

4  Stanley Hoffmann, 'America Goes Backward', *New York Review of Books*, 50:10 (2003).

5  Ibid. The US was dissuaded from this position by Tony Blair.

6  Byers, 'Agreeing to Disagree', 166.

7  Hoffmann, 'America'.

8  Chantal Mouffe, 'Schmitt's Vision of a Multipolar World', *The South Atlantic Quarterly* 104:2 (2005): 245–51, 246.

9  Ulrich K. Preuss, 'The Iraq War: Critical Reflections from "Old Europe" ', in this volume.

10  Nico Krisch, 'Imperial International Law', *Global Law Working Paper* 01/04 Hauser Global Law School Program, NYU School of Law 1–61, 40.

11  Mouffe, 'Schmitt's Vision', 246.

12  Jean-François Kervégan, 'Carl Schmitt and "World Unity" ', in Chantal Mouffe (ed.), *The Challenge of Carl Schmitt* (London: Verso, 1999), 54–74, 61–2.

13  Mouffe, 'Schmitt's Vision', 246–8. A primary example was the 'contract of intervention' signed with Cuba after the US defeated Spain in 1898

which allowed the US to station troops and maintain military bases on Cuban soil.

14 Kervégan, ' "World Unity" ', 62.

15 Mouffe, 'Schmitt's Vision', 248.

16 Krisch, 'Imperial International Law', 41.

17 Simon Dalby, 'The Geopolitical and Strategic Dimensions of U.S. Hegemony Under George W. Bush', unpublished paper (2005): 1–18, 2. I am greatly indebted to Simon Dalby for giving me access to his unpublished work. The evaluation below owes much to his analysis of US geopolitics during the last 15 years.

18 Department of Defense, *Defense Planning Guidance for Fiscal Years 1994–1999* (1992). (Excerpts of the leaked 18 February draft as reprinted in the *New York Times*, 8 March 1992, quoted in Dalby 'U.S. Hegemony', 4.)

19 Dalby, 'U.S. Hegemony', 5.

20 Ibid., 5–6.

21 Mouffe, 'Schmitt's Vision', 250–1.

22 *The National Security Strategy of the United States of America* (Washington: The White House, 2002).

23 Ibid., 15.

24 Dalby, 'U.S. Hegemony', 6–7.

25 Ibid., 7.

26 Nico Krisch, 'Weak as Constraint, Strong as Tool: The Place of International Law in U.S. Foreign Policy', in David M. Malone and Yuen Foong Khong (eds.), *Unilateralism in U.S. Foreign Policy: International Perspectives* (Boulder, CO: Lynne Rienner Publishers, 2003), 41–70, 42.

27 Krisch, 'Imperial International Law', 13.

28 Ibid., 16.

29 *The National Security Strategy*, 17.

30 Krisch, 'Imperial International Law', 31.

31 Cohen, 'Whose Sovereignty?', 18.

32 Giorgio Agamben, *State of Exception*, trans. Kevin Attell (Chicago: University of Chicago Press, 2005).

33 Ibid., 1.

34 Ibid., 22.

35 Ibid., 3. While Agamben's conception of the 'state of exception' is elegant in its formulation, it does not capture the complexities of the division of powers in the US. That the American state may be divided in the determination of exceptionalism is demonstrated in a series of US Supreme Court cases in which the Justices of the Supreme Court argued against the violation of the separation of powers rule that is central to constitutional democracy in the US and in some cases subjected the decision about the status of 'enemy combatant' to limited forms of judicial review. This shows that law will not willingly abdicate its role to a state of exception and will continue to act as an obstacle to the arbitrary authority of the executive branch. See Christiane Wilke, '*War v. Justice*: Terrorism Cases, Enemy Combatants, and Political Justice in U.S. Courts', *Politics and Society*, 34 (2005): 637–69.

36  Andreas Fischer-Lescano, 'Torture in Abu Ghraib: The Complaint against Donald Rumsfeld under the German Code of Crimes against International Law', *German Law Journal*, 6 (2003): 689–724, 691.
37  Schmitt, *Nomos of the Earth*, 354–5. See also Jan-Werner Müller, *A Dangerous Mind: Carl Schmitt in Post-War European Thought* (New Haven, CT: Yale University Press, 2003), 86–103.
38  Kojève, 'French Policy'. For a suggestive analysis of the relationship between Schmitt and Kojeve, see Müller, 'Dangerous Mind', 90–8. See also Auffret, *Alexandre Kojève*, 308–36. Kojève played an important role in negotiating the formation of the European Coal and Steel Community and later was instrumental in the formation of the GATT.
39  Kojève, 'French Policy' (dated 27 August 1945).
40  Ibid., 1.
41  Ibid., 2.
42  Ibid., 2.
43  Ibid., 2.
44  Ibid., 3.
45  Alexandre Kojève, *Introduction to the Reading of Hegel*, ed. Allan Bloom, trans. James H. Nicols (New York: Basic Books, 1969).
46  Kojève, 'French Policy', 7.
47  Ibid., 8.
48  Ibid., 9.
49  Ibid., 9.
50  Ibid., 9.
51  Ibid., 12.
52  Ibid., 12.
53  Ibid., 9–10.
54  Robert Howse, 'Kojève's Latin Empire', *Policy Review*, 126 (2004), *Policy Review Online*, http://policyreview.org/aug04/kojeve_print.html. 1–8.
55  Rosa Balfour, 'Rethinking the Euro-Mediterranean political and security dialogue', *European Union Institute for Security Studies, Occasional Paper* 52 (2004).
56  Kojève, *Introduction*.
57  Alexandre Kojève, *Outline of a Phenomenology of Right*, ed. Bryan-Paul Frost, trans. Bryan-Paul Frost and Robert Howse (Lanham, MD: Rowman & Littlefield Publishers, 2000).
58  Perry Anderson, 'The Ends of History', in *A Zone of Engagement* (London: Verso, 1992), 298–334, 321.
59  Kojève, *Phenomenology of Right*, 160.
60  Ibid., 39–40.
61  Robert Howse and Bryan-Paul Frost, 'Introductory Essay: The Plausibility of the Universal and Homogenous State', in Kojève, *Phenomenology of Right*, 1–27, 17.
62  Kojève, *Phenomenology of Right*, 213.
63  Ibid., 214.
64  Ibid., 221.
65  Ibid., 223.
66  Ibid., 223.

67 Ibid., 224.

68 Ibid., 224.

69 Howse and Frost, 'Introductory Essay', 23. My interpretation of the instability of the synthetic justice of the citizen and of the realization of *Droit* at the transnational level owes much to Rob Howse. I thank him for sharing his views over the years.

70 Kojève, *Phenomenology of Right*, 92.

71 Jürgen Habermas, *The Postnational Constellation: Political Essays* (2001): 58–112. Habermas is more critical of the idea of world citizenship because of problems of democratic legitimacy beyond the nation-state.

72 *Die Tageszeitung*, 24 May 2002, http://portland.indymedia.org/en/2002/06/12210.html.

73 Ulrich Beck, 'Understanding the Real Europe', *Dissent Magazine* (Summer 2003), http://dissentmagazine.org/menutest/articles/su03/beck.htm.

74 Ulrich Beck, 'American Empire, Cosmopolitan Europe', *Europe Review* (Spring 2003), http://www.times-publications.com/publications/ERSpring03/ER_29.htm.

75 Ulrich Beck, 'Make Law Not War', *Der Spiegel* 2 (2003), http://madison.indymedia.org/newswire/display/9278/index.php.

76 Beck, 'American Empire', 3.

77 Ibid., 3.

78 Kojève recognized that while he thought that the era of the nation-state was in decline that it could take some time to establish a plurality of empires in their place. This has been confirmed by the recent refusal of the people of France and the Netherlands to adopt the proposed EU constitution.

79 Jedediah Purdy, 'Liberal Empire: Assessing the Arguments', *Ethics and International Affairs* (2003) (*Online*), http://www.ciaonet.org/olj/cceia_2003_2g.html, 1–9, 1.

80 Purdy, 'Liberal Empire', 1.

81 Cohen, 'Whose Sovereignty', 19.

82 Patrick Tyler, *New York Times* (17 February 2003).

# 9

# Empire's Law and the Contradictory Politics of Human Rights

*Amy Bartholomew*[1]

International law is often viewed as little more than words on paper. Yet, this is not how it is treated by the United States. In the *National Defense Strategy of the United States of America* released on 18 March 2005 (just two days before the second anniversary of the invasion of Iraq) the Pentagon declared that the 'changing security environment' post-9/11 requires 'global freedom of action' for the US to secure and promote its interests. It also maintained that the current milieu reveals both American strengths and vulnerabilities in the coming decade. Among the strengths it outlined are its pre-eminent military power and its 'leading roles' on matters of international concern, while among its vulnerabilities one finds the apparently astonishing claim that: 'Our strength as a nation state will continue to be challenged by those who employ a *strategy of the weak* using international fora, judicial processes, and terrorism.'[2]

One explanation for what was meant by this was offered at a press conference by Douglas Feith, then Under Secretary of Defense for Policy in the Pentagon, when he said 'There are various actors around the world that are looking to either attack or constrain the United States, and they are going to find creative ways of doing that, that are not the obvious conventional military attacks'. He went on to identify 'legal lines of attack' (along with diplomatic and technological ones) as forms of '*asymmetric warfare*' which, alongside international terrorism, may be deployed in attempts to constrain America's 'global freedom of action'. When pressed to provide an example of what might be considered a 'legal line of attack', Feith identified the International Criminal Court (ICC), thus reiterating another theme in the *National Defense Strategy* which points to the need for 'new legal arrangements' that 'support greater operational flexibility' and that 'maximize our freedom' to deploy forces globally, including further 'legal protections' against the possibility of American personnel being tried in the ICC. In his comments to the press, Feith clarified that legal avenues of 'attack' include the 'arguments that some people make to try to, in effect, criminalize foreign policy and bring prosecutions where there is no proper basis for jurisdiction under international law as a way of trying to pressure American officials.'[3]

The *National Defense Strategy* is an expansion of the Bush Doctrine, which Arthur Schlesinger Jr, a former adviser to the Kennedy Administration, called 'a fatal change in the foreign policy of the United States'.[4] Through it the US is attempting to establish a new norm of preventive war which would be available, on *its* view, only to itself – aggressive war 'as an instrument of national policy'[5] – but which from the point of view of international *legality*, could become a norm recognized as available to *all*.[6] The invasion of Iraq is the practical application of that doctrine. Perhaps an even more disturbing aspect of this most recent development of the Bush Doctrine is the US's self-proclaimed *right unilaterally to define and to state* international law – to *constitute* it monologically.

As Jürgen Habermas puts it,[7] the dimension of the Bush Doctrine that rejects international law as a medium for international governance poses a 'revolutionary' challenge to international law. It is important to emphasize, however, that it is not mere rejection and *lawlessness* that lies at the core of the Bush Doctrine, but something even more threatening. If it is successful, the Bush Doctrine means that the 'law' that will rule the globe will be 'empire's law'. With regard to legality, the threat lies in the US's treatment of law as merely a 'derivative of the will of the sovereign'[8] – that is, derivative of its own will as the global sovereign.

It is by now clear that the US evinces a rather complex but nearly always strategic relation to law in its global 'war on terror': it defines 'problem states' as those that 'disregard international law'[9] while it seeks to exempt itself from domestic constitutional norms as well as international and cosmopolitan law,[10] instrumentalizing them where exception is denied, while, most disturbingly, it seeks to re-define legality itself, thus threatening to undermine the halting progress that has been made in human rights commitments and international legal justice in the post-World War II era.

How interesting and possibly perverse it is, then, that the Bush Administration – the pinnacle of the American Empire – should view international and cosmopolitan law and their institutions as 'strateg[ies] of the weak' (listed alongside terrorism at that), and that it should want so desperately to avoid their pull. Is the Bush Administration deluded or is it on to something here? Weren't international institutions – among them international law – developed primarily *by* the US *for* the US in the post-World War II period, and do they not function, as critical scholars have generally maintained, as 'a disposable instrument' of American power?[11] Or is there, in fact, something importantly *correct* about the claim that international and cosmopolitan law and their institutions may function as a 'strategy of the weak', as the Bush Administration maintains? And is it the case that, rather than concern about its 'asymmetric' quality, as Feith insists (or at least not asymmetrical in the *way* that he insists), the Administration's real fear is that a commitment to international and cosmopolitan legality requires a certain *equality*, a condition that no empire will lightly abide? Might that be one of the reasons why American Empire is so insistent on pursuing *another* kind of 'law'? This is what we are calling empire's law: an attempt unilaterally to constitute and impose an illegitimate and unaccountable form of rule by a global power that seeks to arrogate to itself the role of global sovereign by declaring itself to be the exception.

What makes these questions all the more troubling is that it is not only the neo-conservative hardliners in and around the Bush Administration who have pursued illegal aggressive war against, and the occupation of, Iraq and run roughshod over legality by justifying its evasions, exceptions, rejections, instrumentalizations and refoundings in this way. The Bush Administration was supported and encouraged by forces whom I will call the human rights hawks who, drawing on the previous decade's innovations in legitimizing (if not legalizing)[12] humanitarian intervention and 'humanitarian wars', aimed, at least ostensibly, at the protection of peoples from massive abuses of human rights, supported this war on human rights as well as security grounds. In fact, the human rights hawks gave sustenance early on to the aims of American Empire as they articulated the case for 'humanitarian war' against Iraq, a theme that has now become more deeply imbricated within the Bush Administration itself as it fights to 'spread democracy and freedom across the world' aiming to 'end tyranny' in the 'empire of oppression'[13] through continuing war and occupation (both *de jure* and *de facto*). Espousing their humanitarian concern and their sense of cosmopolitan moral solidarity, the human rights hawks also gave sustenance to the project of undermining international and emerging cosmopolitan legality as a mode of regulation. They have thereby encouraged the development of empire's law, a form of rule that is deeply at odds with the post-World War II project of globalizing its obverse, that is, what Ronald Dworkin called in another context, law's empire. In respect to international relations, law's empire may be viewed as the post-World War II development of regimes of human rights and international law that foreshadowed (however imperfectly) a future order of democratic cosmopolitan law. Empire's law aims to derail that project and seeks to do so unilaterally, brutally and by the projection of military as well as economic, cultural, political and even legal power across the globe. Thus is a new phase in the ongoing American imperial project born.[14]

In what follows I will first consider the support of the human rights hawks for this case of military humanism and the result of threatening human rights and international legality with a moralization of politics. Next, I will propose an alternative to empire's law that is grounded in the notion of law's empire. Finally, I will address some of the difficulties that are posed for the position that seeks to generalize and extend law's empire, by the very fact and force of American Empire. It is this that makes a serious analysis of the character and contradictions of that empire so important to our politics. But the core argument that I want to advance is that the defence, extension and reform of law's empire is one means by which we must now attempt at least to 'constrain' American Empire and its 'global freedom of action' while we are figuring out how to *undermine* it. It *is* a strategy to be embraced by 'the weak'.

## THE BUSH ADMINISTRATION AND HUMAN RIGHTS HAWKS: EMPIRE'S LAW THROUGH MORALIZATION OF POLITICS

A consideration of the human rights justifications that have been offered to support the war against Iraq and the expansion of the American imperial project in general reveals some of the contradictions of a cosmopolitan politics of human rights today. This type of argument is designed to convince advocates of human rights to support the American Empire as a benign one aiming at the liberation of peoples.[15] It is an argument that is important to refute because at its heart is a deployment of cosmopolitan moral solidarity that threatens the very legality that is necessary to give human rights and national self-determination their due respect and their practical meaning.

Aligned with the neo-conservative hawks in the Bush Administration, liberal American supporters of the war mobilized republican images of emancipation premised on an imperial vehicle for its realization, as most notably Michael Ignatieff did in his *New York Times Magazine* article entitled 'The Burden', where emblazoned across the front cover of the magazine were the words 'The American Empire – (Get Used to It)'.[16] Perhaps even more surprisingly, the British Marxist political philosopher Norman Geras joined the fray by supporting the war on the basis of moral solidarity with the beleaguered Iraqi people against a brutal dictator.[17] Such positions raise an important cosmopolitan question by asking: By what moral authority does a brutal regime that systematically violates human rights claim a right to unfettered sovereignty? And they challenge us to consider what force we are willing to put behind our human rights commitments, under what conditions and what role legality should play in all of this.

As one of the leading lights among the human rights hawks, Ignatieff emphasized that a 'revolution of moral concern' has transpired since Bosnia and Kosovo such that it is now clear that under conditions of massive human rights abuses and threats to security, the 'agonized ethicist' must make a moral choice between two evils, and the ethicist (and presumably the imperial power) must choose the 'lesser evil'.[18] But what is the lesser evil for Ignatieff?

In responding to critics of the war on Iraq who claimed 'the decision to go to war at this time is morally unacceptable', Ignatieff stated: 'The problem is not that overthrowing Saddam by force is "morally unjustified." Who seriously believes 25 million Iraqis would not be better off if Saddam were overthrown?' He went on to maintain that the ' "consequential" justifications' that some 25 million Iraqis would be liberated clearly trumped the deontological argument that 'good consequences cannot justify killing people'. On this basis – the cosmopolitan aim of liberating (the surviving and presumably also not incarcerated or tortured portion of) 25 million Iraqis – Ignatieff supported the war as the 'lesser evil', while forthrightly admitting that the decision was undertaken in the absence of 'moral certainty'.[19] He did so arguing explicitly against the world-wide anti-war movement, much of world public opinion and the UN Security Council. In these ways, Ignatieff justified, on moral and prudential grounds, the virtually unilaterally decided on and prosecuted war that was, according to almost all serious legal commentators, as well as Kofi Annan, illegal.[20] It was a war that fitted well the definition of aggressive war outlawed in international law and was called the 'supreme international crime' by the Nuremberg

Tribunal which, it should not be forgotten, was largely a creature of the United States.

In doing so, Ignatieff admitted well before the start of the war that the idea of an 'empire's burden', American imperial power at work under what he views as the 'official moral ideology of Empire – i.e. human rights', was far removed from that which is sought by many cosmopolitan human rights activists and lawyers 'who had hoped to see American power integrated into a transnational legal ... order organised around the UN'. He also recognized that, while Europe was more inclined towards preserving a multilateral legal order that might hope to limit American power, 'the Empire will not be tied down like Gulliver by a thousand legal strings'.[21] And yet he plumped for American Empire, thus distancing himself from the legal cosmopolitans while quoting Herman Melville to the effect that the US is an empire that views itself as bearing the 'ark of the liberties of the world'.[22]

Ignatieff views spreading human rights as a republican duty that, under present circumstances at least, requires the American Empire as their chief interpreter and enforcer. Support for the war is given by him even while he explicitly recognizes that 'America's entire war on terrorism is an exercise in imperialism'.[23] He freely admits that 'regime change' is the 'imperial task *par excellence*' when undertaken virtually by a single state, but he maintains that the moral imperative to free the Iraqi people imposed this duty on the US. Further indicating the necessity for empire, he maintains that 'the moral evaluation of empire gets complicated when one of its benefits might be freedom of the oppressed'. For Ignatieff, the 'disagreeable reality' is not just that 'war may be the only remedy' for cases like Iraq,[24] but that the only power capable of addressing this reality is the American Empire, with its 'general world duty':[25] 'The case for empire is that it has become, in a place like Iraq, the last hope for democracy and stability alike.'[26] This is stated, while recognizing that the US campaign of 'pacification' is 'without an obvious end in sight',[27] that the invasion of Iraq may well be just the first 'in a series of struggles'[28] and that the 'real power' in all of the recent cases of intervention 'will remain in Washington'.[29]

To make his case Ignatieff deploys the philosophy of the 'lesser evil'. In the name of security and freedom from 'evil-doers' (the 'axis of evil', the 'terrorists', etc. who are treated as ontologically evil), the empire has the right to undertake acts that amount to the 'lesser evil' in the name of 'us' – we who are by implication ontologically good – to protect our security and to secure the freedom of the world. This is an argument that both flouts international law and exempts political power from legal restraints that apply in 'normal' situations thereby justifying the 'exception' of and for American Empire. It is a moralistic justificatory strategy well designed to accompany the 'war paradigm' that the US has chosen over that of a 'crime paradigm' as the dominant response to 9/11.[30] And it is a position that threatens to break those weak, nascent and 'contaminated'[31] but nevertheless crucial barriers against aggressive war, war crimes and crimes against humanity. It treats international institutions and international law as too 'constraining' to be capable of addressing the existential and political anxiety that empire feels or the burden it bears. His argument is, in these respects, closely in concert with the Bush Administration's position: 'strateg[ies] of the weak' (for Ignatieff, Gulliver will not be tied down 'by a thousand legal strings' issuing from the Lilliputians) may be rejected by liberal empire in so far as they constitute forms of 'asymmetric warfare' aimed at 'attacking' or 'constraining' the US's 'global freedom of action'. It also instrumentalizes human rights and freedom, much as the Bush Administration has, such that the moral argument for cosmopolitan solidarity is used as a justification for the invasion and occupation of Iraq. On both accounts, human rights are instrumentalized as 'swords of empire'[32] while the post-World War II regime of international and cosmopolitan legality is seriously threatened.

Lest it be thought that this embrace of empire in lieu of international and cosmopolitan law is a weakness that could only pervade liberal (and neoliberal) thought, consider the position taken by Norman Geras. Geras chastises his progressive colleagues for failing to address the 'needs of strangers' which, he maintains, required the removal of Saddam's brutal regime by military force – 'regime change'.[33] This is rooted in his analysis of, and fierce and moving opposition to, the 'contract of mutual indifference', that 'brutal moral reality' that describes the 'place of human suffering in an unnoticing cosmos'.[34] Cosmopolitan moral solidarity requires, instead, Geras argues, meeting the 'universal right to aid' through a 'universal obligation'. He also argues that those who opposed the war in terms of anti-imperialism, anti-Americanism and anti-capitalism have failed to appreciate the 'manifold practices of human evil' in places like Saddam's Iraq and he insists that such failure 'is not only to show a poverty of moral imagination, it is to reveal a diminished understanding of the human world'.[35] He accuses the anti-war forces (making no distinction between them) of being disingenuous: they will not attend to the fact that since the war, despite the continued violence and instability, what has 'stopped happening' retrospectively tips the balance in favour of the war. They refuse to face up to this, he contends, because to do so would make it clear that their anti-war position is morally untenable. He concludes with a eulogy for the anti-war Left: 'So much for solidarity with the victims of oppression, for commitment to democratic values and basic human rights.'[36]

How far human rights hawks have travelled from Arthur Schlesinger Jr, who, it will be remembered, has called the Bush Doctrine 'a fatal change in the foreign policy of the United States'. Schlesinger went as far as to liken it to Japanese imperialism prior to the end of World War II, and to predict that it would be the US that would now have to 'live in infamy'.[37] Now, human rights imperialism is the force required of a benign imperium.

However, accepting that cosmopolitan moral solidarity implies that 'manifold practices of human evil' must be addressed, as I agree it does, one does not have to belabour the obvious that with greater hindsight than these analyses could provide there is no plausible argument to be generated that this was a humanitarian intervention, nor has the occupation that is virtually as brutal as the declared war itself been humanitarian. The war and the occupation have been light years away from the sort of liberal policing, rather than military, model that would have to animate any truly humanitarian intervention. In the latter, the intervenors would place civilian safety at least on a par with their own, avoid grave violations of international humanitarian law and refuse to use indiscriminate weapons, including those that will in all probability decimate the environmental, genetic and health future of Iraqis (and likely their neighbours) for centuries to come. The indiscriminate death, pain and destruction unleashed ostensibly in the name of extending freedom, human rights and liberation to the Iraqi people is enough to discredit thoroughly claims of humanitarian aim or consequence.[38]

In fact, these consequences have caused Ignatieff sometimes to doubt his support for the war, maintaining, for example, that he is now convinced that the intervenors' 'intentions' count.[39] But this doubt is tempered by his undermining of the importance of the question of whether the war was legal or even 'necessary'. In November 2004, he claimed, 'The old questions about the war in Iraq – Was it legal? Was it necessary? Was it done as a last resort? – now seem beside the point.'[40] He argues that the UN must be revitalized, with the introduction of a charter on intervention which 'would put America back where it belongs, as the leader of the international community ... Pax Americana must be multilateral ... or it will not survive'.[41] And now he acknowledges the US's blunders in its supposed 'democratization' efforts in Iraq (and elsewhere), but he can still conclude 'And yet ... and yet ... ', while applauding the joining 'together [of] the freedom of strangers and the national interest' and lamenting that 'Never before has America been more alone in spreading democracy's promise', 'the right of people to choose their own path'.[42]

But the truly important point in relation to the question of whether this was a humanitarian intervention is that it did not, in fact, require hindsight to see that this was not going to be a 'humanitarian' intervention in the first place. The American Empire's disregard for humanitarian concerns was as apparent in the run-up to the war as was its disregard for international law, international institutions, the safety, security and human rights of the Iraqi people and global public opinion.[43] From Abu Ghraib to Kandahar, Baghdad to Guantánamo, the US was then, and is now, asserting the sharp edge of empire, governing so-called 'rogue' and 'problem states'[44] through military violence and what Amnesty International has called an 'archipelago of prisons' around the world[45] (which seem to have more in common with concentration camps than they do with prisons). And all the while it was bolstered in its claims of moral and political superiority by the human rights hawks.[46]

It is worth noting that human rights organizations, which tend to support humanitarian intervention, have, in fact, been at pains to argue that the war against Iraq could not be considered humanitarian. Human Rights Watch, for example, refused the overly simple logic that 'something must be done' – that the universal obligation to bring aid fell upon any empire powerful enough to claim that as its motivation. It also refused the far too quick leap of logic that that 'something' needed to be or was justified as a unilaterally decided upon, illegal war.[47]

The human rights hawks' support for the war against Iraq contained within it, then, at least three fatal flaws: an unwavering support for an American Empire charged with the task of liberating the Iraqi people 'by fire and sword'[48] and failing to take into account the nature of that empire, its likely motivations, or the foreseeable consequences of the further entrenchment and expansion of it for human rights; support for a unilaterally declared and pursued preventive war aimed at 'regime change' that threatens the very foundations of international law and human rights protections – characteristics that are necessary to any cosmopolitan project worthy of its name; and, relatedly, a reliance on morality not just as a necessary but also as a *sufficient* guide to the politics of the enforcement of human rights by violent means. In these ways they gave the Iraq war the ideological and moralistic justification the war required to gain, and especially to sustain, support for it. Chalmers Johnson has put the point well (although he fails to identify those supporters outside of the US as also culpable):

> Not since the jingoists of the Spanish-American War have so many Americans openly called for abandoning even a semblance of constitutional and democratic foreign policy and endorsed imperialism. Now, as then, the imperialists divide into two groups – those who advocate unconstrained, unilateral American domination of the world (couched sometimes in terms of following in the footsteps of the British Empire) and those who call for an imperialism devoted to 'humanitarian' objectives.[49]

Ulrich Beck also raises the very considerable concern that the moralization of politics associated with moral cosmopolitanism such as this entails a 'civil–military–humanitarianism threat' to humanity.[50] Furthermore, because these developments occur under conditions where there is no serious obstacle to 'the West', because they are clearly taking shape under a 'specific system of world power', in what Beck calls the 'second age of modernity', human rights are not just a 'system of values', but are also themselves a distinct 'system of power'.[51]

The human rights hawks' arguments have thus encouraged *Lex Americana*, empire's law, a law which, as Ulrich Preuss puts it in this volume, is aimed at 'the creation of a new world order whose law is not yet visible'.[52] And this, of course, is a very particular conception of rule, one that has virtually nothing to do with human rights, but which is aimed, rather, at the expansion by military domination and imperial policing of a neoliberal conception of good governance based on global capitalism.[53] This is combined with the imposition of a political structure via an 'interim constitution' that, far from extending democracy to Iraq, seeks to extend empire's law over it, treating it as mere terrain to be conquered, as Andrew Arato puts it in this volume, to be enveloped within the imperium's thorny embrace, a 'rogue state' to be 'pacified' while being 'free' only in so far as that freedom is in line with the values and interests of empire and 'democracy' is really a name for another client state.

Continuing the long tradition of American exceptionalism, the human rights hawks have combined the potentially cosmopolitan aim of securing universal rights (or is it America's particular understanding of them?) with the agency of a self-appointed imperial power. They have thereby contributed to the 'uninterrogated world monopoly on power and morality' and the 'imperialist abuse' of cosmopolitan goals that Beck[54] identifies with a moralization of politics at the expense of the defence and further development of international and cosmopolitan legality. In fact, their arguments display many of the objectionable qualities that its critics find in moral cosmopolitanism more broadly.[55] Their support for the Iraq war has contributed to the virtually 'unmediated moralization of law and politics'[56] by drawing on the universalism of human rights and the universal humanity to which it refers in a way that participated in, perhaps even fuelled, and certainly has provided justification for, the moral-political crusade of American Empire. They have thereby supported a fundamentalism of human rights by mobilizing an unmediated moral commitment to the other and a monological conception of morality, decision-making and judgment. With this stance they have supported the constitution of empire's law, which threatens existing international law and an erosion of advances towards cosmopolitan legality and the democratic protection of human rights, rather than promoting their advancement. Such analysis reveals that the 'revolutionary' consequences implied by cosmopolitan moral responsibility, to which Beck alerts us, are impelling world politics in a highly unstable and dangerous direction.

These are not the terms in which a progressive politics oriented towards the development of a critical cosmopolitanism[57] ought to display its 'solidarity with the victims of oppression' or its 'commitment to democratic values and basic human rights'. Rather, it is only by rejecting *both* the human rights hawks' moralization of politics and their embrace of American Empire *and* the arguments of those anti-imperialists who would reject legality as a necessary feature of anti-imperial global politics (whether Schmittian or Marxian) that we may be able to *resist* the imperial moralization of politics and the instrumentalization and degradation of human rights, international law and international institutions by empire's version of an American-dominated international 'constitutionalism' and side with the alternative project associated with the forces of 15 February 2003.[58]

This is why we can appreciate Beck's suggestion that addressing the current crisis will require the development of a 'transnational legal order, which, among other things, excludes the possibility of interventions being decided and carried out unilaterally by the hegemonic military power and its allies'.[59] In drawing the distinction between the imperialist abuse of cosmopolitanism and the development of a transnational legal order, Beck demonstrates far more perspicacity than those who have supported the Iraq war on the grounds of cosmopolitan moral solidarity while he also retains the crucial commitment to moral solidarity that underlies a commitment to human rights. The important point is *not* that humanitarian intervention can never be countenanced. Rather, in addition to meeting other stringent criteria of right motivation, discriminating means and extreme necessity, it must be decided upon and closely regulated through legitimate international institutions and legitimate international law for, as Human Rights Watch has put it, the necessity for multilateral deliberations and decision-making, rather than unilateral fiat, lies in the fact that the 'need to convince others of the appropriateness of a proposed intervention is a good way to guard against pretextual or unjustified action'[60] (as Fuyuki Kurasawa and David Coates also argue in this volume).

In the human rights hawks' justifications for the war, however, we saw the human rights norms (so central to what Beck calls the second age of modernity) taking their place, often violently, and certainly without regard for global public opinion or international law, and placed at the disposal of American Empire. Human rights became swords of empire rather than its antithesis. Those who offered justifications for this have contributed to the threat of a global spread of empire's law, when what is so desperately needed instead by those who really care about human rights is an opposite strategy aimed at simultaneously working to protect and reform international law and its institutions, while also working to develop alongside it an even more substantial cosmopolitan law. This 'dualistic' strategy, as Jean Cohen has called it,[61] is what a critical cosmopolitanism that promotes both equal sovereignty and human rights must seek to develop.

## THE ARGUMENT FOR LAW'S EMPIRE:
## FROM ŽIŽEK TO HABERMAS

In addition to Beck, critical scholars such as Slavoj Žižek, Jürgen Habermas and Martti Koskenniemi have challenged the sort of position adopted by the human rights hawks in favour of defending international and cosmopolitan law as the medium through which questions of war, humanitarian intervention and human rights should be addressed. For his part, Žižek advances the idea that the Iraq war placed the future of international law and the 'international community' in peril, arguing that it is not just Iraqi lives (as important as these obviously are as those who bear the heaviest burden of 'moral imperialism') but international rules and frameworks and, in fact, the very category of humanity, that is at stake. He says, '[t]he question should be: who are you to do this? The question is not one of war or peace, it is the well-founded "gut feeling" that there was something terribly wrong with this war, that something will change irretrievably as a result of it.'[62]

It is Habermas, however, who has done the most to publicize the dramatic challenge that the Bush Doctrine in general, with its global 'war on terror', and the war against Iraq in particular, pose to international law and the developing cosmopolitan law of human rights.

In his chapter on the implications of the Iraq war in this volume, Habermas contrasts imperial America's view of its duty with one that is consistent with the 'egalitarian universalism' required in the modern era. The 'universalism' claimed by empires, whether old or new, and whether claiming to be benevolent or not, depends on the assertion of oneself as the 'self-proclaimed' 'trustee' of general interests and perceives the 'world beyond the distant horizon of its borders only from the centralizing perspective of its own worldview'. And this is precisely what the United States has done in pursuing its own 'hegemonic unilateralism'. But, as Habermas contends, the imposition of one's own version of universal 'values' through military (or other) force retains an 'arrogance' that threatens to confuse the universal validity of democratic self-determination and human rights with 'the imperialist claim that the political form of life and the culture of a particular democracy … is exemplary for all societies'. He contrasts this imperial view of the world with 'egalitarian universalism' that 'requires a decentralization of one's own perspective. It demands that one relativize one's own views to the interpretive perspectives of equally situated and equally entitled others' in order, collectively and deliberatively, to be able to assess what is, in each case, 'equally good for all'.[63]

In this and other recent work, Habermas emphasizes the central importance of 'inclusive legal procedures' that have egalitarian universalism at their heart to the adequate deliberation over and judgment of such matters.[64] In fact, he emphasizes law's empire as an antidote to empire's law. In a crucial passage he maintains that, assuming for the sake of argument that the US is genuinely bent on protecting and expanding the protection of human rights:

> [E]ven this best case scenario of the *benevolent hegemon* meets, for cognitive reasons, insurmountable obstacles in identifying those courses of action and those kinds of initiative that accord with shared interests of the international community. The most circumspect state that decides only in [*sic*] its own authority on humanitarian interventions, on cases of self-defense, on international tribunals etc. can never be sure whether or not it actually disentangles its national interests from the shared and generalizable ones. This is not a question of good will or bad intention but an issue of the *epistemology of practical deliberation*. Any anticipation from one side, of what should be acceptable for all sides, cannot be checked but by subjecting a supposedly impartial proposal to an inclusive process of deliberation, by the rules of which all parties involved are equally required to take into consideration the perspectives of the other participants, too. This is the cognitive purpose of impartial judgment that legal procedures are expected to serve, in the global as well as in the domestic arena ... .
>
> Benevolent unilateralism is deficient in terms of a lack of legal provisions for impartiality and legitimacy.[65]

Ignatieff can reject world public opinion and international legal procedures as irrelevant to the judgment of norms and actions and monologically decide on the morality of intervention by calibrating the 'lesser evil' on his own steam while encouraging a counterfactually presumed benevolent and overwhelmingly powerful empire to act. Geras can decide that all those who put reasons forward to oppose the war (including the US's normal allies) are not only morally wrong, but duplicitous. The Bush Administration can mobilize the metaphysical legislation of God to defend its decisions,[66] and the neo-conservative hawks can rely on claims of moral superiority underpinning the 'general world duty' borne by a benevolent empire to spread its liberal values across the world. But it is surely clear by now that cosmopolitan solidarity and morality are insufficiently impartial, as Habermas shows, to guide the 'dangerous politics of human rights'.[67]

In fact, when Ignatieff raises a central insight of the American Declaration of Independence, that we 'must pay "decent respect to the opinions of mankind" ',[68] he seems to acknowledge the kernel of 'egalitarian universalism', but fails to *reject* the promotion of an imperial vehicle for its primary articulation, a move that undermines any serious commitment to the insight. Habermas, on the other hand, thematizes *precisely this aspect* of an anti-imperial politics located pre-eminently by him in the commitment to legality such as can be found in the principles of international and cosmopolitan law. It is defending the symmetry of this law – its 'egalitarian universalism' – that must be a central goal of progressive anti-imperial politics today that, at the same time, is committed to human rights protections, for it has an anti-imperial core. It is, in fact, this that prompts the Bush Administration to view so much of international and cosmopolitan law as 'strateg[ies] of the weak', misrepresenting their egalitarian and principled core as 'asymmetric warfare', while it prefers illegalities, bilateral agreements 'negotiated' with subordinates of empire often while under threat, and attempts to impose a refounding of law.[69]

We would do well, under these conditions of the Bush Doctrine and the aggressive war waged against Iraq, not to mention its occupation, to remember the words of the American Chief Prosecutor at the Nuremberg Tribunal, words that are consistent with Habermas's. The Chief Prosecutor (Associate US Supreme Court Justice Robert Jackson) said that the crime of aggression cannot be justified by *any* political or economic conditions. He went on to say:

> If certain acts in violation of treaties are crimes they are crimes whether the United States does them or whether Germany does them, and we are not prepared to lay down a rule of criminal conduct against others which we would *not* be willing to have invoked against us.[70]

This expresses the most elementary principle of legal justice: that *internally* legitimate law must be universalistic and symmetrical, displaying equal recognition, equal applicability and impartiality. We must now add that, in order for law to be *procedurally* (that is, democratically) legitimate, it must be judged to be *equally* good for all, which, in the contemporary context, means it must issue from processes that include the perspective of *each*. But the Bush Doctrine violates *all* of these dimensions of legitimate legality. Instead, it proclaims the non-reciprocal 'right' of empire to rule as if there are not other equal subjects of sovereignty, to rule the globe and to pursue its self-declared enemies (both external and internal) with force, while claiming the right to act as a self-declared 'trustee' of the interests of the world and, in the course of that imperial project, to reconstruct legality single-handedly into empire's law.

Contrary to these efforts by the American Empire, the commitment to international and cosmopolitan legality is especially important where the coercive enforcement of cosmopolitan moral solidarity's demands is at issue and where enforcement of human rights protections is laden with the possibility of 'collateral damage', conflagration and tragedy, enhanced power imbalances in the form of ramped-up imperial power and undermining the still developing international and cosmopolitan law '*as a medium* for the resolution of conflicts between states, and for the advancement of democracy and human rights'.[71] This indicates one reason why Habermas is correct that the protection of the legal medium – with its in principle commitment to equal treatment and impartiality – is crucial at the international, as well as the municipal, level and why the protection of international law and the further development of cosmopolitan law is necessary to a progressive global politics aimed at developing human rights and sovereignty simultaneously.

The international legal scholar Martti Koskenniemi advances a similar argument by insisting that universalism, the insistence on legal rules, legal processes and formality, renders law the 'gentle civilizer of nations'.[72] But more than this: it can be turned into a 'strategy of resistance, and of democratic hope'.[73] Its spirit pervaded the claims of the opponents of the Iraq war who protested against it not just as a specific war or even as just another act of American imperialism. Recognizing that it is that as well, Koskenniemi emphasizes that the specific 'scandal lies in the mockery that the war has sought to make of the desire for a world of justice and equality'. And he recognizes the 'paradox' that critics, both Left and Right, often claim international law to be dead, useless or entirely the instrument of empire and yet 'never in the past 50 years has there been such a widespread invocation of international law as there is today'. But, he *also* emphasizes the important point that the universal is being conceived in the various oppositions to the war – from Recife to Geneva and Helsinki – as a 'universal violation'.

Reiterating Kant (as well as Habermas and Žižek) in the context of the war against Iraq he says:

> That the war was condemned as a 'violation of international law' or as an attack on the 'rights' of Iraqi civilians is to appeal to something beyond particular interest, [or] privileges .... Such an invocation appeals to something that concerns every member of a projected (legal) community, a violation that touches no one in particular but *everyone in general*. It makes the point that the coalition actions are not an affair between the Iraqis and the Americans (or indeed between Bush and Saddam), but that everyone has a stake in them because the violation is universal. 'I do not condemn it because it is against my interests or preferences. I condemn it because it is objectively wrong, *a violation not against me but against everyone*.'[74]

The recognition of the kernel of anti-imperialism within the form of international legality and the importance of developing a global culture that sustains it is shared by these authors who also share the value of humanitarianism and the commitment to protecting human rights with the human rights hawks. But the insistence on protecting legality, which is true of those who argue for 'law's empire' but not for the human rights hawks, is crucial to a critical cosmopolitanism for reasons of impartiality, adequate judgment based on public reason, self-restraint, insight *and* as a means of resistance and 'democratic hope'. This line of analysis, which both celebrates and analyses the 'gift of formalism'[75] granted by law's empire, is toweringly important as against the contemporary proponents of some version of just war theory and those that treat human rights as 'swords of empire' – from Ignatieff to Geras and many others – whose moral claims impel them to encourage (even if unwittingly) the destruction of legality in light of the moral demands implied by a cosmopolitan understanding of global responsibility and a commitment to human rights.

Moreover, as the Bush Doctrine and those who implement it (not just Saddam Hussein) have shown to be important (if we needed another lesson), it is cosmopolitan legality that may open up leaders to prosecution for crimes against humanity and war crimes, thereby challenging their impunity. A commitment to basic principles of legality also contributes to the protection of the rights of world and national citizens, for example, by protecting the accused against being treated as 'enemy combatants', a category that seeks to strip them of their humanity. This commitment to due process, which it shocks the conscience to have to defend in the twenty-first century, is another one of those 'strateg[ies] of the weak' that the Bush Administration so reviles. And, it *is* legality with its 'gift of formalism'[76] that protects and promotes egalitarian universalism with its demand for public justification, reciprocity and accountability. In fact, the New World Order promoted by the Bush Doctrine and performatively supported by the human rights hawks, at least in relation to the invasion and occupation of Iraq, attacks at least three dimensions of post-World War II legal politics. It attacks international relations based on multilateralism, it attacks the post-World War II regime of international and cosmopolitan law as I have emphasized and it attacks the demand for public justification of law and policies, domestic, international and cosmopolitan. By virtue of the attack on the idea that public authorities must be accountable to the *polis* it threatens the principle of democracy at the domestic level. What we must recognize is that it does the same at the even more vulnerable, because much more thinly developed, level of international and cosmopolitan law. All of this goes some way towards bolstering the contention that the defence and reform of law's empire and the further legalization of international and global relations may hold the promise – even if it is distant – of 'constraining' and possibly even 'attacking' imperial power. In this one regard, the Bush Administration is right, not deluded. International and cosmopolitan law *are* strategies of and for 'the weak'.

## THE IMPERIUM'S CHALLENGE: EMPIRE'S LAW OR AMERICAN EMPIRE THROUGH LAW'S EMPIRE?

Those who argue for the defence and expansion of 'law's empire', then, are right that it is a necessary response to American Empire. However, the very fact of American Empire as an imperial power precludes viewing the project of legalism – of extending law's empire – as a *sufficient* answer to empire's law. An empire must be *expected* to attempt to resist the constraints of law when it is in its interests to do so and to attempt to constitute another law – empire's law – while an empire functioning even *through* international and cosmopolitan law must also be expected to pursue its own interests and sense of responsibility at the expense of others. The critics' argument that legality – international and cosmopolitan as much as if not more than domestic law – does not function as a closed, autonomous system but is, rather, imbricated within, constituted by and constitutive of relations of imperial (and other) power is correct. The nuanced criticism may be stylized as viewing empire as flowing *through* law's empire, through (international and cosmopolitan) legality even when it is not empire's law that is being imposed, thereby dethroning naïve demands for an autonomous realm of law's empire. And this is important for clarifying that law's empire as we have known it and empire's law constitute points on a spectrum rather than distinctly separate entities. This recognition of law's imbrication with power is not enough to *derail* the 'dualistic strategy' for defending international law while advancing a complementary but more substantial cosmopolitan law, but it does demand a sober analysis of what this 'power' is and who wields it, as well as a more sophisticated analysis of international and cosmopolitan law and their institutions.[77]

That American Empire also attempts to rule through law is revealed in the post-World War II development of US-led 'law's empire' as well as in the demand in the 2005 *National Defense Strategy* for 'legal arrangements' that 'support greater operational flexibility' for the US. The now infamous (at least outside the US) Downing Street Memo which reveals Britain's role in convincing the US to attempt a route through the UN prior to war is also telling for what it reveals about the nature of American Empire, its stance towards law and the use of it in this case. The US, which wanted to avoid going to the UN for a second resolution prior to the war, was eventually convinced (enough) by Blair that this strategy would in fact legalize the sought-after war, and thus justify it after Iraq resisted the introduction of weapons inspectors (as Britain predicted it would), that it would give the US what it wanted – the war against Iraq – while meeting Blair's objectives – a war with the legal imprimatur of the United Nations. It was a legal 'strategy to make war possible'.[78] This illustrates the general point that whether or not to avoid legal venues is a *strategic* decision which the imperial power (and others, like its subordinates) makes, rather than an overarching philosophy. Of course, the second resolution that most of the members of the Security Council insisted was necessary in order to justify legal intervention was not to be had and so the US and Britain invaded Iraq illegally. But even then the US Administration's lawyers and friends argued, against overwhelming expert opinion, that a second resolution was *not* required to legalize the war. It continued to claim it was working within the bounds of legality.

*Both* law's empire *and* empire's law have been and are to some great extent determined by American power. The *difference* between them, however, is as important to identify as their continuity. A properly critical account of legality will emphasize its relationship to power and the political as complex with legality conceptualized as a site of struggle, rather than as an 'instrument' either of empire or of cosmopolitan desire. Conceived in this way law's empire constitutes an arena of struggle where international and cosmopolitan law are the site of unequal contests which, however, depend in principle on impartiality, on the internal legitimacy of law. As such, even the powerful are enveloped in its universalism such that they must sometimes submit to the internal logic of international and cosmopolitan law.[79] Empire's law, on the other hand, seeks exceptions, evasions and 'legal' arrangements that accommodate its needs and desires while *in principle* marginalizing others – treating them as law's mere objects, not its equal subjects or authors. That the American Empire seeks to reconstitute and refound the law virtually by unilateral fiat, with enormous pressure placed on its 'coalition' and 'allies', to say nothing of its enemies, both attacks the *internal* legitimacy of law – its egalitarian universalism – and further degrades its *procedural* (or democratic) legitimacy. It is, therefore, inadequate, as the *National Defense Strategy* illustrates, to assume that the Bush Administration's position in relation to law is one merely of acting 'lawlessly'. Its implications are much more threatening than this. This is why, as Andreas Fischer-Lescano puts it (in relation to a discussion of the so far unsuccessful attempt to have Donald Rumsfeld and others investigated under Germany's universal jurisdiction law), the question is whether the 'fundamental constitutional idea of a legal construction and limitation of power can be asserted or whether global law will be pushed back by the totalizing demands of the international political system to perpetuate a global state of exception'.[80]

## CONCLUSION

While we must expect imperial power (and not just the Bush Doctrine) to seek to subvert and to colonize legal initiatives, resisting American Empire does not require a rejection of the dualistic project of legalization. On the contrary, it makes it all the more crucial for the very reasons that Habermas emphasizes: even a 'benevolent hegemon' (should one in fact be possible) must be imbricated within law. Under conditions of a *real* imperium the demand for *internally* legitimate law, not just morality, is critically important in so far as law's 'inclusive procedures' institutionalize the reciprocal expectations demanded by egalitarian universalism. This insistence makes it more, rather than less, likely that imperial power may be held to account, be open to shaming and denunciation for its violations, be hoist with its own petard. In these ways, legalization may contribute to checking the to-be-expected evasions and subversions of legitimate law by imperial power. As Peter Fitzpatrick has argued, conceptualizing the 'definitive difference between imperium and *a community of law*' is crucial. But as he also says: 'It is not as if law's determinate content, responding as it does to the demands of predominant power would be likely to pose a ruptural challenge to American empire.' Rather, for Fitzpatrick, the challenge 'would come from an ethics of the existent within law, from ... an insistence on equality ... and impartiality within law and an insistence on a regardful community of law'.[81] But that 'regardful community of law', that global culture committed to legitimate legality, is what must now be sought, what must be conjured up and forced into existence. And this struggle will also require concerted attempts to find ways to produce procedurally (that is, democratically) legitimate international and cosmopolitan law. The question with which we are confronted is: How can such a global culture and democratic legitimation processes be encouraged into existence, not out of the nothingness of a hypothetical original position or out of an idealist conception of an 'international community', both of which ignore at their peril the constitutively unequal structure of relations implicit in American Empire, but, rather, out of a global context that is dominated by an American imperial project?

Not much is clear about the answer to this question except for the overly general response that we will require contestatory politics that are anti-empire in orientation, not *just* the politics of pursuing a return to or a reform of multilateralism and the post-World War II project of legality, and certainly not just anti-war politics. Under these conditions, politics must be oriented towards contesting the *US's imperial position* – whether it emanates from the Project for a New American Century and the human rights hawks' support for empire's law or from 'benevolent' future administrations which may themselves be *expected* to promote imperial versions of legality 'led' by the US. The project must include support for a *critical cosmopolitanism* that is aimed at 'pacifying the imperial power' in part, but only in part, through international and cosmopolitan legality and through its democratic legitimation. Facing up to this task raises serious questions for the project of legalization (and global constitutionalism), for if it is true, as Habermas argues, that that project will require the US to be in the 'forefront' of these developments, even assuming the move back to a more multilateral imperial America, we can expect the egalitarian universalism that is 'immanent in law and its procedures'[82] to be sorely tested if not repeatedly undermined, evaded or instrumentalized, and we can equally expect serious resistance by it to our attempts to open up law to forms of democratic legitimation. American Empire can hardly be expected to be in the 'forefront', or to be the motor force, of this sort of project (as opposed to leading the oxymoronic 'American internationalist' project). Nor can it be expected to be compliantly constrained by such a project on its own. Indeed, it can be *expected* to have 'bad intention[s]',[83] if by this we mean the intention of organizing global relations in its own and capital's global interests.

So, while I have argued that supporting and reforming law's empire is a crucial move against imperialism, the extent to which it will be resisted, undermined and instrumentalized, and the extent to which empire will attempt to install another 'law', can only be addressed with a more developed analysis of American imperium. This suggests that a critical cosmopolitanism needs to be developed that takes the American imperial project into account far more seriously by beginning with the sort of analysis that Leo Panitch and Sam Gindin provide in this volume.

The project for a critical cosmopolitanism must be modest about the immediate prospects for any project of legalization even while it demands it. This requires a commitment to a 'dualistic strategy', involving a defence and constitutionalization of international and cosmopolitan law while aiming at the development of a cosmopolitan global legal culture and the democratic legitimation of law. To be serious, though, this strategy will necessarily involve engaging in contestatory politics aimed at enforcing the conditions that are necessary to that defence and development. This must involve a contestation of American imperium, of the self-declared non-reciprocal 'right' of American Empire to rule and to constitute another 'law', not just a critique of unilateralism and the Bush Doctrine.

Jean-Paul Sartre perceptively recognized the importance of defending the norms of international legality in his Inaugural Statement to the Bertrand Russell War Crimes Tribunal convened during the Vietnam War. He stated in relation to the paucity of international agreements aiming to limit *jus ad bellum* prior to World War II that 'the nations which had built their wealth upon the conquest of great colonial empires would not have tolerated being judged upon their actions in Africa or Asia'. He recognized that the Nuremberg Tribunal, which passed judgment on the belligerent power by the victors of that war, represented victors' justice, with the consequence that no tribunal was ever constituted to judge the bombing of Hiroshima, Nagasaki or Dresden. But he also recognized that once the principle of legality is invoked, it becomes difficult for those powers to avoid its reach due to its 'implicit universality'.[84] The Nuremberg Tribunal thus created an 'ambiguous reality', he argued, in which an 'embryo of a tradition', a 'precedent', was created that, while it was never extended after the Tribunal to the victors, nevertheless 'created a real gap in international affairs'. That 'gap' lay in the fact that no institution had been created to affirm the universality that necessarily dwells at the principled heart of the Nuremberg judgment. But that gap '*must* be filled', Sartre argued, and where no official institution would do so, it was up to the people. He maintained that the Russell Tribunal should

> have no other function in this inquiry and its conclusions, but to make everybody understand the necessity for international jurisdiction – which it has neither the means nor the ambition to replace and the essence of which would be to resuscitate the *jus contra bellum*, still born at Nuremberg, and to substitute legal, ethical laws for the law of the jungle.[85]

Today, as one aspect of anti-imperial politics, we would do well to take up Sartre's orientation by defending the laws against aggressive war and pursuing those 'strateg[ies] of the weak' that seek to 'criminalize foreign policy'. This should be aimed as much at publicizing the crimes of an 'empire that is no longer concealed'[86] as it builds a case (or, better, a set of linked, world-wide cases) against it. It should also aim to extend the egalitarian universalism in international and cosmopolitan legality while constituting a transnational legal culture that imposes upon empire the demand that it work through rather than undermine legitimate legality. Equally, we might press upon the human rights hawks the crucial role of legality to a future where respect for human rights and equal sovereignty may be expected. And the 'gap' between a post-World War II project of establishing internally legitimate law and the lack of democratic legitimation of that law can become a focus of our politics. Finally, the Left must not reject this sort of legal politics, but rather should work it into broader movements that contest empire. With such an orientation we may be able to address the contradictions of a politics of human rights while we contest empire's law. It is ultimately the aim of undermining American Empire's 'global freedom of action' that must guide our politics.

## NOTES

1  Many thanks to Leo Panitch, Peter Swan, Chris Whitehead and Trevor Purvis for reading and commenting on an earlier draft of this chapter. Thanks as well to Richard Falk who shared his unpublished work with me.

2  United States of America, *The National Defense Strategy of the United States of America* (1 March 2005), issued by the Secretary of Defense, Donald H. Rumsfeld, http://www.globalsecurity.org/military/library/policy/dod/nds-usa_mar2005.htm, emphasis added.

3  Quoted in John J. Lumpkin, 'America at War: Terrorism Report Decries "Strategy of the Weak" ' (19 March 2005), http://www.capitolhillblue.com/artman/publisher/printer_6428.shtml. Also see John Hendren, 'Policy OK's First Strike to Protect US', *Los Angeles Times* (19 March 2005), http://www.commondreams.org/cgi-bin/print.cgi?file=/headlines05/0319-01.htm.

4  Arthur Schlesinger Jr, 'Eyeless in Iraq', *New York Review of Books*, 50:16 (23 October 2003), http://www.nybooks.com/articles/article-preview?article_id=16677.

5  Outlawed in the Kellogg–Briand Pact of 1928, reiterated in the Nuremberg Charter. For the former, see http://www.yale.edu/lawweb/avalon/imt/kbpact.htm; for the latter, see http://www.derechos.org/nizkor/nuremberg/judgment/cap5.html.

6  See Nehal Bhuta, 'A Global State of Exception? The United States and World Order', *Constellations* 10:3 (2003): 371–91; and Lori Fisler Damrosch and Bernard H. Oxman, 'Agora: Future Implication of the Iraq Conflict: Editors' Introduction', *American Journal of International Law* 97 (2004): 553.

7  Jürgen Habermas, 'Interpreting the Fall of a Monument', this volume.

8  Bhuta, 'A Global State of Exception?' 380.

9  USA, *National Defense Strategy 2005*.

10  The distinction between international and cosmopolitan law roughly maps the distinction between the international law of states, pre-eminently equal sovereignty and the law of non-interference, and the law that addresses human rights and individuals. See Jean L. Cohen, 'Whose Sovereignty? Empire versus International Law', *Ethics and International Affairs* 18 (2004): 1–24 and Pavlos Eleftheriadis, 'Cosmopolitan Law', *Ratio Juris* 9 (2004): 241–63.

11  Tariq Ali, 'Re-colonizing Iraq', *New Left Review* 21 (May–June 2003): 5–19, 15.

12  On legality and legitimacy, see Richard Falk, 'Legality and Legitimacy: The Quest for Principled Flexibility and Restraint', forthcoming in a special issue on 'Force and Legitimacy', *Review of International Studies (UK)*, ed. J. S. Armstrong; and Jürgen Habermas, 'Bestiality and Humanity: A War on the Border between Legality and Morality', *Constellations* 6:3 (1999): 263–72.

13  President George W. Bush, The White House, *State of the Union Address* (February 2005), http://www.whitehouse.gov/news/releases/2005/02/20050202-11.html.

14  See Leo Panitch and Sam Gindin, 'Theorizing American Empire', this volume.

15  See, for example, Samantha Power, *A Problem from Hell: America and the Age of Genocide* (New York: Basic Books, 2002).

16  Michael Ignatieff, 'The Burden', *The New York Times Magazine* (5 January 2003): 22.

17  Norman Geras, 'A Moral Failure', *Wall Street Journal.com Opinion Journal* (4 August 2003), http://www.opinionjournal.com/forms/printThis. html?id+110003834.

18  Michael Ignatieff, 'Mission Possible?' *The New York Review of Books* 49:2 (19 December 2002), http://www.nybooks.com/articles/15931. Also see Michael Ignatieff, 'Barbarians at the Gate?', *The New York Review of Books* 49:3 (28 February 2002), http://www. nybooks.com/articles/15146; and *The Lesser Evil: Political Ethics in an Age of Terror* (Princeton, NJ: Princeton University Press, 2004).

19  Michael Ignatieff, 'I am Iraq', *New York Times Magazine* (23 March 2003); 'Friends Disunited', *Guardian* (24 March 2003), and *The Lesser Evil*.

20  'Iraq War Illegal, Says Annan', BBC News (16 September 2004). For a smattering of the arguments that the war was illegal, see International Commission of Jurists, 'Iraq – This War Must be Conducted Lawfully', http://www.icj.org/news.php3?id_article=2774&lang=en. Also see Bhuta, 'A Global State of Exception', and the Center for Economic and Social Rights, *Tearing up the Rules: The Illegality of Invading Iraq* (18 March 2003), http://cesr.org/node/view/523?PHPSESSID=c1ca6c2db5fb05a16786679c2f7a459d. For a list of some legal opinions on the war, see http://www.robincmiller.com/ir-legal.htm.

21  Ignatieff, 'The Burden', 50.

22  Ibid., 24.

23  Quoted in David Harvey, *The New Imperialism* (Oxford: Oxford University Press, 2003), 3.

24  Ignatieff, 'The Burden', 25–6.

25  Theodore Roosevelt, quoted in Panitch and Gindin, 'Theorizing American Empire', this volume.

26  Ignatieff, 'The Burden', 54.

27  Ignatieff, 'Barbarians at the Gate'.

28  Ignatieff, 'The Burden', 25.

29  Ibid., 53.

30  See David Golove and Stephen Holmes, 'Terrorism and Accountability: Why Checks and Balances Apply Even in "The War on Terrorism"', *The NYU Review of Law and Security* 2 (April 2004): 2–7, www.law.nyu. edu/centers/lawsecurity/publications/quarterly/spring04.pdf.

   For discussions of Ignatieff, see Amy Bartholomew and Jennifer Breakspear, 'Human Rights as Swords of Empire', in Leo Panitch and Colin Leys (eds.), *The New Imperial Challenge, Socialist Register 2004* (London: Merlin Press: 2004), 125–45; and Ronald Steel, ' "The Lesser Evil": Fight Fire with Fire', *New York Times* (25 July 2005).

31  See Pheng Cheah, 'Posit(ion)ing Human Rights in the Current Global Conjuncture', *Public Culture* 9 (1997): 233–66.

32  See Bartholomew and Breakspear, 'Human Rights as Swords of Empire'.

33  Geras, 'A Moral Failure'. Also see his 'Normblog', http://normblog. typepad.com/normblog/.

34  Norman Geras, *The Contract of Mutual Indifference: Political Philosophy after the Holocaust* (London: Verso, 1998), 45 and 8, respectively.

35  Geras, 'The Reductions of the Left', *Dissent Magazine* (Winter 2005), http://www.dissentmagazine.org/menutest/articles/wi05/geras.htm/.

36  Geras, 'A Moral Failure'. Also see Maurice Chittenden, 'Stormin' Marxist is Toast of the Neocons', *Sunday Times* (6 February 2005).

37  Arthur Schlesinger Jr, 'Today, it is We Americans Who Will Live in Infamy', *Los Angeles Times* (23 March 2003), http://www.commondreams.org/ views03/0322-01.htm.

38  See the Introduction to this volume for more details and sources. On civilian and other casualties, in addition to the controversial report published in *The Lancet*, http://www.thelancet.com/journals/lancet/ article/PIIS0140673604174412/fulltext, which projected deaths in Iraq of over 100,000, see the 'IBC [Iraq Body Count] Response to the Lancet Study Estimating "100,000" Iraqi Deaths' (7 November 2005), at http://www.iraqbodycount.net/press/. The ICB projects approximately 25,000 *confirmed civilian deaths due to the war to date* in Iraq and acknowledges, in the report above, that 'our own total is certain to be an underestimate of the true position, because of gaps in reporting or recording'. Also see Carl Conetta, 'Vicious Circle: The Dynamics of Occupation and Resistance in Iraq' (18 May 2005), http://www.comw.org/pda/ 0505rm10.html.

   On the state of Iraq hospitals under occupation, see Dahr Jamail's important report 'Iraqi Hospitals Reeling Under Occupation', http:// www.commondreams.org/views03/0322-01.htm. Also see Ghali Hassan, 'Iraqi Women under Occupation', *Crosscurrents* (9 May 2005), http:// www.countercurrents.org/iraq-hassan090505.htm; and David Cortright, 'Iraqi Social Conditions Worse under US Occupation than under Hussein', *Christian Science Monitor* (7 June 2005), http://www.occupationwatch. org/analysis/archives/2005/06/iraqi_social_co.html. Finally, see the fine testimony of eye-witnesses and experts at the Istanbul session of the World Tribunal on Iraq, http://www.worldtribunal.org/main/.

39  Michael Ignatieff, 'The Year of Living Dangerously', *New York Times Magazine* (14 March 2004), 13, at 16.

40  Michael Ignatieff, 'The Terrorist as Auteur', *The New York Times Magazine* (14 November 2004), 50, at 51.

41  Michael Ignatieff, 'Why Are We in Iraq? (And Liberia? And Afghanistan?)', *New York Times* (7 September 2003).

42  Michael Ignatieff, 'Who are Americans to Think that Freedom is Theirs to Spread?' *The New York Times Magazine* (26 June 2005), www.nytimes.com/css/page_type/article/print.css.

43  See Ken Roth (for Human Rights Watch), 'War in Iraq: Not a Humanitarian Intervention' (2004), www.electronicIraq.net/news/printer1354.shtml.

44  The term is used in *The National Defense Strategy* 2005.

45  Amnesty International USA Executive Director, William Schultz, 'Guantánamo Bay: A "Gulag of Our Times" or a "Model Facility"? A Debate on the U.S. Prison & Amnesty International', *Democracy Now* (1 June 2005), hosted by Amy Goodman. Transcript available at: http://www.democracynow.org/article.pl?sid=05/06/01/1441204.

46  It is in this way that the human rights hawks have bolstered what Richard Falk has called the 'militant version of Wilsonian idealism' expressed by the Bush Administration. Richard Falk, 'What Future for the UN System of War Prevention?', www.transnational.org/forum/meet/2003/Falk_UNCharter.html (23 June 2003).

47  Roth, 'War in Iraq: Not a Humanitarian Intervention'.

48  This is an early translation of Habermas's that is more evocative in this regard than the subsequent one found in 'Interpreting the Fall of a Monument', this volume. See 'What Does the Felling of the Monument Mean?', http://slash.autonomedia.org/analysis/03/05/12/1342259.shtml.

49  Chalmers Johnson, *The Sorrows of Empire: Militarism, Secrecy and the End of the Republic* (New York: Metropolitan Books, 2004), 7.

50  Ulrich Beck, 'The Cosmopolitan Perspective: Sociology of the Second Age of Modernity', *British Journal of Sociology* 51:1 (2000): 79–105, 86.

51  Beck, 'The Cosmopolitan Perspective', 85.

52  Preuss, 'The Iraq War'.

53  See Herbert Docena, ' "Shock and Awe" Therapy: How the United States is Attempting to Control Iraq's Oil and Pry Open its Economy', speech delivered at the World Tribunal on Iraq, Istanbul, 24 June 2005, http://www.focusweb.org/pdf/Shock%20and%20Awe%20Therapy%20Final.pdf; and Naomi Klein, 'The Rise of Disaster Capitalism', *The Nation* (2 May 2005), http://www.thenation.com/doc.mhtml?i=20050502&s=klein.

54  Beck, 'The Cosmopolitan Perspective', 85, 87.

55  See Cohen, 'Whose Sovereignty? Empire versus International Law'.

56  Habermas, 'Interpreting the Fall of a Monument'.

57  The idea of 'critical cosmopolitanism' is beyond the bounds of this essay. See Bartholomew and Breakspear, 'Human Rights as Swords of Empire'; and Robert Fine, 'Crimes against Humanity: Hannah Arendt and the Nuremberg Debates', *European Journal of Social Theory* 3:3 (2000): 293–311.

58  See Bartholomew and Breakspear, 'Human Rights as Swords of Empire'.

59  Ulrich Beck, 'The Cosmopolitan Society and Its Enemies', *Theory, Culture and Society* 19:1/2 (2002): 17–44, 37.

60  Roth, 'War in Iraq: Not a Humanitarian Intervention'. Also see Bartholomew and Breakspear, 'Human Rights as Swords of Empire'.

61  For an important discussion of the importance of a dualistic strategy, see Cohen, 'Whose Sovereignty? Empire versus International Law'.

62  Slavoj Žižek, *Iraq: The Borrowed Kettle* (London: Verso, 2004), 16 and 51 respectively.

63  Habermas, 'Interpreting the Fall of a Monument'.

64  Jürgen Habermas (interview with Eduardo Mendieta), 'America and the World: A Conversation with Jürgen Habermas', *Logos* 3:3 (Summer 2004): n.p. transl. Jeffrey Craig Miller, http://www.logosjournal.com/issue_3.3/habermas_interview.htm.

65  Jürgen Habermas, 'Dispute on the Past and Future of International Law: Transition from a National to a Postnational Constellation', unpublished paper delivered at World Congress of Philosophy, Istanbul, 2003, second emphasis added.

66  See, for example, Doug Thompson, 'Bush Leagues', *Capitol Hill Blue* (4 June 2004), where he reports that White House personnel willing to talk off the record present a view of 'an administration under siege ... led by a man who declares his decisions to be "God's will" and then tells aides to "fuck over" anyone they consider to be an opponent of the administration'; www.capitolhillblue.com/artman/publish/article_4636.shtml.

67  Jürgen Habermas, 'The Nation, the Rule of Law, and Democracy', in Ciaran Cronin and Pablo De Greiff (eds.), *The Inclusion of the Other: Studies in Political Theory* (Cambridge, MA: The MIT Press, 1998), 129–53 at 149.

68  See Ignatieff, 'Friends Disunited' and 'Why we are in Iraq'.

69  Andreas Fischer-Lescano, 'Torture in Abu Ghraib: The Complaint against Donald Rumsfeld under the German Code of Crimes against International Law', *German Law Journal* 6:3 (2005): 689–724.

70  Quoted in Marjorie Cohen, 'Aggressive War: Supreme International Crime', *Truthout* (9 November 2004), www.truthout.org/docs_04.

71  Habermas (interview with Eduardo Mendieta), 'America and the World'.

72  Martti Koskenniemi, *The Gentle Civilizer of Nations: The Rise and Fall of International Law, 1879–1960* (Cambridge: Cambridge University Press, 2001).

73  Martti Koskenniemi, '"The Lady Doth Protest Too Much": Kosovo, and the Turn to Ethics in International Law', *The Modern Law Review* 65 (2002): 159–75, 174.

74  Martti Koskenniemi, 'What Should International Lawyers Learn from Karl Marx?', *Leiden Journal of International Law* 17 (2004): 229–46, 244–5.

75  Anne Orford, 'The Gift of Formalism', *European Journal of International Law* 15:1 (2004): 179–95.

76  Orford, 'The Gift of Formalism'.

77  For efforts towards the latter, see Bartholomew and Breakspear, 'Human Rights as Swords of Empire'.

78  Mark Danner, 'The Secret Way to War', *The New York Review of Books* 52 (no. 10) (9 June 2005), http://www.nybooks.com/articles/18034.

79  See 'Fundamentalism and Terror: A Dialogue with Jürgen Habermas', in Giovanna Borradori, *Philosophy in a Time of Terror: Dialogues with Jurgen Habermas and Jacques Derrida* (Chicago: University of Chicago Press, 2003), 25–43, at 42. Also see Andrew Arato, 'Empire's Democracy, Ours and Theirs'; and Trevor Purvis, 'Looking for Life Signs in an International Rule of Law', in this volume.

80  Fischer-Lescano, 'Torture in Abu Ghraib', 690–1.

81  Peter Fitzpatrick, ' "Gods would be needed ...": American Empire and the Rule of (International) Law', *Leiden Journal of International Law* 16 (2003): 429–66, 466, emphasis added.

82  Habermas (interview with Eduardo Mendieta), 'America and the World', 20 and 18 respectively.

83  Habermas, 'Dispute on the Past and Future of International Law'.

84  Jean Paul Sartre, 'Inaugural Statement', Bertrand Russell Vietnam War Crimes Tribunal, http://web.archive.org/web/20041025164511/www.911review.org/Wget/www.homeusers.

85  Ibid.

86  Panitch and Gindin, 'Theorizing American Empire', this volume.

# III

# Occupation, Democracy and Contradictions of Empire in Iraq

# 10

# A New Bonapartism?

*Nehal Bhuta*

When the French in 1792 invaded Italy, they had no scruple in summoning the invaded populations to repudiate all allegiance to their sovereigns ... Nys may tell us that the French generals 'limited themselves' to breaking the ties between invaded peoples and their princes and to convoking assemblies to determine the form of government. There is no doubt that the assemblies would never have been permitted to reinstate the princes, or to establish any form of rule distasteful to the Republic; it was practically a reversion to the old type of conquest by occupation; the later decree ... directing the military authority to suppress all existing authorities, taxes, feudal government and privileges, in reality goes very little further. The whole drastic proceeding was a consequence of the breaking away of France from the sphere of international law, and of her desire to replace it by a new Law of Nations of which the first article should be – 'no state may be organised on any but a soi-disant republican system'. It was not that a monarchical state was necessarily, as she expressed it, her enemy; it was not even a lawful enemy.[1]

## INTRODUCTION

The United States' invasion of Iraq was not jurisgenerative in any direct sense. Without authorization from the Security Council, the arguments for the legality of the invasion as 'preventive self-defence' were tenuous at best[2] and did not receive wide acceptance from the preponderance of states.[3] The ensuing military occupation of Iraq was one of the few self-declared[4] belligerent occupations since World War II,[5] revivifying a category of international law which had fallen from use in the language of state practice.[6] The concept of belligerent occupation, born of the nineteenth-century intra-European land order, was to be applied as the legal framework regulating an ambitious project of transforming the material and formal constitution of the Iraqi state. It was quickly observed by commentators that the determinate content endowed to the concept of belligerent occupation by its nineteenth-century context of formation was inadequate to the US objective of 'occupation as liberation'.[7]

Noting that, since the end of the Cold War, international institutions had authorized and promoted transformational 'state-building' projects with minimal reference to occupation law,[8] some advocated that the scope of permissible action under occupation law should be expanded if the occupied society requires 'revolutionary changes in its economy (including a leap into robust capitalism), rigorous implementation of international human rights standards, a new constitution and judiciary, and a new political structure (most likely consistent with principles of democracy) ...'.[9] Consistent with the contemporary revival of what Simpson terms 'liberal anti-pluralism', the objective of instituting – even imposing – a democratic governance regime where previously there was none is asserted as the value relative to which positive legal rules should be adapted.[10] It may be that the revision of occupation law which is argued for is, like Hegel's Owl of Minerva, simply a recognition of a reality which has already formed. But if this is the case, it may also be an opportune moment to re-examine the provenance and evolution of the idea of belligerent occupation, and ask what is implied in giving a legal-conceptual imprimatur to the project of 'transformative occupation'.

In this chapter, I revisit the classical concept of *occupatio bellica*, and situate its emergence and conceptual determinacy in the particular conditions and needs of the intra-European land order, as it evolved after the Congress of Vienna in 1815. I argue that the development of *occupatio bellica* as a legal institution can be seen as part of the wider effort to re-found and restore the concrete spatial order that was a precondition for the efficacy of the *jus publicum Europeaum*, in response to the twin perils of revolutionary war and wars of liberation. As such, the concept of *occupatio bellica* crystallized the equilibration of a set of competing geopolitical interests and conflicting principles of political legitimacy, and formed a functional mechanism by which the problem of intra-European land appropriation could be mediated. Its (internal and external) order-conserving function leads me to develop a parallel between the classical concept of *occupatio bellica* and the domestic constitutional law idea of a state of exception, wherein the role played by the occupying power is analogous to that of a commissarial dictator.

The shift from the classical concept of belligerent occupation to the endorsement of 'transformative occupation' has certain elective affinities with a shift from commissarial to sovereign dictatorship. Yet this move is fraught with political risk, as it implies that the occupant must achieve a much higher threshold of effective power over the territory and its inhabitants: rather than preserving an extant material and formal order as a temporary measure, the occupant must create conditions under which a new political order can be established and legitimated. The capacity to impose a new order that is resilient depends on a precarious dialectic of subordination and legitimation. In the concluding section of this chapter, I contend that the US attempt to realize a transformative model of military occupation in Iraq has failed because of its inability to obtain the degree of subordination – by force, acquiescence or consent – necessary to ensure sufficient normality and stability for the legitimation of the new order. The heavy burdens of legitimation and subordination entailed by the transformative vision of military occupation reveal the antinomies of democratic imposition under conditions of military dictatorship.

## BELLIGERENT OCCUPATION AND THE AGE OF EUROPEAN PUBLIC LAW: COMMISSARIAL DICTATORSHIP AND THE MEDIATION OF TERRITORIAL AND CONSTITUTIONAL CHANGE

The notion of 'military occupation' occupies an anomalous place within the classical international law of war rights and territorial acquisition. Unlike the post-UN Charter legal environment,[11] classical international law did not limit a state's right to go to war against another state or to acquire legal title to the territory of another state by means of war. Although the actual practice of intra-European land appropriation in the seventeenth and eighteenth centuries was complex, acquiring effective control over a territory was recognized as a sufficient legal basis to assert a right of conquest and obtain full sovereign rights over it.[12] In medieval doctrine, this entitlement was based on the identity of *imperium* and *dominium*, in which a lord's territory was his private property and the inhabitants' allegiance to a prince implied the latter's reciprocal obligation to maintain his territory against foreign invaders. Seizing effective control of the prince's territory severed the foundation for allegiance between a prince and his subjects, and entitled the conqueror to demand an oath of allegiance from the inhabitants and exercise *dominium* over the prince's territory. By the time of Vattel, the differentiation between the prince and his subjects had developed to the point where the presumed identity between public and private property was diminished,[13] and the right of the invader to incorporate territory into his sovereign domain was 'perfected' only after a peace treaty. Verzijl similarly observes that, after the Treaties of Utrecht (1713), effective occupation of territory was construed as 'operating a change of sovereignty under the *condition suspensive* of a peace treaty with retroactive effect'.[14] But no characterization of 'belligerent occupation' as a distinct legal category, conferring specific rights and obligations and distinguishable from sovereign power, emerged until after end of the Napoleonic Wars and the reconstruction of the European order at the Congress of Vienna in 1815.

Lauterpacht dates the first usage of 'belligerent occupation' to 1844, in the writings of the German publicist Hefter.[15] *Occupatio bellica* develops as a legal status defined in contraposition to *debellatio*. The former is quintessentially a temporary state of fact arising when an invader achieves military control over a territory and administers it on a provisional basis, but has no legal entitlement to exercise the rights of the absent sovereign.[16] The latter is a legal category describing a condition of 'subjugation' in which the original sovereign is not merely temporarily prevented from exercising his powers due to the presence of the occupying military forces, but is completely defeated: his institutions of state destroyed, his international legal personality dissolved, with no allies continuing to fight on his behalf.[17] *Debellatio* implies, in other words, a certain *quality of subordination* that is achieved by the invader, and which permits him to re-found the political order of the territory afresh. Full sovereignty over territory was thus obtained either through a thorough destruction of the juridical and political institutions of the sovereign and the state, or by a treaty of cession at the formal conclusion of the war in which an orderly transfer of populations and allegiances was effected.

In contrast to *debellatio, occupatio bellica* is an intermediate status between invasion and conquest, during which the juridical and material constitution is maintained. The authority of the occupant derives purely from his factual power – his military capacity to exercise functions of administration and issue enforceable commands, rather than any sovereign right. The paradox of exercising a part of the sovereign's rights (control over public property, maintenance of order) in the absence of legally recognized sovereign authority was explained by publicists and jurists as international law's accommodation of the sheer facticity of the occupant's military power of command. Thus, Funck-Brentano and Sorel write that the authority exercised by the occupant is based only on the force at his disposal and exists only where this physical force manifests itself,[18] while Hall insists that 'rights which are founded on mere force reach their natural limit at the point where force ceases to be efficient. They disappear with it; they reappear with it; and in the interval they are non-existent'.[19] Correlative with international law's recognition of the occupant's factual power of command, however, was the imposition of an obligation to restore and ensure public order, respect the property rights of private citizens and refrain from interfering in private economic relations governed by contract and other financial laws in force in the territory.[20] The occupant is entitled to seize moveable public property, but has only use-rights (for the duration of the occupation) in relation to public immovable property. Subject to derogation only in response to military necessity, the occupant is effectively obliged to preserve the economic order of the territory.

The ordinary laws of the territory might be partially suspended in the name of military necessity (such as to ensure the security of the occupying military forces) or provisionally supplemented in order to meet the exigencies of preserving order under conditions of war, but otherwise the law in force in the territory was to be respected by the occupant, unless 'absolutely prevented'.[21] Crucially, the fundamental principle of occupation law accepted by nineteenth-century publicists was that an occupant could not alter the political order of territory.[22] All laws implicating the population's political relationship with the former sovereign – such as those conferring political privileges or mandating conscription – could be suspended, but not enforced vis-à-vis the occupant. The political constitution could similarly be suspended to the extent that it interfered with the occupant's entitlement to protect its forces and pursue legitimate war aims, provided that the occupant did not attempt to impose obligations akin to duties of allegiance or loyalty on the occupied population. The population was deemed to owe a factual, rather than legal, duty of obedience to the occupant, arising out of an acceptance of the occupant's power to enforce his commands and in return for the preservation of public order. Thus, as Schmitt observed, the legal institution of *occupatio bellica* recognizes a direct relationship of protection and obedience between the occupying power's military commandant and the territory's inhabitants,[23] potentially mediated by local laws and institutions, but in the last instance arising from the occupant's 'naked power',[24] which is at once legitimated and constrained by international law's precarious balance of 'military necessity' and order-conservation.

The characterization of belligerent occupation as a legally sanctioned extra-legal power that is plenary in its mandate to pursue specified aims (military victory and order-preservation), but constrained in its *order-constitutive* authority, invites an obvious comparison with the Roman public law institution of commissarial dictatorship. Fraenkel notes that the occupying power's entitlement to preserve order and protect the security of its military forces is analogous to the police power of the Executive in 'continental political theory',[25] while nineteenth-century publicists such as Hall and Lieber recognized the law of occupation as a variety of martial law transposed to the international plane.[26] Like the Roman commissarial dictator, the military commander or administrator exercises 'complete authority',[27] which unifies the different limbs of constituted power, and suspends the normal legal order on a temporary or provisional basis with the exclusive purpose of 'bringing about a concrete success'[28] – a return to the state of law in the case of the Roman dictator, or military victory in the case of the military commander. Schmitt gets to the heart of the matter when he points out that in *both* a state of exception and *occupatio bellica*, there were 'no *juridical* answers to any of the important questions consistent with the real circumstances'.[29] The procedures and powers of the dictator are given content by the *concrete situation* that he is called upon to meet.

Analogously, the notion of 'military necessity' as a regulative principle in international law expands and contracts, depending on the actuality of the threat to be contained and of the enemy to be defeated.[30] Von Glahn writes that 'the interests of the occupant are paramount and every act and measure undertaken by military government has to be judged by the yardstick of military necessity and usefulness in concluding the conflict successfully and preserving order in the occupied area'.[31] Nineteenth- and early twentieth-century commentators noted that the twin imperatives of military necessity and order-preservation allowed the occupier to extend his control 'over practically all fields of life',[32] particularly if faced with local resistance to his military control.[33] Spaight observes that 'the secret of successful occupation is really the disciplining of the conglomeration of more or less disaffected persons who made up the population of an occupied province',[34] and in nineteenth-century law the measures permitted to bring about this disciplining included collective penalties, the taking and execution of hostages,[35] and reprisals.[36] Occupation forces were expected and entitled to be 'severe'[37] in as much as pacification was necessary to the carrying out of legitimate military operations and the efficient administration of the territory: 'in military government, the mission is paramount and controls the form'.[38] Nevertheless, an important limitation remained: neither the commissarial dictator nor the belligerent occupant exercise constituent power and are thus the opposite of the sovereign dictator: the former uses unlimited power in extraordinary circumstances to bring about the termination of his power, while the latter uses unlimited power over an indeterminate duration to create a radically new order.[39]

Andrew Arato observes the Roman dictatorship was an 'institutional attempt to solve the problem of republican order within a republican identity'.[40] I suggest that the peculiar legal institution of *occupatio bellica* should be understood as a legal product of the nineteenth-century European political order's preoccupation with modulating the problems of territorial and constitutional change within Europe. As a matter of principle and practice, belligerent occupation in its nineteenth-century manifestation was applied exclusively to land wars between European sovereigns. A state of belligerent occupation could arise only in the context of a state of war, and only sovereigns could declare war upon one another. Sovereignty was a 'gift of civilization'[41] and was, almost exclusively, a recognized attribute only of members of the 'European family of states'.[42] The anomalous (from a classical international law point of view) distinction between effective control and sovereign rights over territory which lies at the heart of the law of occupation, and the law's enjoining of fundamental constitutional change by the military occupant, had no application to colonial wars or 'police actions' against less civilized – and therefore non-sovereign – peoples and territories.[43]

Hence, the British deemed military occupation to be a sufficient basis to assert sovereign rights, such as the right to demand allegiances, over the territories of Egypt that were seized from the Ottoman Empire,[44] while Russia declared the laws of military occupation to have no application to its acquisition of Bulgaria from the Turks.[45] After all, reasoned Feodor de Martens (one of the leading proponents of the laws of land warfare), the very point of the war was to liberate a population from the antiquated and despotic constitutional system of the Ottoman Empire, and it would therefore be senseless to refrain from introducing a modern social and legal order.[46] The Russian action was 'approved by many observers'.[47] Similarly, the strict division between public and private property encoded in the law of occupation was not sensibly applied to peoples and civilizations whose chieftains were not 'public authorities' in any sense recognized by European law, and whose social orders did not themselves distinguish common and private property in the manner of European states. Thus, occupation law's restraints on seizing private property as the dominium of the occupant were predicated on a common – Eurocentric – standard of a constitutional order that distinguished between public and private law, and between state and state-free (economy, property) society.[48]

When placed in the context of late eighteenth- and nineteenth-century European politics, these characteristics of *occupatio bellica* take on a functional intelligibility. The French Revolution, and the subsequent revolutionary and Napoleonic Wars, challenged the legal foundations of the eighteenth-century intra-European political order and threatened to transform the nature of European warfare permanently. The revolutionary government in France renounced the right of conquest and offered instead 'fraternity' with peoples who rejected the dynastic principle of legitimacy in favour of popular sovereignty. International conflicts over treaties and defined legal rights thus became struggles over fundamental political principles, in which the French claim that rights based on popular sovereignty transcended those based on treaties. Instead of annexing territories which came under their effective control, French armies replaced the religious and dynastic political authorities with popular committees, under revolutionary guidance from France. In other words, the revolutionary wars, and the Napoleonic Wars that followed them, initiated *constitutional change* in place of conquest and (under Napoleon in particular) attempted radically to transform the nature of the state and the accepted bases for territorial control.

Revolutionary warfare also brought with it the phenomenon of the 'nation-in-arms', in which the total human resources of a territory were potentially mobilized in the name of patriotic duty. Napoleon's enlistment of inhabitants of recently annexed or 'liberated' territories to fight on behalf of the empire exacted a new and potentially destabilizing kind of allegiance from the populace, that of national citizenship. Koselleck notes that by the beginning of the nineteenth century, the notion of a national *Bildung*, and associated ideas of an integrative relation between a people, a heritage and a territory, were emerging as political 'metaconcepts'.[49] In 1808–9, in the middle of the Napoleonic Wars, Viennese newspapers extolled the unique relation that an individual has with the fatherland, and the undesirability of foreign rule because of the close relationship between the native political system of one's land and the customs and traditions that one shares with the inhabitants of the land.[50] The Austrian elites, inspired by the Spanish *guerillero* resistance to Napoleonic rule, created a civil militia (*Landswehr*) for the defence of 'the fatherland', and engaged poets and writers, such as Friedrich Schlegel and his brother, to propagate patriotic sentiment and mobilize the populace against Napoleon.[51] In a dialectical movement that neither Hegel nor Marx would fail to notice, the reaction's determination to defeat Napoleon led them to cultivate and unleash forces that would in the future erode their own legitimacy:

> shared resentment of Napoleon could metamorphose into the proto-nationalism that was to prove a major source of instability in Restoration Europe. ... When they employed national rhetoric, [ousted rulers] implicitly recognised that popular will rather than dynastic right was the basis of sovereignty.[52]

Moreover, although the Austrian and Prussian attempts to incite a patriotic war were unsuccessful relative to the Spanish partisan campaign, both the revolutionary nation-in-arms *and* the reactionary effort of fomenting popular resistance undermined classical international law's presumption of warfare as 'cabinet matter' conducted between aristocratic warrior castes or professional soldiers. Clausewitz recognized patriotism as a powerful military asset, but the military scholar Werner Hahlweg notes that the endorsement of armed civilian resistance against the existing order (even when embodied in a foreign occupation) was also extremely dangerous, because it was 'something simultaneously outside the legal state'.[53]

The defeat of Napoleon confronted the Great Powers with the challenge of re-founding an international legal and political order that was capable of stabilizing and moderating the contradictory historical and political tendencies unleashed by two decades of war and revolution. The Congress of Vienna was, in this sense, less a 'restoration' than a re-constitution, which repudiated the revolutionary imperative of universalizing a specific political order while simultaneously tolerating the continuation of constitutional settlements that incorporated changes wrought by the revolution, retained Napoleonic institutions or endeavoured wholly to reject the revolutionary era.[54] The stabilization of political plurality within an agreed range of territorial and institutional parameters was at the heart of the new order. Just as the Peace of Westphalia bracketed the religious question, the Vienna settlement tried to bracket the constitutional question and create a spatial regime which permitted the coexistence of absolutism, liberal parliamentarism and enlightened authoritarianism in a kind of *complexio oppositorium*, preserved by a system of treaties that 'legalized' the hegemony of the Great Powers. As Broers observes:

> The cooperation and competition of the Great Powers preserved the territorial integrity of the intra-European borders from reimposition of the uniform, internationalist doctrines of the French Revolution. In practice, this meant that existing rulers could not be overthrown by their own subjects or an outside power, and in no circumstances could they be replaced by anything resembling the revolutionary regimes of pre-1814. Within these limits, the states could evolve by their own volition.[55]

I suggest that it is this equilibration of ideological-political conflict and geopolitical interest that explains the determinate content of the concept of belligerent occupation. The debt to the experience of Napoleonic rule is apparent in *occupatio bellica*'s basic distinction between the occupant's authority and sovereign right, which presupposes the possibility of a clear demarcation between a sovereign, a state administration (falling into the hands of the occupant) and a people under occupation. Napoleonic rule was a 'major catalytic agent'[56] for the centralization and modernization of the state, and at efforts at sweeping away the institutional remnants of feudal society. In France, and to greater or lesser degrees in other polities that had come under Napoleonic rule, the social and material bases for a distinct legal conception of the state as a moral and juridical person were set in place: the model of a centrally controlled, hierarchical and uniform administration which assumed that 'the executive chain descends without interruption from the minister to the administered and transmits the law and the government's orders to the furthest ramifications of the social order'.[57]

By enjoining the occupant from changing the political order of the occupied territory, and by interdicting the legal transfer of sovereignty until the state of war was formally concluded, the legal category of belligerent occupation effectively facilitated the mediation of territorial and constitutional change. A state of war could not be concluded until all allies had ceased to fight on behalf of the state the territory of which was occupied, and hence, through the intermeshing web of alliances between Great Powers and smaller states, the negotiated concurrence or acquiescence of the Great Powers was a practical precondition for the appropriation of territory. The revolutionary transformation of the domestic order of a state through the intervention of another state was effectively bracketed, making possible the coexistence of two contradictory principles of political legitimacy – the dynastic and the popular democratic. The consolidation of territorial boundaries along 'national' lines over the course of the nineteenth century was equally compatible with occupation law's preservationist imperative, which could be interpreted retrospectively (and often was) as an embrace of the intrinsic connection between a peoples and their 'soil' and of their inherent right to determine their own political future. Similarly, the codification of the laws of land warfare aimed to revive classical international law's clear distinction between combatant and non-combatant, reflected in occupation law's delegitimation of civilian resistance (such as its circumscription of the *leveé en masse*) and its authorization of severe measures to deter partisan and irregular combatants.[58]

## TOWARDS TRANSFORMATIVE OCCUPATION: THE ANTINOMIES OF SOVEREIGN DICTATORSHIP

The law of belligerent occupation did not fare well in an epoch of total war. Mechanized aerial warfare, and the full engagement of a state's economy and society in the war effort made the distinctions between 'private property' and appropriate military objects unsustainable. The work and wealth of 'private' economic actors were indispensable to war production, and victory over another state that had placed its entire economy and society on a war-footing implied not just the defeat of its armed forces, but the debilitation of the state's institutional and economic capacities. Even if the occupying state did not expressly aim to overthrow the enemy's social order, it was hard to imagine that the order would survive the measures necessary to bring about defeat. World War I shattered what remained of the Vienna settlement, and led to a peace settlement which consciously revised external territorial boundaries while internal constitutional revolutions remade political systems across Central and Eastern Europe. At the same time, the 'well-ordered police state' of the nineteenth century had given way to a range of interventionist state-forms, from social democracy to fascism and communism, blurring or collapsing altogether the presumption of 'state' and 'state-free' society on which occupation law was based.

By the middle of the twentieth century, and in the wake of a second total war that transformed economies and societies, jurists wrote with some scepticism about the concrete determinacy and relevance of the idea of *occupatio bellica*. Feilchenfeld commented that the 'old rules' were essentially defunct by 1914, and that the only reason they were not denounced between 1918 and 1935 was 'they were not tested again through major occupations resulting from major wars'.[59] Stone similarly noted that the social, economic and political foundations for the institution of belligerent occupation had disappeared,[60] but concluded that the rules survived 'as a result of two contending imperatives: Allies concern in both world wars to fix Germany with guilty violations of the rules, and Germany's desire ... to exploit the great leeways for occupation *machtpolitik* left by the rules'.[61] It was widely accepted that new political orders imposed by the US on Germany and Japan entailed an exercise of power which exceeded the bounds of occupation law.[62] The conclusive considerations justifying the exercise of this power were self-evidently not legal, but political: the turning of former enemies into allies, and their economic and political re-integration into the emergent 'Western bloc' of anti-communist states. The factual circumstances which made possible this exercise of sovereign power (equivalent to conquest, but without annexation) were inherent in the aftermath of total war and total defeat. Germany was reduced to a condition of *debellatio*, in which its state institutions and constitutional order were destroyed and its population exhausted and demoralized. Japan's institutional continuity was preserved, but the capitulation of the Emperor, the exhaustion of the populace and the shadow of nuclear annihilation assured the cooperation of political elites. Thus, in both cases, the exercise of sovereign power by a foreign state was rooted firmly in the completeness of the subordination achieved over the defeated territory and the acquiescence of its inhabitants.

The humanitarian concerns encoded in occupation law were reaffirmed and strengthened in the Fourth Geneva Convention of 1949, which specifically prohibited certain kinds of violence against civilians (such as reprisals and hostage-taking) that had previously been accepted under the law of war.[63] But the preservationist principle at the heart of occupation law seemed particularly anachronistic in light of the new geopolitical landscape after World War II, in which the antagonists oversaw two 'large areas' within which their respective economic and political principles were applied and upheld. In this environment, as Stalin recognized with brutal clarity, 'whoever occupies a territory also imposes on it his own social system. Everyone imposes his own system as far as his army can reach.'[64] The law of occupation was redundant, in a sense, because there was no longer a single spatial order within which competing principles of legitimacy had to be mediated. There was instead a global order of two domains, and a series of proxy confrontations in the hinterlands of each. Neither power considered its interventions within its own *Grössraumen* as 'occupations', relying instead on 'invitations' from local political forces and other kinds of indirect control. Perhaps wary of a *tu quoque*, the Cold War powers do not appear to have actively resuscitated the notion of belligerent occupation even in respect of their adversary's conduct: if the Soviet Army in Budapest and Prague was an 'army of occupation', so too was the US military presence in Saigon and Seoul. Roberts noted in 1985 that the plurality of kinds of intervention undertaken during the Cold War, and the reluctance to invoke the law of occupation, led the category to lose much of its determinacy as a concept capable of clear application.[65]

Security Council Resolution 1483 expressly recognized the US and UK as 'occupying powers' in Iraq,[66] and required them to comply 'fully with their obligations under international law including in particular the Geneva Conventions of 1949 and the Hague Regulations of 1907'.[67] The Security Council resolution's declaration of the applicability of the law of occupation to the situation in Iraq returned the question of the content of *occupatio bellica* to the centre of international politics. Resolutions authorizing peacekeeping and 'state-building' missions under international auspices throughout the 1990s had been conspicuously silent on the application of occupation law, an implicit recognition that the emergent phenomenon of 'internationalised transitional administration' could not be subsumed under the laws of belligerent occupation.[68] The Security Council's explicit reference to occupation law in Resolution 1483 could thus be interpreted as an effort at restraining the occupant's authority to undertake unilaterally a 'transformative occupation', and careful legal analyses have offered persuasive reasons to construe the resolution as not entitling the US and UK to derogate from the preservationist core of occupation law.[69]

But the Security Council resolutions are also political documents, expressing a *modus vivendi* between the US and UK, and the Security Council permanent members which had strongly opposed the war.[70] Hence, Security Council Resolutions 1483 and 1500 are sufficiently ambiguous to permit a colourable claim of legitimation – if not legalization – of the idea that the occupying power is authorized, in the interests of the population, to exceed its order-preserving functions and embark on a project of state-building. The resolutions exhorted, without specifically mandating, the occupying powers to set in motion (with the 'advice' and 'assistance' of the UN Special Representative) a process for the formation of a new political and economic order, including the establishment of 'national and local institutions of representative government', the promotion of 'economic reconstruction and the conditions for sustainable development' and the promotion of 'legal and judicial reform'.[71] The claimed legitimacy of imposing a new institutional and constitutional structure was also strengthened by the emergent practice of the international administration of territories that has emerged since the end of the Cold War.

In Cambodia, Bosnia-Herzegovina, Kosovo and East Timor, treaties or Security Council resolutions established internationalized administrations which undertook to exercise, to a significant degree, sovereign powers over the territories in question.[72] These genuinely international governance structures were not completely subordinate to the controlling power and financial resources of one state – as in the case of the US occupation of Iraq – and thus may be optimistically regarded as exemplifying the mediation of interest-driven power politics through international law and multilateral institutions.[73] However, their emergence also coincided with a renewed willingness to consider some states or territories as properly subject to international tutelage or undeserving of full sovereign equality – either because of their undemocratic government or their 'rogue status' as persistent violators of international law (or both).[74] By the time the terrorist attacks of 11 September 2001 induced a 'forward-leaning' posture in favour of military intervention and 'regime change', both the ideological and technical-practical bases for 'transformative occupation' were well developed.

The US made it clear early in the occupation that *it* would determine the proper allocation of competences and roles in the transformation of Iraq, rejecting any substantial political coordination or oversight function for the UN[75] and 'retaining something akin to plenary power within the transition; if a controversy were to arise as to which component of the transition is properly to perform some specific function, it would seem to be [the occupying power's] task definitively to allocate competence'.[76] In other words, the final power of decision over the form and substance of the transitional process was retained by the US-controlled Coalition Provisional Authority (CPA). The CPA exercised this power of decision extensively, promulgating hundreds of orders and regulations which went far beyond the exigencies of preserving order and ensuring compliance with international law. As Fox has documented in his detailed review of the scope of CPA legislation, the occupying powers sought radically to remake economic life in Iraq and completely retrench the established role of the state in production and distribution of goods and services.[77]

The CPA established and appointed the Interim Governing Council (IGC) as an Iraqi organ of 'interim administration', but the IGC lacked both decision-making and implementation powers, and its legislative proposals were subject to CPA veto. Feldman recalls that '[t]he Governing Council governed no-one. Its "decisions" were more in the nature of recommendations. While it named technocrat transitional ministers to run Iraq's various ministries, the Governing Council [had] little or no say in the ministries' day-to-day operations.'[78] Under the shadow of the CPA's veto, the IGC negotiated the Transitional Administrative Law (TAL) but lacked the legal or political representative capacity to proclaim or enforce it as an 'interim constitution'. In the days before the dissolution of the CPA and formation of a (CPA-appointed) 'interim government' under Ayad Allawi, the CPA issued orders addressing the post-occupation period, which stipulated critical political procedures such as the electoral law, the political parties law and criteria disqualifying individuals from holding political office. All rules and orders created by the CPA were maintained in force by the TAL, and can only be overturned by a politically cumbersome 'opt-out' procedure.[79]

The real constituent power behind the creation of the new Iraqi political system – and the sole arbiter of exceptions to it – was the United States.[80] It would appear that the US invasion of Iraq has revived the category of *occupatio bellica*, but not the essential distinction between sovereign power and occupant authority. Rather, through its effective exercise of political power in multilateral fora such as the Security Council, the US obtained a reasonable degree of international acquiescence in its project for 'transformative occupation'. It carved a space in which the exercise of sovereign power over Iraq was, if not mandated, then tolerated, by the European bloc which had strongly opposed the war. The concrete result was that the US achieved a relatively free hand, at the international level, to exceed the limits imposed by the conservationist principle of occupation law. In its transformative vision, the military occupation of Iraq shifted from a category analogous to commissarial dictatorship, to one which approximated a sovereign dictatorship, wielding plenary power to institute a new constitution, both formal and material.

Like a sovereign dictatorship, transformative occupation exceeds the legal order that authorizes its provisional assumption of control, in the name of 'a new and better order'. It derives its legitimacy, in other words, from *the promise of the order to come*, a horizon of expectation that is invoked to relativize the legal rules which bind it in the present. The occupying power as sovereign dictator essentially undertakes a gamble, in which the illegality of the present will become moot or even cured by the concrete legitimacy of the future order: *ex factis jus oritur*, or as Machiavelli put it, 'when the act accuses him, the result should excuse him'. However, because the 'concrete success' to which the military occupant *qua* sovereign dictator is oriented is nothing less than the concretization of a new political order, he assumes a much greater burden than simple military victory: he must bring about a certain quality of subordination, under which conditions receptive to the fostering of a new order can take root. As noted above, in the case of Japan and Germany, this degree of subordination was achieved by exhaustion or acquiescence.

The dilemma of attempting to exercise constituent power through military occupation arises from the reality that, in the last instance, the occupant's authority derives from pure facticity – something well recognized by the jurists who rationalized and refined the nineteenth-century concept of belligerent occupation. The occupant's ability to legitimate a new order in place of the old depends on his capacity to engender among the occupied population the belief, *post facto*, in the legitimacy of the occupant's 'naked power' as a precondition for the new basic norm to which the occupied is subjected. To the extent that the occupant is rendered incapable of normalizing its constitutive coercion – and thus allowing the coercion to become less visible – it continues to inhabit a 'zone of risk' in which its capacity to produce a firm basis for political legitimation is either static or constantly diminishing.

According to a recent military inquiry, there were 15,257 attacks against coalition forces throughout Iraq between July 2004 and March 2005.[81] The success of the insurgency in Iraq has been to prevent the consolidation of normality, and thus to constrain the occupant's opportunity to create the conditions under which its imposition will be acquiesced to. The resistance, aided in no small part by the occupying power's failure to undertake effective advance planning to restore services and guarantee security, has successfully employed the two-fold tactic of compelling occupying forces to treat the occupied population as the enemy, and encouraging the alienation of the population from both the occupant and the political structures which the occupation has created. The invisibility and indistinguishability of the 'terrorist' or insurgent from the general population, and the devastating effectiveness of terrorist bombings, invites counter-terror from the occupant – whether in the form of widespread arbitrary detention, torture (in a desperate effort to make the invisible visible and penetrate the opacity of the insurgent enemy) or highly intrusive raids and searches. The insurgent cannot function without the consent or acquiescence of the occupied population,[82] and thus the occupant tries to cleave combatant from non-combatant by raising the costs of non-cooperation with the occupier.[83] But in so doing, the occupant forces the population to *choose who it regards as the real enemy*.

The structure of the relationship between occupant and insurgent is thus the structure of a gamble, in which the strategy of the insurgent is a kind of mirror of the occupant's response. The insurgent also tries to raise the costs of collaboration and so deny the multiplication of sites and opportunities in which the population might be encouraged to accept the constitutive coercion of the occupier. Instead, the insurgent seeks to coerce a different, thinner, kind of acquiescence: a depoliticization and reluctance to make political decisions, bred by constant insecurity, fear of both sides and perpetual abnormality.[84] The insurgent tactic of attacking essential infrastructure, in order to disrupt reconstruction and the restoration of essential services, can be seen as forming part of a strategy of ensuring a permanent state of abnormality[85] so as to prevent an exit from the occupant's state of exception. The coercive power of the occupant can thus never recede into the background, but is always visible and present – a constant reminder of the foreign provenance of the new political environment. As long as such a condition persists, the insurgent does not necessarily win, but the occupant cannot but lose. As Chalmers Johnson recognized in 1962, 'the willingness of the population to support the insurgent 'is not necessarily related to the ultimate goals of the guerilla leadership … . The population will support the guerillas if it is convinced that the guerrillas are operating effectively against the enemies of the people.'[86]

## CONCLUSION

The US experiment with sovereign dictatorship in Iraq has clearly failed to create and stabilize a new order. Many historical and political factors have contributed to this failure, but I have argued that using a military occupation as a vehicle for democratic imposition is by its very nature contradictory and fraught with a high risk of failure. The success of transformative occupation is precariously dependent on the quality of the subordination that it achieves over the occupied territory, and the military occupier *qua* sovereign dictator therefore locates itself in a paradox: it has to subordinate before it can legitimate effectively, and the more it tries to subordinate, the harder becomes the legitimation. An interview study conducted in July 2003 revealed a deep mistrust of US intentions among the Iraqi population,[87] but a willingness to cooperate for a limited period of time, provided concrete improvements in daily life (such as security and essential services) were forthcoming. This narrow window of opportunity for cooperative stabilization quickly closed.

The profound difficulties encountered by the US in realizing its vision of 'transformative occupation' has put radically into question whether the legal recognition of such a notion is either desirable or useful. I contended in the first half of this chapter that the law of belligerent occupation is indeed inappropriate for situations in which the occupant wishes to exercise sovereign power and remake the state, having its origins in the stabilization of the nineteenth-century European order. By maintaining attempts at 'transformative occupation' as outside legality and within the realm of sheer political power, we are of course unlikely to impose any real constraint on those states that possess substantial political power. But at the same time, we maintain one of the most important legacies of the nineteenth-century legal order: the formal sovereign equality of states, and a (formal) rejection of any one state's legal entitlement to impose a single model of political order. Just as the concept of *occupatio bellica* crystallized in the conflict between the dynastic and the popular-sovereign principles of political legitimacy, it seems that the future content of the law of occupation is hinged between imperial democratization (and the supporting framework of liberal anti-pluralism) and the pluralistic notion of nation-state self-determination.

## NOTES

1  Thomas Baty, 'The Relations of Invaders to Insurgents', *Yale Law Journal* 36 (May 1927): 966–84, 983.
2  See Nehal Bhuta, 'A Global State of Exception? The United States and World Order', *Constellations* 10 (September 2003): 371–91, at 372.
3  During the Security Council debate concerning the use of force against Iraq (open to Security Council members as well as non-members) convened on 26 and 27 March 2003, the 'overwhelming majority' of states condemned the US attack as illegal and called on the Security Council to 'end the illegal aggression'; UN Press Release SC/7705, 4726th meeting, 26 March 2003.
4  After an initial reluctance to refer to the presence of their military forces in Iraq as constituting an 'occupation', the US and UK representatives to the United Nations notified the Security Council that their respective countries considered that the international laws of belligerent occupation applied: *Letter Dated 8 May 2003 from the Permanent Representatives of the United Kingdom of Great Britain and Northern Ireland and the United States of America to the United Nations Addressed to the President of the Security Council*, UN Doc. S/2003/538 (2003). This legal position was confirmed by the Security Council in Resolution 1483 of 22 May 2003: UN Doc. S/RES/1483 (2003).
5  Simon Chesterman, 'Occupation as Liberation: International Humanitarian Law and Regime Change', *Ethics and International Affairs* 18 (2004): 51–64, 51; Eyal Benvenisti, *The International Law of Occupation* (Princeton, NJ: Princeton University Press, 2004 [1993]), ix–xiv, 149.
6  See generally Adam Roberts, 'What is a Military Occupation?', *British Yearbook of International Law* 55 (1985): 249–305.
7  David Scheffer, 'Beyond Occupation Law', *American Journal of International Law* 97 (October 2003): 842–60, 842; Benvenisti, *The International Law of Occupation*, viii.
8  See, for example, the cases of Bosnia-Herzegovina, Kosovo and East Timor, discussed in Simon Chesterman, *You, the People: The United Nations, Transitional Administration and State-Building* (Oxford: Oxford University Press, 2004), Chapters 1–2.
9  Scheffer, 'Beyond Occupation Law', 849. For evidence concerning an earlier effort to induce a 'leap into robust capitalism', see Robert Service, *Russia: Experiment with a People, from 1991 to the Present* (London: Macmillan, 2002).

10   Gerry Simpson, *Great Powers and Outlaw States: Unequal Sovereigns in the International Legal Order* (Cambridge: Cambridge University Press, 2003), 55, 299–316.

11   See generally UN Charter, Articles 2(4) and 51; Declaration on Principles of International Law Concerning Friendly Relations and Co-operation among States in accordance with the Charter of the United Nations, GA res. 2625, Annex, 25 UN GAOR, Supp. (No. 28), UN Doc. A/5217 at 121 (1970).

12   Sharon Korman, *The Right of Conquest: The Acquisition of Territory by Force in International Law* (Oxford: Clarendon Press, 1996), 8–9; Hans Kelsen, *General Theory of Law and State* (New York: Russell and Russell, 1961), 215; Friedrich August Freiherr von der Heydte, 'Discovery, Symbolic Annexation and Virtual Effectiveness in International Law', *American Journal of International Law* 29 (1935): 446–71, 448, 450. J. H. W. Verzijl, *International Law in Historical Perspective – Part IXA, The Laws of War* (Utrecht: Sijthoff and Noordhoff, 1978), 151.

13   E. Vattel, *The Law of Nations* (Philadelphia: J. W. Johnson, 1849 [1758]), Bk. III, Ch. XIII. At §200, Vattel differentiates between the property of the defeated sovereign and the property of 'private individuals'. The former may be seized by the conqueror, but not the latter; private individuals owe the conqueror their allegiance to the new order he imposes. Schmitt notes that European wars of the seventeenth and eighteenth centuries were pursued largely as wars of succession. The eighteenth-century occupier took the place of the former sovereign, but 'largely left in tact the former law, in particular private law and the societal structure as a whole'. Carl Schmitt, *The Nomos of the Earth in the International Law of the Jus Publicum Europaeum*, trans. G. L. Ulmen (New York: Telos, 2003), 201.

14   Verzijl, *International Law in Historical Perspective*, 151.

15   Lassa Oppenheim, *International Law: A Treatise, Volume 2: War, Peace and Neutrality*, ed. Hersh Lauterpacht, 5th edition (London and New York: Longmans, 1935), 344.

16   W. E. Hall, *A Treatise on International Law* (Oxford: Clarendon Press, 1884), 444; 'Actes de la Conférnce Réuni à Bruxelles, du 27 Juillet au 27 Août 1874, pour Régler les Lois et Coûtumes de la Guerre', *Nouveau Recueil Général de Traités*, 2nd series, 1879–80, IV, 219–24, Article 41 (the Brussels Declaration); 'Cinquième Commission – Réglementation des Lois et Coutumes de la Guerre', *Annuaire de l'Institut de Droit International* 5 (1881): 159–70 (the Oxford Code), Articles 6, 41; Convention (II) with Respect to the Laws and Customs of War on Land and its annex: Regulations concerning the Laws and Customs of War on Land. The Hague, 29 July 1899, Articles 42–3 (The Hague Convention of 1899); Convention (IV) respecting the Laws and Customs of War on Land and its annex: Regulations concerning the Laws and Customs of War on Land. The Hague, 18 October 1907, Articles 42–3 (The Hague Convention of 1907).

17   Verzijl, *International Law in Historical Perspective*, 470, 480; Benvenisti, *The International Law of Occupation*, 92–3; Roberts, 'What is Military Occupation?' 267–88.

18  T. Funck-Brentano and Albert Sorel, *Précis du Droit des Gens* (1877), quoted in Doris Graber, *The Development of the Law of Belligerent Occupation, 1863–1914* (New York: Columbia University Press, 1949), 50.

19  Hall, *A Treatise on International Law*, 444. See the Brussels Declaration, Article 1, the Oxford Code, Articles 6, 41; The Hague Conventions of 1899 and 1907, Article 42.

20  The Brussels Declaration, Articles 6, 38; the Oxford Code, Articles 1, 49, 54; The Hague Conventions of 1899 and 1907, Articles 23(g) (h), 46, 53.

21  The Hague Conventions of 1899 and 1907, Article 43.

22  See Graber, *The Development of the Law of Belligerent Occupation*, 124–53; Gerhard von Glahn, *The Occupation of Enemy Territory* (Minneapolis: University of Minnesota, 1957), 276.

23  Schmitt, *The Nomos of the Earth*, 206.

24  Julius Stone, *Legal Controls of International Conflict* (New York: Rinehart, 1954), 723; von Glahn, *The Occupation of Enemy Territory*, 34, 234.

25  Ernst Fraenkel, *Military Occupation and the Rule of Law: Occupation Government in the Rhineland, 1918–1923* (Oxford: Oxford University Press, 1944), 194–5.

26  US War Department, Instructions for the Government of Armies of the United States in the Field, General Orders No. 100 (24 April 1863), Articles. 1–4; Hall, *A Treatise on International Law*, 431 n 2; H. de Watteville, 'The Military Administration of Occupied Territory in Time of War', *Transactions of the Grotius Society* 7 (1921): 133, 143. Lieber's code, considered the first effort to codify and apply the law of belligerent occupation, was famously applied by the Union army during the US Civil War. The concept of 'military necessity' (defined by Lieber in his code), was also invoked by Abraham Lincoln in domestic political environment, to justify the expansion of presidential powers at the expense of the legislature: see Andrew Arato, *A Conceptual History of Dictatorship and its Rivals*, manuscript of 23 June 2003, 26. My thanks to Professor Arato for providing me with a draft of this book.

27  von Glahn, *The Occupation of Enemy Territory*, 265.

28  Carl Schmitt, *Die Diktatur*, quoted in John P. McCormick, *Carl Schmitt's Critique of Liberalism* (Chicago: University of Chicago Press, 1999), 124.

29  Schmitt, *The Nomos of the Earth*, 207.

30  Military necessity in the first half of the twentieth century was the rule under which, subject to the principles of humanity and chivalry, a belligerent was justified in applying any amount and any kind of force to compel the complete submission of the enemy with the least possible expenditure of time, life and money: US Army Field Manual, 1940. Similarly, in *New Orleans v. Steamship Co.*, 20 Wallace 387, the US Supreme Court held that 'the occupying power … may do anything necessary to strengthen itself and weaken the enemy. There is no limit to the powers that may be exercised in such cases, save those which are found in the laws and usages of war.'

31  von Glahn, *The Occupation of Enemy Territory*, 265.

32  E. Feilchenfeld, *The International Economic Law of Belligerent Occupation* (Washington, DC: Carnegie Endowment, 1942), 86.

33  H. R. Droop, 'On the Relations between an Invading Army and the Inhabitants', *Papers Read before the Juridical Society* 3 (1871): 705–24.

34  Spaight, *Rights of War on Land*, 323. As Nabulsi comments, the notion of military necessity was invoked by all nineteenth-century military occupiers to justify a variety of punitive measures against inhabitants: Karma Nabulsi, *Traditions of War: Occupation, Resistance and the Law* (Oxford: Oxford University Press, 1999), 29–30.

35  See, for example, US Army Field Manual, 1940, Art. 358(d), permitting the taking and execution of hostages to prevent assassination of members of the occupying forces. Similar provisions can be found in the early twentieth-century military manuals of Great Britain and France. Spaight, *Rights of War on Land*, 349–50; Stone, *Legal Controls of International Conflict*, 702.

36  Most of these measures have now been specifically proscribed by the 1949 Geneva Conventions.

37  von Glahn, *The Occupation of Enemy Territory*, 264; de Watteville, 'The Military Administration of Occupied Territory in Time of War', 150.

38  Ralph Gabriel, 'The American Experience with Military Government', *American Political Science Review* 37 (1943): 417, 437. Davidonis comments that the 'logical conclusion' of the principle of military necessity was an enlargement of the occupant's powers, particularly where the inhabitants of occupied territory are not 'docile': A. C. Davidonis, 'Some Problems of Military Government', *American Political Science Review* 38 (1944): 460, 470–2.

39  McCormick, *Carl Schmitt's Critique of Liberalism*, 130; Arato, *A Conceptual History of Dictatorship*, 44.

40  Arato, *A Conceptual History of Dictatorship*, 2.

41  Martti Koskenniemi, *The Gentle Civilizer of Nations: The Rise and Fall of International Law, 1870–1960* (Cambridge: Cambridge University Press, 2001).

42  Paul Schroeder, *The Transformation of European Politics, 1763–1848* (Oxford: Oxford University Press, 1994), 9; Anthony Anghie, 'Finding the Peripheries: Sovereignty and Colonialism in Nineteenth Century International Law', *Harvard International Law Journal* 40 (Winter 1999): 1.

43  Korman, *The Right of Conquest*, 56, 61.

44  Baty, 'The Relations of Invaders to Insurgents', 973. See also Chatterjee's fascinating account of the British annexation of Awadh: Partha Chatterjee, 'Empire after Globalization', *Economic and Political Weekly* (11 September 2004).

45  Graber, *The Development of the Law of Belligerent Occupation*, 133.

46  Schmitt, *The Nomos of the Earth*, citing Martens, 215.

47  Graber, *The Development of the Law of Belligerent Occupation*, 258, n.1.

48  Feilchenfeld, *The International Economic Law of Belligerent Occupation*, 10–11, 25.

49  Koselleck, 'On the Anthropological and Semantic Structure of *Bildung*', in *The Practice of Conceptual History: Timing History, Spacing Concepts* (Stanford, CA: Stanford University Press, 2002), 171–207.

50  Walter Langsam, *The Napoleonic Wars and German Nationalism in Austria* (New York: Columbia University Press, 1930), 19.

51  Ibid., 93.

52  David Laven and Lucy Riall, 'Restoration Government and the Legacy of Napoleon', in David Laven and Lucy Riall (eds.), *Napoleon's Legacy: Problems of Government in Restoration Europe* (New York: Berg, 2000), 6.

53  Hahlweg, cited in Carl Schmitt, *Theory of the Partisan* (1965), translated in *Telos* 127 (Spring 2004): 11–73, 41. For further evidence of military concern at the emergence of partisan warfare, and the threat it represented for standing armies, see Nabulsi, *Traditions of War*, chs. 2–4.

54  Michael Broers, *Europe after Napoleon: Revolution, Reaction and Romanticism, 1814–1848* (Manchester: Manchester University Press, 1996), 13.

55  Broers, *Europe after Napoleon*, 11.

56  Ibid., 379.

57  Laven and Riall, 'Restoration Government and the Legacy of Napoleon', 2; Michael John, 'The Napoleonic Legacy and Problems of Restoration in Central Europe: The German Confederation', in Laven and Riall (eds.), *Napoleon's Legacy: Problems of Government in Restoration Europe*, 83–96.

58  See Nabulsi, *Traditions of War*, 21–36; and Droop, 'On the Relations between an Invading Army and the Inhabitants'.

59  Feilchenfeld, *The International Economic Law of Belligerent Occupation*, 23.

60  Stone, *Legal Controls on International Conflict*, 727.

61  Ibid.

62  See, e.g., Hans Kelsen, 'The Legal Status of Germany According to the Declaration of Berlin', *American Journal of International Law* 39 (1945): 518–26, 518; and von Glahn, *The Occupation of Enemy Territory*, ch. 21; Benvenisti, *The International Law of Occupation*, 93; Roberts, 'What is Military Occupation?', 269–71.

63  Geneva Convention relative to the Protection of Civilian Persons in Time of War, 75 U.N.T.S. 287, *entered into force* 21 October 1950.

64  Stalin, quoted in Chesterman, 'Occupation as Liberation', 51.

65  Roberts, 'What is Military Occupation?', 299–301.

66  Securing Council Resolution 1483, UN SCOR, 58th Sess., 4761st mtg., U.N. Doc. S/RES/1483 (2003).

67  Ibid., para. 5.

68  Chesterman, *You, the People*, 7. Scheffer, 'Beyond Occupation Law', 852.

69  See Gregory Fox, 'The Occupation of Iraq', *Georgetown Journal of International Law* 36 (April 2005); and Marco Sassoli, 'Legislation and the Maintenance of Public Order and Civil Life by Occupying Powers', forthcoming, *European Journal of International Law*.

70  Thomas D. Grant, 'The Security Council and Iraq: An Incremental Practice', *American Journal of International Law* 97 (October 2003): 823–42, 823, 827.

71  Security Council Resolution 1483, para. 8.

72  See generally Chesterman, *You, the People*.

73  Although as Chesterman notes, for the most part these administrations created new orders through forms of imposition, with greater or lesser degrees of local elite involvement: ibid., 239.

74  Simpson, *Great Powers and Rogue States*, ch. 10; Jose Alvarez, 'Hegemonic International Law Revisited', *American Journal of International Law* 97 (October 2003): 873–88, 873; Alexandros Yannis, 'The Concept of

Suspended Sovereignty in International Law and its Implications in International Politics', *European Journal of International Law* 13 (November 2002): 1037–52, 1040–2.

75 Larry Diamond, 'What Went Wrong in Iraq', *Foreign Affairs* 83 (September/October 2004): 34–56, 46–7.

76 Grant, 'The Security Council and Iraq', 853.

77 Fox, 'The Occupation of Iraq', 16–22.

78 Noah Feldman, *What We Owe Iraq* (Princeton, NJ: Princeton University Press, 2004), 110. See also Larry Diamond, 'Lessons from Iraq', *Journal of Democracy* 16 (2005): 9–23.

79 Transitional Administrative Law, Article 26(C).

80 For a detailed recounting of the ways in which the US controlled the evolution of the transitional political framework in Iraq, and of its decisive capacity to change the direction of that framework in accordance with its needs to manage crises, see Andrew Arato, 'Interim Imposition', *Ethics and International Affairs* 18 (2004): 25–50; and Andrew Arato, 'Bush v. Sistani', *Constellations* 11 (June, 2004): 174–92.

81 Report of Inquiry into the death of Nicola Calipari, 2 May 2005.

82 Chalmers Johnson, 'Civilian Loyalties and Guerilla Conflict', *World Politics* 14 (July 1962): 646–61.

83 For example, the rationale for aerial bombardment of 'terrorist safehouses' in Fallujah in October 2004 was explained as follows: ' "If there are civilians dying in connection with these attacks, and with the destruction, the locals at some point have to make a decision", one Pentagon official said, "Do they want to harbor the insurgents and suffer the consequences that come with that, or do they want to get rid of the insurgents and have the benefits of not having them there?" ' Thom Shanker and Eric Schmitt, 'Terror Command in Falluja is Half Destroyed', *New York Times* (13 October 2004). See also Michael Walzer, *Just and Unjust Wars: A Moral Argument with Historical Illustrations* (New York: Basic Books, 1977), 189–93.

84 See, e.g., Sabrina Tavernise, 'Iraq's Violence Sweeps Away All Norms', *New York Times* (6 May 2005), A1.

85 Ahmed S. Hashim, 'Iraq's Chaos: Why the Insurgency Won't Go Away', *Boston Review* (May 2004), http://bostonreview.net/BR29.5/hashim.html.

86 Johnson, 'Civilian Loyalties', 657.

87 International Center for Transitional Justice and Human Rights Center, University of California at Berkeley, *Iraqi Voices: Iraqi Attitudes Towards Transitional Justice and Social Reconstruction* (May 2004). The author was a co-investigator and author of the report.

# 11

# Empire's Democracy, Ours and Theirs

*Andrew Arato*

## THE CONFISCATION OF DEMOCRACY

We must recover and repossess our democratic discourse and our democratic politics, which have been confiscated, taken over, co-opted, instrumentalized in an imperial project. The world today is not an empire, not yet in any case. As Jean Cohen has argued, the global legal political order is an uneasy and highly conflictual combination of two principles: international law and a new type of imperial hegemony.[1] I speak of hegemony because there is no question of directly dominating most of what the remaining superpower hopes effectively to control or strongly influence. I call it imperial because of that superpower's extreme solicitude for its own sovereignty, coupled with its cavalier and aggressive attitude to the sovereignty of all others.[2] I insist on a struggle between two principles, because international law, while not a 'legal order', remains a reality, however threatened, and international organizations and regulations repeatedly stand in the way of imperial aspirations on both symbolic and policy-making levels.

During the late Cold War period and in the years immediately following, 'democratization' belonged to the world of international law, with its key concept of sovereign equality. Not only were international agreements used to promote democratic change, and occasionally as sanctions against dictatorships, but new democracies sought to recover their sovereignty with respect to the two superpowers, Central and East Europe from the Soviet Union and Latin America from the United States. The international organizations they sought to join or revitalize, the European Union and the Organization of American States, were, on balance, sovereignty-enhancing. Even today this trend continues to some extent, as the recent cases of Georgia and the Ukraine show. Of course, even in that epoch democratization was both an internal and an external political matter. From the 1970s in Spain and Portugal to the most recent cases,

democratization involved significant outside influence or even
'intervention' – positive and, in the case of Gorbachev's withdrawal of
support from some ruling communist parties, negative. Nevertheless,
two salient facts characterized the outside–inside relationship: interventions were soft in the sense of remaining well within the UN
Charter which bans aggressive wars, even wars of liberation; and liberation and regime change were achieved on the whole by internal
reformist, (most often) radical civil society or (rarely) revolutionary
forces.

The war in Iraq and subsequent developments in that country
indicate that we have entered a new period where international law
is no longer the primary framework or reference point for democratization projects. Indeed, the war occurred in the clearest possible
violation of the UN Charter,[3] one opposed moreover by the
immense majority of citizens and governments the world over. In
Iraq liberation was not endogenous, and, so far at least, neither
was regime change: they were both externally imposed.[4] Even
Afghanistan, after a Security Council Article 53 authorized war, with
the Northern Alliance doing the bulk of the fighting and international organizations (UN and EU) deeply involved in the political
transition, turned out to be a transitional case. Iraq is a clear sign of
something new, but it is not the only sign.

For almost four years foreign policy pronouncements from the
US Administration have been repeatedly and increasingly clothed
in the language of democracy, human rights, quite often civil society and even women's rights. While the invasion of Iraq was initially justified (illogically and mendaciously) more in terms of the
fear of weapons of mass destruction (WMD), here too the minor
motif, democratic regime change, has long since become the primary one. Since the motivations of all states can always be
assumed to be primarily *raison d'état*, or, as here, particular political,
i.e. sub-state, interests, it is useless to point out that the real reasons
for the war were different: geopolitical, institutional, party-political,
or their likely combination. The ideology of justification carries its
own particular force, especially where people suffer from dictatorships or have been recently emancipated from such rule. Given
the self-image of the Americans, and a shared reading of their
history across the political spectrum as a shining city on a hill, a
beacon to all others, the power of this language over both ordinary citizens and intellectual strata in the US should never be
underestimated.

Thus, the recently announced 'struggle against tyranny', to many Europeans the seemingly pathetic successor to the failed Bush Doctrine, and the mere renaming of the ongoing 'war against terror', represent the most powerful challenge to all those to whom the norms and values of democracy, human rights, civil society and the public sphere remain the unsurpassable ideals of the present historical epoch (the 'us', 'we', 'our' and 'ours' of this chapter). While the illegal and, on the whole, unjustifiable military intervention in Iraq already tested *us*, the defining feature of that adventure, the use of military force and its disastrous consequences, still allowed perhaps the majority of the veterans of recent struggles to draw a line between the *imperial* democratization project and *ours*. But now, when military force is, at least for the moment, no longer readily available for imperial democratization, we have every reason to expect that there will be an attempt that is far more extensive and determined than any before to alienate and instrumentalize the soft power and soft forms of intervention of civil society organizations.[5] Indeed, this has already happened in the midst of the hard intervention in Iraq.[6]

One possible response to alienation and instrumentalization is to leave the field and tacitly concede to the other side the whole complex range of issues connected to political democracy. Not only do I believe that we ought not to concede defeat for very valid normative reasons, however – because our democracy is democratic and the imperial one is not – I also believe that we can win both the battle of ideas and influence over the relevant political processes. I would like to show this in the hardest possible case of Iraq, where 'we' were only marginally present as an independent set of actors, where the imperial project could rely on all possible instruments at its disposal: hard as well as soft power of every conceivable variety. My thesis, based on the study of the Iraq adventure, is that we can win only if we recognize that three democracies rather than two are struggling for control of the shared political meanings: *imperial* democracy, *our* liberal democracy and *their* autonomous but not necessarily liberal democracy. Whatever success the imperial project of externally imposed democracy has had so far, it depended on a split on our side between *imperial* liberals and *anti-imperial* democrats, the latter of whom have more or less withdrawn from the field. Its defeat will depend not only on healing that split, but also on a new understanding, if not yet an alliance, between 'our' democracy and '*theirs*' – namely, of people and groups fighting for autonomy and self-government under various forms of authoritarian rule ranging from the old dictatorships to dictatorial impositions by the external power.

## OUR WEAKNESS AND THE PERFORMATIVE CONTRADICTION OF IMPERIAL DEMOCRATIZATION

We have been weak and indecisive in response to the crisis in Iraq because we faced the Scylla of instrumentalization and the Charybdis of passivity. All right, they said (to us, to governments, to the various NGOs, to the agencies of the UN), you opposed the war, but it happened. Are you not ready to do what you did elsewhere? Come to Iraq and help, not us, but the Iraqis, to develop and establish the institutions of democracy, of civil society, to make a constitution. Help us redeem even what you think is unredeemable. Luckily, in their desire to secure jobs for mostly incompetent clients and acolytes, they did not ask too many of our friends. Of those asked, some refused. Some who did not refuse, the imperial liberals, eventually produced peculiar *mea culpas* in book form. Some still feel self-righteous and deny having been used at all.

How difficult it was to get involved without being instrumentalized is shown by the particular case of Lakhdar Brahimi's UN missions to Iraq, whose chief of staff I had the opportunity of briefly, if informally, advising. After more or less fully disregarding the United Nations and paying only the slightest attention to Sergio di Mello before his tragic death, the US government suddenly needed the UN. The Grand Ayatollah Sistani was willing to accept the delay of elections in early 2004 only if so advised by a representative of the Secretary General. At a later date, the legitimacy of interim governmental arrangements depended on Brahimi's imprimatur, and, as I was directly told, the diplomat and his team were initially very determined not to accept a mere transmogrification of the US-appointed Governing Council as a supposedly sovereign interim government. Moreover, the team was very interested in dramatically expanding the bargaining process in Iraq, leading to a transitional formula, and it is regarding this problem area that I repeatedly offered advice based on Central European and South African models.

The first UN visit, the 'fact-finding mission' of February 2004, did not go badly.[7] In the conflict between the Americans and Sistani, Brahimi proposed a compromise formula that nevertheless put the

Iraqi elections, with their probable Shia victory, safely after the US elections. Equally important, his team, pushing towards the election of a single legislative and constitutional assembly, 'helped' Sistani quash the idea of creating an unelected, co-opted transitional legislature that would remain the seat of government through the making of the permanent constitution, through December 2005 at the very least. It was during the second and third visits, when in fact American dependence on Brahimi's activities was growing because of the US elections, that an independent UN role collapsed. Brahimi now accepted the American imposition of the Transitional Administrative Law (TAL), the interim constitution, although he sought rhetorically to play down its significance.[8] More fatefully, during the third visit in May 2004, he accepted the leading role of the Governing Council (GC) in establishing the interim government, its controlling role in organizing a (therefore) meaningless and unrepresentative national conference, and the prime ministership of Ayad Allawi, a prominent GC member reputedly close to the CIA.[9] Brahimi – and his sophisticated chief of staff, Jamal Benomar – clearly had the opportunity, because of Bush's electoral vulnerability, and certainly the diplomatic skills and superior knowledge of the situation, to obtain much more. Instead, they put up with their own instrumentalization without much complaining.[10]

Would it have been better to forget about Iraq altogether and not get involved, as the UN staff following di Mello's death would have liked? Or to try to support whatever force there attempted to throw the invaders out, no matter how ugly and dangerous? The latter option has been and remains almost unthinkable, and I don't know anyone belonging to the 'we' label of this chapter wanting the defeat of the Bush Administration to the extent of openly affirming it. The former option, however, was the choice of most European governments and intellectuals who had previously opposed the war. Thus, contrary to Afghanistan, the American government and its civil allies, mainly semi-independent NGOs, were more or less the only foreign actors that mattered in Iraq for the last two years, if we don't count the inexplicably weak representatives of the UN, who privately explain their weakness by the lack of support they had for an independent stance even from the governments that opposed the war. The international conference of key members of the Security Council with the representatives of Iraq and neighbouring countries at Sharm el Sheik held just before the US elections was a case in point. Such a meeting on Iraqi peace and security should have taken place much earlier, but in principle it was still a good idea – even if called for by the US government probably in part to counteract John Kerry's electoral complaint of unilateralism. Michel Barnier, the French Foreign Minister, quite sensibly proposed some conditions on participation, like the inclusion of hitherto excluded Iraqi actors and the discussion of a schedule for the withdrawal of foreign troops. I had the good fortune to be able to ask his German counterpart, Joschka Fischer (whom I would certainly include under the 'we' of this chapter), whether Germany would support this French initiative. To my surprise his answer was an unconditional no, thus ensuring that the conference would amount to absolutely nothing. Here there was no question of instrumentalization, because the US could gain very little by having a meaningless meeting culminating in empty declarations. Rather, Fischer expressed a desire to remain as passive as possible, to avoid doing anything that might, in Habermas's words, 'redeem the unredeemable'. One can understand that desire, but the passivity was nevertheless wrong. An opportunity to prepare the ground for a broader Iraqi compromise was lost – and not for the first or last time.

We should not, in our weakness however, imagine that the imperial project clothed in the language of democratization is itself all-powerful. Its own weakness lies in a fundamental performative contradiction. An empire, even an imperial project, cannot really afford democratic provinces. Democratic or even partly democratic states develop their internal and external policies in large or small part in response to internal actors, to whom they are to greater or lesser extents accountable. Depending on the circumstances, these policies can oppose those of the imperial or hegemonic power even if the states in question owe their liberation to that power. When the imperial state is a former or present occupier, the likelihood of conflict is even greater. Thus, the aim of imperial democratization is self-contradictory to the extent that it seeks *both* democracies *and* countries friendly to the US and its policies; the procedural goals are in conflict with the substantive ones.

Undoubtedly, in an Orwellian imperial system non-democracy could simply be renamed democracy. While there are efforts in this direction, it is obvious that under current conditions of international publicity a negative utopia where war could be renamed peace, and dictatorship democracy, is not in the cards. More to the point, in a more traditional imperial system, like the former British Empire, it would have been possible to resolve the contradiction through a variety of devices like colonial (partial) self-government formally deprived of the right to make foreign and defence policy or protectorates, where the dominance of the imperial centre is established through powerful, institutionalized informal mechanisms. Mandates and trusteeships gave recognition to these devices in international law. In our age, however, the duality of imperial and international law arrangements means precisely that such limits to internal sovereignty can receive at best only very temporary world recognition. The language of democratization, though mobilized for an imperial purpose, thus lands the bearers of the discourse in an international legal field that does not allow democracy to be openly replaced by its opposite. The democratic justification binds, at least to some extent, even those who use it in bad faith.

Instead of arguing this point in general, let me show how it works in the case of Iraq. Here it was possible for a supposedly democratizing external power to argue, even if in a mendacious way, that elections could not be organized at a given time, but not that they would have to be postponed indefinitely. Ayatollah Sistani's demand for elections to a constituent assembly could be thus deferred, but not entirely denied. It was only very late in the game that elections were 'spun' as a great victory for the American project. In the absence of any pressure from representatives of 'our' democracy, Sistani was and remains (I hope) a great example of a political actor who has seen the performative contradiction of the American project of imperial democratization – the conflict between the norm and the practice – and utilized it as much for the purpose of Iraqi autonomy as he could (and can). In my opinion, it is only because of the unexpectedly ferocious Sunni insurrection (stoked in part by American repression), with its anti-Shia violence, that Sistani has not (yet?) emerged as the nationalist leader who could end the occupation altogether. But in any case he managed to push through his elections and block (so far at least) the effort of American clients to steal it or to deform it entirely. The fight is not over as I write, because there is further opportunity for interference and deformation around the formation of a coalition government. Nevertheless, in principle, as I will argue, a very small window of opportunity is now open to Iraqi reconciliation and to ending the occupation.

What I am arguing for the moment, though, is that the democratic justification of the imperial venture also puts its proponents between a Scylla and a Charybdis, as illustrated by the case of Iraq. If they fail to establish something that looks like a democracy, they fail on the level of justification. This would interfere with other, similar future projects as presented in the 2005 Inauguration and State of the Union speeches with their invocations of struggles against tyranny. If they succeed to any extent, however, it is unlikely that they will get a friendly government or be able to stay and secure military bases, and they will thus fail in terms of their probable motives. Undoubtedly if they fail they will try to spin it as victory, in the sense that anything is better than Saddam. And if they are thrown out of Iraq, that too will be presented as a mark of incredible success. We, who hope to recover control of the discourse of democracy, must be ready in either event, to offer our alternative interpretation of the whole process of (failed) imposed democracy.

Unfortunately, however, we cannot, like the owl of Minerva, satisfy ourselves with such *post festum* diagnoses. A failed state or a purely majoritarian and entirely illiberal democracy in Iraq will not and should not fill us with any sense of triumph. There is still time to contribute to something better than either. We, like Sistani, must try to enter the performative contradictions of imperial democracy, and even those of autonomous democracy, hoping for a productive dialogue between our democracy and theirs.

## IMPOSING A DEMOCRACY?

Let us then look more closely at the performative contradiction(s) of 'imposed democracy' in the Iraqi case, comparing it with a few others. Is the external imposition of democracy possible? Is it ever justifiable? If it is not justifiable, why is it nevertheless tried? I take the second and third questions first. Defenders of the Iraq adventure like to point to the post-World War II French, Japanese and German cases to support their claims. I will do them the favour of forgetting the huge difference between just and unjust wars of liberation: France, Germany and Japan were liberated, or occupied, as the result of the aggression of the latter two countries; Iraq was liberated, or occupied, in a war in which we were, like Napoleon's France 200 years earlier, the aggressor.[11] It is necessary in any case to distinguish, as Hannah Arendt did, between 'liberation' and 'constitution' in the process of democratic regime change. Assuming that external liberation can be justified in the three postwar instances, it does not follow that constitutional imposition by the liberating power can be as well. Indeed, international law forbids the latter.

In Iraq the case for external liberation cannot be said to be entirely without merit. What speaks for it is the apparent damming up of internal processes that in 1991, for example, showed themselves to have a great political potential – revolts which broke out because of our promises and failed, in the South, because of our lack of support. The American responsibility in the subsequent repression of the Shia – and in part even the Kurds – is thus very serious. What speaks against the external liberation in 2003, of course, are the lies needed to sell the policy, which are entirely unacceptable in democratic countries; the weakness of the Saddam state, which could very well have been made to collapse in other ways; and the damage done to international law and mutual trust through the unilateral and illegal action of the US and the pathetic coalition of the willing.

Still, it seems undeniable that in the midst of all that was wrong with the war, the overthrow of the Saddam regime and the freeing of political energies in Iraq were, (very) abstractly considered, a good thing. From this judgment it does not follow that all the subsequent American attempts to control the pace and parameters of democratization, and to impose a series of quasi-dictatorial arrangements on the Iraqis, were also good, legitimate in any way, or even fully legal in terms of international law. In the case of the making and authorization of the Transitional Administrative Law, the interim constitution that is still in effect today and may remain so for a long time,[12] international law was manipulated in order to barely satisfy Article 43 of the 1907 Hague Convention: 'the authority of the legitimate power having actually passed into the hands of the occupant, the latter shall take all steps in his power to re-establish and insure, as far as possible, public order and safety [civil life], while respecting, unless absolutely prevented, the laws in force in the country'.[13]

While I consider Article 43 to be a case of almost hopeless under-regulation, at its normatively valid core remains the idea that if there is to be the creation of a new legal and constitutional system in a country under foreign occupation, the decisions concerning how such a system is to be created belong to agents that can legitimately speak in the name of the country's own population and not to the occupying power or its agents.[14] This idea converges with the common sense of democratic theory. We assume that democracy is a system that emerges from the autonomous activity of its (potential) citizens and is never, or rarely, the gift of political elites, who would seek to preserve undemocratic advantages hidden in new institutions.[15] The theory of democratic legitimacy can further clarify the matter. Any set of modern democratic institutions has distributional consequences and implies the rule of political elites through mechanisms of representation. We therefore assume that strong legitimation requirements have to be satisfied during the beginning of a new democracy that do not require the mythological attribution of purely democratic constituent power as the source of the new regime, but which must go well beyond the idea that elites (especially foreign ones) have imposed it because they had the power to do so.[16]

This idea of the democratic legitimacy of constitutions is, of course, very well known to Americans from their own history, and they have taken it seriously during the few previous liberation-occupation regimes to which they now like to refer. Before Iraq they never openly pretended that constitutional imposition, direct or through a local agent, could be justified. Here comparisons of Iraq with France, Germany and Japan should be helpful. In all three of these earlier cases external armies accomplished the main task of liberation. In France, where the internal liberation forces were strong and where the Free French contingent under Charles de Gaulle was in a position to organize civil power in all liberated territories from the first day, there was no external imposition. The constitution of the Fourth Republic was the result of an unusually democratic process, in which the French Left played a dominant role. In Germany, especially in the American but later in the other Western zones, local, provincial and regional democratic powers based on free elections were organized with unusual rapidity. The constitution-making process was rooted in freely elected provincial governments and newly organized 'national' parties, and American interference was kept to a minimum.[17] In Japan, where there was the clearest case for American constitutional imposition, the Japanese state structure, with its symbolic unification in the emperor, was nevertheless untouched, governments continued to be formed, and a new Imperial Diet involving women's suffrage was elected in 1946 – all under the inherited Meiji Constitution. It was this new Diet that passed the American-imposed Constitution under the amendment rule of that 1883 Constitution, formally satisfying the Article 43 requirement of the Hague Convention. The fact of imposition was a carefully guarded secret.[18]

Thus, all three cases are dramatically different from that of Iraq, where (unlike in France) the Americans assumed direct occupation power, where (unlike in Japan) they destroyed the inherited state, where (unlike in Germany) they did not begin from the ground up and organize freely elected local governments, where (unlike in France and Germany) they imposed a constitution, although supposedly an interim one, and where (unlike in Japan) they made little effort to hide that imposition or the clientelistic nature of various interim governments.

It is worth asking why this difference, especially since the democratic justification of the Iraq war of 'Operation Iraqi Freedom', should have implied greater rather than lesser solicitude for local autonomy and self-government than in the 'guilty' nations of Japan and Germany. The first answer will not please many Left critics of US imperialism, who prefer to see the welfare state and international law as parts of the same overall strategy as neoliberalism and unilateral foreign policy. The US today is not the same as it was in 1945–48, when its politicians and even military leaders believed in the democratic welfare state and in the international institutions this country helped to create. Where in 1945 the rather new idea of the sovereign equality of states was still taken seriously, today it is not. Where in 1945 it was understood that an effective political community requires state integration, today this idea is rejected. Where in 1945 the US sought to create an effective alliance of states with itself as *primus inter pares*, today it is seeking imperial hegemony, and strong states, whether dictatorial or democratic, are in the way.

There is, however, another way to look at the matter – from the point of view of international politics. The cases mentioned occurred in different international constellations, as Japanese writers were the first to point out.[19] Leaving France aside, where the Americans ready to install an occupation government were entirely outmanoeuvred by de Gaulle, Japanese constitution-making occurred at a time when the US was unchallenged in the Pacific, before the victory of the Chinese communists and before the outbreak of the Cold War. The Japanese were not thought of as potential allies, which explains their relatively harsh treatment compared to Germany. In (West) Germany the making of the *Grundgesetz* was an intrinsic part of the Cold War division (of the country and of Europe), and it was clear that the new Federal Republic would have to be an important ally on the very frontier between West and East. It was, moreover, important to demonstrate the superiority of American-supported autonomous democracy to Soviet-imposed pseudo-democracy next door, in the Eastern zone, and further to the East. Given this train of thought, we can see that in an epoch of one-sided American dominance, Iraq is seen as its terrain rather than its partner. There is no other social-political model around that would require the demonstration of the superiority of the American model. Moreover, the outcome of a genuinely democratic process in Iraq is likely to be very different from the point of view of American interests than in Germany in 1948 or Japan in 1946–47.

It is well and good to define democracy minimally as procedural uncertainty.[20] Given the Japanese and German electorates, that uncertainty had sufficient built-in certainty that a generally pro-American and certainly anti-Soviet government would emerge in either country in free elections. The defeated Right in both countries clearly preferred the Americans to the Soviets, and the same was true of all groups, including the democratic Left (with the exception of the small communist parties of course). In Iraq the situation is very different. There is now no outside power threatening Iraq to whom the Americans are preferred. In the case of the majority Shi'ites, most of the people and the main political groupings would probably be on Iran's side in the event of a conflict with the US. Even more importantly, with the exception of the Kurds, the main political forces in Iraq are anti-Israel, and the US is generally identified with that country and its policies. Most important, the liberation itself has been experienced by most Arabs as a humiliating occupation, even by Shi'ites, who remember both the slaughter in 1991, and which country allowed Saddam to carry it out. Among the Sunni, anti-American feelings are much more intense. Moreover, the decentralized or loose federal framework demanded by the Kurds was bound to establish powerful local governments and parties intensely hostile to the US in the Sunni triangle. Had there been fully open and generally contested elections, the chances of some of these parties making their way into the national assembly would have been excellent, and into a coalition government rather good. There was probably always this much certainty in the high uncertainty of a potential Iraqi democracy.

But if I am right, democratization in Iraq linked to free elections always was and remains a questionable proposition for the United States. This point was first clearly articulated by Brent Scowcroft, national security adviser to George H. W. Bush, who earlier probably opposed the war for the same reason: the US could not have gotten rid of Saddam only to bring new enemies like the friends of Iran to power in Iraq.[21] Thus, in early 2003 free elections on the local level were either not permitted or, if they did take place, their results were declared void. And, of course, national elections were going to be delayed until the end of 2005 in favour of various provisional arrangements involving governments and rules of the game imposed by the occupying authority, eventually named the Coalition Provisional Authority (CPA), endowed with the full powers of a military dictatorship over most of Iraq (technically all, but the CPA in fact did not rule over Kurdistan).

A (foreign) dictatorship in the name of (indigenous) democracy? This is the performative contradiction I have in mind. Could it possibly work? Can democracy be externally imposed? Let me admit again that there have been conditions all over the world historically, like the various mandates after World War I, when this contradiction has been manageable. But I believe it is never manageable when a powerful enough actor supported by broad social strata steps into its framework and blows it wide apart. This is the meaning of the phenomenon of the Grand Ayatollah Ali Al-Sistani, and this is precisely what he has done. An actor like Sistani is capable, in other words, of entering into a process of the imposition of liberal democracy and transforming it into both a much more autonomous and, alas, a far less liberal one.

I have elsewhere detailed the series of fatwahs issued and mass actions promoted by Sistani to achieve his single-minded goal: relatively early free elections for a constituent assembly that would give Iraq its new constitution.[22] His statements echo the radical democratic traditions of Thomas Paine and Emmanuel Sieyès. We have no way of knowing whether the style was adopted sincerely or for American and international consumption. I favour the former interpretation. In any case, it is not really worthwhile to say either that he was sure of his majority in free elections or that he hoped to establish some kind of Islamic republic through such a process. The first statement may be true, but does not detract from the justice of the demand. The second statement means only that he is a majoritarian democrat, not a liberal one. There is no evidence whatsoever that he wishes, Iranian-style, to use his majority to make sure that the most important future incumbents will never be exposed to the contingency of free elections, that he wants to use democracy against democracy itself.

There is thus at the very least something on the procedural level in common between *his* democracy and ours, allowing a possible future interaction and mutual enrichment. From our point of view, crossing the two democracies would have the aim of liberalizing and constitutionalizing majoritarianism, and we do not know to what extent, if any, he would resist constitutional restraints on future majorities. What we do know, however, is that he has strongly, and in part successfully, resisted constitutional-type restraints imposed by the occupying power.

## IMPOSING A CONSTITUTION?

The interim constitution, the Transitional Administrative Law (TAL), was the terrain on which the three democracies first met in Iraq, but, it appears, with liberal democracy as an ally of imperial democracy against autonomous democracy. How the given alliance came about is not too difficult to explain.

From a normative point of view, sustained by experience from Spain to South Africa, the purpose of interim constitutions in contemporary democratic transitions is to introduce constitutionalism into the process of making constitutions, to produce legitimacy for inevitably non-democratic beginnings, and to allow constitutional learning before later constitutional self-binding or insulation. I have hopefully demonstrated in other writings that the badly drafted, hastily imposed TAL accomplishes these purposes in a remarkably deficient manner.[23] I argue, however, that its motivations were rather different: to evade the requirements of international law and to give Sistani his elections for a constituent assembly while imposing a constitution that such an assembly would not really be able to change. It is the second dimension that produces the alliance between liberal and imperial democracy.

As to the first dimension, the evasion of international law, it involves a simple matter. As I noted, the Hague Convention forbids the occupying power from changing the legal order of the occupied country. This blanket requirement, which emerged for traditional European states still in a supposedly Westphalian order, is, in fact, quite absurd in cases of formerly totalitarian or violently repressive pseudo-legal orders, where any occupation would have to change the laws immediately. Even if concrete measures were substituted for only a finite period (like the CPA regulations and decrees), they would certainly have irreversible consequences. Thus, we need an entirely new type of regulation of these matters, formulated to inhibit poorly motivated, illegal or unjust interventions, but which regulate the consequences of all interventions more effectively than the radical Hague requirement. But for now the Convention stands, as it stood in 1945–46 when General MacArthur's staff (SCAP: Supreme Commander for the Allied Powers) formed a 'constitutional convention' in its own Government Section[24] and formally evaded it by passing the imposed draft through the legal and orderly inherited Japanese process. At that time, the Americans were forced to operate under international law, and the Convention that was evaded therefore had consequences. Almost from the beginning, when the American draft was translated into Japanese, through the various parliamentary discussions, a unique Japanese interpretation of the imposed constitution emerged which changed many of its meanings for the better – or, from a liberal point of view, for the worse.[25]

In Iraq there was no orderly process, based on a normal parliament, that could be manipulated from behind the scenes. But here the international law prohibition (twice reaffirmed by the Security Council for the present case of Iraq!),[26] taken together with Sistani's challenge, was to have a far more potent and conflictual result: the interim constitution. (Nothing similar to the mass mobilization promoted by Sistani could exist in Japan, where socialists and communists played a passive role after producing interesting constitutional drafts.) Again, this is what I mean by acting in a double legal field constituted not only by imperial dominance but also by international law. After trying various ridiculous formulas to impose a new constitution through its creation, the Governing Council, the Americans chose as their method of evasion an interim constitution to be drafted by the GC with CPA approval and authorization. Accordingly, it could be claimed that Iraq's legal order would be modified by Iraqis (this was legally worthless) and only temporarily, provisionally, and in a way fully reversible by the freely elected assembly, with the dates for the elections initially brought forward to March 2005 to placate Sistani.

Again, there were concessions within the evasion. Once a serious relevant demand from below emerges, earlier elections are better than later elections. If there are to be elections, they require rules of the game guaranteeing free competition and its prerequisites to all legitimate contenders. An interim constitution, had it been legitimately introduced, would have been the appropriate legal instrument at that stage. Neither the promise of earlier elections nor the downscaling of the constitutional project to an interim one would have taken place without the converging counter-pressures of international law and oppositional politics. Yet these concessions were also meant to keep the process in its original imperial framework, and thus represented evasions of the spirit of the law and of the democratic demand.

The Grand Ayatollah was, however, impossible to fool, especially since the CPA-GC agreement of 15 November 2003 that first pointed to an interim constitution would have involved the creation of a co-opted rather than elected national assembly. The freely elected constitution-writing body would only have been a weak convention of the American type, one that would not have been the locus of the provisional government. Even after Sistani denounced the formula and obtained the junking of the co-opted assembly with UN help, the interim constitution was drafted and promulgated, in spite of a brief protest by some of his adherents in the GC and his own attacks. And this interim constitution, the TAL, involved powerful procedural limits on the ability of the freely elected constituent assembly (no longer a mere convention) to produce its constitution: amending the TAL required the votes of three-quarters of the members of the National Assembly and the consent of all three members of the presidential council, and the famous veto of any permanent draft was given to two-thirds of the voters of any three provinces. The likelihood of the interim becoming permanent was enhanced by the TAL's own failsafe provisions enacted for the possible or even likely failure of ratification or even the drafting of a permanent constitution (TAL: Article 61 E and G). This is the point where the international prohibition against an occupier changing the laws of an occupied country was potentially subverted. Assuming that a strong, regionally dominant minority is fundamentally attached to the American-imposed TAL – and this is the case for the Kurds – if the freely elected drafters changed the TAL significantly, the new constitution would not be ratified and the TAL would remain in effect. Thus, either way, the temporary would become permanent or quasi-permanent.[27]

Let me note, however, what Sistani gained in this round by exploiting the performative contradiction of the American project: not only an even earlier date for elections (no later than 31 January 2005), but also a powerful, freely elected rather than co-opted National Assembly that would be the seat of governmental powers. This concession can no longer be understood as mere evasion or subterfuge. Nevertheless, Sistani remained so dissatisfied with the imposition of the interim constitution that he went so far as to block its formal approval in Security Council Resolution 1546. What he objected to was the obvious legal condition that the constituent powers of the assembly he had fought so hard for and now attained would be bound.[28] In fact, this legal condition corresponds to the emerging model of 'post-sovereign constitution-making', which has broken with the idea of unlimited constituent power or an assembly with the plenitude of all powers. The constitution-making assembly in South Africa, for example, had to put up with a far more restrictive set of limitations, including a series (34) of almost unalterable constitutional principles enforced by a new constitutional court. There was, however, one fundamental difference between the emerging model and what was done in Iraq: the restrictions in Iraq, very heavy on the procedural level, did not emerge in a legitimate, consensual or broadly representative process, but were simply imposed by the fiat of the occupying power. It is hard to say whether it was the restrictions or the fiat to which Sistani most objected; probably in his mind they became inseparable. It is very important to note that, in spite of UN proposals to this effect, no political force was there at any time to help accomplish the separation in theory or in practice![29] In other words, the option of consensually-imposed, and therefore self-imposed, limitations on the power of the majority to make a constitution was not rejected by Sistani because no one seriously represented that option.

Evidently, the restrictions on majority rule were first and foremost demanded by the Kurds, who understandably did not, even for a moment, wish to try majoritarian democracy when they already had *de facto* federal and autonomous power in their provinces. Such restrictions also converged with US interests, to the extent that the denial of sole power to Iranian allies or friends remained a key desideratum, and the preservation of Kurdish influence over the process as a whole represented a potential opening for strong American influence as well. Finally, however, the same limitations were important to all those who found the table of rights in the TAL – and its requirement for significant political participation of women – very much worth preserving in the face of a potential majority suspected of wishing to install an 'illiberal democracy'. Here is where liberal democracy encountered imperial imposition and autonomous democracy and had to make a choice.

### STRUGGLES OVER WOMEN'S RIGHTS IN THE TAL:
### CONSTITUTIONALISM VERSUS DEMOCRACY?

Once again, the right way of promoting the very same rights and the same binding of the constituent majority would have been in a legitimate process, supervised by a valid international authority, involving the free agreement and mutual binding of all major Iraqi forces. There is no reason why such a process, if initiated well before the insurrection, could not have included significant representation of many hitherto excluded groups, for example, women's groups. Such a process was, however, not possible on the ground of an endless occupation, since many key actors, especially but not only among the Sunni, were uncompromisingly hostile to what they saw as national humiliation. Despite UN efforts in this direction, the American authorities certainly always resisted calling a genuinely representative roundtable or multi-party negotiating forum with decision-making powers. So the choice for the Kurds, liberals and women was imposed rights (how real?) or the prospect (certainly exaggerated, but to what extent?) of having no rights at all. Many, unsurprisingly, chose the former. We have only some clues as to how this happened during the closed and secretive process of drafting the TAL, in relation to three interrelated controversies: the question of the role of the Shari'a in the interim constitution; the question of guaranteeing women's political participation; and the particular issue of the three-province veto over the final constitution.

The first question came up because the Interim Governing Council (IGC), not known for undertaking initiatives independent of the superior American authorities, nevertheless decided independently on 29 December 2003 to pass Resolution 137, which (voiding a law of 1959) was to make the Shari'a the foundation of family and civil law. The new regulation was to be incorporated both in a so-called Personal Status Law and in the interim constitution that was then supposed to be completed by 28 February 2004. As far as I can reconstruct, during early and mid-January this proposal was strongly challenged in the streets of Baghdad by a series of women's demonstrations ranging from hundreds to thousands of participants. Undoubtedly, the anger of the demonstrators was fuelled by the dramatic worsening of the condition of women in many parts of the country, the return of honour killings, the enforcement of strict Islamic dress, sackings from many jobs, as well as reprisals and threats against women political activists.[30] While up to 85 groups were said to participate,[31] the leading role was played by two civil society organizations: the OWFI (the Organization of Women's Freedom in Iraq)[32] and the Women's Alliance for a Democratic Iraq (WAFDI).[33] There is much to admire in their statements and actions under difficult circumstances. Both belong to the 'we' of this chapter, and obviously represent the cause of secular, liberal rights for women to the best of their abilities.

Nevertheless, the differences are also striking. The OWFI, allied with small, left-wing groups, makes its demands to Iraqi society and to international opinion. It regards the CPA as a foreign occupier that should leave Iraq, and the Governing Council (later the Interim Government as well) as its illegitimate creature. The Women's Alliance does not contest the legitimacy of the GC, but addresses Ambassador Bremer, the real source of authority in their eyes. Their attitude to the occupation is unabashedly positive, and it is for this reason that I would apply to them the label of *imperial liberalism*. They claim to represent hundreds of women activists who advocated the (foreign) liberation of Iraq and who now, among other things, fear for the fate of ' "the forward strategy of freedom in the greater Middle East" that is a cornerstone of President Bush's policy'. With all that said, their letter,[34] after applauding Bremer's veto of Resolution 137, culminates in important suggestions for strengthening women's representation in the interim constitution and building national as against merely local organizations capable of competing with the established parties. In contrast, many of the activists of the OWFI are very close to supporting at least secular insurrectionists against foreign domination.[35] It is not clear in their case, however, how they hope to secure the rights of women if the Americans are forced to leave, given the shifting of the political organization of Iraqi society to political parties, none of which (not even the main Kurdish groupings) is sensitive to women's rights.

Unsurprisingly, the two positions are close to one another in their uncompromising hostility to what they both call political Islam or the Islamist parties. Nevertheless, they clearly undercut each other on the strategic level. The Women's Alliance lends legitimacy to the occupation (although less so to the Allawi government),[36] which the OWFI rejects, while the latter considers the former's proposal for women's electoral quotas irrelevant, since the established parties can find women to fill these who are supposedly enemies of women's rights. The OWFI has also supported the boycott of the elections, while undoubtedly members of the Women's Alliance campaigned (and were nominated?) for Allawi's list. Neither activity obviously contributed to the success of the other.

Yet both groups have had some success. It was above all the larger and more radical demonstrations led by the OWFI that led to the Governing Council voting again on and repealing Resolution 137, although Bremer's veto threat also had a major role to play. That threat may have been influenced by the appeals of the Women's Alliance, and it is even more likely that the requirement that one-quarter of the National Assembly be female was written into the TAL as a consequence of their demand. Assuming that the figure represented a compromise between two factions of the GC,[37] Bremer's changing one-quarter to every third person on electoral lists was probably influenced by demands addressed directly to him.[38]

These victories, however, do not show the rightness or viability of either the *imperial liberal* or the *leftist sectarian* strategy. Appealing to the occupier, however we are to judge it normatively, puts women's rights on the side of the occupation, in opposition not only to political Islam but to Iraqi nationalism and political self-determination as well. It implies either that the occupier would (and should!) stay, one way or another, forever, or entirely unrealistic expectations about liberal and secular development during an occupation that has itself defined representation in Iraq in terms of religious and ethnically-based political groupings. At the same time, waiting for a radical popular but secular revolution in Iraq is senseless today. The anti-occupation feminists who reject both the secular political groupings tied to the occupation and the Islamic parties have almost nowhere to go for allies. In this sense, having a more attractive normative position is paid for by an even greater remoteness from political power and influence.

Let me quickly admit, however, that in the very fluid political situation, both groups already have new political opportunities. The one-third women representatives now in Parliament, or their more secular part, are potential partners in dialogue for the Women's Alliance, if much less so for the OWFI. On the other hand, recent attempts on the part of the more radical feminists to establish links with the Sunni Association of Muslim Scholars (AMS), which is strongly opposed to the occupation but also to the more radical wing of the insurrection, may be a promising sign on their part. Nevertheless, even here the uncompromising anti-Islamic party stance is likely to hurt alliance-building or even dialogue. The women representing Islamic parties should be open to considering many women's issues, but not if they are raised by groups unwilling to recognize any of the aims of Islamic parties as legitimate. Similarly, the AMS is now involved in intense negotiations with the followers of Moktada Al-Sadr, who represent the most theocratic wing of the Shi'ite constellation. It makes little sense to be participating in discussion with the Sadrists and to reject entirely more moderate Islamist politicians in Parliament. Nor would it be a good idea to force the AMS to choose between feminists and Sadrists. What I am arguing for, therefore, is the beginning of a dialogue, within Parliament and outside, between 'our' democracy, represented by women's movements in civil society, and 'their' democracy, represented by the Shia parties and the AMS.

It should be frankly admitted that the interim constitution, its status (resented by the Shia) and its contents (supported by women's movements) represent roadblocks to this dialogue that cannot simply be dismissed. Women's movements in civil society see themselves as having contributed to the making of the interim constitution, the TAL, which is distinguished by many strong affirmations concerning rights. Islam is said to be 'the official religion of the State and is to be considered a source of legislation' – *a* source, but not the only source, as Resolution 137 had it. While 'No law that contradicts the universally agreed tenets of Islam … may be enacted during the transitional period', the same is affirmed in the very same sentence regarding 'the principles of democracy, or the rights cited in Chapter Two of this Law' (Article 7A).

The strong Chapter Two affirmations of rights concerning civil equality, non-discrimination, due process, and so on were to an important extent unenforced during the supposed restoration of Iraqi sovereignty under the Interim Government, its various states of emergency, and the activities of the almost entirely uncontrolled and unmonitored American military forces. This lack of enforcement does not, characteristically enough, diminish the symbolic weight of the TAL to both sides. To Iraqis, from Sistani to the Association of Muslim Scholars, the document remains an externally imposed constitution, a badge of oppression, one well endowed with mechanisms by which it seeks to perpetuate itself. They well remember that Ambassador Bremer threatened to delay transferring sovereignty if the five Shi'ite members persisted in their opposition. Of course, most important Sunni groups did not agree to the document at all. And yet, at the very time when, under Sistani's pressure, five Shia members of the Governing Council were still refusing to sign the TAL because of its three-province veto, the Kurds, who controlled three provinces, already regarded the document as something like their Magna Carta. To them, other minorities and liberal women, it represents constitutionalism against the potential tyranny of the majority, and its spirit and perhaps its very content should indeed be perpetuated.

Thus, it is the very characteristic that involves the outmanoeuvring of both international law and the Shia movement led by Sistani that makes it so valuable to minorities and liberals of various colours. To the majority, however, the same features represent tyrannical external attempts to subvert their rights, supported at best by their own coerced agreement. It is this situation that puts constitutionalism in direct conflict with democracy. It is not in the interest of minorities and of women that the conflict continue and even be exacerbated – because in the end both constitutionalism and democracy are likely to be sacrificed.

## FROM SUBSTANCE TO PROCEDURE?

Its defenders support the TAL because of its substantive contents, which they would like to see preserved in a permanent constitution – or, secretly, in the interim made permanent. Its opponents reject the imposed procedure that brought the interim constitution about and its potential deformation of future democratic processes. The reason for the great gap between procedure and substance lies, however, in a faulty and illegitimate procedure. It is perhaps not too late to remedy this problem, now that elections have actually taken place but without any guarantee that a functioning government and legitimate constitution-making are to follow.

We have good reason to believe that comprehensive, multi-party negotiations, where actors have incomplete knowledge of the future, have the best chance to produce constitutional safeguards supported by mutual promises and commitments. Such negotiations did not take place in Iraq because the Americans did not want them. But now a different force could be in charge – if it wants to be in charge and escape American manipulation and tutelage, and it remains in its interest to move toward a large-scale, comprehensive historical compromise. There is no point in inheriting a state that is no state at all, or making a constitution that is no more than a piece of paper.

The Sunni boycott of the elections as well as the looming conflict over Kirkuk dramatize the issue. There are no major Sunni forces in the recently elected National Assembly, and it is unthinkable that a new constitution be drafted without the participation of this central population group, to which so much of the professional and military elite belong. Thus, there is some reason to hope that a large-scale negotiating process, in or out of Parliament, may still be cobbled together to produce a pre-constitutional bargain.[39] Similarly, the Sunni have a great interest in Kirkuk, since without a share in its oil resources, their part of the country would be permanently impoverished. If there is ever to be civil peace in Iraq, they must be brought into the negotiating process concerning the fate of this city, territory and resources.

A constitution cannot be viable if it is not made for an existing state, or if a new state is not created through agreement on a basic law. In Iraq the old state was destroyed in a wholly irresponsible manner by the American occupiers, and they have put only themselves and their means of violence (hardly a legitimate monopoly) in its place. The interim constitution was not made for a coherent state, nor did it create one through agreement or successful conquest. Thus, the document, and the process based on it, cannot be effective. Its successor's viability presupposes that a state is structured or restructured that is capable of enforcing law and monopolizing, more or less, the legitimate means of violence in Iraqi territory. This would mean a binding agreement among all the armed political forces about the role and subordinate status of the many militias now in existence. It would also mean ending the large-scale involvement of the Sunni community in the ongoing insurrection. That is possible only if there is a clear and timely perspective for ending the occupation. Assuming that, only comprehensive negotiations among all the major political forces, especially those linked to organized means of violence, could re-establish a viable state power in Iraq. The key to constitutional legitimacy is effective state-making, which presupposes a horizontal agreement among Iraqis, freed of the burden but also the supposed advantages of the occupation, concerning the major political rules of the game including the relationship of federal and central authorities. Only with the end of the occupation, as demanded by the AMS and the Sadrist movement but also the OWFI, can Iraqis learn that the problems of security can be solved only by their own state, and that they cannot substitute a foreign political intermediary to establish its sovereign powers.

Admittedly, in such a state bargain civil society groups that do not possess means of violence do not have a natural role. Fortunately, however, any bargain would have to be agreed to by a freely elected parliament, where their influence can be easily brought to bear. Here any political bargain will require the assent of women and secular deputies, many of whom are linked to civil organizations. If they manage to divest themselves of their uncompromisingly hostile attitude to the Islamic parties, it is hard to believe that parliamentary arithmetic will not favour the reassertion of many important rights. Already, the Kurds do not accept the imposition of an Islamic theocratic state in Iraq, although it is hard to know where they will draw the boundaries. Once a government is formed, however, all coalitions will be weak and probably temporary, working on an issue-by-issue basis. A powerful secular caucus including women, and another, a women's caucus including Islamic women, would have a strong role to play in political bargaining if they could be formed. If some kind of pre-constitutional negotiating process emerges with Sunni groupings like the AMS drawn in, anti-occupation women's groups like the OWFI can play a role through their agency as well. What is important is that it be recognized that a democratic process ties all the participants together, and that process logically entails at the very least the maintenance of the *political* rights that makes the participants able to participate.

There is little evidence that even the Islamic parties currently wish to attack political, participatory rights, which now include the electoral law with its guaranteed seats for women. I could be wrong. But, in any case, in the political bargaining process there will be room to reaffirm these rights further as well as many civil rights as well. If the imperial democracy had its performative contradiction, so does 'their' democracy, Shia democracy in Iraq, and it is this. There is now a commitment to democratic procedure and political rights, affirmed through a series of fatwahs, but not to the civil rights and civil equality without which political participation is ultimately without value. Here too the best politics would be based on the immanent and practical critique of the performative contradiction. Sistani's method should be used against Sistani himself. But this would mean first recognizing the authenticity of *their* struggle, which is, I believe, for the Shia as well as the Sunni, in spite of the different means used, directed first and foremost against the illegitimate occupation.

# NOTES

1  Jean Cohen, 'Whose Sovereignty? Empire versus International Law', *Ethics and International Affairs* 18:3 (2004): 1–24.

2  Zbigniew Brzezinski, *Global Domination or Global Leadership* (New York: Basic Books, 2004), 11.

3  See Nehal Bhuta, 'A Global State of Exception? The United States and World Order', *Constellations* 10:3 (September 2003): 371–91. Supporters of the legality of the war used to cite Attorney General Lord Goldsmith's 'legal opinion' as the major piece justifying their views. We now know that his actual legal opinion given to the Blair government maintained that legal action could be expected against the UK in a domestic or an international court in the absence of a new Security Council resolution. It went on to point out that 'regime change cannot be the objective of military action'. The one-page report to Parliament, before the relevant vote, was in fact written by aides of the Prime Minister, Lord Falconer and Lady Morgan. For a summary of the events, see *Guardian* (10 and 12 March 2005). For analysis of the legal advice published in late April, see *Guardian* (29 April 2005).

4  See Andrew Arato, 'The Occupation of Iraq and the Difficult Transition from Dictatorship', *Constellations* 10:3 (September 2003): 408–24; Andrew Arato, 'Sistani v. Bush: Constitutional Politics in Iraq', *Constellations* 11:2 (June 2004): 174–92; and Andrew Arato, 'Interim Imposition', *Ethics and International Affairs* 18:4 (2004): 25–51.

5  Thus Paul Wolfowitz has been transferred precisely to where the next battles are likely to take place, where the large-scale funds for development will be allocated, and where the preferred civil society organizations and NGOs are likely to be targeted.

6  See Haifa Zangana, 'The Three Cyclops of Empire-Building', in this volume for a discussion of the use of 'soft' power in occupied Iraq.

7  See the excellent report 'The Political Transition in Iraq: the Report of the Fact Finding Mission' (New York: United Nations, 2004). I was gratified to find a trace of my proposals in paragraph 28.

8  Ibid.

9  Anne E. Komblut, 'In Prime Minister, Presidential Race Gets a Touchstone', *Globe Staff* (24 september 2004), http://www.boston.com/news/globe.

10  To be fair, Brahimi did complain a little afterwards, and moreover in sociologically accurate terms. See Terence Neilan, 'U.N. Envoy Urges Iraqis to Give New Leaders a Chance', *New York Times* (2 June 2004). 'Mr. Brahimi struck a mildly surprising note when, in answer to a reporter's question, he referred to the American occupation administrator, L. Paul Bremer III, as "the dictator of Iraq." "He has the money," he said. "He has the signature. Nothing happens without his agreement in this country." ' These lines indicate that Brahimi ultimately blamed Bremer rather than the Governing Council for being outmanoeuvred.

11  According to Benjamin Constant 'The French revolution saw the invention of a pretext for war previously unknown, that of freeing peoples from the yoke of their governments which were supposed to be illegitimate and tyrannical ... the worst of all conquests is the hypocritical

one', in *The Spirit of Conquest and Usurpation and their Relation to European Civilization* [1813/1814], in B. Fontana (ed.), *Political Writings* (Cambridge: Cambridge University Press, 1988), 65. In the same passages Constant vividly unmasks the lies used to justify pre-emptive wars.

12   Arato, 'Interim Imposition'; and Andrew Arato, 'How Many Methods Are There to Enact a New Constitution in Iraq?', *Informed Comment* (21 February 2005), http://www.juancole.com.

13   The Avalon Project at Yale Law School, *Laws of War: Laws and Customs of War on Land* (Hague II), 29 July 1899 (Washington, DC: Government Printing Office, 1968).

14   The regulation actually is broader, and seems to exclude not only the process of creating the new political and legal system, but even the decision whether there would be a new order at all issuing from the jurisdiction of the occupying power. However, where war is between regimes and not only governments, and can lead to the destruction of a regime before occupation, the decision concerning the creation of a new regime of some indeterminate type is taken with the overthrow of the old one. Any occupation government will therefore imply some new regime-building, and it is this process that is poorly regulated by either the blanket negative rule or the phrase 'unless absolutely prevented'. For a different perspective, preferring a conservative interpretation of the Hague Convention, see the outstanding article by Gregory H. Fox, 'The Occupation of Iraq', *Georgetown Journal of International Law* 36 (April 2005): 195. Fox shows that the radical evasion of Hague requirements has been much broader in Iraq than merely the matter of imposing the interim constitution, and extended to the economic and administrative fields as well.

15   Today a great external power certainly cannot take on the mantle of the disinterested foreign law-giver, a figure that has in any case been universally abandoned since the modern democratic revolutions.

16   See Andrew Arato, 'Forms of Constitution Making and Democratic Theory', in Andrew Arato, *Civil Society, Constitution and Legitimacy* (Lanham, MD: Rowman & Littlefield, 2000), 250–5 where I outline a set of procedural principles (consensus, plurality, publicity, fiction of legality and empirical veil of ignorance) that allow the attribution of democratic legitimacy. These principles are further developed in 'Constitutional Learning', *Theoria* (South Africa) 106 (April 2005): 1.

17   Peter H. Merkl, *The Origin of the West German Republic* (New York: Oxford University Press, 1963).

18   Koseki Shoichi, *The Birth of Japan's Postwar Constitution* (Boulder, CO: Westview Press, 1997). See also the lively discussion in John Dower's *Embracing Defeat. Japan in the Wake of World War II* (New York: Norton, 1999), 346–404, and the very useful bibliography, 608–9. Unfortunately, this first-rate book came to my attention only after completing the present chapter.

19   Hideo Otake, 'Two Contrasting Constitutions in the Postwar World: The Making of the Japanese and the West German Constitutions', in Yoichi Higuchi (ed.), *Five Decades of Constitutionalism in Japanese Society* (Tokyo: University of Tokyo Press, 2001), 43–71.

20   Adam Przeworski, *Democracy and Market* (Cambridge: Cambridge University Press, 1991), 10ff and 40ff.

21   Walter Gibbs, 'Scowcroft Urges a Wider Role for the UN in Post War Iraq', *New York Times* (9 April 2003).

22   Andrew Arato, 'Sistani v. Bush: Constitutional Politics in Iraq' and 'Constitution Making in Iraq', *Dissent* (Spring 2004).

23   Arato, 'Interim Imposition'.

24   Shoichi, *The Birth of Japan's Postwar Constitution*, 79.

25   Ibid., chs. 6, 8 and 9.

26   Security Council Resolutions 1483 (5) and 1511 (1).

27   Professor Nathan Brown, whom I greatly respect, disagrees with my claim that the rejection of the new constitution and the preservation of the TAL could occur an indefinite number of times, because, according to him, the TAL does not allow the extension of the time limit of the interim period by amendment (Article 3A). But the indefinite number of failed attempts at ratification and preservation of the TAL requires no amendment, following the plain text of the TAL (Article 61E) that does not limit in any way the number of times this can occur. Of course, politically, the greater likelihood is either the drafting of a final constitution that largely corresponds to the TAL, and thus can be ratified, or the majority, the first or second time around, repudiating the TAL altogether. The second of these options could occur if there are two blocs stopping ratification: a pro-TAL Kurdish bloc and an anti-TAL Sunni bloc.

28   He did not buy the many reassurances, of Brahimi and Allawi among others, that a freely elected assembly could not be bound in any case, a position that I also maintained especially after Security Council Resolution 1546 did not underwrite the TAL. Sistani had probably already thought through at that time the interrelated difficulties of government formation (according to the TAL, and having some consensual elements) and majoritarian repudiation of the TAL. See Arato, 'Interim Imposition'.

29   I am thinking of Jamal Benomar, 'Constitution Making after Conflict: Lessons for Iraq', *Journal of Democracy* 15:2 (April 2004): 81–95, and the report of the first Brahimi visit, 'The Political Transition in Iraq: the Report of the Fact Finding Mission' (New York: United Nations, 2004), probably written mostly by Benomar, which stressed, at least implicitly, both the need for consensual process and constitutional limitations on constitution making.

30   Rod Norland et al., 'Iraq's Hidden War', *Newsweek* (7 March 2005).

31   Bill Weinberg, 'The Civil Opposition In Iraq', *World War 4 Report* 98 (May 2004).

32   See statement of 14 January 2004.

33   See letter of 23 January 2004.

34   Women's Alliance for a Democratic Iraq *Letter to Ambassador Bremer* (23 January 2004), available at http://www.womenforiraq.org/.

35   'U.S. Troops Will Have to Leave Now and We Will take Care of Iraq', interview with Yanar Mohammed in *Democracy Now* (13 September 2004).

36 See Judge Zakia Hakki's critique of the formation of the co-opted Interim National Council, 'Peace Needs Women, and Women Need Justice', lecture at *Conference on Gender Justice in Post Conflict Situations Co-Organized by the United Nations Development Fund (UNIFEM) and the International Legal Assistance Consortium (ILAS)* (15–17 September 2004).

37 Yochi J. Dreazen, 'Long Way from Indiana', *The Wall Street Journal* (12 April 2004).

38 CPA Order 96, 4 (3).

39 For several alternatives see my three guest editorials on Juan Cole's website, *Informed Comment* (28 December 2004, 4 February and 21 February 2005). Of course, other options are conceivable and perhaps viable, http://www.juancole.com.

# 12

# The Three Cyclops of Empire-Building: Targeting the Fabric of Iraqi Society

*Haifa Zangana*

Colonialism pulls every string shamelessly. (Frantz Fanon, *The Wretched of the Earth*, 1961)

'What we would tell the children of Iraq is that the noise they hear is the sound of freedom.' (Army Brigadier General Mark Kimmitt, spokesman for the occupation forces, replying to an Iraqi reporter, who asked what he would recommend Iraqi mothers tell their children frightened by low-flying helicopters. Baghdad, February 2004)

At the front, the banner of 'liberating' Iraq was carried by high-tech soldiers. The message was the readiness to use unbridled US military force in the face of any opposition to the exercise of its imperial power anywhere in the world. At the rear, there was a different kind of troop marching to accomplish a different 'mission': to tackle a deeper and longer-term remoulding of Iraqi society in the aftermath of military invasion.

The military scenario was supposed to end with the media event celebrating victory as 'mission accomplished', as George W. Bush landed on the USS *Abraham Lincoln*. 'Mission accomplished' it is not. 'At least 100,000 excess Iraqi civilian deaths had occurred since the 2003 invasion; most of those violent deaths were caused by coalition air strikes';[1] 1,710 occupation troop deaths, and more than 10,000 wounded.[2] With no end in sight, the body count is still mounting. We also witnessed the fall of the 'weapons of mass destruction' (WMD) banner, which was carried by US-led troops in an attempt to justify the military invasion of Iraq. WMD has proved to be a mirage, despite all the money and time invested to prove otherwise.

But what about the brightly coloured banners of religious freedom, civil society and women's liberation? These have been used by the occupiers to justify their neocolonial policy and to cement in 'civilized manner', their presence within Iraqi society. In the demise of the military banners, they have become especially important.

While military invasion, the front line of colonization, was carried out by highly publicized US-led hi-tech soldiers with the help of a few Iraqi groups set up or supported financially by the CIA and MI6,[3] issues of freedom, religious freedom in particular, building civil society and empowering Iraqi women were left to organizations representing 'the supply line of colonialism': NGOs, missionaries and women's organizations. Unlike military invasion and violence, the work of these organizations is directed at the very fabric of society and has received much less publicity. But these invasions – these three Cyclops of empire-building – are crucial to analyse for the occupation they envisage is one that threatens to go much deeper even than military occupation. The 'building of civil society' both implies that Iraq lacks such a society and consolidates the colonial portrait of the Iraqi people as passive victims, unable to manage or transform their own country. In order to examine the reasons for this level of colonial organization and the implications of the work of these 'soft' occupiers, and to evaluate the likelihood of their success or failure, we need, first of all, to leaf through a few pages of Iraq's modern history. Although, being an Iraqi, I am tempted to start even earlier.

In Iraq we do not just read history, but carry it within ourselves. History plays a decisive role in our understanding of both our present and our future. Events which took place thousands of years ago are engrained in our daily life. With 10,000 archaeological sites, a constant reminder of ancient history, many aspects of our lives are woven together both consciously and unconsciously with related historical events. No wonder we see present-day events – invasion, occupation, mandate and the nominal hand over of sovereignty to 'Iraqis', as well as elections – as a revival of the same sort of colonial occupation that we fought in the past: occupations that have been desperate to control our natural resources, primarily oil.[4]

On 28 April 1920, Britain was awarded a mandate over Iraq by the League of Nations to legitimize its occupation of the country. This immediately led to the 1920 revolution, in which an estimated 10,000 Iraqis were killed. In the revolution's aftermath the overt occupation was replaced with a provisional Iraqi government, 'assisted' by British advisers under the Authority of the High Commissioner of Iraq, but the problems proved to be enormous. The British High Commissioner had to devise a solution to reduce the loss of British lives and the costs to the empire. He did so in the form of a 'suitable ruler'. Finding one to install was not easy, but the British finally settled on Emir Faisal, the son of Sharif Hussain of Hijaz.[5] To the British government, control of Iraq and its oil was a strategic necessity. But Iraqi national liberation movements called for *Istiqlal al Tamm*, complete independence, which was seen by the British as 'the catchword of the extremists here'[6] and as an 'idiot phrase which the extremists of Baghdad, and no one else, added to the referendum papers: cut off from the control of anyone'. Any protest against British-imposed monarchy was regarded as the work of 'extremists'.[7]

In 1932, Iraq was declared an independent state, but only after signing a new treaty that allowed the British to retain their military power, to control land and resources and to coordinate foreign policy for the next 25 years. Iraqi forces had to be trained by the British and arms were to be provided by them. Unsurprisingly, another popular uprising erupted against the oppressive regime of the monarchy which failed to understand the depth of feeling among Iraqis against occupation, which was seen as collective humiliation. In the years that followed, many opposition leaders were executed, elections were manipulated and force was used against popular demonstrations. The cost of living was high; poverty was widespread. In 1935, hundreds of members of the Yazidis minority group were arrested, six were hanged and the rest were imprisoned. Military *coups d'état* and more popular uprisings followed; all demanding significant social and political reforms. In 1941, the Iraqi government refused to allow passage of British troops through Iraqi territory and declared its support for Germany, acts that led to the Anglo-Iraqi war and the re-invasion of Iraq by British troops.

Just this small slice of Iraqi history clarifies that the question we are confronted with today is the following: is this pattern of occupation, violence and resistance what Iraq now has to look forward to?

The enemies of today's US-led occupation were the enemies of yesterday's British rule. In 1921, Miss Bell, Oriental Secretary to the High Commissioner, wrote:

> The villain is Saiyid Muhammad Sadr, the son of old Saiyid Hasan Sadr. Saiyid Muhammad, a tall black bearded Alim (cleric) with sinister expression. He was little more than the son of Saiyid Hasan, but a month

later he leapt into an evil prominence as the chief agitator in the disturbances. In those insane days he was treated like a divinity .... We tried to arrest him early in August and failed. He escaped from Baghdad and moved about the country like a flame of war, rousing the tribes .... In obedience to his preaching the tribes attacked Samara but were beaten off. He then moved down to Karbala and was the soul of the insurgence on the middle Euphrates .... It's a hand-to-hand conflict between us and him. We have won the first round .... He is in a black rage and I feel as if we were struggling against the powers of evil in the dark. You never know what Shi'ahs are up to.[8]

Contrary to Miss Bell's claims, Shias, like the rest of Iraqis, knew exactly what they were 'up to': complete independence.

Three major events have shaped our national identity: the 1920 revolution; the revolution of 1958 which finally and definitively ousted the British Empire from Iraq; and the Palestinian issue. At the heart of the three lies the struggle to end occupation. Occupation has always been perceived as a process to rob us of our identity and dignity. The British failed to understand the depth of feeling among Iraqis against occupation and towards the Palestinian issue. Now, in partnership with the US, they are repeating the mistake. To sever links with history and to erase our memory, to be silent about the daily killings of Iraqis resisting US-led occupation and Palestinians fighting Israeli occupation, these have become the blueprint to create the 'new Iraqi'. Here we come face to face with the same old colonial racist spirit whispering 'Iraqis are not yet sufficiently developed to stand wholly by themselves'. They have to be taught how to build their country, to implement democracy and, above all, to welcome the US-led troops.[9]

Since 1979, Iraqis have suffered 24 years of oppression under Saddam Hussein, 43 days of continuous bombardment which caused the destruction of their country's infrastructure and the killing of tens of thousands of their people during the first Gulf War. Iraqis were shocked and confused by this: it seemed bizarre to punish them for the crimes of their persecutors. Confusion turned to numbness when people discovered they were to be subject to one of the 'most comprehensive campaigns of economic sanctions in [modern] history'.[10]

On 6 December 1995, I sent an A4 padded envelope to my nieces and nephews in Mosul city, in the north of Iraq. It contained one pencil case, three erasers, three pencil sharpeners, six fountain pens, two markers, one glue-stick and two ball point pens. It was marked 'gift for children'. The envelope was returned, stamped: 'Due to international sanctions against Iraq, we are not able to forward your packet.' Thirteen years of sanctions which caused the death of half a million Iraqi children, five years of sporadic weekly bombing by the British and US air forces supposedly enforcing the no-fly zones established after the first Gulf War and, finally, the cluster bombs and depleted uranium (DU) of the campaign of 'shock and awe' in March and April 2003 – these military forays and the sharp edge of 'hard power' were quickly to prise open the door for the evangelist missionaries to accompany the military to the long-denied land, the enforcement of US policy through colonial feminists selling 'women's initiatives', and government-sponsored NGOs.

## GOVERNMENTAL NGOs

In the aftermath of September 11, Bush's words 'You are either with us or against us' became the mantra that governs all aspects of the American state's policy, including its policy towards non-governmental organizations (NGOs). The 'war on terror' has reformulated many aspects of world politics, and the NGO sector has not been spared. Former Secretary of State Colin Powell outlined the new vision of relief work when, addressing NGOs in 2001, he argued, 'Just as surely as our diplomats and military, American NGOs are out there serving and sacrificing on the front lines of freedom. NGOs are such a force multiplier for us, such an important part of our combat team.'[11]

Andrew Natsios, the Administrator for the US Agency for International Development (USAID), bluntly spelled out the same vision. He told international humanitarian leaders that 'NGOs and contractors are an arm of the US government' and that in order to serve Washington's political and military objectives, aid agencies 'should identify themselves as recipients of US funding'.[12]

How does this redefinition of policy reflect on American NGOs working in Iraq, a country the US government deems vital to its national interests?

Several American NGOs that accepted initial US government funds for work in Iraq have decided against applying for additional resources. Others have chosen the 'pragmatic' path by attempting a balancing act between theoretical neutrality and factual submission to US policy. In fact, as a reward for choosing the pragmatic path,

'Five NGOs – Mercy Corps, International Relief and Development, Inc., ACDI/VOCA, Cooperative Housing Foundation International and Save the Children Federation, Inc. – received cooperative agreements, and initial funding of $7 million, as part of USAID's Iraq Community Action Program'.[13] This is just a small sample of the many American and British NGOs which descended on Iraq immediately after the invasion, although many just as hurriedly left after the attack on the UN building in Baghdad.

To Iraqis it became obvious that these NGOs, much like the Iraqi Governing Council and Iraqi Interim Government, are nothing but subcontractors acting on behalf of the occupation forces. Otherwise, why were they created, in some cases, within two months of the invasion? As I will address the role of colonial feminists in Iraq in a later section, I will concentrate here on women's NGOs funded by the US in order to identify the common grounds characteristic of US-backed Iraqi women's organizations which assert their 'neutrality' while under US–UK neocolonial tutelage.

The common grounds characteristic of US–UK-funded Iraqi women's NGOs are that Iraqi women's NGOs that began working in Iraq immediately after 'mission accomplished' and that accompanied the arrival of the occupation forces, were established primarily in the US, with only a few originating in the UK; most of them acquired their birth certificates within three months – before or after – the occupation; they are all carrying out US–UK policy by proxy; and they have no roots in Iraqi society.

Although these organizations are registered under a variety of names, and claim varying objectives and programmes, they have, in fact, been established and run by just a handful of Iraqi women. Ms A. Talabani, a member of the Patriotic Union of Kurdistan (PUK) Party, for example, co-founded Women for a Free Iraq in February 2003, then The Iraqi Women's High Council, in October 2003. Rend Rahim Francke, the Executive Director of the Iraq Foundation, moved on to co-found Women for a Free Iraq. Some members of the same group established, within two months, Women's Alliance for Democratic Iraq. The differences among these organizations are nominal; but they are much needed by the US Administration to broadcast the false impression that there is widespread popular Iraqi support for the invasion and occupation.

Reading the 'achievements' of these organizations, before and after the invasion, it is worth noting that, in addition to their clear lack of 'neutrality', their implementation of US–UK policies in Iraq has led to their total silence on Iraqi women's suffering. Furthermore, their failure to address women's daily priorities such as lack of security and health care, widespread imprisonment and collective punishment must be seen in this context. Despite this lack of tangible concern, two new programmes for Iraqi women were announced by Colin Powell on 8 March 2004: the US–Iraq Women's Network, and Iraqi Women's Democracy Initiative.

According to John S. Burnett, what was left out of all the official announcements to grant funds by the US is:

> A condition that each grantee agree to clear any and all publicity or media-related matters tied to their funded-activities through USAID first, and to repeatedly and consistently publicise the U.S. government's funding of their efforts throughout each phase of their on-the-ground service delivery, reflecting the Administration's belief that recipients of federal grants are agents of the U.S. government and its policies.[14]

The obstacles facing these NGOs are enormous, a fact which has forced many of the 80 or so international aid agencies operating in Iraq to relocate their international staff outside Iraq, leaving only local staff on the ground. This is because the NGOs, and their non-local staff, are correctly regarded as extensions of US–UK political and military agendas.[15] Ordinary Iraqis are justifiably sceptical when the NGO relief agencies that moved to work in Iraq did so while accepting funding from the very governments that had created – and continue to cause – so much of the destruction in the first place.

Sadly, due to the arrogant American policy of forcing US-funded NGOs to publicize US interests and backing, and a palpable lack of understanding of, or consideration for, the Iraqi people's feelings against occupation, most aid workers and NGOs, no matter how independent they are, are perceived in the mayhem of Iraq under occupation as tools of the occupation used to infiltrate and undermine or 're-shape' Iraqi society and grass-roots organizations.[16]

## COLONIAL FEMINISTS

In late September 2004, the US State Department announced the names of organizations that would share in $10 million worth of grants allocated under the 'Iraqi Women's Democracy Initiative' to train Iraqi women in the skills and practices of democratic life. Paula Dobriansky, US Under Secretary of State for Global Affairs, said, 'We will give Iraqi women the tools. We will provide the information and experience they need to run for office, lobby for fair treatment in Iraq's emerging institutions.' The fact that the money will go mainly to organizations embedded with the US Administration – such as the Independent Women's Forum (IWF) founded by Dick Cheney's wife, Lynn Cheney, who has worked tirelessly over the years to oppose progress on women's issues in the United States – was not mentioned nor was it revealed that Paula Dobriansky, who announced the grant, has also served on the IWF's board of advisers. Also missing was the fact that the IWF's staff 'consists primarily of former Republican activists with extensive government and lobbying experience but little or no experience in democracy promotion, international affairs, or the Middle East'.[17]

Of all the blunders by the US Administration in Iraq, the greatest is its failure to understand the Iraqi people, and Iraqi women in particular. The main misconception is to perceive Iraqi women as silent, powerless victims in a male-dominated society in urgent need of sexual and political 'liberation'.[18] The most striking example of this failure comes from the CPA's representative, Joanne Dickow, who began working with Iraqi women in April 2003. Recalling the timid response she received in a meeting from Iraqi women, she says: 'There was this incredible sense by the Iraqi women of "Oh my goodness, what do you mean we are going to get involved in politics?" ... And there was this sense of "Oh, these are doctors, lawyers and engineers." ' Dickow explained that women had been largely excluded from the political process. 'Getting them to understand that this was their time was probably the hardest job of all at the beginning,' she said.[19]

This image fits conveniently into the overall picture of the Iraqi people as passive victims who would welcome the occupation of their country. And it is specifically founded in a view of Iraqi women as victims of massive sexual oppression.

The reality is, of course, entirely different. Iraqi women have been actively involved in public life going as far back as the Ottoman Empire. This can be seen in Iraq's public schooling, in the media and in women's participation in political life. In 1899 the first primary and secondary schools for girls were established, and 90 girls were enrolled. *Layla*, the first Iraqi women's magazine, was published on 15 October 1923 and ran monthly for two years. By 1937 four women's magazines were being published in Baghdad: *Al Subh* magazine published by Nihad Al Zehawi (1936), *Fatat Al Iraq* (Iraqi Girl) by Hassiba Raji in 1936, *Al Mar'aa Al Hadetha* (Modern Woman) by Hamdiyaal A'araji in 1936, and *Fatat Al Arab* (Arab Girl) by Maryam Narmah in 1937. The well-known *Sawt Al Mar'aa* (Woman's Voice) magazine was published in 1943.[20]

Women were also involved in political activity, including combat, going back at least to the 1920 revolution against the British occupation. Feda'aha al Ezairjiya of Amara, the 'poetess of the Twenties revolution', joined the fighters to replace her brother who was killed in battle. Nazik al Malaika (b. 1924), the most important poet and critic in the Arab world, blended Iraqi nationalism and solidarity with Palestinian and Algerian struggles against occupation as well as broader struggles for freedom and social justice. Women were active in various political parties during the entire period, and, by 1952, there were 150 women political prisoners.

The Communist Party (CP) established The League for the Defence of Women's Rights in 1942 with Amina al Rahal as the first Iraqi woman in the central committee of the CP in 1941–43. This was followed by the efforts of other political parties to open up to the participation of women. All of this reflected the same principle: fighting alongside men, women were also liberating themselves. This was proved in the aftermath of the 1958 revolution which ended the British-imposed monarchy when, within two years, women's organizations achieved what over 30 years of British occupation failed to: legal equality.

These struggles and achievements, the result of slow organic processes, led UNICEF to report in 1993:

> Rarely do women in the Arab world enjoy as much power and support as they do in Iraq. The 1970 constitution affirmed the equality of all citizens before the law, and guaranteed equal opportunities without discrimination by sex. According to labour law number 71 enacted in 1987, men and women must receive equal pay for equal work. Women working in the government sector are entitled to a one-year maternity leave, receiving their full salary for the first six months and half salary for the next six months. A wife's income is recognised as independent from her husband's. She has the right to vote, hold office, acquire and dispose of agricultural land. In 1974, education was made free at all levels, and in 1979/80 it was made compulsory for girls and boys through the age of twelve. These legal bases provide a solid framework for the promotion of women and the enhancement of their role in society. They have had a direct bearing on women's education, health, labour and social welfare.[21]

Other developments were also reported by UNICEF in 1998: women's industrial employment increased from 13 per cent in 1987 to 21 per cent in 1993; in the same year, female employees constituted 79 per cent of the service sector, 43.9 per cent of the professional and technical sectors, and 12.7 per cent of administrative and organizational posts.[22] Iraq also had one of the highest literacy rates in the Arab world, 22 universities, 45 vocational colleges and approximately 14,000 schools. There were more professional women in positions of power than in almost any other Middle Eastern country.

Despite all this progress, the tragedy was, of course, that women were living under Saddam's oppressive regime. Members of the National Assembly were not elected but appointed. There was no legal protection for victims of crimes of the regime. It is true that women occupied high political positions, including 27 of the 250 seats in the National Assembly, but they did nothing to protest the injustices inflicted on their sisters who opposed Saddam's regime. The same is now happening in 'the new democratic Iraq'.

After 'liberation', Bush and Blair shared a vision for Iraq that trumpeted women's advancement as a centrepiece of their policy of 'democratization'. And, indeed, in the White House and Downing Street carefully selected Iraqi women recited what Bush and Blair desperately needed to hear, justifying the invasion of Iraq. On 28 June 2004, US Administrator Paul Bremer was replaced by the *de facto* governor, US Ambassador John Negroponte. Nominal sovereignty was handed over to a US-appointed Iraqi Interim Government (IIG), which included six women cabinet ministers. They were not elected by the Iraqi people. Under Ayad Allawi's regime, 'multinational forces' remained immune to legal redress, rarely held accountable for crimes committed against Iraqis. All decisions approved by the IIG, those affecting women included, were made to protect the interests of the US-led occupation, not the Iraqi people.

The gap between those women who were members of Allawi's puppet regime and the majority of Iraqi women widened by the day. While cabinet ministers and the US–UK embassies are cocooned inside the fortified Green Zone, Iraqis are denied the basic right of walking safely in their own streets. The rights of the road are for American humvees and tanks bearing the warning: 'Itha tetejawaz al ratil teta'radh lilmawt' ('If you pass the convoy you will be killed'). Iraqi women's daily lives are marked by this violent turmoil. Lack of security and fear of kidnapping make them prisoners in their homes, effectively preventing them from participating in public life. They witness the looting of their country by Halliburton, Bechtel, mercenaries, contractors and local subcontractors while they are denied clean water and electricity. In a land coveted for its oil, they have to queue nine hours every day to buy kerosene, gas or petrol. According to a study conducted by Iraq's Health Ministry in cooperation with Norway's Institute for Applied International Studies and the UN Development Programme, severe malnutrition has doubled among children. This figure translates into roughly 400,000 Iraqi children suffering from 'wasting', a condition characterized by chronic diarrhoea and dangerous deficiencies of protein.[23] Unemployment at 70 per cent is, of course, exacerbating poverty and increasing prostitution, backstreet abortions and honour killings.

According to Isam al-Khafaji, the Director of the New York-based Iraq Revenue Watch, corruption has become an 'open secret' within the Iraqi government.[24] Nepotism is widespread among the IIG. Hassan Al Naqib, Minister of the Interior, admitted that he had appointed 49 of his relatives to high-ranking jobs, although he was careful to point out that they were 'qualified'. Ediba Nouman, a distinguished Iraqi academic who was dismissed by Saddam's regime in the 1980s, applied for her old job as a lecturer at Basra University. In order to start the process she was asked to provide a letter from al Hawze (the Shia religious scholar authority) to prove her affiliation with one of the sectarian parties controlling the IIG.

In addition to all this, the killing of academics, journalists and scientists has not spared women: On 27 October 2004, Liqa Abdul Razaq, a newsreader at Al sharqiaya TV, was shot with her two-month-old baby in the Aldoura district of Baghdad. Layla Al-Saad, Dean of Law at Mosul University, was slaughtered in her house. Yet, the silence of the 'feminists' in Ayad Allawi's regime was deafening: their response to the daily violations of human and women's rights has been highly selective. The suffering of their sisters in cities showered by US jet fighters with napalm, phosphorus and cluster bombs, the destruction of archaeological sites, the daily killing of civilians by occupation forces, all of these are met with transparently thin rhetoric about 'training for democracy'. Is it any wonder that most Iraqi women perceive initiatives by US–UK-sponsored NGOs, no matter how nobly packaged, and colonial feminists as meaningless, paying lip-service to the idea of democracy, but never meaning to implement it?[25]

## MISSIONARIES

Before the subject of Christian missionaries can be discussed, some background is required. Some of the oldest Christian communities in the world live among the 27 million predominantly Muslim people of Iraq. As in neighbouring Syria, some of them still use the language of Christ of the gospels in speech and print. Peaceful co-existence between religious groups, including in mixed villages and urban neighbourhoods, is the norm in Iraq and the rest of the Middle East. For centuries under Ottoman rule and earlier, religious communities, however widely dispersed they were in the realm, administered their own family and property affairs independently from the state. These practices were partly a reflection of the traditional Islamic principle of protecting the 'People of the Book'. This regards the three monotheistic religions as stemming from Abraham, a common genealogical as well as theological ancestor of all people in the region. The holy books are seen as chapters of the same Eternal Book revealed at successive times through the prophets. In turn, this reflects more ancient notions of the oneness of mankind in the Mesopotamian cultures extant millennia before the Bible collection of the myths of the region.

Such background should explain why bans on proselytizing among the 'believers', as opposed to pagans, is in operation all over the Middle East. This ban has maintained social peace even throughout the centuries of European crusades carried out under the banner of Christianity. Throughout all colonial rule in the region, the Arab Christians stood politically beside their compatriots denouncing aggression. Hence, even when Arab and other Middle Eastern Christians became part of worldwide church organizations, they maintained a clear loyalty to their respective countries and their ethno-linguistic groups in the face of foreign aggression.

There are around 900,000 Christian Iraqis, the majority of whom are Chaldean Catholic, with various Orthodox and Eastern Catholic denominations as well. There is also a handful of Protestant evangelicals. Ethnically, the majority of Christians are Arabs, with some Kurdish and Assyrian minorities. Iraqi civil society and successive Iraqi governments highlighted the rights of religious minorities and the duty of Muslims to protect them ('Dhimma'). Politics was separated from religion in political parties, all of which, until recently, were cross-sectarian.

Unlike what the US-led occupation would like observers to believe, political affiliation rather than ethnic identity, religious affiliation or sectarian orientation was the yardstick against which various Iraqi governments determined which groups or individuals would be subject to persecution. Just one illustration of this is the fact that evangelical churches are illegal in most Middle Eastern countries, Iraq included, for the reasons noted above. 'In 1969, under the Ba'ath regime, all American missionaries were expelled from the country and their schools nationalized or closed. However, Iraqi non-evangelical Christians continued to practice and churches continued to function under national leadership.'[26]

The Christians who chose to flee Iraq in large numbers under Saddam's rule did so mostly for reasons other than religious ones: 'faced with economic hardship, the oppressive nature of Saddam Hussein's regime, and the effects of UN sanctions, thousands of Iraqis chose to flee the country. Many Christians were among those who fled, mainly to Europe and the USA'.[27] In fact, one observer noted that 'Religious minorities have been favoured by Saddam Hussein if they demonstrated political loyalty. Christians have had increasing freedom for worship since 1968.'[28]

The language of 'crusade' was used by George W. Bush in the run-up to the war on Iraq, when he told reporters: 'This crusade, this war on terrorism, is going to take a while.' It was not a single slip of the tongue. The same 'crusade' was revived by the Bush–Cheney election campaign in Autumn 2004.

With his religious background, it is easy to see how Bush's evangelical bent, his repeated biblical references and his vision of freedom spreading out from a saved Iraq, gave the missionaries – the professional proselytizers – the green light to move into Iraq immediately after declaring 'mission accomplished'. Conveniently, Bush became the embodiment of both the military and evangelical mission to spread Christ's word not just in Iraq, but also in the whole Middle East.

American evangelical organizations, including the Oklahoma-based Voice of the Martyrs (VOM), the Southern Baptist Convention and the Pennsylvania-based Association of Baptists for World Evangelism, have said they will focus much of their proselytizing on Muslims in Iraq and surrounding nations. It is worth noting how open and widespread the proselytizing zeal has been in the Iraqi adventure. VOM missionaries have organized groups to distribute Christian tracts in Baghdad, among other activities. One can imagine how these operate at traffic jams under the protection of occupying troops. Todd Nettleton of VOM explained why they do so even though this jars with public sensibilities: 'Yes, sharing Christ's love causes conflict. But the alternative is allowing people to go to hell.'[29] This is a general attitude among missionaries, and despite much controversy surrounding their work, the Southern Baptist Theological Seminary leader, Albert Mohler, sees what the missionaries are doing in Iraq as completely in keeping with the traditional role of Christian relief agencies and equates proselytizing with 'liberty': 'It would be an appalling tragedy if America were to lead this coalition and send young American men and women into battle, to expend such military effort, to then leave in place a regime that would lack respect for religious liberty.'[30] That is presumably why, within eight months of the invasion, at least nine evangelical churches have opened in Baghdad, supported by American organizations. More than 900,000 Bibles in Arabic, along with hundreds of tons of food and medical supplies, have been sent to Iraq. The National Biblical Christian Federation Church has distributed more than 60,000 aid boxes prepared by Samaritan's Purse, an organization headed by the US evangelist Franklin Graham.[31]

Kyle Fisk, Executive Administrator of the National Association of Evangelicals, explained that the strategic advantage of establishing mission bases in Iraq draws its inspiration from George W. Bush: 'President Bush said democracy will spread from Iraq to nearby countries,' Fisk said. 'A free Iraq also allows us to spread Jesus Christ's teachings even in nations where the laws keep us out.'[32]

Thus, humanitarian aid became the cloak that many missionaries chose to wear in order to enter Iraq. And, missionaries perceived Iraq as a base to convert the rest of the region.

How does all of this play in Iraq itself? Most Iraqi Christians believe that Bush's missionary invasion will affect them negatively, rather than giving them greater promised religious freedom.[33] *The World from Rome* reported, for example, that 'The Chaldeans say that the growing presence of American Protestant evangelical missionaries in Iraq is not helping.' By openly seeking Iraqi converts in the wake of the US-led invasion, these missionaries have promoted the impression that all Christians are part of the coalition forces.[34]

The view of the invasion as a religious war cuts across a confessional divide within the Muslim population. Sheik Fatih Kashif Ghitaa, the head of Baghdad's Strategic Studies Centre, is in no doubt that 'most Iraqis think that the US wants to erase Islam, so this would have fed into the thinking of the attackers at Mosul.' 'There will be more such attacks,' he said. Furthermore, 'after Saddam, the Iraqi religions are enjoying their own revival, so Christians will be seen as Crusaders – and that's very dangerous'.[35] 'Extremists, whether Muslims or evangelicals, inspire violence and hatred,' said Mahmoud Othman, a secular Kurdish member of the Iraqi Governing Council: 'The newspapers are screaming about a Christian conspiracy.'[36]

Muslim clerics rallied to the defence of the Churches declaring attacks on Iraqi Christians another stratagem for undermining national unity. They suspect that attacks on civilians, and especially on mosques, churches and clerics of any kind, are as likely to be the work of mercenaries in the pay of the occupation forces or Israel's Mossad as they are of religious fundamentalists and deranged individuals.

Minas Yousifi, spokesman for the Iraqi Christian Democratic Party, relayed how the Sunni Association of Muslim Clerics and the Shia Khalisi School in Baghdad responded readily to his suggestions for gestures to allay the fears of the Christians in Baghdad and Mosul after the August 2004 spate of attacks on churches. They promptly organized groups to visit churches on Sundays, staying all day with the congregations. On one Sunday in Mosul alone about 20 taxis were needed to transport about 45 Muslim clerics with guards to churches in villages. This position was echoed by the young cleric Moktada Al-Sadr, who heads a mass Shia movement, in offering to protect all Christian churches in the country.[37] Yousifi regards the claims of a massive exodus of Christians from Iraq as malicious scaremongering. He estimates the number of families who fled the Baghdad area to Syria and Jordan at around 200 at the height of the scare, with about twice that number from Mosul. He did not have data on Basra and the South, but thought that the worst was over by the end of 2004. 'These figures may not be different from the average exodus from any other group,' he said. Mr Yousifi is one of the 15-member Secretariat Committee of the Iraqi National Foundation Congress, a cross-sectarian, cross-ethnic political umbrella of anti-occupation academics, clerics and veteran politicians who were in opposition to Saddam's regime but who also oppose the occupation.

To most Iraqis, the spectre of American missionaries settling in their country, in the aftermath of the military invasion, feels like a second invasion. This is seen as undermining the nation's stability, and will make a precarious situation that much worse. Iraqi Christians are no exception.[38]

## CONCLUSION

These three Cyclops of empire–building in Iraq – US and UK government-sponsored NGOs, colonial feminists and missionaries – bear the face of 'soft power' which advances just behind the steel of 'hard' military power. But Iraqis are not unaware of their purposes which, varied as they may be in particulars, are generally aimed at the successful occupation of Iraq by the US and its closest, favoured 'allies', its imperial subordinates. We may go further. They are part of the processes of establishing informal imperialism in Iraq. Perhaps not a relation of colonialism, exactly, but certainly a form of imperialism with the penetration and pacification of Iraq as its aim, a country so vital to the global capitalist order and to the role of American Empire in it. In fact, any long-term 'success' on the part of the occupiers would require a successful reconstruction of Iraqi civil society such as we see attempted through government-sponsored NGOs, colonial feminists and missionaries. What the occupiers and aspiring imperial relations ignore, however, is that Iraqis have been through this before. They are virtually born with the historical memory of the occupations and colonialisms of the past written into their DNA. And they are politically savvy. The difference between the 'soft occupation' of the three Cyclops and the real liberation of Iraqi women, religious freedom and a thriving civil society is clear to most Iraqis. As earlier occupiers have found, this one too will meet its deserved fate – and it is unlikely to be a soft one.

## NOTES

1 Les Roberts et al., 'Mortality Before and After the 2003 Invasion of Iraq: Cluster Sample Survey', *The Lancet* (29 October 2004).
2 Occupation casualties as of 31 March 2005, more statistics are available at http://icasualties.org.
3 One good example is the Iraqi National Accord (INA), headed by Ayad Allawi, backed by the CIA and MI6, and which is seen in Iraq as 'a Western stooge' who 'lacked domestic credibility'. *Telegraph* (24 September 2004).
4 See Edith Penrose and E. F. Penrose, *Iraq: International Relations and National Development* (Boulder, CO: Westview Press, 1978).
5 Ghassan Atiyyah, *Iraq 1908–1921: A Political Study* (Beirut: Arab Institute for Research and Publishing, 1973).

6   Gertrude Bell, *Letters* (21 August 1921), http://www.gerty.ncl.ac.uk/letters/l1447.htm.

7   Ibid.

8   Ibid.

9   The American counterpart of the British Miss Bell, Deputy Defense Secretary Paul Wolfowitz, told Congress in April 2003 why he could not put a time to form a permanent Iraqi government: 'We want to push it, but we want to make sure that when the training wheels are off, the bicycle doesn't fall over.'

10  In 1997, US State Department spokesperson James Rubin described the embargo against Iraq as 'The toughest, most comprehensive sanctions in history'. A 2000 report by the UN Commission on Human Rights similarly concluded that 'the sanctions against Iraq are the most comprehensive, total sanctions that have ever been imposed on a country'.

11  Remarks to the National Foreign Policy Conference for Leaders of Nongovernmental Organization, Secretary of State Colin L. Powell, Washington, DC (26 October 2001).

12  Andrew Natsios, speaking on the last day of Interaction's three-day forum (9 June 2003).

13  *USAID Awards Grants for Iraq Community Action Program* (28 May 2003), http://www.usaid.gov/press/releases/2003/pr030527.html.

14  John S. Burnett, 'In the Line of Fire', *New York Times* (4 August 2004).

15  Sir Nick Young of the British Red Cross said of a visit to Baghdad in 2004: 'I had a very strong feeling that we were regarded as the occupying powers … and this was something I hadn't felt before.' Christian Aid submission to the International Development Committee Inquiry on development assistance in Iraq, Addendum (10 January 2005).

16  Ibid., 'Since the Spring 2003 intervention, coalition leaders have consistently tried to present the political/military mission as a humanitarian one, giving humanitarian tasks to coalition military units, and giving coalition military officers the job of coordinating humanitarian work. As a result, any distinction between the neutral role of humanitarian organisations and the role of the coalition military is now quite unclear to most members of the Iraqi public, many of whom now resent all international organisations, or even internationally funded organisations, as "occupiers". Humanitarian space, as aid agencies describe the ability to reach those in needs, has been severely compromised as a result and may not be recovered for many years.'

17  Jim Lobe, 'Politics: Anti-Feminist Group to Train Iraqi Women in Politics', *IPS-Inter Press Service* (5 October 2004).

18  Haifa Zangana, 'Quiet or I'll Call Democracy', *Guardian* (22 December 2004).

19  See   http://www.iraqcoalition.org/transcripts/20040426_women_net.html.

20  'Iraq Women's Panel Presents Paper on Role in Public Life', *Gulf News* (29 January 2002).

21  UNICEF Report, 'Iraq: Children and Women in Iraq, 1993'.

22  UNICEF Report, 'Situation Analysis of Children and Women in Iraq' (30 April 1998).

23 Karl Vick, 'Children Pay Cost of Iraq's Chaos', *Washington Post* (21 November 2004).

24 Dexter Filkins, 'Missing Money: Mystery in Iraq as $300 Million is Taken Abroad', *New York Times* (22 January 2005).

25 'To date, women have not played an active role in the new Iraqi governing bodies. Only three women have been appointed to the 25-member Interim Iraqi Governing Council, and the three women on the Council did not have the right to serve on the Presidential Council. No women were appointed to be governors of the 18 provinces in Iraq nor were any women appointed to a committee overseeing the drafting of the new Iraqi constitution.' Women for Women International (WWI), 'First Post-War Survey of Iraqi Women', press release (7 January 2005).

26 'The Forgotten Church in Iraq – a Fact Sheet', http://www.ekklesia.co.uk/content/services/iraqchurchfactsheet.shtml.

27 Ibid.

28 Global Mapping International, 'Operation Change – Iraq', http://www.gmi.org/ow/country/iraq/owtext.html.

29 Charles Duhigg, 'Evangelicals Flock into Iraq on a Mission of Faith', *Los Angeles Times* (18 March 2004).

30 Broward Liston, 'Missionary Work in Iraq (Interview with Albert Mohler)', *Time* (15 April 2003).

31 David Rennie, 'Bible Belt Missionaries Set Out On a "War for Souls" in Iraq', *Telegraph* (27 December 2003).

32 For example, 'Jon Hanna, an evangelical minister from Ohio who has recently returned from Iraq, applied for a new passport to travel there, describing himself as a humanitarian worker.' Dominic Volonnino, 'Evangelicals Invade Iraq', *Peace and Conflict Monitor* (20 March 2004).

33 'God and the president have given us an opportunity to bring Jesus Christ to the Middle East', said Tom Craig, an independent American missionary working in Iraq and Cyprus. 'This is my commandment. No amount of danger will stop me.' 'The Recent Attack of American Missionaries Makes Iraq a Minefield', *Christian Today* (24 March 2004).

34 John Allen 'The World from Rome', *National Catholic Reporter*, 3:50 (6 August 2004).

35 Paul McGeough, 'In God's Name', *Sydney Morning Herald* (26 March 2004).

36 David Rennie, 'Bible Belt Missionaries Set out on a "War for Souls" in Iraq', *Telegraph* (27 December 2003).

37 To Delegates at the Pan-Arabic Islamic Conference in Beirut (4 December 2004).

38 'The Pastor of the Light Independent Church of Baghdad accused the foreign missionaries of attaching strings to offers of financial assistance: "When we asked them for money they said that we would have to be like them. They made big mistakes in going to Mosul and they are causing security problems for all of us. Muslims are committed to God, too, so it would be better for these people to encourage Muslims to be good Muslims than for them to switch to Christianity. I don't seek converts." ' Paul McGeough, 'In God's Name', *Sydney Morning Herald* (26 March 2004).

# IV

# Resisting Empire: Room for Manoeuvre?

# 13
# Drifting Away from the Edge of Empire: Canada in the Era of George W. Bush

*Reg Whitaker*

As the US and UK governments sought frantically to line up UN support for their long-planned invasion of Iraq in early 2003, global attention was focused on the recalcitrant French, Germans and Russians. When the invasion was denied Security Council sanction, the world paid less attention to a rebuke much closer to home for the Americans: their two NAFTA partners, Canada and Mexico, both refused to support Bush's illegal war. In Mexico's case, as a member of the Security Council, it had to cast a 'No' vote, thus provoking open threats of retaliation for this act of insubordination. In Canada's case, intimidation was less direct, but clear: negative economic consequences could be expected, as the US Ambassador to Canada grimly expressed his government's 'disappointment' at the Canadian decision.

Canada's decision to stay out of the so-called 'coalition of the willing' (more accurately described as the coalition of the bribed, the bullied and the bilked) may have attracted little attention from a wider world fixed on the contest of wills between Bush and Blair vs. Chirac and Schroeder, but in the North American regional context it was a matter of some considerable significance. It was a strikingly independent position for a country that had until that point seemed on an inevitable trajectory toward closer economic – and, it was assumed, political – integration with the American superpower. For Canadians, it was a defining moment in their long and tortured relationship with the 'elephant'. Never before, as the right-wing opposition in Parliament indignantly pointed out, had Canada refused to stand by its closest friends, America and Britain, beside whom it had fought in two world wars as well as in regional conflicts in Korea, the Gulf and, most recently, Afghanistan. What was more, the decision proved immensely popular; indeed it was the single most popular act of the decade-long Liberal government of Jean Chrétien.

With the Iraq decision, something had changed on America's northern border. When George W. Bush visited Canada in late 2004 and publicly bullied Chrétien's successor, Paul Martin, to accept Bush's faith-based ballistic missile defence shield (BMD), the Canadian reaction, never in doubt over similar issues in the past, was very different. Despite the expectations of the right-wing media, the Canadian armed forces and defence industries, and usually influential pro-Americans strategically situated in key positions in the private and public sectors, a decision that would in the past have been routine instead had become a political minefield. In fact, Bush's aggressive public confrontation of Martin turned out to be the kiss of death for Canadian acceptance of BMD. Faced with strongly anti-Bush public opinion which had turned decisively against BMD, a minority Parliament with two opposition parties vociferously in opposition and large sections of Martin's own party in open revolt, the Prime Minister announced in February 2005 that Canada would not support the plan. Like the Iraq decision, the 'No' to BMD was more symbolic of selective autonomy than a substantive rebellion against American hegemony (as a North American Aerospace Defence (NORAD) partner, Canada is already in a sense practically involved with BMD, just as it had sent Canadian forces into Afghanistan even as it said 'No' to Iraq). Yet it was precisely the symbolism of Canadian support that Bush had demanded, and failed to achieve. It seems that the American Empire is fraying just a little on the northern edge of the homeland. But even that little represents a significant change.

Canada's new-found *de facto* autonomy on key security issues for the Bush Administration – not of course a veto, but certainly an op-out – requires some explanation, not least from Left analysts, who have argued consistently that politics follows from economics, and find it difficult to explain how decades of continental integration, from the Canada–US Free Trade Agreement in 1988, to the implementation of the North American Free Trade Agreement (NAFTA) in the early 1990s, could have led to *greater* political autonomy for Canada. Equally difficult to explain is that the Chrétien government in the mid- and late 1990s had actively pursued a neoliberal economic agenda that was seen to tie Canada into even closer lockstep with the American-dominated North American market. I will argue that Canada's recent trajectory instead illustrates a surprising observation, one that will certainly seem perverse in Marxist analysis: intensified

North American economic integration, along with fiscally conservative policies on the part of Canadian governments, actually fosters
greater scope for Canadian *political* autonomy.

A little historical background helps gauge the extent of the shift.
Forty years before the Iraq decision, Canada faced a crucial test of its
national sovereignty on a key international security issue. In 1963,
Canada faced a demand that BOMARC anti-aircraft missiles stationed
on Canadian soil under NORAD be armed with nuclear warheads.
Relations between the aggressive Cold Warriors in the Kennedy
Administration and the Progressive Conservative government of
Canadian Prime Minister John Diefenbaker had become quite
strained, especially during the heart-stopping Cuban missile crisis in
1962, when Diefenbaker showed reluctance to mobilize Canadian
forces at Kennedy's request (or demand). In fact, American pressures
drove deep divisions within the governing Conservative Party, setting
the hawkish Minister of Defence against the dovish Minister of
External Affairs, a division that the dithering Diefenbaker was unable
to resolve. When his Defence Minister quit over his inability to commit on nuclear warheads, Diefenbaker's minority government fell and
an election was precipitated. With the Kennedy Administration and
the US media in Canada openly intervening against the Tories, the
Liberals, led by Nobel Peace Prize winner Lester Pearson, took the pro-
American position, promising to accept nuclear warheads in order to
fulfil NORAD obligations. The election campaign was fought as a
virtual referendum on Canada's relationship with the US, and the
Liberals won.

This election led the conservative nationalist philosopher George
Grant to write his grimly pessimistic *Lament for a Nation: the Defeat
of Canadian Nationalism*,[1] inspiring a generation of young nationalists, most, oddly enough, on the Left. What Grant saw as the impossibility of (pre-modern) conservatism in his era meant, in his mind,
the impossibility of Canada. The Left nationalists read Grant more
straightforwardly: it was the Liberal continentalists who sold out
the Canadian nation, and only a socialist nationalism could save the
country. This party-line interpretation withstood some turbulence
in the great free trade election of 1988, fought over ratification of
the Canada–US Free Trade Agreement, the predecessor to NAFTA,
when it was the Conservative ministry of Brian Mulroney that
championed continental integration and the Liberal leader of the
opposition, John Turner, who led the passionate opposition to

ratification. But the Mulroney government's re-election seemed to confirm the results of 1963. Once again, Canadian nationalism had lost out to continentalism.

In 2003, George Grant was stood on his head. A clear choice was posed by the American demand for support on Iraq. This time it was a Liberal government that said no, and the Conservative opposition that vainly demanded that Canada adopt a 'ready, aye ready' stance towards Canada's 'best friends'. In the 2004 election, the Liberals, trailing the Conservatives in the polls because of domestic scandals, ran negative ads suggesting that if the Conservatives had been in office in 2003, Canadian troops would have been sent to Iraq. This helped turn the tide and gain a last-minute Liberal minority. Clearly, the party-line interpretation has no basis. In any event, parties in liberal democracies are electorally opportunistic and notoriously lacking in long-term principles, so no one should be surprised at the ideological adaptability of the Liberals, who have dominated federal politics for more than a century. More interesting is the question of why the Liberals seized on the Iraq issue and why it proved so successful for them. Another pertinent question is how this could be related to another example of Liberal opportunism of a different kind: the Chrétien Liberals had abandoned their 1988 opposition to free trade to become enthusiastic supporters of NAFTA and even a wider free trade area of the Americas.

Behind these shifts was the backdrop of the end of the Cold War. Throughout the Cold War era, Canada played a somewhat schizophrenic role as both junior partner to the US hegemon on the committed Western side (founding member of NATO; NORAD partner; member of American-led intelligence network; military contributor to the Korean War; willing partner to the US in Cold War diplomacy; enthusiastic supporter of anti-communist ideological offensives, etc.) and advocate of international and multilateral arrangements outside the Cold War framework (as Foreign Minister, Lester Pearson won the Nobel Peace Prize for inventing UN peacekeeping missions). Canadians tried to be both good Cold Warriors and liberal internationalists at the same time. It was not always easy, as Canada's juggling act fell foul of the Americans from time to time. Even Pearson, after becoming Prime Minister in 1963 with American sanction, soon put himself in Lyndon Johnson's bad books by daring to suggest a peace strategy in Vietnam.

Despite occasional abrasive flare-ups, Canada continued to the very end of the Cold War to be a generally loyal junior partner, albeit one that sat out some direct involvements such as Vietnam, and at the same time a respected player on the international stage. Sometimes the latter involved a certain amount of hypocrisy on Canada's part. For instance, the Canadian members on the Tripartite International Control Commission on Indochina were sometimes employed for intelligence-gathering by the Americans as the regional conflict with the Communists widened in the late 1950s and early 1960s. Canada's predilection for multilateralism could also be assimilated into the bipolar Cold War strategy of the US. From the 1940s through the 1980s, the US showed an aptitude for leading *through* rather than around coalitions, alliances and multilateral institutions, which wiser American leaders, from both the Democratic and Republican parties, understood actually amplified, rather than diminished, American power and influence. Independent diplomatic action by Canada could sometimes prove quite functional to American purposes, when rigid bipolar confrontation prevented the US from initiating moves. Thus, the creation of a UN peacekeeping force in Gaza after the Anglo-French fiasco of Suez was helpful to the US in resolving a difference among Western allies, while the East–West conflict had escalated over the Hungarian revolt. Pierre Trudeau's action in recognizing Communist China, viewed at the time as a brave independent move, actually facilitated Richard Nixon's celebrated subsequent visit to Beijing and his playing of the 'China card' against the Soviets.

With the end of the Cold War came the end of the bipolar division of the world. With America as the only remaining superpower, unchallenged by any rival nation or bloc of nations of even roughly comparable weight, its need to cultivate alliances and govern through multilateral institutions has faded. At home, a mood of post-Cold War triumphalism along with a rising tide of America First nationalism drove both Congress and White House in the 1990s towards a curious blend of isolationism and interventionism. This culminated in the election of the aggressively unilateralist George W. Bush in 2000. 9/11 cemented the new mood, providing an alibi – the global 'war on terror' – for a series of new wars abroad, and the rationale for the Bush Doctrine of pre-emptive regime change with or without UN sanction. This was an unpleasant prospect for Canada, a country attached to multilateralism and its international boy scout image. But a unipolar world also meant the loss of its semi-officially sanctioned independent role – the junior partner that could take on alliance missions that the bloc leader preferred to delegate. A cottage industry has grown up in Canada bemoaning our 'lost place' in the world, and lamenting the demise of the 'golden age' of Canadian diplomacy in the 1940s and 1950s.[2] Golden ages, of course, always look more gilded with the passage of time. But the present is certainly anything but golden. In 2003 the skilful Canadian ambassador to the UN, Paul Heinbecker, tried to broker a sensible compromise over Iraq between the US/UK and France/ Germany/Russia that could have averted war. In the new post-golden age era of the 'war on terror', not even the legendary diplomat Lester Pearson could have played his part any longer. Heinbecker was simply ignored, as Bush and Blair readied their big battalions and prepared to roll over the UN, not to speak of Iraq.

Iraq was, however, only one of a number of blows delivered by the Bush Administration to Canadian susceptibilities. The disdain demonstrated towards alliance partners, thinly veiled by former Secretary of State Colin Powell's diplomatic cover, was mirrored in the attitude towards international institutions, and indeed to any international treaty or protocol that might be seen as in any way limiting America's sovereign 'right' to do as it pleases, free of any external impediment or limitation. Multilateralist Canada witnessed with shock a series of existing treaty abrogations, along with a flat refusal to sign up to any new multilateral agreement. Among a blizzard of unilateral acts, the anti-ballistic missile treaty was ditched to open the way for BMD; the Kyoto Protocol on climate change was rejected; and – especially galling to Canada, which had taken a special interest in this initiative – the US renounced the International Criminal Court (ICC), denying its jurisdiction over American citizens. Worse, they bullied a string of Third World and former communist states not to challenge the American exemption by threatening to cut off assistance if they refused to comply. Congress even passed the 'Hague Invasion' resolution, giving the President power to rescue any American held for war crimes. Not that the Americans denied the relevance of the Court to other, lesser nations, nor refrained from delivering war crimes suspects from elsewhere to the Hague; rather, they claimed the right of exemption from the rule of international law they expected everyone else to adhere to. That this is more than self-righteousness soon became evident with revelations about terror, torture and murder in American prisons strung like an archipelago of gulags from Guantánamo to Abu Ghraib to Bagram, not to speak of those unlucky enough to be 'rendered' by the US to outsourced torture in countries with notorious human rights records.

The Bush Administration, and Congress behind it, seemed to be saying that America not only insisted on its own way, always, but even rejected the very notion of negotiating common responses to common problems in a globalized world. Even on Bush's own terms, this seemed self-defeating: how could any one state, even the US, combat the borderless threat of global terrorist networks without extensive international co-operation provided on a voluntary, rather than coerced, basis? Early in Bush's second term, a charm offensive, test-marketed first in Canada, was launched to recoup lost support from allies in Europe. This was followed by the appointment of State Department superhawk John Bolton to the post of ambassador to the UN – a man who had once declared that the UN 'does not exist', and who described the day the US abrogated its commitment to the ICC to be the 'happiest' of his public career. Adding insult to injury, Bush then dumped the chief architect of the Iraq war, neo-con fanatic Paul Wolfowitz, on the 'World' Bank as its president.

Clearly, Canada was in for a rocky relationship with Bush's America. But Canada was also the most precariously situated of potential dissident nations. Immediately after 9/11, the US slowed traffic of both people and goods across the Canada–US border to a painful crawl, citing 'security' concerns (unfounded rumours of a 'Canadian connection' to the 9/11 conspirators abounded in the American media and among US politicians, although none was ever verified). This action had serious, potentially catastrophic, implications for Canadian economic interests. It also had serious implications for American economic interests, since Canada is America's largest trading partner, but the US was apparently willing to bear the costs – proportionally less in any event than in Canada – in the name of responding to threatened national security. The immediate response of Canadian capital, much of the business-owned media and many conservative politicians was to call for what amounted to immediate unconditional surrender to the US. The call went out for the establishment of a Fortress North America security perimeter within which Canadian policies on defence, security, immigration and refugees would be 'harmonized' with American policies. Conservative think tanks seized the opportunity to suggest that the moment was propitious to trade national security for economic security with various 'big ideas' for deepened continental integration: a customs union; American dollarization of the Canadian currency; a common labour market, etc. None of these schemes came with any meaningful suggestions for how a Canadian political voice could be guaranteed from a unilateralist 'America First' White House and Congress that rejected in principle any foreign limitation on American national sovereignty. In other words, the 'big idea' people in Canada wanted a military, security and economic Europe without any of the forms of political voice the European nations enjoy in the Council of Europe and the European Parliament. While this vision commended itself to neoliberal Canadian capital, which sees Canadian sovereignty as no more than a nuisance impeding continental market forces, and actively dislikes somewhat more liberal Canadian economic and social policies (a national medical care plan, higher tax levels), it proved to have limited purchase on the popular Canadian imagination.

9/11 presented itself to Canadians in a double guise. The threat of terrorism was real enough, and Canadians shared in the sympathy with American losses that echoed around the world in the early days after the fall of the Twin Towers. Canadians too were frightened and alarmed that terrorists could strike at them, as well as at the US. They were also uneasily aware that any evidence of terrorists using Canada as a base or staging ground for further attacks on the American 'homeland' would have horrendous consequences for Canada. But the terrorist spectre has never loomed as menacingly over Canada as it has over the US, hardly surprising given the American hegemon's position as primary target for the globally disaffected.[3] Contributing to the global 'war on terror' – in Canada's case, passing an omnibus Anti-Terrorism Act, reallocating several billions of dollars to security and sending Canadian forces to Afghanistan – was only one front, albeit a highly public one, in a two-front war. The second, covert, front was quietly dedicated to limiting the damage to Canadian sovereignty entailed in the new security-first agenda in Washington.[4] Despite a vociferous and highly influential domestic lobby from big business, with the prestigious Canadian Council of Chief Executives leading the charge, big media, policy think tanks, the conservative opposition in Parliament and several provincial premiers, Fortress North America never commended itself as a model to the federal Liberal government. To capital, the bottom line alone counted, but the Liberals understood that as politicians they had to submit themselves to the voters, who value Canadian sovereignty, as well as economics.

The Liberal answer to the challenge of 9/11 was to launch the Smart Border initiative, a brilliantly conceived method of allaying

American national security concerns, guaranteeing Canadian economic security while minimizing the loss of sovereignty. The Smart Border negotiations, which are still ongoing, have achieved a series of agreements on various mechanisms for ensuring effective security while facilitating the smooth flow of people and goods, including the application of better technology to travel documents and border inspections, fast-tracking pre-approved persons, pre-clearance and tracking of goods transported across the border, etc. The key to understanding the Smart Border process lies in its incrementalism and specificity. Instead of negotiating within a 'big idea' framework looking towards new, overarching structures, the negotiations were strictly on a step-by-step, case-by-case basis. This focused the attention of the Americans on specific, achievable agreements. In their entirety, they added up to a win/win for both sides, but it also took American, not to speak of conservative Canadian, minds off the big picture of continental integration, which is dangerous ground for Canada. The yawning gap in all the big idea schemes for structural integration remains the missing Canadian voice, raising the spectre of taxation without representation. The Smart Border agreements have already delivered many of the security guarantees that the US would gain from a grand security perimeter while leaving Canadian authority largely, although not entirely, intact. Right-wing political opponents initially attacked the negotiation process as a stop-gap and lacking in 'vision' (which was the point), while nationalist opponents on the Left overestimated the degree to which Canada was surrendering sovereignty in practice. More recently, critics have tended to fall relatively silent, as the Smart Border initiative has proved visibly successful.

Capital, however, has simply moved on to argue that these agreements are only a first step towards the yet deeper integration they wish to see. Following the re-election of George W. Bush in 2004, the integrationist chorus rose once more.[5] In early 2005, a tripartite American–Canadian–Mexican task force, including the former Liberal Finance Minister and Deputy Prime Minister, John Manley, recommended yet another scheme for broad integration on security and economic matters. Once a contender for the Liberal leadership, Manley is now, temporarily at least, out of politics and thus beyond the reach of the voters. His former colleagues in the federal cabinet, however, were quick to dismiss his group's ideas, rejecting any 'Big Bang' schemes, as one source put it, while relying on incrementalism. To critics on the Left, in the social democratic New Democratic

Party (NDP) and the Quebec sovereignist Bloc Québécois, Liberal incrementalism is no more than doing in stages what the big thinkers would do in one mega-deal. This misses the subtlety of the Liberal strategy, which sees incrementalism as a substitute, rather than a staging post for wider integration. While some individual Liberals, perhaps including Prime Minister Martin, might prefer wider integration, unlike Manley they have not been released from accountability to the voters, and are reluctant to abandon a politically advantageous Canadian nationalist stance. Even as editorial writers praised its vision, the Manley plan was widely written off as politically unrealistic.

Of course, the Smart Border approach represents no significant departure from the logic of the American Empire. But Canada had, and has, little choice but to engage the Americans constructively on the terrain of border security, where American anxieties are most acute and where these anxieties are inextricably entangled with Canadian security standards and practices.[6] Senator Hillary Clinton, one of the more outspoken (and ill-informed) Congressional critics of alleged Canadian border laxity, has stated as a primary axiom of post-9/11 American policy that 'security trumps economics'. This has proved invalid in relation to the Iraq and BMD decisions, which have not led to economic retaliation, but these involve political agendas of the Bush Administration in foreign and defence policy that cannot convincingly be tied to fundamental American homeland security requirements. A terrorist-related security breach, or even significant risk on the US's northern border, would be tied in this way, and would almost certainly result in security trumping economics, with disastrous consequences for a range of fundamental Canadian economic interests, despite the associated American costs. Less than full engagement in bilateral anti-terrorist cooperation was never an option for Canada.

Despite the voices of alarmism about Canada in Congress and in the right-wing US media, the Bush Administration has recognized in practice that Canada has delivered on the key security issues. Thus Canadians have been given a unique exemption from the new and controversial requirement for foreign visitors to the US to present biometric identification upon entry and exit, indicating a degree of trust extended to Canadians denied even to America's faithful British allies – not to speak, of course, of US economic self-interest given the degree of cross-border shopping and tourism. But the real point of the Smart Border route is that it has left Canada space in other areas to assert its independence, avenues that might well have been closed had Canada submitted to a Fortress North America alternative with extensive harmonization of policies in areas beyond border security alone.

The question remains why Canadian opposition to the wider Bush agenda beyond the basic security cooperation level has been so pronounced, and why it has influenced to such a degree the ruling Liberal Party in Ottawa. Hostility and distrust towards the Bush White House have been endemic almost everywhere in the world, and are sufficiently recognized to be taken as a fact of life of today's international scene. Even those countries whose governments have most closely allied themselves with the US Iraqi adventure – Britain, Italy and Spain before the defeat of the pro-Bush Aznar government – show very much the same levels of popular anti-Bush sentiment as those countries – France, Germany – that publicly opposed the administration. Yet Canada, so precariously close geographically, economically and culturally to the US, with such little history of visible independence from the American imperial image, presents a puzzle. After all, Australia, like Canada a white settler Commonwealth dominion, has, with the John Howard government's re-election, apparently accepted a role as gun-toting junior partner to the US in Iraq, and quite likely anywhere else Bush wants to lead the empire. Admittedly, Australia's geopolitical position as an Asian nation is very different from Canada's, but the divergence in outlook between the two countries remains quite striking. Even New Zealand, whose decision a number of years ago to refuse harbour to US nuclear submarines caused significant strains in its relationship with Washington, sent a small contingent of troops to Iraq (later to be withdrawn). The Canadian government is clearly offside from the English-speaking alliance, or 'Anglosphere' as some are beginning to refer to it. In some surveys of international opinion, Canadians actually score as among the most sceptical anywhere of the Bush Doctrine and America's democratizing mission to the world.

One basis for the Canadian difference is Quebec. Sometimes appearing in the guise of national disunity with the secessionist, or sovereignist movement, represented in the Quebec National Assembly by the Parti Québécois and in the federal Parliament by the Bloc Québécois, Quebec is also a heavy anchor dragging Canadian opinion and the federal government towards liberal social attitudes at home and anti-imperialism abroad. Although previous PQ governments in Quebec looked to the US for help against

Ottawa – and to a North American economic bloc as a check against the power of the federal government – following the Bush Administration's arrival, Quebec nationalist opinion has turned strongly anti-American. Moreover, dominant Quebec social values are at cultural loggerheads with the born-again Christian Right worldview of the Bush Republicans. Quebec opinions are doubly influential in Canadian politics. Not only is Quebec the second largest province, representing about a quarter of the electorate, but the dominant role played by the sovereignist parties at both levels means that English Canadian politicians are particularly sensitive to 'what Quebec wants'. After all, the sovereignists came within a whisker of winning a referendum on secession in 1995.

Although conservative politicians and commentators in English Canada regularly grumble about the federal government pandering unduly to Quebec, the importance of Quebec in determining overall Canadian attitudes is easily exaggerated. Quebec is one factor among a number that have tilted Canadian attitudes moderately leftward and away from the American mainstream. When the Chrétien government made its Iraq decision, it was no doubt significant that Quebec was the most strongly opposed to the Iraq war of any province, and that the decision was made in the midst of a Quebec election. However, the decision was approved by majorities across the country, which continued to build in the aftermath of the fiasco of 'victory' and occupation. Similarly, the BMD decision was undoubtedly helped by strong anti-BMD sentiments in Quebec, but a national poll indicated that the decision was approved by two-thirds of Canadians, including a majority in every province.[7]

Behind the ephemera of partisan politics lies a fascinating narrative of national particularity that has not only resisted the effect of globalization and continental economic integration, but in a curious and almost perverse way has actually been stirred into action by the very processes that were supposed to assimilate and homogenize such differences. A major survey of North American social values suggests that since 1988, the year that Canada–US free trade was formalized, Canadians have actually been diverging sharply from their American counterparts.[8] While Americans, especially from the politically dominant South, have been turning more conservative, more religious, more patriarchal and more closed and fearful of outsiders, Canadians have been moving in exactly the opposite direction: more liberal and egalitarian, less religious and more open to the world. It is hardly surprising in light of these trends that Canadians should react unfavourably to George W. Bush, his evangelicals and neo-cons. Values do not necessarily follow the economic base, it would seem, despite the fears of the nationalists in the 1980s that the coming of free trade would inevitably doom Canadian distinctiveness. Perhaps there is a dialectical process at work in which the very invasion of American imagery sets off cultural resistance. Perhaps the two societies simply follow different rhythms, reflecting different forces at work, despite the pressures of economic integration. In any case, the disjuncture between economics and culture/politics is interesting, whatever challenges it poses to Marxist determinists.

There is, however, one nuance in this picture that does reflect the importance of class in determining values. The features of Canadian public policy that distinguish Canada from the US are precisely those that dovetail with more liberal and egalitarian Canadian popular values, especially the national single-payer health care system and a greater role for government in social and cultural policy. The obverse of this is a tax structure that is more progressive than in the US, especially since Bush's regressive programme for massive tax relief for the super-rich. This America does appeal to the Canadian corporate elite, who yearn for similar capital-friendly policies in Canada, and see greater continental integration as an effective route to undermining Canadian redistributive tendencies. For precisely the same reason, working-class and many middle-class Canadians are apprehensive about the penetration of the American model and increasingly receptive to nationalist defences of the 'Canadian way'. There is a growing gap between liberal, nationalist mass public opinion, and conservative, pro-American opinion on the part of the economic elite and the media they largely control, a gap displayed over the Iraq and BMD decisions. To the frustration of the economic and media elites, political opportunism if nothing else dictates that when Bush comes to shove, the governing Liberal Party will look to the wider public where the votes are.

In this changing context, NAFTA as the framework for North American integration presents a curious paradox. NAFTA is no economic base generating a continent-wide political and ideological superstructure. It was never constituted as anything but a limited commercial arrangement at the corporate level. No political superstructure, as in Europe, was ever contemplated – indeed any suggestion of political integration was anathema to nationalist American politicians sensitive to the need to reject any potential limitation on American sovereignty. Even joint dispute resolution panels to resolve trade issues have been received with deep suspicion in the US. Any idea of a common labour market sets off visceral fears of cheap Mexican labour flooding into the US; indeed, a selling point for NAFTA in the US was the idea of encouraging low-wage production on the Mexican side of the border. The provisions for a freer flow of people within NAFTA relate strictly to business and professional classes required by transnational capital. Ironically, the narrow economic focus of NAFTA, designed to protect American political sovereignty, crucially limits the capacity of the US government to enforce a common political line on its partners. Faced with Canadian and Mexican resistance over Iraq, the Bush Administration found it difficult to enforce its will through threatened retaliatory economic measures. The integration of the North American economy with its binding rules handcuffed Bush and vindictive elements in Congress. Economic retaliation in response to a political challenge would not only be illegal, but, if effective, would mean the US biting off its economic nose to spite its political face. In other words, being locked into a continental market narrowly conceived in economic terms alone has proved a constraint on America's capacity to bully its partners over its own foreign and defence policy agenda. By the same token, NAFTA offers Canada, as well as Mexico, a certain political space. Granted, autonomy is unlikely to be exercised very often, but it was, by both countries, over Iraq. Another unilateral US move in the near future – against Iran, Syria, North Korea, etc. – could very well again fail to gain the support of one or both NAFTA partners, representing one more pinprick in the pretensions of the cowboys in the White House – not perhaps very constraining in itself, but taken in tandem with Bush's difficulties with 'old Europe', something that will have to be factored into future imperialist adventures.

If the Left critics of NAFTA, and of economic globalization more generally, have missed this paradoxical effect of a continental market model without political integration, a similar observation can also be made about the other half of the globalization phenomenon, the adoption of a neoliberal domestic agenda by successive Canadian governments. Neoliberalism at home seems inextricably connected to the triumph of globalization abroad: each represents the elevation of markets over politics in the authoritative allocation of resources. The corrosive effects of the 'competitiveness' agenda on national social welfare systems is familiar around the world, and certainly not absent in Canada at both the national and provincial levels of government. The best and most detailed critical study of the contemporary

Americanization of Canada argues that Canadian governments have carried neoliberal ideology further than the external forces of globalization.[9] Stephen Clarkson writes that NAFTA and the World Trade Organization (WTO) form a kind of 'supra-constitution' within which Canadian governments at all levels are forced to operate, but much of the actual heavy lifting of neoliberal implementation is in fact done in Canada itself. Yet even Clarkson, writing before the Iraq war decision, predicted wrongly that this process was forcing Canada into lockstep with American foreign and defence policies. While the evidence of neoliberal undermining of the social welfare state cannot be denied, any more than the evidence of continued North American economic integration, there is still a disconnect between economics and politics that requires explanation.

At the centre of the Left nationalist critique of the record of Liberal governments since 1993 is the deficit elimination policy pursued by then Finance Minister Paul Martin in Jean Chrétien's cabinet. The Conservatives under Brian Mulroney (1984–93) had made a lot of noise about deficit elimination as the centrepiece of a new market-oriented neoliberal programme of privatization and deregulation and, of course, free trade which they inaugurated in 1988. They actually left a deficit as large as they had begun with by the time they were driven from office, and a greatly expanded cumulative debt. The Liberals talked little about neoliberalism, but Martin, in the mid-1990s, made huge cuts in the federal transfer payments to the provinces in support of health, education and social welfare, and, by 1997, had eliminated the deficit and set the federal government on the road to years of successive surpluses. Critics point to the slash-and-burn cuts in the fabric of health, welfare and education as evidence of a corporate Liberal agenda. The Liberals themselves always insisted that they simply wished to put the country's finances in order so that they could return to funding social programmes. They also claimed that it was necessary to establish sound fiscal management to reduce Canadian vulnerability to lenders, bond rating agencies and foreign governments that came with a high debt load, the majority of which, in the Canadian case, was owed abroad. Although critics have been scornful and dismissive of Liberal claims, the fact is that by the time of the 2004 election, fiscal conservatism had become a pillar of consensus across the board. Every party, even the NDP and the Greens, were pledged to keep the books in the black. Programme spending had begun to rise again, but this time on a fiscally sustainable basis. This Canadian consensus is in stark contrast to the reckless fiscal irresponsibility of the Bush Administration which, through gigantic tax cuts to the super-rich and profligate spending on defence, security and corporate welfare, is awash in oceans of red ink, with twin deficits on the federal books and the external account of close to a trillion dollars a year.

A few years earlier, an infamous editorial in the *Wall Street Journal* had painted Canada as a Third World banana republic about to hit the 'debt wall'. The destabilizing effect this kind of foreign attack could have on the Canadian economy was sobering indeed. In response, the country set about to make itself less vulnerable, and has succeeded, to the degree that it was able to act independently over Iraq. It is not widely appreciated that it is fiscal conservatism that has provided Ottawa with the confidence and capacity for autonomous action. The Americans' dominant position in the world economy may permit them the luxury of bad economic behaviour and an ability to export their difficulties to other countries, for a time at least. Such options were never available to smaller economies like Canada. For the latter, sustained solvency is empowering, both domestically and abroad.

Citing NAFTA and conservative fiscal policy as the basis for a degree of Canadian independence from the Bush Administration may strike some as perverse and paradoxical. But this is only the case where it is assumed that independence from the American Empire can only rest on an anti-capitalist foundation. The crisis that has split Europe and set parts of Europe at odds with Bush's America arises not from a revolt against capitalism, but from the contradictions of capitalism itself. The same holds for the growing estrangement of Canada, and Canadians, from Bush's America. The unilateralism, some would say pig-headedness, of the neo-cons in Washington is not only seen as counterproductive to an effective and cooperative 'war on terror', but US economic policies are seen as self-destructive and radically dysfunctional to the workings of the global economy. If the US fails to follow the rules of international conduct expected of law-abiding nations, it also fails consistently to follow the rules expected of a member of the World Trade Organization and of a regional economic pact like NAFTA. Two of the biggest economic issues in Canada for many years have been the disastrous impact of the US softwood lumber lobby's illegal duties on Canadian imports, and the closure of the US border to Canadian cattle over BSE ('mad cow disease') fears. In the former case, Canada has appealed to NAFTA and the WTO and won repeatedly – but so far to no avail, as the protection continues. So angry have Canadian supporters of free trade become that recently the number two Canadian negotiator with Washington over the original free trade agreement in the 1980s has publicly raised the spectre of 'the administration's attack dogs [let] loose to savage America's closest trading partner', and speculated that 'today, the lumber industry is the principal target. Tomorrow, we can expect these tactics to be applied to everything from energy to agriculture, and ultimately to strip the protections from the free-trade agreement itself.'[10]

Together with deep anxieties about the threat Bush's fiscal policies pose for the collapse of the US dollar and a general crash of the global economy, it is increasingly evident that a common capitalist front under US hegemony cannot be sustained forever. America First nationalism may have profound political resonance in 'red state' America with its born-again antediluvian conservatism and its xenophobic and authoritarian outlook on the outside world, but it can only spawn counter-nationalist revolts among America's erstwhile alliance partners. Canada's drift away from the looming shadow cast by its powerful but sick neighbour to the south shows just how far this process has already progressed.

## NOTES

1  George P. Grant, *Lament for a Nation: the Defeat of Canadian Nationalism* (Toronto: McClelland & Stewart, 1965).

2  Andrew Cohen, *While Canada Slept: How We Lost Our Place in the World* (Toronto: McClelland & Stewart, 2003).

3  Kent Roach, *September 11: Consequences for Canada* (Montreal: McGill-Queen's University Press, 2003).

4  Reg Whitaker, 'More or Less than Meets the Eye? The New National Security Agenda', in G. Bruce Doern (ed.), *How Ottawa Spends 2003–2004: Regime Change and Policy Shift* (Don Mills: Oxford University Press, 2003), 44–58.

5  Reg Whitaker, 'Living with Bush's America', *Literary Review of Canada* 13:1 (January/February 2005): 3–5.

6  Reg Whitaker, 'Securing the "Ontario–Vermont Border": Myths and Realities in post-9/11 Canadian-American Security Relations', *International Journal* LX:1 (Winter 2004–5): 53–70.

7  Alexander Panetta, 'Martin Move on Missiles Politically Correct', *Canadian Press* (22 March 2005).

8  Michael Adams, *Fire and Ice: the United States, Canada, and the Myth of Converging Values* (Toronto: Penguin Canada, 2003).

9  Stephen Clarkson, *Uncle Sam and Us: Globalization, Neoconservatism, and the Canadian State* (Toronto: University of Toronto Press, 2002).

10  Gordon Ritchie, 'Who's Afraid of NAFTA's Bite?' *The Globe & Mail* (Toronto) (15 February 2005).

# 14
# A 'Just War', or Just Another
# of Tony Blair's Wars?[1]

*David Coates*

New Labour came to power determined to do good in the world. Its 1997 election manifesto contained that commitment. Its first governmental statement of foreign policy principles put ethical concerns at the heart of the UK's overseas agenda. That made sense in 1997, since the new government came to power attempting to be, at one and the same time, both qualitatively different from and morally superior to the government it was replacing. That government – the government of John Major, and still in image the government of Margaret Thatcher – was one whose ethical stance, both abroad and at home, was by then seriously in question; put there, in part at least by Labour's exposure, when in opposition, of a string of dubious arms deals struck with ministerial connivance between UK-based companies and the regime of Saddam Hussein.[2]

New Labour also came to power with Iraq as a pre-established item on its governmental agenda. British troops had played an important supporting role in the Gulf War triggered by Saddam Hussein's invasion of Kuwait, and British military planes were currently helping the US to police the no-fly zones that had been created over northern and southern Iraq in the wake of that war. The New Labour government in 1997 found itself in an active military alliance with the United States in the Middle East, and from the outset was entirely comfortable in that alliance. Indeed, as time passed, its comfort level visibly rose. Postwar UK Prime Ministers had long chosen to 'punch above their weight' as the United States' key European ally, and the New Labour Prime Minister soon caught the habit. For reasons of international status as well as of international morality, Blair's government, like UK governments before it, proved entirely willing to deploy British forces abroad on military missions with only the most tenuous connections to immediate UK security interests. It did so in Sierra Leone and it did so in Kosovo.

As Tony Blair picked up the victory laurels of his series of small wars,[3] he proved increasingly willing to advocate such military interventions into the internal affairs of sovereign states in a post-Cold War era, and to lay out the criteria that should guide them. Before an audience in Chicago in 1998 he discussed those criteria, and before a smaller gathering in Texas in 2002 he explained their context and their relevance to the Iraqi case. In Chicago, he said this:

> I think we need to bear in mind five major considerations. First, are we sure of our case? War is an imperfect instrument for righting humanitarian distress; but armed force is sometimes the only means of dealing with dictators. Second, have we exhausted all diplomatic options? We should always give peace every chance … . Third, on the basis of a practical assessment of the situation, are there military operations we can sensibly and prudently take? Fourth, are we prepared for the long term? … having made a commitment we cannot simply walk away once the fighting is over … . And finally, do we have national interests involved?[4]

In Texas, Blair then used his sense of global interconnectedness to define those national interests in a new and expansive way – one indeed that stretched straight to Baghdad. 'I advocate,' he told his Texan audience:

> … an enlightened self interest that puts fighting for our values at the heart of the policies necessary to protect our nations. Engagement in the world on the basis of these values, not isolationism from it, is the hard-headed pragmatism for the 21st century. Why? In part … because the countries and people of the world today are more interdependent than ever … and … the surest way to stability is through the very values of freedom, democracy and justice. Where these are strong, the people push for moderation and order. Where they are absent, regimes act unchecked by popular accountability and pose a threat: and the threat spreads. So the promotion of these values becomes not just right in itself but part of our long-term security and prosperity. Not all the wrongs of the world can be put right, but where disorder threatens us all, we should act … . We cannot, of course, intervene in all cases, but where countries are engaged in the terror or weapons of mass destruction business, we should not shrink from confronting them … leaving Iraq to develop weapons of mass destruction, in flagrant breach of no less than nine separate UN Security Council resolutions, refusing still to allow weapons inspectors back to do their work properly, is not an option … . The message to Saddam is clear: he has to let the inspectors back in – anyone, any time, any place that the international community demands.[5]

Given views of this kind, it was not surprising that, fresh from playing a leading role in orchestrating the coalition of nations that had fought in Afghanistan, Blair should then have proved vulnerable to the Bush Administration's call for a move against Iraq. Nor is it entirely surprising that, in advocating such a move, the Prime Minister should have added an explicitly moral dimension to the justifications for military action being proposed. The military intervention in Afghanistan had enjoyed widespread popular support, both globally and in the UK. That global popular support had been the legacy of a generalized revulsion against the attacks on the World Trade Center and the Pentagon on 9/11. Invading Afghanistan in search of al-Qaeda had been widely seen as legitimate and ethical in both its purposes and its implementation. The war looming in Iraq, by contrast, enjoyed no such widespread global popular support and no such generalized sense of legitimate moral purpose; which was presumably why, in February 2003, as a million people prepared to demonstrate in London against the impending invasion, Blair felt obliged to put the moral case for war to them. He did so in a strongly argued piece in the London paper most likely to be read on that demonstration: the *Observer*. He wrote this:

> What brings thousands of people out in protests around the world? .... It is a right and entirely understandable hatred of war. It is moral purpose, and I respect that. But the moral case against war has a moral answer: it is the moral case for removing Saddam. *It is not the reason we act. That must be according to the UN mandate on weapons of mass destruction. But it is the reason, frankly, why if we do have to act, we should do so with a clear conscience.* Yes, there are consequences of war ... but there are also consequences of 'stop the war'. There will be no march for the victims of Saddam, no protests about the thousands of children who die needlessly each year under his rule, no righteous anger over the torture chambers which, if he is left in power, will remain in being .... If there are 500,000 on the [Stop the War] march, that is less than the number of people whose deaths Saddam has been responsible for. If there are one million, that is still less than the number of people who died in the wars he started. So if the result of peace is Saddam staying in power, not disarmed, then I tell you there are consequences paid in blood for that decision too. But these victims will never be seen, never feature on our TV screens or inspire millions to take to the streets. But they will exist nonetheless.[6]

The need to do good in the world, the interconnected nature of the world that made doing good essential, and the status of Iraq as the most pressing example of where good was required – these were linked by Blair into a justificatory structure for the war itself. The invasion of Afghanistan, Blair had told Arab journalists in 2001, had been a 'matter of justice'.[7] It had been a modern example of a 'just war', and the invasion of Iraq would be another.

The question before us is whether that claim had any substance to it. It will be the argument of this chapter that it did not.

## JUST A WAR?

Even in choosing to explore the issue in this way – even to pose the question of whether the movement of US and British troops into Iraq in March 2003 was just – is to run the risk of framing the invasion in an entirely misleading fashion. It is to run the risk of giving far too much ground to the retrospective defenders of what was, from its outset, seen by many as a controversial act of modern imperialism. For no matter what the main players now argue, with the event well behind them, it is vital to remember that concerns with democratization and human rights were *never* the key driver of policy when the invasion was being planned and implemented. It is also vital to remember that the internally repressive nature of the Saddam Hussein regime was not even the key legitimating element when the invasion was launched. The invasion was originally presented as part of the 'war on terror', as an attack on one component of 'the axis of evil', with the manner and urgency of military intervention justified by the existence of links between Saddam Hussein's Iraq and al-Qaeda. Then, when those links proved elusive, the invasion of Iraq quickly became a war legitimated by Iraq's possession of weapons of mass destruction. It was even legitimated for a while as an exercise that gave voice to the UN's own resolutions, when that body was supposedly immobilized by French intransigence. It was only when the adequacy of these main-line legitimating arguments began to be undermined by the emergence of powerful evidence of a counterfactual kind that the 'democratic and human rights' case for invading Iraq – Bush and Blair's 'moral' case for invading Iraq – was moved centre-stage, where it now remains.

Because it is now so centre-stage, we need continually to remember that even Blair – the key moralizer in this story – is on record, on more than one occasion, as insisting that it was Iraq's possession of weapons of mass destruction, not questions of democracy and human rights, which triggered and legitimated the invasion.[8] We also need to remember that his position in the run-up to the invasion, which differed significantly in this regard from that of the Bush Administration, was that if Saddam Hussein voluntarily disarmed, the coalition would not (and could not legally) insist on regime change in Baghdad. We need to remember too the dating of Washington's repositioning of the Iraq invasion as part of a wider crusade for freedom and democracy. That repositioning took place long after the invasion, and in response to the resistance to it. It took place predominantly in 2004, most notably in the President's State of the Union address to Congress. For by then, even George W. Bush was backtracking on the claims about al-Qaeda links and Iraqi weapons of mass destruction, telling his audience that the unilateral invasion of Iraq had been a legitimate military operation, not because it made America a safer place but because it made Iraq a *freer* one.[9] But that was the Bush Administration's 2004 story. The 2003 one had been entirely different, terrorist-focused and largely morality-free.

Of course, it would be churlish of us not to welcome a US change of heart here, if issues of democracy and human rights have genuinely, if belatedly, come to prevail in the White House. In giving that welcome, however, we would do well to maintain our guard, for there are still issues of timing and connivance that remain in need of explanation here. If this invasion was genuinely driven by revulsion at the internal brutality of the Iraqi regime, and by the use of terror and weapons of mass destruction (WMD) on Iraq's own people and on their immediate neighbours, as is now so often claimed – why, then, was the invasion not triggered in 1983 (when the regime used chemical weapons against the Iranian army) or in 1988 (when it used them in Halabja against the Kurds)? If the Bush Administration suddenly in 2003 found the Iraqi regime so distasteful as to warrant regime change, why was the key architect of the invasion, Donald Rumsfeld, happy to visit Baghdad (and Saddam Hussein) within months of the 1983 use of chemical weapons, advocating stronger business and diplomatic ties between the regime and the US? Why did an earlier UK government secretly help to finance and build a chemical facility in Iraq in the 1980s, the very facility described by Colin Powell (before the UN in February 2003) as evidence of the potential of the regime for the aggressive use of WMD? And why did Blair not support, when in opposition, Early Day Motions condemning the Iraqi regime?

It is also hard to square the claim that the motives of those directing this war were driven by concerns for democracy and human rights when there is now so much evidence of exaggeration, deceit and inconsistency in the justifications used. Paul Wolfowitz and Richard Perle have been the clearest of the inner circle of the Bush Administration on this: conceding their willingness to use, and their dexterity in deploying, any argument (even that about WMD) in order to trigger support.[10] Colin Powell has not been quite so candid: but even he was obliged obliquely to concede in 2004 that there was no linkage between Iraq and al-Qaeda, though he had been adamant before the UN as late as February 2003 that such a link was there, and was potent.[11] Given this, it is hard to escape the conclusion that the Bush Administration's decision in 2004 to foreground its newly discovered concerns with Iraqi civil rights and democratic potential was in reality an exercise in damage control: as one disgruntled former insider after another publicly recorded the administration's long-established determination to 'get Saddam Hussein' and its willingness to use any excuse, including the events of 9/11, as a cover for that purpose.[12] The list of lost opportunities here – the list of moments when policy towards Iraq might have been driven by moral revulsion but was not – is a lengthy one. Not least among them, as we now know from the exchange between Senator Byrd and Secretary Rumsfeld before the Senate Armed Forces Committee, was that period in the 1980s when the US and UK actually connived at the arming of Iraq: a lost moment that had the ironic consequence of leaving the leading partners in the 'coalition of the willing' as the source of at least some of the weapons of mass destruction against which the coalition then mobilized.[13] So if moral sensibilities did suddenly drive US foreign policy here, the most we can safely say is that those moral sensibilities were remarkably late in coming.

## A JUST WAR?

We also know that the tests of what constitutes a 'just war' are very demanding. Those tests, and the moral discourses underpinning them, are matters that have attracted serious scholarly attention and development over many centuries – to the point, indeed, of establishing a clear 'tradition'[14] of argument whose general message is reasonably clear. It is that for a war to be just, both the going to war and the conduct of the war have to meet exacting standards. A just war has to be undertaken for the right reasons and fought in the right way. There has to be *jus ad bellum*: just cause, competent authority and right intention. War has to be waged only as a last resort, when all non-violent options have been exhausted. And there also has to be *jus in bello*. The violence used in the war has to be proportional to the suffering triggering it, and it has to be applied in ways that discriminate between combatants and non-combatants. There has to be legitimate authority behind the war, and a reasonable hope of a successful (that is, peaceful) long-term outcome.[15]

Yet, even when allowing for the 'sliding scale' argument – that the greater the justice of one's cause, the more rights one has in battle – the invasion of Iraq fails these tests across virtually their full range. A just war can invoke the spectre of immediate national danger as its cause, as the Bush Administration initially did when linking Saddam Hussein to al-Qaeda and the events of 9/11. They do not make that linkage now, as we have just seen; and in consequence the 'right intention' behind the invasion is currently extremely difficult to fathom. In any case, no matter how 'just' the original intention might have been, all the non-violent routes to the achievement of the invasion's stated goals had not been exhausted when the war began. Hans Blix has been on record repeatedly since the invasion, establishing this.[16] The illegitimate nature of the 'rush to war' was, in any case, abundantly clear to a number of major governments at the time. It was certainly clear to the French government, and arguably to the German, Russian and Chinese governments too. 'Seven noes, one aye ... the ayes have it' might have worked for Abraham Lincoln, but it was bad policy here; and even the normally reticent Kofi Annan, the UN Secretary General, is now on record as rejecting the legality, and calling into question the justice, of such a unilateral a move to war. As he told the BBC in September 2004, 'the decision to take action in Iraq contravened the UN Charter and should have been made by the Security Council, not unilaterally'.[17] If the US and UK had been set on launching a just war, they should, at the very least, have waited for Blix to complete his work, and should then have acquired a second and clear UN mandate. They did not.

Moreover, the aerial bombardment of Iraqi cities did not, because it could not, differentiate between combatants and non-combatants; and even for the ground war and the subsequent occupation, the calculus of proportionality remains unresolved. US military commanders invariably claim, of course, that as they resist the insurgency they differentiate carefully between the two categories of potential victims, and do their utmost to limit what they call unavoidable collateral damage; but even now we cannot judge whether the war took more lives than it saved, because we do not know the Iraqi casualty totals. What we do know, however, is that the Pentagon does not even keep a record of Iraqi civilian casualties: 'We don't do body counts', General Tommy Franks once famously told the world's press. We also know that whenever those that do count bodies publish their findings, their numbers are invariably dismissed by the advocates of the invasion as both speculative and inflated. Speculative they have to be, since data-gathering is so difficult; and depending on the methodology used, the scale of the death toll does indeed vary significantly. But low or high, it remains substantial. Anywhere between 15,000 and 100,000 Iraqi civilians are thought to have died since the invasion, depending on the source used; and a commensurate number are thought to have died between the two Gulf Wars, as the consequence of the UN sanctions regime then in place. Those are the numbers that have to be set against the evidence of Iraqi suffering at the hands of the regime that is now emerging from the mass graves of Hussein's victims; and when that is done, it is not self-evident that this invasion was a just one proportional in its violence to the suffering it relieved.

Nor do we yet know, of course, if the invasion will achieve its stated ends. Iraq's political future remains uncertain, the US military has yet to find weapons of mass destruction – indeed, even the Bush Administration has been obliged to concede that it will not[18] – and the networks of international terrorism remain unbroken. Arguably those networks have actually been strengthened by the invasion itself.[19] But we do know that the invasion lacked legitimacy. It lacked legitimacy within the formal institutions of the international community and among huge swathes of the global population, both in the Middle East and in the electorates of the participating governments. It even lacked legitimacy, as the continuing resistance and protests within Iraq demonstrates, among many of those Iraqis who were so forcefully liberated. Which is why no less a personage than Nobel Prize winner President Jimmy Carter was among those who, even before the invasion, denied it the status of a just war: 'As a Christian and as a president who was severely provoked by international crises,' he wrote in the *New York Times*, 'I became thoroughly familiar with the principles of a just war, and it is clear that a substantially unilateral attack on Iraq does not meet these standards.'[20]

## A WAR WITH JUST OUTCOMES?

It is therefore relatively straightforward, and politically extremely important, to deflate the more ambitious of the claims that the invasion of Iraq was designed and delivered as some kind of just war. But as we have seen, the criteria associated with the notion of a 'just war' are, quite properly, very demanding ones. They set the bar extremely high. It is harder to drain this exercise of ethical elements when the bar is lowered to questions of the unintended consequences of both war and the lack of war. Against this lower bar, the argument needs to be different and involves a balancing of any immediate and specific ethical gains against the weakening of structures capable of generating more long-term and general ethical advantage. It needs to be as follows.

If 'just war theory' is not to be our yardstick here, we need some other set of benchmarks; and if those are not to be either simply idiosyncratic in origin – as Blair's Chicago criteria clearly were – or culturally-specific in design and relevance, they need to possess some form of universal (transcultural) applicability and legitimacy. The most immediately obvious set of criteria that meets those requirements are the 30 Articles of the UN's own *Universal Declaration of Human Rights*; and against those at least, it is clear that a powerful, if secondary, case for the morality of the war *can* be made. For the removal of Saddam Hussein from power has clearly increased the number of people who are able to enjoy the rights asserted for them in that UN Declaration. This is especially true for the Kurds in the north and for the Shia in the south of Iraq; in both cases the outcome of this second military confrontation between US and Iraqi arms has proved to be significantly better than was the outcome of the first. But it might also become true more generally for Iraq as a whole, at least to the degree that solid democratic structures with entrenched civil rights are eventually created. It is also clearly preferable from a moral point of view to see the removal from the Middle East of a regime willing to launch military strikes against Israeli non-combatants; to see regimes that had hitherto refused to allow the international inspection of their weapons programmes now beginning to do so; and to see the recent emergence of incremental (if still heavily managed) democratic openings in places such as Saudi Arabia and Egypt.

So what is the problem here? Why do these potential gains not make the case for the invasion, if only by default? They do not do so because of the methods by which they were achieved. It is the ramifications of *how* Saddam Hussein was removed from power that erode their impact.

There can be no serious doubt that, by insisting on unilaterally instigating 'regime change' in Baghdad in the face of general UN resistance, the US and UK seriously weakened the international institutions that alone can, over the long period, sustain a morally just global order. The UN is, of course, an imperfect vehicle for this task – it is in need of extensive reform, that much too is clear – but even so it *is* such a vehicle, and the Pentagon most definitely is *not*. As the Bishop of Durham put it, 'for Bush and Blair to go into Iraq together was like a bunch of white vigilantes going into Brixton to stop drug-dealing. This is not to deny there's a problem to be sorted, just that they are not credible people to deal with it.'[21] In fact, even if in principle they had been credible people to do this job, the long-established and extensive use of double standards by the US and UK in relation to the implementation of UN resolutions would still have undermined their claim for moral legitimacy here; and even after the war, the Bush Administration proved unwilling for a long period to cede control, or indeed influence, to the UN in the design and implementation of new political institutions in Iraq. The UK government has been more sympathetic to UN involvement throughout, but it has not been calling the shots.

Nor is it clear that the US and UK have the staying power, capacity and inclination to deliver a 'democratic' Iraq, as Bush and Blair now promise. The jury is still out on this, of course, but certainly the experience of post-liberation Afghanistan gives very little cause for optimism here. Constitution-building on the basis of the Sharia in the context of persistent warlordism is hardly an unambiguously democratic step forward for the Afghans; and neither the US nor the UK seems to have learned from this that, if nation-building of a democratic kind is the objective, as much planning has to go into post-invasion reconstruction as into the invasion itself. No such pre-war planning happened in the Iraqi case: or rather, what limited planning the State Department initiated the Pentagon chose to ignore. In consequence civil strife is, for the moment at least, much deadlier in Iraq now than it was prior to the invasion, and the major forces in position to win power in a democratic Iraq seem likely to be Islamic, even fundamentalist, in kind. So Iraq's future may actually be Iranian; and if that is its future, then in terms of the UN's Universal Declaration of Human Rights the issue of progress will become more problematic, especially for Iraqi women.

Of course, defenders of the invasion are prone to draw parallels, not with the Iranian Revolution, but with the successful postwar, US-led reconstruction of West Germany and Japan; but the parallel is a forced one. At best the legitimacy of US reconstruction of West

Germany and Japan was generally accepted both internationally and internally, as the legitimacy of the US-led reconstruction of Iraq is not: and the democratic and capitalist rebuilding of both countries remained a high priority for the United States (and absorbed huge amounts of US aid and capital) primarily because of the strategic position each occupied on the frontline of the Cold War after the Communist Party took power in China in 1949. Iraq has no such global and long-term strategic significance for the United States, though it may have a more short-term regional one. Nor is there large-scale popular support in the United States for the injection into Iraq of large amounts of American resources. On the contrary, with levels of relative poverty at an all-time high in the US, with the US budget deficit rising dramatically and with the Republicans in control of both the legislative and the executive branches of the federal government, the electoral base, fiscal surpluses and political leadership for an Iraqi 'New Deal' are quite simply not there. In their absence, the social and economic preconditions for the successful consolidation of a German/Japanese-type democracy are not there either. It will not be electorally expedient for the US to fund the reconstruction of an adequate Iraqi health service, for example, when 40 million Americans cannot afford health care for themselves.

Even more problematic is the likely effectiveness of the newfound enthusiasm of the Bush Administration for the expansion of democracy in the Middle East. That enthusiasm looks in any case paper-thin, cosmetic rather than principled. Egypt is currently the recipient of the second largest amount of US foreign aid. Israel is the recipient of the most. Yet only very recently has there been any evidence of even limited US pressure on the Egyptian regime significantly to deepen the democratic process, and none at all on Israel to negotiate in good faith its withdrawal from the West Bank. Instead, the Bush Administration is pushing a road map that prioritizes democratic reform and the control of militants by the *Palestinian* Authority, without until very recently providing any of the political (Israeli restraint) or economic (investment and aid) underpinnings that might give Palestinian moderates any hope of winning popular support in the region. Indeed, one of the main barriers to the US fully backing democratic transitions in the Middle East is that – and in large measure only because of past and present US policy in the region – the victors in any fully democratic elections in many of the Arab states are likely to be parties that are hostile to Washington. There is a genuine paradox of policy here. US support for democratization in the region is hesitant because, from an American perspective, its outcomes are likely to be destabilizing; and yet the longer that hesitancy continues, the more likely that the outcomes will in fact take this destabilizing and anti-American form.

This paradox is then compounded by the issue of Israel. For by pursuing a 'war on terror', that legitimates unilateral American strikes outside its national borders against groups and states hostile to the US, the Bush Administration has, by example if not by design, given the Israeli government a green light to go on doing the same. In consequence, the administration is ostensibly pursuing a roadmap to peace in the Middle East while simultaneously implementing policies that build ever higher barriers to the successful implementation of that roadmap. So before we swallow whole the argument that an indirect but desirable consequence of the invasion of Iraq is that it will open the way to a democratized Middle East, we would do well to consider the alternative argument: that, on the contrary, if democratizing the Middle East was the goal of policy, unilaterally invading Iraq was the least likely way of effecting it. The rhetoric may invoke moral purposes; but the policy consolidates immoral practices.

## JUST WAR

The argument of this chapter runs entirely counter to the claims now made about the invasion of Iraq by those who initiated it. 'Our coalition came to Iraq as liberators', George W. Bush told a London audience in November 2003, Tony Blair by his side, 'and we will depart as liberators'.[22] 'We have no desire to dominate, no ambitions of empire.'[23] Like crusaders from an earlier age, the architects of this invasion speak one language and practise another, and in the process both delude themselves and muddy the waters for the rest of us. It is possible to conceive of conditions in which external intervention of a military kind is necessary and legitimate in the cause of justice. There can be just wars.[24] But the invasion of Iraq was not one of them. The war that Bush and Blair commissioned never met even the weakest, let alone the strongest, of the criteria conventionally laid out for a just war. It failed to meet even Blair's Chicago criteria for intervention in a just cause, let alone the more philosophically anchored and long-established requirements for a war that is just.

The invasion was always a war in which claims of high moral purpose sat alongside, and invariably served to obscure, less moral and more imperial/post-imperial attitudes and ambitions. So when its advocates now claim that they were engaged from the outset in a profoundly moral exercise – and that those of us insisting on a second UN resolution were inadvertently conniving at tyranny – they insult both our integrity and our intelligence. There is, after all, something profoundly offensive in the way in which American neo-conservatives, long the champions of US *realpolitik*, now lecture us on the need for international justice. Sunday school teaching by the princes of darkness rarely transmits sound theology, and it certainly is not doing so in this particular case.

## NOTES

1  The argument in this chapter draws on the volume written jointly by the author and Joel Krieger (with the help of Rhiannon Vickers), *Blair's War* (Cambridge: Polity Press, 2004). The reader is referred to that volume for a fuller statement of the argument and supporting evidence. The author would also like to thank David Weinstein for help with the literature on just wars, and Joel Krieger for guidance on the matters at hand.

2  Culminating in the 1996 report of the Scott Inquiry set up in 1992.

3  See John Kampfner, *Blair's Wars* (London: The Free Press, 2003); also see Richard Little and Mark Wickham-Jones (eds.), *New Labour's Foreign Policy: A New Moral Crusade?* (Manchester: Manchester University Press, 2000).

4  Tony Blair, speaking to the Economic Club in Chicago, 24 April 1999.

5  The full text is available at http://www.pm.gov.uk/output/Page1712.asp.

6  Tony Blair, 'The Price of My Conviction', *Observer* (16 February 2003), 20 (emphasis added).

7  Press conference given by the Prime Minister to Arab journalists, 19 October 2001.

8  Explicitly so in the *Observer* piece quoted above ('The Price of My Conviction'); and again to the Liaison Committee of the House of Commons as late as July 2003. See Coates and Krieger, *Blair's War*, 128.

9  George Bush, addressing Congress, 20 January 2004. The summer of 2004 witnessed the publication of the reports of a number of high-level investigations, all of which found serious defects in the intelligence information that had prompted the war. That was true of both the report by the Senate Intelligence Committee on the CIA, and the report of the Butler inquiry into MI6, both of which reported in July. The later report of the 9/11 Commission was equally dismissive of the claim of a link between al-Qaeda and Saddam Hussein's regime.

10  Paul Wolfowitz conceded, in a widely cited article in *Vanity Fair*, that the Bush Administration 'focused on alleged weapons of mass destruction as the primary justification for toppling Saddam Hussein by force because it was politically expedient ... because it was the one reason everyone could agree on'. See Coates and Krieger, *Blair's War*, 78. Similarly,

Richard Perle was reported as conceding openly that, in terms of international law, the invasion was illegal, but that he did not care. See Richard Ingram, 'Perle and His Whines', *The Observer* (23 November 2003).

11  Donald Rumsfeld quietly made a similar concession, before the Council on Foreign Relations. See the *Guardian* (6 October 2004).

12  The key insiders here were former Treasury Secretary Paul O'Neill and former counter-terrorism chief Richard Clarke. O'Neill testified that the invasion of Iraq was planned within days of President Bush coming to office, and a full 18 months before the attacks of 9/11. See Ron Suskind, *The Price of Loyalty: George W. Bush, the White House and the Education of Paul O'Neill* (New York: Simon and Schuster, 2004). Richard Clarke's memoir was more damning still. See Richard Clarke, *Against All Enemies* (New York: The Free Press, 2004).

13  Appearing before a Senate committee, Rumsfeld was pressed by Byrd on the veracity of a *Newsweek* article documenting the secret arming of Saddam Hussein in 1982 by the Reagan Administration – armaments that included tanks, computers and video cameras for political surveillance, helicopters, and 'most unsettling' to the Senator, 'numerous shipments of bacteria/fungi/protozoa' to the Iraqi Atomic Energy Commission. Noting that the Reagan Administration first denied, and then conceded, that it knew that the Iraqis had used chemical weapons against the Kurds, and that Rumsfeld himself had – at Reagan's behest – travelled to Baghdad immediately after the event, Byrd asked him, 'Now, can this possibly be true ... Are we in fact now facing the possibility of reaping what we have sown?' (Hearings: The Senate Armed Forces Committee, 19 September 2002).

14  See J. H. Yoder, *When War is Unjust* (New York: Augsburg Publishing House, 1984), 17.

15  For outstanding recent examples of work within this tradition, and of commentaries on it, see Michael Walzer's *Just and Unjust Wars* (New York: Basic Books, 2000) and *Arguing about War* (New Haven, CT: Yale University Press, 2004); Jeff McMahan, 'War and Peace', in Peter Singer (ed.), *A Companion to Ethics* (Oxford: Blackwell, 1991), 384–95; and Brian Orend, 'Just War Theory', in Edward Zalta (ed.), *The Stanford Encyclopedia of Philosophy* (Winter 2001 edition), http://plato.Stanford. edu/archives/win2001/entries/war/#2.

16  A typical example is the BBC report 'Blair "Clinging to Straws" – Blix', *BBC News* (10 October 2004).

17  *BBC News* (17 September 2004).

18  The final report of the Iraq Study Group in 2004 finally put the issue to rest. There were no weapons of mass destruction in Iraq at the time of the invasion.

19  This is the view of, among others, President Chirac (*BBC News*, 17 November 2004); the International Institute for Strategic Studies (*Guardian*, 20 October 2004); and even senior US officials working for the Bush Administration (*New York Times*, 22 October 2004).

20  Jimmy Carter, 'Just War, or Just a War?' *New York Times* (9 March 2003).

21  'Blair under Fire from Top Clergy', *BBC News* (29 December 2003).
22  President Bush speaking in Whitehall Palace, London (19 November 2003).
23  President Bush, *State of the Union Address to Congress*, Washington, DC (20 January 2004).
24  For this argument in detail, see Coates and Krieger, *Blair's War*, 130–55.

# 15

# The Uses and Abuses of Humanitarian Intervention in the Wake of Empire

*Fuyuki Kurasawa*

To intervene or not to intervene, that is the question. Indeed, whether external military force can and ought to be used in a given country to respond to human rights violations represents one of the most contested and urgent topics of our time. It has become so since the end of the Cold War, with the gradual collapse of the bipolar logic of mutually assured destruction that negated the very prospect of intervention lest the latter escalate into a full-blown nuclear confrontation between the Eastern and Western blocs. Moreover, the current period of ambiguity, located between an international and a global order, is marked by the rise of an infrastructure of formal institutions and agreements (such as the Kyoto Protocol, the World Trade Organization and the International Criminal Court), civil society actors (e.g., NGOs and social movements), and transnational corporations that are putting into question the principle of state sovereignty underpinning the Westphalian system of governance. And all of this is occurring in the context of the consolidation of US hegemony, which has revealed its more belligerent and unilateralist face during George W. Bush's presidency.

The stakes at play in the debates about humanitarian intervention are perhaps most starkly underscored by juxtaposing two well-known recent catastrophes. The first is the Rwandan genocide of 1994, when more than 800,000 Tutsis were slaughtered as the international community looked on, yet chose to do little more than be a bystander. In the following years, apparently remorseful Western leaders and UN officials sought to explain their inaction by taking refuge behind unconvincing claims about lack of information, inability to realize the scale of the disaster, bureaucratic mistakes and delays, and political indecision. Despite such disingenuous *mea culpas*, the Rwandan genocide's aftermath – coupled with the memory of belated and botched interventions in the former Yugoslavia and East Timor during the 1990s – marked something of a watershed. Indeed, a newfound resolve to act to stop or avert mass atrocities took hold in certain international circles; the title of the influential report of the International Commission on Intervention and State Sovereignty, *The Responsibility to Protect*, captured the mood of the time.[1] Some analysts even foresaw, and enthusiastically embraced, the dawn of a new era of military cosmopolitanism and muscular humanitarianism, a humanitarian ethos with teeth that would metamorphose the lofty dream of universal respect for human rights into a tangible reality due to a host of factors: multilateral collaboration between states (notably within the UN Security Council), an emerging body of cosmopolitan law supporting extraterritorial jurisdiction and prosecution, as well as the willingness to exercise military power to enforce humanitarian principles. As a result, perpetrators of mass atrocities would no longer be able to exploit the notion of non-intervention in a nation-state's domestic affairs to commit their deeds.

The war in Iraq quickly put an end to any grandiose predictions of a new world order in which might could always be at the service of human rights. The flaws of muscular humanitarianism came to the fore: it was easily appropriated, subsumed under and redeployed in the name of the US-led 'war on terror'. If we should not forget that misleading, fear-mongering allegations about the imminent threat posed by Saddam Hussein's stockpiles of weapons of mass destruction and his ties to al-Qaeda were by far the most significant factors in rallying Anglo-American public opinion and legislators behind the invasion of Iraq, what cannot be denied is that humanitarian rhetoric played a strategic role in legitimizing it. This was undoubtedly a hollow, cynical and opportunistic appropriation of human rights discourse emptied of all substantive content, yet the Bush Administration half-heartedly resorted to it while the Blair government did so with more conviction in order to muster support for the war – or quell domestic and international opposition to it. The argument that the invasion was necessary to liberate Iraqis from the clutches of Saddam's regime, even if such an objective was an ancillary benefit that paled in comparison to the doctrine of pre-emptive self-defence, contributed to tipping the balance.[2] Consequently, many on the Left, who were already deeply suspicious of military power under any guise due to its imperialist credentials, have portrayed humanitarian intervention as the latest ideological device serving to consolidate 'full-spectrum' US global domination.

In some progressive circles, opposition to the invasion of Iraq has revived an anti-imperialist absolutism that is sceptical of the discourse of human rights as such.

Undeniably, muscular humanitarians and their anti-imperialist absolutist colleagues raise important points. At the same time, I want to contend that we need to carve out a third way that navigates between the two polarized perspectives' normative and political flaws, preserving the possibility of humanitarian intervention in instances of massive violations of human rights but guarding against its instrumentalization in the service of the American Empire. In other words, the position proposed here – which can be characterized as weak interventionism – can simultaneously enable the Left to uphold the duty to protect populations from crimes against humanity and to remain firm in its condemnation of imperialism cloaked as humanitarianism. The invasion of Iraq highlights the imprudence of embracing intervention without qualification, but conversely, Rwanda (and more recently Darfur) indicates the moral bankruptcy flowing from a total rejection of it. To my mind, the task of any progressive theory of humanitarian intervention is to accommodate both of these limit-cases and be vigilant about the complexities, dangers and potential paradoxes entailed in the articulation of coercion and human rights. We must move away from deterministic and ontological understandings of intervention, according to which the latter is intrinsically humanitarian or imperialist. Rather, we should seek a more nuanced and circumstantial view of it, one that portrays it as a social construct whose uses and effects are determined through political struggle, institutional mechanisms, as well as analytical and normative framing. Therefore, this chapter will proceed in three steps. The first two sections will advance a critique of the moral and political limits of muscular humanitarianism and anti-imperialist absolutism, respectively. In the third section, I will elaborate a model of weak interventionism that stresses conditionality in the exercise of force, modesty in what we believe it can achieve, and the need to have it enframed by a set of participatory processes of multilateral decision-making and public deliberation.

## THE PITFALLS OF MILITARY COSMOPOLITANISM

At the heart of muscular humanitarianism lies a bold programme of swift and dramatic restructuring of the global system along cosmopolitan lines, to be accomplished via the substantive and universal realization of human rights. Among its most controversial aspects is the connection between humanitarian ideals and military power, a connection that has profound implications for both sides of the equation: the exercise of violence potentially resulting in the loss of lives is anathema to humanitarianism's long-standing credo of doing no harm in the process of assisting victims in need, whereas the pursuit of humanitarian objectives represents a serious departure from the armed forces' function as the ultimate guardians and guarantors of national self-interest. Equally contested is military cosmopolitanism's readiness to jettison one of the cornerstones of international law, the tenet of state sovereignty, in the name of human rights. Supporters of military cosmopolitanism assert that if and when a particular government violates higher-order cosmopolitan norms in relation to its citizens, it forfeits the right to non-interference in its domestic affairs; in fact, under such circumstances the international community has a duty to intervene, by force if necessary. What should be noted is the fundamentally affirmative, even utopian, character of muscular humanitarianism, which holds that military power is a legitimate means by which to promote cosmopolitan universalism. Backed by coercive means, compliance with a human rights agenda in all corners of the earth can finally be secured.[3] In some instances, muscular cosmopolitans will even support military action with non-humanitarian motives or objectives if it offers the prospect of latent or derivative humanitarian gains.[4]

This kind of hawkish cosmopolitanism suffers from a case of overstretch, in two senses of the term. First, for the sake of an internal consistency that averts the trap of selectivity, muscular humanitarianism provides weak grounds to oppose the invasion or attack of any country deemed by one or more of its counterparts to violate human rights. When coupled with the potential generalization of the precedent set by the Bush dogma of pre-emptive warfare, the dismissal of international law and state sovereignty can rapidly deteriorate into a scenario of perpetual and virtually unrestricted use of violence in world affairs. Second, the liberal idealism that underpins muscular humanitarianism frequently overlooks the fact that military power is inappropriate, or simply useless, when dealing with many of humanity's most urgent and serious crises. Force is a blunt tool that can provide a quick fix in certain political situations, but it cannot tackle the sorts of structural socio-economic and cultural injustices that are affecting the world's population (mass poverty, gender domination, etc.). By improperly acknowledging the limited effectiveness of coercive measures to achieve humanitarian objectives, military cosmopolitans implicitly divorce human rights from substantive questions of material and symbolic distribution and recognition that are integral to any conception of global justice.

Military cosmopolitans also provide few tools when confronting the reality of humanitarian imperialism, which in our epoch takes the form of the US aiming to maintain its status as a global hegemon by unilaterally threatening to wage war against rival, 'rogue' nation-states (or actually doing so in the case of Iraq) while invoking the rhetoric of human rights to justify the relentless and reckless pursuit of geopolitical and economic American self-interests. To be fair, because still basking in the post-Cold War glow of multilateral collaboration, few thinkers writing prior to the 2000 US election and 11 September 2001 could predict the radicalism of the Bush Administration's belligerent unilateralism. Yet muscular humanitarianism prior to and since those events has prescribed insufficient limits on or low thresholds for the use of force to defend human rights, being rather cavalier about the serious potential for abuse of humanitarian intervention in the context of empire.[5] Today, this reality cannot be ignored: aside from the fact that the US version of human rights standards is invariably limited to formally legitimate elections and neoliberal capitalism – the freedom to vote occasionally and to consume often, the former exercise being modelled on the latter – the White House and Congress have appointed themselves as the sole judges, juries and executioners of what human rights are worthy of being implemented internationally (and conversely, of being ignored), and of what countries urgently need to be 'democratized' and introduced to the joys of free market shock therapies. Furthermore, the US is free to implement selectively even its own stripped-down humanitarian code when strategic and commercial considerations are at stake, as is clear from the treatment of Pakistan, Saudi Arabia, China (in Tibet) and Russia (in Chechnya), to say nothing of the prisoners in Guantánamo Bay and Abu Ghraib.

Put differently, muscular humanitarianism suffers from an analytical and normative under-specification of the conditions under which military power can legitimately be employed to defend human rights. This sort of logic comes uncomfortably close to reviving the West's civilizing mission, for it would have 'us' patronizingly presume that 'we' must liberate 'them' from oppression for their own good. Whatever appeal it holds, it cannot serve as the basis for a progressive theory of humanitarian intervention.

## ANTI-IMPERIALIST ABSOLUTISM AND ITS IMPASSES

If seeds of doubt about humanitarian intervention were planted within the Left due to the belated and deeply flawed 1992–93 US mission in Somalia, as well as the NATO bombing of Kosovo six years later, they blossomed with the invasion of Iraq in 2003. Indeed, as is widely recognized, Bush and Blair's rhetorical strategy included appealing to human rights to legitimize the toppling of Saddam Hussein, whose long-ignored (and even tacitly supported) crimes against the Iraqi population suddenly became a rationale for war that was seamlessly blended in to the portrayal of the Iraqi state as an immanent menace to international security (support of al-Qaeda, weapons of mass destruction, and so on). Within this Manichean framework, to oppose the invasion was tantamount to being 'soft' not only on terrorism, but also on mass atrocities.

Although American 'liberal hawks' largely accepted this dubious equation, many critics have refused to play the game of intellectual blackmail in such terms by convincingly insisting that the humanitarian justification was at best an afterthought, or at worst an ideological distraction that obscured the fundamental socio-economic and strategic dynamics underpinning the war. Masterfully transformed into floating signifiers, human rights served as a potent semantic device through which to validate imperialist aims – discursive 'swords of empire'.[6] At the same time, however, another group of thinkers called the US's and Britain's bluff by carving out a stance of anti-imperialist absolutism that went a step further in throwing out the baby of humanitarian interventionism (and human rights more generally) with the bathwater of empire, asserting that all manifestations of the former are intrinsically instruments of the latter. Put differently, anti-imperialist absolutists do not differentiate between the principle of humanitarian intervention and how it has been abused *de facto* in the case of Iraq. To have firm grounds on which to oppose the American Empire and the invasion necessarily means, according to this position, rejecting humanitarian intervention under any and all circumstances, and a growing cynicism towards the discourse of human rights itself. Echoing Carl Schmitt, this leaves little room for manoeuvre, since reference to human rights is always already interpreted as a veiled claim for the extension of power; the two are fused, and attempts to decouple them merely play into the hands of the US.[7]

To shore up its critique of humanitarian interventionism, anti-imperialist absolutism often allies itself to two distinctive worldviews: pacifism and international legalism. The first argues that humanitarianism and warfare are strictly incommensurable, for the practice of killing in order to save lives is a performative contradiction that undermines the core of the humanitarian project.[8] As admirable as it may be, moral purity of this sort skirts round the difficult reality that the use of violence may be both justified and required as the only way to stop armed forces or paramilitary groups from carrying out genocide, ethnic cleansing or systematic rape against civilian populations. No pacifist plea would have halted the mass slaughters in East Timor, the former Yugoslavia or Rwanda. Under most circumstances, perpetrators of atrocities are only deterred from attacking their 'enemies' by having to stare down the barrel of a gun. The question, then, is not whether force ought to be employed in humanitarian crises at all, but under what conditions and according to whose directives.

For its part, international legalism is of an entirely different order from pacifism, asserting that state sovereignty is a basic regulatory tenet of international law that must be upheld to prevent or control the use of force by nation-states against each other. By putting into question this principle, humanitarian intervention eases the way towards an anarchic condition of survival of the fittest in world affairs. Accordingly, interventionism's challenge to state sovereignty made the invasion of Iraq and the 'war on terror' possible by easing the US's and Britain's breaching of international law; Bush and Blair used human rights exceptionalism, calling on a series of precedents to justify military action. In this respect, international legalists assert that such exceptionalism makes warfare more probable because it is less strategically and formally costly for nation-states. It has also helped to supply a foothold for empire by implicitly and informally assisting the Bush Administration's assumed right to strike unilaterally and pre-emptively any country it declares to be threatening its security – whether this threat is actual or fictional, or yet again, whether it is immediate or anticipated.[9]

International legalism fruitfully alerts us to the risks of muscular humanitarianism's dismissal of state sovereignty, which offers a formal buffer against military incursions by Western powers in the global South.[10] At the same time, it cannot serve as an absolute in the face of mass slaughter. If military cosmopolitanism potentially produces perpetual warfare in the name of human rights, the defence of state sovereignty as a *sine qua non* of world affairs effectively results in standing by as mass atrocities take place. Under certain circumstances, then, the need to deter or halt the carrying out of large-scale crimes against humanity may trump the rule of domestic non-interference. The difficulty of determining the threshold at which this 'trumping' occurs and a government fails the basic test of humanity by abusing its power, should not permit us to evade the task of doing so.

Ultimately, anti-imperialist absolutism relies on an unpersuasive 'slippery slope' argument, whereby contemplating humanitarian intervention *per se* provides the US with *carte blanche* to engage in unilateral warfare against whoever it wants, whenever it wants. This reasoning is frequently joined to a belief that the very essence of interventionism is imperialist, and thus that all uses of coercion in the name of human rights are solely and inherently intended to reproduce global American hegemony (or will be reoriented for this purpose). As I will explain in the next section, what is missing here is a recognition that humanitarianism and imperialism ought to and can be decoupled, and that interventionism is neither intrinsically humanitarian nor imperialist. Instead, its uses are socio-politically and normatively circumstantial, being determined by its insertion in processes of discursive and socio-political struggle at the level of global and national institutions.

Similarly puzzling is anti-imperialist absolutism's *Realpolitik*-like neglect of the problem of Western governmental and public indifference towards distant suffering. Without offering an alternative means to stop or prevent mass slaughter, the denunciation of interventionism because of its apparent imperialist essence amounts to abandoning large numbers of human beings to their fate; 'we' let ourselves off the hook by asserting that 'they' should sort things out by themselves. By contrast, though by no means a panacea and loaded with hazards, the willingness to contemplate humanitarian intervention is one way to turn towards a politics of global solidarity that cultivates a sense of responsibility towards those subjected to crimes against humanity, regardless of where they may live or of what their ethnicity, race, religion, class or gender may be. The norm of universal moral equality means nothing if not that their lives, no less than our own, are worthy of being protected – by the use of force, if necessary and as a last resort.

## TOWARDS A WEAK INTERVENTIONISM

Having discussed the limitations of muscular humanitarianism and anti-imperialist absolutism, I want to propose a critical paradigm that aims to disentangle the dynamics of humanitarianism from those of US imperialism in order to resist the kind of logic deploying the latter in the name of the former. Military intervention may be required to halt crimes against humanity under certain circumstances, yet we must simultaneously be vigilant about the instrumentalizing abuses of interventionism to consolidate American hegemony (e.g., the 'war on terror' being fought in the guise of exporting human rights and democracy to the non-Western world). As mentioned in the previous section, what leads us in this direction is a circumstantial view of interventionism that understands its uses as socially and politically constituted – by contrast to an ontological argument that searches for its essence. Instead of debating whether interventionism is always already humanitarian or imperialist, the challenge consists in proposing some of the normative, socio-political and institutional conditions that will steer it in a more progressive direction. This should, therefore, allow the Left to support humanitarian interventions in Rwanda and Darfur, as well as to oppose its unjustified invocation in the case of Iraq.[11]

The position advocated here can be labelled 'weak interventionism'. Its 'weakness' distinguishes it from the hawkishness of muscular humanitarianism, since it is a reflexively circumscribed and self-limiting conception that recognizes what military power can accomplish but, just as significantly, what it cannot do. To be clear, I am arguing that humanitarian intervention can never serve as a device to sustain a thick conception of global justice that works towards the comprehensive realization of socio-economic, civil and political rights for all human beings. Although the project of global justice is tremendously valuable, it cannot be achieved via coercive means that are utterly ill suited to securing freedom of expression or redistribution of material resources around the world, to take but two examples. In the same vein, interventionism is incapable of overcoming nationally or globally rooted structural injustices and socio-economic inequalities (such as the North/South divide, or gender domination), nor should it be employed for such purposes. Furthermore, weak interventionism is indubitably negative in that it advocates military action only to avert or halt mass slaughter, never as an affirmative mechanism to advance an emancipatory human rights agenda and even less to remake the world order – whether through Bush's 'democratic' messianism or, at the other end of the political spectrum, a cosmopolitan vision of the global system.

More modestly, humanitarian intervention can be a way to help stop massive suffering and crimes against humanity, and perhaps prevent further severe violations of the civil and political rights of targeted populations. Admitting its limited effectiveness and range signifies that it must not be overstretched to become a cure-all for humankind's ills, for it represents a device mismatched to the task of global justice (something that can only be achieved via long-term and complex dynamics of domestic and transnational struggle and structural transformation in various settings).[12]

Because of its self-limiting character, weak interventionism prescribes high thresholds that need to be met if force is to be deployed in specific humanitarian emergencies. I thus want to propose a two-fold evaluative typology, with each dimension containing multiple conditions:

1. Analytical appraisal of the humanitarian crisis:

   a) Kind and scale: Does it involve a large-scale loss of life (through genocide, ethnic cleansing, famine, etc.)?
   b) Timing: Is it imminent or ongoing, rather than in the past or merely potential?
   c) Evidence: Is information about it valid, does such information come from credible sources, and has it been substantiated by independent observers?

2. Socio-political assessment of the military action:
   a) Intentionalism: Is its primary objective to prevent or halt large-scale death and suffering, and what other interests are at play?
   b) Decision-making: Is it called for and approved by progressive national and global civil society groups (Human Rights Watch, etc.), and has it been subject to democratic processes of public debate and deliberation within nation-states participating in it?
   c) Appropriateness: Are the means to be used proportional to the situation, and will only the minimal amount of force necessary to remedy it be employed?
   d) Consequentialism: Is it likely to be effective in improving the predicament of victimized populations in the short term

(rather than worsening it), and is it designed to minimize unintended and unforeseen consequences in the medium to long term?

Despite being deliberately circumscribed in its advocacy of the deployment of force, weak interventionism is robust at the level of public deliberation and democratic decision-making. Indeed, it understands humanitarianism less as a norm than as a mode of socio-political practice located in fields of action enframed by existing national and global democratic institutions. Correspondingly, humanitarian interventions themselves should be preceded and followed by the work of publicity, that is to say, of civil society actors (notably human rights organizations, social movements and diasporic groups) alerting citizens and governments around the world to the plight of victimized populations. As a practice, humanitarianism must attempt to cultivate a sense of responsibility with these populations, underpinned by a notion of transnational solidarity affirming the fact that all human beings are deserving of the same protection against mass slaughter and suffering. This, in turn, may generate sufficient 'trickle-up' pressure to prompt states and international organizations to intervene in a crisis. Thus, on the one hand, what must be overcome is public indifference and governmental reluctance to send troops into a region with little or no national strategic value.[13] On the other hand, the work of publicity consists of civil society involvement in both the analytical and socio-political dimensions explained above, by way of providing decision-making bodies with information about specific situations, monitoring how and why they decide to take action (or refuse to do so), as well as holding them accountable for taking such action (i.e. whether humanitarian interventions are multilateral, appropriate, and effective).

A key component of weak interventionism's humanitarian practice consists of advocating for structural transformations of the system of global governance, in order to create institutional conditions that would maximize public participation in and enforcement of interventionism and thereby satisfy the analytical and socio-political criteria set out above. While a comprehensive description of reforms of the world order are beyond the scope of this chapter, a few building-blocks should be specified. In the first instance, what is paramount is the development of an enforceable body of international law specifying rules for humanitarian intervention, as well as a

consolidation of the International Criminal Court's universal jurisdiction and central role in prosecuting perpetrators of crimes against
humanity (which could thus have a deterrence effect on political
and military leaders). Second, inter-governmental decision-making
processes and fora need to be substantially democratized. In the
short term, this means that approval for military action can be
sought in a modified UN Security Council – one without permanent
member-states or that eliminates their veto power – or better yet, a
shift of executive power to the General Assembly. Although such
measures would not necessarily ensure that military force would
always be legitimately used or, conversely, that action would be
taken in the face of large-scale disasters, they would at least lessen
the possibility of unilateral responses. Likewise, the armed forces
deployed for humanitarian interventions should be multinational
in composition and under the command of the United Nations.
Aside from acting as a buffer against specific countries' imperialist
aims, a UN military contingent devoted to humanitarian operations
would be able to respond to emergencies more rapidly and
efficiently than nationally-based troops.

Yet in the longer term, weak interventionism envisages a more substantial procedural and institutional reconfiguration. Applying the
cosmopolitan idea of a Global Peoples' Assembly to the problem at
hand, we can envisage a representative world parliamentary body having decision-making power surrounding questions of humanitarian
intervention.[14] Because it would include representatives from national
and global civil societies, this kind of body would be more open to
popular input and oversight, as well as capable of serving as an arena
where claims about unfolding crimes against humanity could be
assessed and debated within strict time-frames; advocacy groups
(human rights NGOs, social movements, diasporic communities, etc.)
could put forth demands for intervention and have them be publicized, deliberated over and acted upon if deemed to be legitimate. Here
again, a participatory model cannot entirely rule out the prospect of
unresponsiveness nor that of imperialist manipulation. None the less,
it fosters a more just application of force and is in a better position to
fulfil the analytical and socio-political norms laid out here.

## CONCLUSION

The globally-minded Left finds itself in an unenviable predicament,
caught between and living in the shadows of two defining human

rights catastrophes: Rwanda and Iraq. The first situation was one where military intervention was justified and desperately needed to halt the genocide of Tutsis yet never seriously forthcoming from the international community, whereas humanitarianism was instrumentalized as part of the flawed US and British efforts to legitimize the toppling of Saddam Hussein's regime. Accordingly, the perils of transnational indifference and of imperialist abuse must frame our responses to humanitarian intervention. The Rwandan genocide and other humanitarian disasters of the 1990s gave birth to muscular humanitarianism, which advocates military intervention to avert or halt massive human rights abuses around the world. Though laudable in certain respects, this sort of hawkish cosmopolitanism is vulnerable to an anti-imperialist critique because it has not formulated an adequate framework to sort out legitimate and illegitimate instances of humanitarian intervention, and nurtures an over-zealous belief in the right entirely to disregard state sovereignty in order to enforce and impose a universal human rights regime. It is not difficult to see how muscular humanitarianism can be transformed into an ideological tool of empire, called upon unilaterally to wage war against declared enemy states.

For its part, the Iraq war gave renewed credence to anti-imperialist absolutism, which discards humanitarian intervention *in toto* on the grounds that it is inherently designed to be a handmaiden of Euro-American power and a means through which the Bush Administration can expand its 'war on terror' by giving it a more acceptable appearance. Here again, these concerns are to be taken seriously, but drawing the conclusion that intervention must always be opposed is unwarranted; it overlooks the cosmopolitan argument that numerous perpetrators of mass slaughter have exploited the doctrine of national sovereignty to carry out their plans without having to worry about outside interference. Moreover, it risks fortifying governmental and public bystanding in the face of crimes against humanity at a time when transnational solidarity and intervention can contribute to preventing them.

Consequently, I am advocating a weak interventionism that seeks to articulate each position's merits while simultaneously buffering itself against their respective weaknesses. To be viable, this viewpoint distances itself from deterministic conceptions of humanitarian intervention to embrace a socio-political constructivist (and thus circumstantial) understanding that is informed by discursive and material practices, analytical and normative principles, as well as institutional mechanisms. Weak interventionism is minimalist and self-restrictive in its vision of the possible applications and effectiveness of the use of force in international affairs, which can only serve to stop or thwart immanent and unfolding large-scale humanitarian emergencies. Weak interventionism demands that military action meet high analytical and socio-political thresholds to be considered legitimate; and conversely, that satisfying these thresholds ought to trigger a duty to intervene in order to assist the victims of carnage and extreme suffering. At the same time, weak interventionism adopts a strong vision of global institutional transformation and publicity to shift humanitarian interventions towards more consistently multilateral and democratic processes. In this regard, the opening up of deliberation and decision-making to civil society actors would mark an important step as long as the criteria I laid out are kept in play.

None of this is to claim that weak interventionism guarantees the proper use of military power for humanitarian purposes. Any and all concepts are dangerous and contested when entering the political arena, for they are liable to being appropriated in paradoxical, unexpected and even unintended ways. To my mind, however, the recognition of this peril does not constitute a reason to reject humanitarian intervention out of hand. Instead, as I have tried to do here, it calls for an elaboration of the circumstances under which intervention is both necessary and desirable, as well as a commitment to forms of political action that struggle against its abuses while supporting its just uses. We must remember the lessons of Rwanda and Iraq, and find in them a path that enables us to help our fellow human beings in dire circumstances and to resist the providential fantasies of the latest version of *Pax Americana*.

## ACKNOWLEDGEMENTS

The research and writing of this chapter were made possible by a Standard Research Grant from the Social Sciences and Humanities Research Council of Canada. I would like to thank Patti Phillips and Philip Steiner for their research assistance.

## NOTES

1  Gareth Evans and Mohamed Sahnoun (chairs), *The Responsibility to Protect: Report of the International Commission on Intervention and State Sovereignty* (Ottawa: International Development Research Centre, 2001).

2  The appeal to the defence of Iraqis' human rights to justify the invasion played out differently on each side of the Atlantic. While humanitarian considerations were hardly meaningful among the US neo-conservatives who run the White House, referring to them did curb attacks from moderate Democrats in Congress and rallied certain hawkish liberal public intellectuals to support the war (most prominently among them, Christopher Hitchens and Michael Ignatieff). However, since backing for the invasion was much more precarious in Britain, the human rights rationale was vital to Blair's tactic of appeasing the public as well as both rank-and-file members of the Labour Party and his own cabinet. For an excellent analysis of why the war was not a legitimate humanitarian intervention, see Ken Roth's report on behalf of Human Rights Watch, available at http://www.hrw.org/wr2k4/3.htm, accessed 18 February 2005.

3  Jacques deLisle, 'Humanitarian Intervention: Legality, Morality, and the Good Samaritan', *Orbis*, 45:4 (2001): 535–56; Michael W. Doyle, 'The New Interventionism', in Thomas Pogge (ed.), *Global Justice* (Oxford: Blackwell, 2001), 219–41; Michael Ignatieff, *Empire Lite: Nation-Building in Bosnia, Kosovo and Afghanistan* (Toronto: Penguin, 2003); Nicolaus Mills, 'The Language of Slaughter', in Nicolaus Mills and Kira Brunner (eds.), *The New Killing Fields: Massacre and the Politics of Intervention* (New York: Basic Books, 2002), 3–17; and Peter Singer, *One World: The Ethics of Globalization* (New Haven, CT: Yale University Press, 2002). On the problems that such a stance has entailed for humanitarian non-governmental organizations, see David Kennedy, *The Dark Side of Virtue: Reassessing International Humanitarianism* (Princeton, NJ: Princeton University Press, 2004); David Rieff, *A Bed for the Night: Humanitarianism in Crisis* (New York: Simon and Schuster, 2002).

4  This was one of the principal reasons advanced to support the invasion of Iraq. More generally, see Nicholas J. Wheeler, *Saving Strangers: Humanitarian Intervention in International Society* (Oxford: Oxford University Press, 2000).

5  Consequently, prominent figures such as Ignatieff came to support the invasion of Iraq during the run-up to it – despite their recent misgivings and about-faces on the topic. See Michael Ignatieff, 'The Burden', in *New York Times Magazine* (5 January 2003), 22ff; George Packer, 'The Liberal Quandary over Iraq', in *New York Times Magazine* (8 December 2002), 104ff. For a critique of Ignatieff's position, see Amy Bartholomew and Jennifer Breakspear, 'Human Rights as Swords of Empire', in Leo Panitch and Colin Leys (eds.), *Socialist Register 2004: The New Imperial Challenge* (New York: Monthly Review Press, 2003), 125–45.

6  Bartholomew and Breakspear, 'Human Rights as Swords of Empire'.

7  David Chandler, 'International Justice', in Daniele Archibugi (ed.), *Debating Cosmopolitics* (New York: Verso, 2003), 27–39; Noam Chomsky, *The New Military Humanism: Lessons from Kosovo* (London: Pluto, 1999); Peter Gowan, 'The New Liberal Cosmopolitanism', in Archibugi (ed.), *Debating Cosmopolitics*, 51–66; Gary Teeple, *The Riddle of Human Rights* (Aurora, Ontario: Garamond Press, 2004).

8  Iain Atack, 'Ethical Objections to Humanitarian Intervention', *Security Dialogue*, 33:3 (2002): 279–92; Jean-Hervé Bradol, 'Introduction: The

Sacrificial International Order and Humanitarian Action', in Fabrice Weissman (ed.), *In the Shadows of 'Just Wars': Violence, Politics and Humanitarian Action* (Ithaca, NY: Cornell University Press, 2004), 1–22.

9  For an alternative approach based on reforming international law and state sovereignty – by contrast to the *status quo* advocated by international legalism – see Jean L. Cohen, 'Whose Sovereignty? Empire versus International Law', *Ethics & International Affairs*, 18:3 (2004): 1–24.

10  Of course, Euro-American nation-states have frequently ignored the principle of non-intervention in practice since Third World nations gained political independence, either through invasions to topple governments, covert funding and training of rebel groups, support for friendly regimes, or economic interference and control of national industries.

11  For a nuanced position that is in many ways similar to the one I am advocating, see Michael Walzer, *Arguing about War* (New Haven, CT: Yale University Press, 2004). However, to my mind, Walzer is not sufficiently critical of humanitarian interventions' imperialist potential.

12  Of course, this is not to say that armed intervention can contradict the principles of global justice, but only that it is too much to believe that the former can spread the latter. In other words, external military action ought not, at the very least, worsen the condition of victimized populations.

13  The failure to do just that was evident in the West's and the United Nations' half-hearted efforts to stop the Rwandan genocide, with the American feet dragging being compounded by memories of its debacle in Somalia in 1993.

14  Richard Falk and Andrew Strauss, 'The Deeper Challenges of Global Terrorism: A Democratizing Response', in Archibugi (ed.), *Debating Cosmopolitics*, 203–31.

# 16
# Taking Empire Seriously: Empire's Law, Peoples' Law and the World Tribunal on Iraq

*Jayan Nayar*

The authors in this volume confront the implications of the ascendancy of empire. Although the essential fact of brute force – the invasion, occupation and domination of Iraq by the US-led 'coalition' – provides the immediate impetus for these contributions, more is at play in the objective realities of our time. Brute force alone is unsurprising to any student of international relations – the violations of law in a world of unequal power are, after all, a commonplace. That there is a claim to the normalization of the right to unilateral use of force through the use of normative languages is that which is thought to transform the present time into a time arguably of empire's rule through empire's law.

But power exercised through violence is seldom without rejection and resistance. An unprecedented popular opposition to the invasion of Iraq has resulted in major citizens' actions aimed to support the resistance within Iraq and to denounce the claims of empire. An example of such is the World Tribunal on Iraq (WTI).[1] Born out of a series of anti-war gatherings, the plans for a world-wide peoples' tribunals initiative were finalized in Istanbul on 27–29 October 2003 with the preparation of a 'Platform Text' for the WTI. Since its coming into being, the WTI, organized as a horizontal network of activists and coordinated through an internet discussion list with periodic 'international coordinating meetings', has conducted no fewer than 20 national tribunal/hearing sessions addressing the issues surrounding the invasion and occupation of Iraq. A culminating session of this international tribunals process took place between 23 and 27 June 2005 in Istanbul.

The WTI initiative raises important issues relevant to an imagination of resistance to empire. In this chapter I consider some of the implications of recognizing empire, and of the 'constitutional' ordering of empire's law. While theorizations of ideal situations enabling the restrictions of empire through re-rationalizations of international law continue to be important, I argue for a peoples' law perspective; a counter-theorization of law that seeks to be informed by real human struggles against empire's violence. Finally, I discuss the World Tribunal on Iraq (WTI) initiative in light of the competing implications of empire's law and peoples' law.

## EMPIRE'S LAW: A CONSTITUTIONAL PERSPECTIVE ON EMPIRE'S RULE

Although we freely speak the word 'empire', how might we envisage it in terms that are relevant to law?

Empire's law, I suggest, is more than the sum of individual legal assertions which have come to gain prominence. It is, instead, an assertion of a constitutional superiority backed by the power of violence. Empire's law overrides all other legal orders, in fact. This new constellation asserts the following:

1. Within the empire, all laws are not equal.
2. There is no international law deriving from the UN Charter that can be interpreted as applying to prevent the US (as empire's politico-military centre) from undertaking unilateral action to maintain or establish the global political conditions necessary for the proper functioning of empire's activities.
3. All international laws supporting empire's fundamental interest in the unrestrained movement of capital across territorial boundaries shall be inviolable, and shall be enforced through international enforcement agencies.
4. All laws at the national or subnational levels that aim to preserve and protect the political, economic and cultural needs of empire shall be inviolable, and must be respected through effective enforcement by the relevant authorities.
5. All laws that seek to preserve national or subnational self-determination in matters pertaining to the conduct of empire's activities are repugnant to the idea of empire's law and shall thereby be non-enforceable by reason of unlawfulness, and shall instead be subject to harmonization to facilitate the smooth progress of empire's activities.

If these are indeed the fundamentals of empire's law, what implications arise for a possible resistance-imagination of law within the context of empire?

Let us begin with a brief review of that which happened and that which did not.

The invasion of Iraq on 20 March 2003 by the US-dominated 'coalition' happened. It was followed by an unrepentant occupation, leading subsequently to an ongoing process of manipulative political engineering in the name of political transition to Iraqi 'democracy'. Not by happenstance; not without design. Invasion, occupation and political domination of Iraq (field-tested first in Afghanistan) followed from a new and explicit claim to power, asserted as both right and inevitable,[2] the 'unipolar moment' to be seized with the confidence of a preordained destiny,[3] its manifestation the right to domination, 'full spectrum' no less, in a new 'American Century' that is to be established with the assistance of whatever 'coalitions of the willing' that might be mustered.[4] We were thereby introduced to the new language of unilaterally decided 'pre-emptive'/'preventive' strikes, a language designed to demand recognition of a new order(ing) of international political realities. The gauntlet was thrown down, the challenge stark in its simplicity: Domination is fact. Domination is right. Who dares dream otherwise?

Might otherwise have been possible? What might have happened but did not?

It did not happen that we were delivered a UN system which censured and suspended US and UK (and cohorts) membership for their contemptuous disregard for the global will against the invasion of Iraq.

It did not happen that an anti-empire international community of states arose to reject the presumptuousness of empire by withdrawing collectively from relevant global institutions that stand dominated by the US and UK – the WTO, the World Bank, the IMF, thereby insisting on a post-imperial world order.

It did not happen that the global community of law-workers/ thinkers brought about a paralysis of the discredited legal order by an indefinite 'vigil for law' by lawyers outraged by the US–UK disdain for law, through a worldwide strike action to uphold the sanctity of their ideals and demonstrate the power of the legal community to stall the machinations of power against law.

None of the above (im)possibilities was to be. Neither the institutions of inter-state relations nor the institutions of 'law' were able or willing to take real action against the violent satisfaction of imperial desire. Instead of action based on a determination of legality, the realism of a hierarchically ordered political system has prevailed;

a 'transition' to 'interim' Iraqi self-government was granted solemn UN endorsement; purple-fingered Iraqi elections, UN sanction; a 'liberated' Iraq on the road to 'democracy', UN promotion, and along with it a collective forgetting of multilateral and legal failure to halt empire. All but in the violated consciousness of the people of Iraq resisting empire and the confined circles of agonized anti-war activists and 'Leftist' international lawyers, the transition from the hitherto asserted world order of 'sovereign equality' to the new order of US 'full spectrum dominance' has come to pass smoothly without undue rupture of international affairs. A new world order of imperial whim and impunity, it would seem, has come into being. Constitutional Principles (1) and (2) of empire's law as outlined above apparently apply.

But more than the assertion of the New American Century defines a transition to empire; see Principles (3), (4) and (5). If the war on Iraq serves to 'remake the world' over and above being yet another example of belligerent disregard of law by the powerful, then it is because military domination serves to introduce and consolidate other features of contemporary world ordering that deviate from the foundational assumptions of the UN conception of international relations and international law. These can be summarized as follows:

- There is the ascendancy of power (whether of action or persuasion) of private and multilateral actors, particularly those whose motivation is the ever-expanding accumulation of capital and profit capable of overriding the capacity of states to protect traditionally conceived 'national interest' concerns;[5] TNCs,[6] business-related 'civil society' actors such as the International Chamber of Commerce,[7] International Financial Institutions such as the World Bank and the IMF, and institutionalized regimes of governance as exemplified by the WTO, all increasingly wield practical vetoes over potentially offensive state action.[8] This ascendancy provides the material force which seeks to reorient sovereignty and thereby the regulatory functions of the state, and its various multilateral manifestations, away from socialism to corporatism.
- The reorganization of the global 'public space' of economic governance to serve the 'private' domains of corporate lust is accompanied and facilitated by a greater centralization of 'police' power with respect to political governance. We see this clearly in the recent upsurge in the assertions of the growth industry that is the 'anti-terror'/'security' discourses within national political

entities wherein recalcitrant domestic populations are soundly 'managed' with the instrumentalities of 'law and order'. Finally, we have common ground between North and South, East and West! The effect of these tendencies towards the monopolization of violence has been the twofold manifestation of greater political suppression of the social majorities and the outbreak of isolated and dramatic expressions of rejection and counter-violence. 'Security' has become the code for (legalized) political violence.[9] The 'war on terror', as espoused by those who seek the monopoly to the 'right to violence', brings to vision all of these upon one screen.

Explicit in the new order of empire's constitution is the transformation of the idea and reality of the state, and of 'sovereignty' as traditionally understood – a recognition that the sovereignty idea is perceptibly losing its state-centric quality (if such was indeed ever possessed) thereby re-forming the nature of the state as a political actor vis-à-vis its regulatory capacity, authority and orientation. This is now well appreciated. From an historical perspective, however, what this implies is familiar; a re-emergence of the old colonial structure of governance which is formed by centres of power in the cores and 'local chieftaincies' in the peripheries, the former determining matters of general policy through various levels of elite contestations, the latter handling the day-to-day exigencies of 'management' and 'control' in order to implement desires so formulated. Empire, it would seem, entrenches colonial governance upon the global space.

Under the rule of empire's law, in stark contrast to the world as envisaged by the UN conception of international law's order, the state increasingly serves not to mediate some collective 'national interest' at the international level, but to mediate the transnational interest at the national level.[10] We thus see a reconfigured transnational society where solidarities derive from human situatedness within the matrix of empire's order, according to the hierarchy of materialities and psychologies of livelihoods.[11] And accordingly, empire's law may be seen as serving the following functions:

- Law as Emancipation: It facilitates and enables the citizens of empire within the empire's First Worlds, with its unbounded social space of leadership, entrepreneurial competition, social mobility and the consumerism of 'global cultures', promised to all but inhabited by the few who are the transnational elites for whom empire provides order, for whom empire is order.

- Law as Regulation: It regulates and disciplines the subjects of empire within the Second Worlds, with its located social space of labour, service, work-space competition, social rootedness and pop consumerism, inhabited by aspirants, always dreaming of the possibility of graduation, constantly living the threat of relegation, caught between the promise and the danger of human possibilities within empire.

- Law as Exclusion: It excludes the outcasts of empire within the Third Worlds, with its ruptured social space of flight, capture and subsistence competition, lying in the underground of 'civil-ized society', its inhabitants, the disposables of the ordering of civil-ization, either incapable of being, or unwilling to be, the servile service-providers that would enable their survival in the Second World.

The description above is not intended to suggest that all law as formulated serves as such within the context and conditions of empire. What it does aim to set out is a perspective on the social function of empire's law as the new ordering of empire is effected. Viewing 'law' within empire from a perspective that recognizes the conflicts inherent in the confrontation between the three worlds outlined above suggests that, notwithstanding the promise of law, and suggestions for its democratization,[12] law exists within a reality of imperial influence and control, not as a social institution subject to rational negotiations for either a national or universal good.[13] Humane law, as it might be described, stands subjected, therefore, to the constitutional primacy of empire's law. And thus, we witness law's abdication of justice. Issa Shivji is persuasive, I believe:

First, I want to suggest that the empire's lawlessness in the sense described here can no longer be explained in terms of the divergence between the ideal and the real. It is no more a question of double standards or not matching deeds with words. Rather, the very 'word' is wanting. The Law and its premises, the liberal values underlying law, *Law's empire* itself needs to be interrogated and overturned. In other words, fascism is not an aberration, it is the logical consequence of imperialism, and when imperialism runs amok, you get 'Iraq'.

Second, whatever the achievements of Western bourgeois civilization, these are now exhausted. We are on the threshold of reconstructing a new civilization, a more universal, a more humane, civilization. And that cannot be done without defeating and destroying imperialism on all fronts. On the legal front, we have to *re-think* law and its future rather than simply talk in terms of re-making it. I do not know how, but I do know how not. We cannot continue to accept the value-system underlying the Anglo-American law as unproblematic. The very premises of law need to be interrogated. We cannot continue accepting the Western civilization's claim to universality. Its universalization owes much to the argument of force rather than the force of argument. We have to rediscover other civilizations and weave together a new tapestry borrowing from different cultures and peoples.[14]

Taking American empire seriously means that we need to revitalize an imagination of decolonization relevant for the present time. It is not institutions – the state system, the idea of 'law', etc. – that are of primary importance in this respect; they are instruments whose worth for the cause of struggle against empire remain subject to critical examination. Instead, it is the dream of freedom from oppression and violation which serves as the guiding point for thought-action that ought to be remembered as we set out on new visions, or more accurately, as we register and dignify struggles for other possibilities. One of these is peoples' law.

## A THEORIZATION FOR RESISTANCE: A PEOPLES' LAW PERSPECTIVE

A peoples' law perspective of resistance against empire's rule would begin with a series of demystifications necessary as a first act of repudiation:

- Despite attempts to claim the opposite, there exists no inviolable right, on the part of the powerful, to govern, rule, order, the weak.
- Regardless of the ideological claims being advanced, there exists no unifying or unified civilizational consensus on the naturalness of a corporate-dominated, militaristic imperialism as comprising the common values, truths, visions of human futures that prescribe a universal course for humanity's social evolution.
- Notwithstanding attempts to convince otherwise, there exists no pre-ordained rationale for, eternal truth of, inevitability, regarding, forms of socially constructed orders that form the institutions of governance, including the form of 'law'.

How, therefore, might we theorize law for resistance to empire?

Decolonization histories, as histories of struggle against the claimed 'truths' of empire, have seldom flowed from law's generosity. Everything, the world so to speak, is up for grabs. And it is precisely this grabbing that is being pursued by the powerful, the dominant, in their appropriation of the idea of 'law', and through it, the mechanisms of governance for empire. Given the materialities and the ideological thrusts of current world orderings as discussed above, a perspective of peoples' law, therefore, would recognize the right of peoples to speak the words and act the actions of law from a position of opposition to the violence of empire. The words of the Mazarain in Punjab serve as an illustration and inspiration:

> The myths by which your laws persist fail to sustain in the South. ... [W]e are excluded, we are omitted, we are disposable, yet cannot be a sacrifice. To talk then of state law is to talk of the monopolisation of violences and to lay claim to lie making. But it's a deeper movement that inheres the greatest violence. The colonisation of the ideas of law.
>
> What we seek to imagine is a peoples law. The Mazarain seek to establish their own truths concerning their living and dying. Why does this truth not carry the normative weight ascribed to law? It is no less law than the states truths concerning living and dying. And so the Peoples of the Damaan seek to tell their own truths. Both truths uncover the violences of dominant law. The forms of this uncovering are vast and varied − public hearings, poetic recitals, music, testimony and story-telling. They all lay out the peoples' law. And all are experiments with the truth.[15]

The reclaiming of the idea of law, therefore, entails a thorough reorientation of the ideas underpinning political practice as we have been made to understand them. In reality, such reorientations are daily happenings within communities of the violated who have asserted their rebellious consciousness; for them the living of peoples' law is less a matter of theoretical preference than one of survival.

The idea of peoples' law, as an opposition to empire's law, is something more than an articulation of protest. It is not preoccupied with urging empire to reform. It is not intended to seek an invitation to speak with the powers who seek to implement empire's projects. Rather, it is about creating a different authority for judgment and action altogether, based on other 'Word-Worlds' of law that are authored by peoples in action:[16]

- Peoples' law as a process of reclaiming Histories and Futures. An underlying thrust of the conceptual and practical implication of peoples' law is the reclaiming of violated peoples' rights to 'truth', manifest in the reappropriation from dominant sites and processes the narratives of histories of suffering and futures of emancipation.[17] An elaboration of peoples' law, therefore, impinges on the very basis upon which ideological constructions of the 'world' are maintained and promoted. Much of what can be seen as peoples' action in this regard has been to re-tell history as a means of reclaiming the power of memory and judgment of violation.
- Peoples' law as a manifestation of reclaiming Political Action. Running through the entire range of violated peoples' political initiatives in opposition to 'power' is a fundamental reclaiming of the 'right to act'.[18] Peoples' law, therefore, brings to the fore ideas of political action which counterposes the mainstream conceptualization of democratic politics with the radical reappropriation by peoples' groups to initiate what might be termed 'grass-roots democratic action' of and for law.[19]

Clearly, the rejection of the 'certainties' of mainstream political-legal imaginations by the growing peoples' movements represents mounting resistance to the powers of domination that have ruled thus far. The manifestation of these movements also represents a reclaiming of peoples' power to narrate their own stories and project their own visions. The functionaries of empire would have it be that the 'wretched of the earth' are gripped by the manifolds of misfortune – 'terror', 'underdevelopment', and the like – which are to be eradicated through empire's visionary action. The peoples subjected to the 'globalization' projects of empire tell a different history. Suffering is less the condition of misfortune; they resoundingly condemn it as a consequence of violations.[20] From this original stance of resistance and rejection of empire's 'authority' arises the possibility of a more thorough reorientation of the very idea of law as a means and manifestation of a reclaimed peoples' authority-sovereignty.

I submit the following principles as describing the foundations of a peoples' oriented perspective of law in opposition to empire's law:

- *Judgment*: the right/power of peoples to judge the 'realities' that are inflicted upon them and to name as violation that which is otherwise proclaimed as normality by the dominant powers.

- *Authorship*: the right/power of peoples to author/create 'law' and to define the structures and nature of social relationships conducive to a life of security and welfare.
- *Control*: the right/power of peoples to control (and not merely 'participate' in) the processes of decision-making and judgment in relation to the matters which affect the daily life-conditions of their communities.
- *Action*: the right/power of peoples to effect the 'implementation' of their alternative visions of social relationships in ways that reinforce and celebrate the diversity of humanity, for humanity.

Empire's law and peoples' law posit two conflicting movements, one real and in motion, the other nascent, for the (re)constitution of global orderings. We are familiar with empire's law as it projects the desires of empire onto global life-worlds. We are less so with peoples' law. We see empire and credit its rule with a normative content of 'law' even if we reject its motivations and implications. The aim of introducing a peoples' law perspective is to give equal dignity to peoples' actions of resistance as amounting to a rebellious legal imagination outside of empire's predefinition of the 'law-idea'. A reconciliation, or harmonization, of desires and visions is not contemplated here – empire's law and peoples' law projects would stand fundamentally in conflict.

The theorization of peoples' law as presented, therefore, does indeed contravene the universalist requirement of law as conventionally demanded. It also places a somewhat minimized role for conventional legal thinking as a means for emancipatory imaginations. This is done not as a rejection of the possibilities of 'victories' against empire that might be achieved by recourse through law. Rather, it is based on a recognition that while struggles against empire are an everyday truth for people, 'emancipatory law' seldom is. Hope, therefore, is vested not in wishing resistance through 'law', but rather, in thinking resistance against (empire's) law. In this sense, it is not a theorization which seeks to reclaim a lost majesty of law. It is, on the contrary, one that de-theorizes empire's law's majesty. It is, in other words, an attempt towards a decolonization from and of 'law'.

## THE WORLD TRIBUNAL ON IRAQ: EXISTENTIAL HESITANCIES BETWEEN EMPIRE AND PEOPLES' LAW?

Where in between empire's law and peoples' law, then, might the World Tribunal on Iraq fall?

The rejection of empire, its manifestation perceived through the prosecution of the unprovoked invasion of Iraq, lies at the very heart of the motivation underlying the WTI; there is no ambiguity about this. The Istanbul Platform Text which serves as the constituting 'charter' of the WTI movement, declares its existence precisely upon this rejection:

> A war of aggression was launched despite the opposition of people and governments all over the world. However, there is no court or authority that will judge the acts of the US and its allies. If the official authorities fail, then authority derived from universal morals and human rights principles can speak for the world.[21]

It might be argued, as a preliminary to any critical analysis of the WTI, that this underlying bias so explicit in the Platform Text exposes the political motivation of the undertaking, thereby undermining the credibility of the WTI, as a 'tribunal', from the very start. This criticism would be valid if we adopted a standpoint which maintains the assumption of primacy accorded to 'law' as conventionally understood, with all its purported prerequisites of 'neutrality'. The Istanbul Platform Text begins, after all, with a judgment, rather than a statement of investigation. If, however, the WTI is a creature of a different species, then a different analytical lens must be applied.[22] Viewing the WTI imagination as one that derives from a peoples' law orientation, it might be regarded that this explicit positioning of opposition is exactly the necessary statement of the power of judgment that makes it significant as a challenge to empire's law and a reason why it is potentially significant as a peoples' law doing.

As a product of its time, however, the WTI was born from no one 'vision'. Neither has it come to be without essential conflicts of imaginations. Carrying with it the burden of a 'crisis' of emancipatory aspiration, the WTI has been constructed out of various cultural biases of political and legal imagination. The debates within the WTI are therefore symptomatic of the more general challenges posed by a recognition of empire to political and legal thought. A brief description of the recurring tensions may be useful.

### a)  WTI as a site of competing imaginations of judgment

Two visions of the WTI undertaking and its underlying aims may be seen as having moved the WTI process; one, of the legalist tendency whose aspirational motivation lies in the concern to preserve the sanctity of international law in a world where is witnessed the ascendancy of empire's law and with it political malfeasance – theirs might be understood as the claiming of a peoples' right to legal judgment upon empire's rule and its attendant violations of 'international law'; the second vision, one arising from a movement-grounded political tendency whose motivation stems from a broader rejection of violence understood as inherent in the political-economic order maintained by empire for its projects of profit and domination – theirs might be viewed as the claiming of a peoples' right to a politico-ethical judgment of empire's rule. Both of these find voice in the Platform Text. Both have continued to have influence over the course of the practical construction of the WTI international tribunals process.

### b) WTI as a site of competing imaginations of activism

A related issue that has dominated much internal debate within the WTI relates to the role it is to play in a wider environment of political activism against the war on Iraq. In specific terms, the issue was to what extent the WTI should attach its name to campaign statements of the anti-war movements. At the heart of competing perspectives here is the meaning assigned to the 'tribunal' form. One view has been that as a tribunal activity the WTI should maintain some distance between itself and the ongoing anti-war campaigns that maintain a clear political rejection of the violence against and domination of Iraq. This view holds that legitimacy for the 'tribunal' aspect which is central to the WTI undertaking would be jeopardized by such overtly articulated campaigning postures, that instead, the WTI should dignify itself by judgments formed during the tribunal sessions. The contrary position is that, as an outcome of the anti-war movements, the WTI has to maintain a significant political profile in support of campaigning work that is the political activity of these movements. Legitimacy, according to those who urge for an active campaigns presence, is seen more from the perspective of the movements; the concern being that should the WTI be seen as detached from the politics of anti-war campaigning, it would lose credibility among the movements as a serious political actor against the war.

Both of these issues of internal contention derive from perspectives on the idea of a peoples' tribunal and the implications of 'doing' that follow, the essential questions being why a peoples' tribunal? And, how a peoples' tribunal? I am not sure whether these questions have seriously been addressed by the participants of the WTI initiative to the point of reaching a consensus resolution. In this respect, the WTI initiative has emerged less as a coordinated undertaking where the individual sessions consciously contribute to a coherent framework of investigation, than a series of individualized, national sessions based on participant preoccupations, orientations and motivations. Desiring a pragmatic outcome of realization, a claim to a unity of diversity has been the preferred option for the mediation of contentions.

My view is that what is more important than the reality of differences within the WTI imagination is how these might be understood and addressed. What follows is a suggestion of how the WTI might be self-imagined from a peoples' law perspective, where the debates outlined above become a meaningful aspect of a coherent process of thinking and acting resistance against empire. I discuss this by reference to the issues, first of 'legitimacy', then of the substantive 'tasks' envisioned for the WTI process.

## 1. Legitimacy

The issue of legitimacy lies at the heart of the seemingly competing visions of the WTI outlined above. Notwithstanding the stated 'sources' from which legitimacy is claimed in the Istanbul Platform Text, the differences may be stated thus:

- For the 'legalist' – legitimacy derives from an approximation of the WTI undertaking to the processes and languages of institutions of law.
- For the 'politico-ethicist' – legitimacy drives from an approximation of the WTI undertaking to the processes and languages of the anti-war movements.

I suggest that both are demonstrative of an unnecessary preoccupation.

The perceived need to seek external 'legitimizations', whether from institutions of power (UN accreditation, recognition by 'authority' figures, etc.) or from 'the movements', reveals a need for reassurances that the doing of a peoples' tribunal is sanctioned by some reference-point of authority. The desire for legitimacy in this way, aside from inadvertently legitimizing the 'way-of-the-world' as it is constructed by dominant conceptions of authority, is overly constraining because it defines the limits of imagination and because it defines the limits of action. In practical terms, rather than beginning with the question of what needs to be done in contemplating the role of a peoples' tribunal in developing a serious and critical examination of the nature and realities of empire's rule, the dominating question becomes what can (permissibly) be done by reference to the perceived prerequisites set by those from whom legitimacy is sought. Thus, we become preoccupied with issues of 'credibility', whether by mimicking institutions and practices of power in the doing of 'law' or by pandering to the agendas of (mostly) institutionalized 'movements' of the North. Neither leads to creative and potent praxes of resistance.

A peoples' law orientation might rather begin by distinguishing 'legitimacy' from 'recognition'. Legitimacy, seen from this perspective, is self-defined; an assertion of being, based on a confidence of being legitimate by virtue of critical self-consciousness and of conscience. Legitimacy, therefore, is not externally sought or deemed to be so generated, existence is not to be sanctioned by accreditation. Legitimacy lies in the very self-assertion of being 'actors'. The separate issue of 'recognition', that which is often confused for legitimacy, would be accepted as being open to be gained. Legitimacy gives meaning to the assumption of the power to act, recognition the subsequent test by which that action may be judged by various publics. Although the legacy of the Bertrand Russell Tribunals is much repeated as a basis from which the WTI has been imagined, and is reflected in the Istanbul Platform Text, its statement on legitimacy as deriving from the self-confident claim to being is worth recalling:

> We are perfectly aware that we have not been given a mandate by anyone; but we took the initiative to meet, and we also know that nobody could have given us a mandate. It is true that our Tribunal is not an institution. But, it is not a substitute for any institution already in existence: it is, on the contrary, formed out of a void and for a real need. We were not recruited or invested with real powers by governments: but, as we have just seen, the investiture at Nuremberg was not enough to give the jurists unquestioned legality. ... The Russell Tribunal believes, on the contrary, that its legality comes from both its absolute powerlessness and its universality.[23]

I make this point about 'legitimacy' not to undermine the significance of the WTI but, on the contrary, to emphasize it. Rather than regarding the self-creation of the WTI as an embarrassment, it should be understood as a conscious act of claiming power.

The credibility of the process and its outcomes, as well as whatever recognition flows from its doing of judgment, comes not from some claimed derivation of external authority but from its integrity of doing and its quality of substance. From this position of confidence, based on the reclaimed 'rights' of peoples' judgment and voice, may the WTI be an impetus for the emergence of a movement of peoples' tribunals against empire's rule.

## 2. Tasks

The conception of the WTI included a series of 'tasks' that formed the basis upon which the international process of tribunal sessions was undertaken:

> The first task of the tribunal is to investigate the crimes committed by the US government in launching the Iraq war. ...
>
> The second task is to investigate allegations of war crimes during the aggression, crimes against laws of occupation, humanitarian law and crimes against humanity, including genocide.
>
> The third task is the investigation and exposure of the New Imperial World Order. The tribunal would therefore consider the broader context of the doctrines of 'pre-emptive war' and 'preventive war' and all the consequences of those doctrines: 'benevolent hegemony', 'full spectrum dominance' and 'multiple simultaneous theatre wars'.... As part of this process, some hearings will investigate the vast economic interests involved in this rationalised war-logic.
>
> The tribunal, after having examined reports and documentary evidence and having listened to witnesses (Iraqi and international victims and various experts), will reach a decision.[24]

From a reading of these tasks, some uncertainties arise regarding the questions: Why a peoples' tribunal? And how a peoples' tribunal? What is meant by 'investigations' and 'decision' since there already appears to have been a predetermination of judgment? Does investigation here relate to detached investigations of 'legality', 'criminality', 'legitimacy' (in which case, the predetermination which has been articulated as giving origin to the WTI makes this a superfluous if not a disingenuous claim), or does it pertain to an investigation of 'facts' in order to put on record the realities and outcomes of the illegal and criminal act (in which case what is meant by a 'decision')? And, what is the purpose of the sessions by conducting such investigations? Does it hope to present a 'judgment' of 'crimes' and 'illegalities', to present judgments on the implications of such crimes and illegalities, to present a record of facts? Or something else? At issue, is the underlying nature of interventions against empire that the WTI seeks to initiate.

The challenge to bring coherence to the diversity of orientations and the ambiguities of aspirations that have been the reality of the international WTI process, falls upon the 'culminating session' in Istanbul in June 2005. At the time of writing the signs were encouraging that a more rigorous elaboration of a peoples' law orientation might be enabled in Istanbul.

The Framework Text of the Istanbul Session sets out two major lines of enquiry for the proceedings:[25] first, an investigation of the wrongs committed against the people of Iraq; second, an investigation of issues related to the implementation of justice.

Such a framework provides the conceptual space which may permit reconciliations of the various competing visions and resolution of some of the inconsistencies thus far highlighted. I discuss this potential for coherence by suggesting that we should see the tasks set as following from an identification of three significant functions of the WTI, corresponding to the original repudiations from which a peoples' law imagination is born:

- *The Declaratory Function*: rejecting the claim to 'inviolability' of empire's rule/law.
- *The Deliberative Function*: reflecting on the realities of empire's rule and their implications for thought-action thereby challenging the claim to the 'naturalness' of empire's prescribed orders. And,
- *The Mandating Function*: imagining strategic action for continuing peoples' law initiatives to follow from the WTI thereby challenging the claim to the 'inevitability' of empire's rule.

### a) The Declaratory Function

It was noted above that a key contemporary feature of empire's rule, as evidenced by the claim to the right to unilateral violence, is the attempt to normalize the 'constitutional' ordering of empire. It was also observed that the institutions in which faith for a humane 'international law'-based order have come to be placed – the state, the UN system, national and international legal institutions – appear to have divested themselves of this obligation to resist empire's usurpation of 'law' in favour of bit-part benefits to be gained as participants in empire. Thus, we see the statement of rejection with which the Istanbul Platform Text of the WTI begins. And this, I suggested, may be the very necessary claim to power which might move peoples' law beginnings.

The rejection of the inviolability of empire's rule is the first act of 'decolonization'. It is only through a 'No' to oppression and violence that imaginations of other possibilities may be born. The 'declaratory function' of the WTI, therefore, pertains to an undertaking to place on record the substantive rejection, by a peoples' process of investigation and judgment, of the realities of empire's rule and its efforts to impose the constitutional order of empire's law through the prosecution of the war on Iraq. Various issues, therefore, become necessary as being the subject of such a declaration.

First, the claim to 'legality' made to justify the actions undertaken on behalf of empire – here the legal declaration of illegality/criminality is a necessary act of rejection against empire's assertions of the normative content of its actions. Law-based considerations are a priority in this aspect of the tribunal's proceedings. The 'rebellious' lawyer would be the central protagonist to bring to public notice this legal declaration of violation.[26] There would be no contradiction therefore that the already formed judgment of illegality/criminality which moved the WTI into existence should be followed with the aim of undertaking a public process of declaring such a judgment based on a comprehensive presentation of evidence. The argument of illegality/criminality in this case would be more a matter to be presented by the session, rather than one to be determined. In this way, the unnecessary pretence of a 'judicial' process can be avoided, thus also avoiding the accusations which may follow if such a claim were made given that a detachment in judgment is not, and neither should it be, present in the WTI imagination.

Second, the claim to legitimacy made to justify the actions undertaken on behalf of empire – here the politico-ethical declaration of the illegitimacy of empire's desires in prosecuting the war also serves as a rejection of the claim to the benevolence of empire's rule. This would entail a presentation of rejections based on the ordering principles sought to be imposed by empire for normalization. Here also would arise the distinctive 'listening' function of a peoples' tribunal which recognizes the dignity of voices of suffering. What is significant in the declarations of illegitimacy which follow is not that these consequences of empire's designs have been claimed to possess legal sanction, but they are judged to be wrong. A presentation of evidence demonstrating the motives of empire, its mechanisms of control and deception and its agents of domination, and the human consequences that flow from violence and domination, all serve to record a public rejection of empire and reclaim a peoples' voice of judgment against such desires.

Third, the silence/inaction by the institutions entrusted with the aspirations of a humane political-legal order – in this case, a declaration of rejection (opposition?) against the betrayal by mainstream institutions and processes – serves to record a peoples' rejection of complicity and acquiescence to empire's rule leading to the seeming entrenchment of the constitutional ordering of empire's law. Such a declaration would place as contested the claims to legitimacy accorded to the very institutions of politics and law and locate them within the ambit of empire, having served as they have as functionaries of empire for all the imposing rhetoric prior to the invasion of Iraq. A peoples' judgment so declared would also bring to focus the necessary problematization of 'international law' within empire.

It may be noted that the declaratory function as described does not conform to what might conventionally be understood as the object of work of a tribunal. This is consciously so, for it is based on a perspective that sees the judgments on these violations and betrayals not as an embarrassment to be disguised by a veil of pretend 'objectivity' but as the very basis from which a peoples' action flows. Rather than the staging of a mock 'judicial' proceeding, it is the recording of judgments based on the exposure of truths that is of primary significance. The declaratory function would, as it were, make an honest 'doing' out of the WTI. Put differently, it serves to announce to the world the reason for existence of the World Tribunal on Iraq, and from this, follows what potentially are the creative and creating contributions of this historical process of a peoples' tribunal doing relevant to our time.

## b) The Deliberative Function

In truth, the 'declaration' of 'illegality', 'criminality' and 'illegitimacy' in the context of the invasion, occupation and ongoing control of Iraq through both the violation and the application of the UN Charter canon of international law is far from breaking news. That a peoples' tribunal so declares it, or so 'finds' it, would cause little ripple in the political consciousness of the majority of the global citizenry. There is no Russellian 'crime of silence' in this respect which would be redressed by a WTI judgment. 'Illegality' and 'illegitimacy' have been shouted literally and figuratively from the rooftops, not solely after the event, but from before its prosecution, to little avail it would seem. If this were the sole ambition of the WTI, then it would be not too difficult a task. The question is, what remains subject to 'silence' requiring a peoples' judgment to give it voice?

Aside from the violence inflicted as fact by empire, also critical in empire's projection of dominance is the imposition of a colonized imagination by which 'the people' are brought to believe in the 'naturalness' of the ordering so imposed. If the declaratory function of the WTI serves to place on record the peoples' findings of the failures of the international political-legal order in the specific context of the war on Iraq, then the 'deliberative function' initiates a necessary process of judgment upon the implications which follow from such a finding, enabling a people-oriented reflection of the idea and practice of 'law' under the conditions of empire. This is not easy work for it requires more than statements of protest, more than recounting a litany of violations and its consequences (as a record of reality). Instead, it would provoke a questioning of prevailing assumptions and aspirations that follow from such analyses. That the international political-legal system failed to halt complicity with empire through inaction, acquiescence and silence, that normalization of the unilateral right to violence appears to have been the outcome, that empire's constitutional order means the erosion witnessed of previous gains in the attempt to humanize law, that there is a usurpation of the 'security' discourse to impose by violence human insecurity, all of these would necessitate serious consideration before human-oriented resistance perspectives and possibilities may be charted. Also pertinent to this aspect of deliberation is a critical reflection of past and on-going efforts to resist empire's violence across global landscapes so that understandings may be gained of the politics of resistance. Crucially, such enquiries would locate the war on Iraq within the broader implications of empire's rule. The critical question is how do these realities affect our choices and strategies of intervention? As it stands, the second part of the Istanbul Framework Text appears to provide for these tasks to be undertaken.

A process of deliberation on these issues would challenge the 'naturalness' of the current 'order' which enables empire's violence. In addition, and this is perhaps more important, it would also challenge the limits of possibilities sought to be presented by dominant ideologies as natural. Methods of 'protest', channels of challenge, institutions of recourse, languages of intervention, jurisdictions of action, all of these ordered conditions would be subject to critical re-evaluation. Here also lies a challenge to 'our' own internalizations of a 'colonized' condition, as it may require many 'professional' and 'expert' biases to be cast aside upon examination. In admittedly general terms, the following enquiries may be undertaken as a supplement to those issues already identified in the Istanbul Framing Text:

- To what extent do existing institutional spaces for political articulation and legal challenge, national or international, provide real scope for interventions against empire? From an identification of such possibilities may be devised strategic choices for action in various viable locations.
- What languages of challenge may be most effective under the current context of empire's appropriations and legitimizations? Such determinations may point to the extent to which languages of 'law', 'human rights', etc., given the conditions of articulation and silencings which prevail, promise a real impact on the various audiences, and whether other languages may be more appropriate in given contexts.
- What non-institutional sites and strategies of intervention suggest themselves for potential impact upon the weak spots of empire. From this may be identified creative possibilities for mass mobilization and direct action.

Should the WTI embark on deliberative tasks along these lines, then it may be able to move beyond the usual lamenting that often takes place in outraged gatherings against empire. Aside from setting forward a compiled list of the many sins of empire, and calling ever again for institutions that have proven themselves servile to suddenly rise as saviours, such deliberative courage would at least attempt to take empire, and resistance to it, seriously. Out of such deliberation may be developed a 'mandate' for future peoples' actions.

## c)  The 'Mandating Function'

The WTI exists in a political climate where a peoples' law orientation is nascent. Consistent with the stated aims of the WTI to be a component part of a creative and vital movement for peace and justice, the 'mandating function' would use the opportunity of solidarities fostered by the WTI process to give credence, and provide inspiration, to new directions of peoples' law actions. Through the voice of the WTI, therefore, may be mandated specific future initiatives which build peoples' law movements across time and space, challenging the inevitability of empire's ordering. It is in this connection that I suggest the WTI should envisage future campaigns.

The issue of campaigns, it was stated earlier, has been a matter of some contention during the WTI process. As noted, this debate has been influenced by two different conceptions of the 'tribunals' idea. However, what unites both approaches, I believe, is a tendency to see the WTI process as an adjunct to existing means of protest – whether legal or political. I suggest, instead, an alternative thinking on campaigns which begins with an appreciation of the potential 'newness' of the WTI. The issue, I think, is not whether or not the WTI should be involved in campaigns, but on how we might imagine the WTI itself *as* a campaign. Based on an identification of challenges and locations of action, the WTI might serve as a springboard from which a conscious and confident assertion of a peoples' mandated action against empire could be launched. These, then, would be the campaigns imagined and initiated by the WTI.

Campaigns mandated by the WTI may be formulated by thinking along the following lines:

- Campaigns to intervene in the existing institutional sites identified as potentially amenable to a challenge against empire – the WTI may, therefore, issue a peoples' mandate calling on activist lawyers, media workers, parliamentarians, diplomatic personnel and the like, to effect strategies of intervention as deemed appropriate, specific to the findings of the WTI proceedings.
- Campaigns that aim to communicate and convince ever greater sections of the global public of the violations of empire and the mechanisms by which these are enabled – a peoples' mandate calling on national and international movements, media activists, parliamentarians, etc., to enhance the profile and volume of the recorded rejections of empire declared by the WTI through specifically identified channels of dissemination and intervention.
- Campaigns that seek to build peoples' law movements, uniting communities of solidarity across the diverse issues of empire's violent orderings: a peoples' mandate calling for coordination of

existing tribunals initiatives and exchanges of peoples' law imaginations and experiences.[27]

A mandating function along these lines is suggested to extend the usual practice among many anti-war gatherings to issue generalized 'plan of action' statements to include critically and strategically thought-out programmes of intervention that are specific to aims and locations of action. empire, after all, does not exist in abstract terms of power; it exists only through manifestations within locations of power. It is at these locations that a peoples' intervention may serve to repel the specific avatars of empire. Significantly also, may it be seen that these actions of resistance stem not from isolated and aberrant instances but rather that they flow from a confident and conscious reclaiming of a peoples' power to act. Such would be, I believe, the symbolic potency of mandates issued by the WTI.

## CONCLUSIONS AND BEGINNINGS?

The context of empire as it emerges and impinges on the global social majorities necessitates that we begin rethinking the assumptions of law's promised order for justice. Whatever our perceptions might be regarding the 'majesty' of law, its violence continues as a daily ordering principle for effecting empire's projects. And however we might wish for 'polite' transformations through law's reclaiming of the terrain of action, peoples' struggles against empire continue often distant from humane law's gaze.

The WTI is a presence within this oppositional reality of empire's law and peoples' law. It is also in many respects reflective of the general uncertainties of imagination wrought by empire's appropriations of hitherto cherished presumptions of a humanity of law. These uncertainties cannot be wished away; they are necessary stages of contemplation from which clearer insights into the possibilities of thought-action against violence and domination may be attained. Despite the discomforts this may give those of us who are still essentially located within empire's comfort-zones, it is worth remembering that these imaginations of 'alternatives' are everyday present at the frontlines of empire's projections of violence.

I believe that the WTI does indeed possess a unique potential. My wish is obviously that it will seize what I believe to be a significant symbolic potency of voice, not merely of protest, but of reclamation. If we can believe that there is nothing inviolable, natural or inevitable about empire's rule, notwithstanding such indoctrinations, if we can recognize within ourselves the internalizations of empire's prescriptions as we find ourselves 'existing' within empire, then we might begin to accord a rightful dignity to those for whom the struggles against empire are more than theoretical postulations. This is simply a matter of choice. The WTI may wish to confine itself to considerations of the specific outrage of the war on Iraq within parameters, and through lenses, already existing – the language of international law, the language of urgings, the language of reformism, the language of strivings – or it may see itself as indeed a creation. May it be that after the culminating session of the WTI in Istanbul, we meet again not to express yet another outrage through a peoples' tribunal with the same statements of rejection and urgings, but that we meet as we build new solidarities and connectivities of a peoples' law and tribunals movements. May it be that the WTI too does not mark yet another dead-end in the course of empire's business-as-usual.

To the extent that the work of the WTI may be concluded with beginnings that go beyond being outraged, it portends the creation of a peoples' law imagination against empire. Decolonization, after all, always begins with dreaming the impossible.

## ACKNOWLEDGEMENTS

I am grateful to the Lelio Basso International Foundation, and to Dr Gianni Tognoni, for the research grant to initiate a Peoples' Law Programme which enabled this work. I am especially grateful to Walter Musco who was my assistant and a constant source of support through some difficult times; Flavia Gasperetti who through work and friendship rescued us at a crucial time; and Ayse Berktay of the World Tribunal on Iraq (Istanbul) whose belief in the Programme has been invaluable.

## NOTES

1  For general information on the origins, aims and sequence of the international process of tribunal sessions initiated as part of the World Tribunal on Iraq, see the website of the WTI at http://www.worldtribunal.org.
2  For a comprehensive statement of the vision which has come to inform current US 'policy' on international security issues, see Thomas Donnelly, Donald Kagan and Gary Schmitt, *Rebuilding America's Defences: Strategy, Forces and Resources for a New Century*, A Report of the Project for the New American Century (2000), at http://www.newamericancentury.org/

Rebuilding AmericasDefenses.pdf; and its official, US government incarnation, *The National Security Strategy of the United States of America* (September 2002). In this connection, see also Thomas Donnelly, 'The Underpinnings of the Bush Doctrine' (January 2003), at http://www.aei.org/publications/pubID.15845/pub_details.asp; and Joshua Muravchik, 'The Bush Manifesto' (2002), at http://www.aei.org/news/newsID.14538/news_detail.asp.

3  See, Philip Bobbitt, *The Shield of Achilles: War, Peace, and the Course of History* (New York: Knopf, 2002). On the idea of unipolarity, see, for example, William C. Wohlforth, 'The Stability of a Unipolar World', *International Security*, 24:1 (Summer 1999): 5.

4  See, for example, Robert Kagan, 'Multilateralism, American Style', *The Washington Post* (13 September 2002), at http://www.newamericancentury. org/global-091302.htm. For a warning on pursuing a multilateral path, see William Kristol and Robert Kagan, 'The U.N. Trap?', *The Weekly Standard* (18 November 2002), at http://www.ceip.org/files/publications/2002-11-18-kaganwklystandard.asp.

5  For a revealing discussion of the military-industrial complex as being central to the control structure, and essential for both political and economic dominance, see William D. Hartung, *Military-Industrial Complex Revisited: How Weapons Makers are Shaping U.S. Foreign and Military Policies*, FPIF, at http://www.fpif.org/papers/micr/.

6  There is a vast amount of literature on the extent of corporate-control and perversion of the so-called democratic space; the issues involved range from corruption, political lobbying and funding of political parties, to the appropriation of political processes and the virtual drafting of international regulations (as in the case of the TRIPS Agreement within the WTO framework). See, for example, David C. Korten, *When Corporations Rule the World*, 2nd edition (Bloomfield, CT: Kumarian Press, 2001); Thom Hartmann, *Unequal Protection: The Rise of Corporate Dominance and the Theft of Human Rights* (Emmaus, PA: Rodale Press, 2002); Greg Palast, *The Best Democracy Money Can Buy* (London: Robinson, 2002); and Belen Balanya et al., *Europe Inc.; Regional & Global Restructuring and the Rise of Corporate Power* (London: Pluto Press, 2000).

7  See factsheets produced by Corporate Europe Observatory on the International Chamber of Commerce, at http://www.corporateeurope. org/icc/factsheets.html.

8  See, for example, Fatoumata Jawara and Aileen Kwa, *Behind the Scenes at the WTO: The Real World of International Trade Negotiations* (London: Zed Books, 2003).

9  See, Richard Falk, 'Will the empire be Fascist?', at http://www.transnational. org/forum/meet/2003/Falk_Fascistempire.html, for a discussion of the current discourse on 'security' and 'anti-terror' on US approaches to international relations and law.

10  See John Braithwaite and Peter Drahos, *Global Business Regulation* (Cambridge: Cambridge University Press, 2000).

11  See, Jayan Nayar, 'Orders of Inhumanity', in R. Falk, L. E. J. Ruiz and R. B. J. Walkers (eds.), *Reframing the International: Law, Culture, Politics* (London: Routledge, 2002), 107, at 120.

12  We recall the so-called 'postcolonial' experience of efforts to challenge empire's law, of the many historic struggles for international legal transformations attempted through such innovations as 'permanent sovereignty over natural resources', the 'Charter for the New International Economic Order', the 'Right to Development'. It seems seldom, if not no longer, the case that these languages of political-legal imagination sustain contemporary resistance-thinking against empire. Why is that? How do we acknowledge that despite so many struggles to dream law as 'emancipation', worlds of 'world order' have changed little for the social majorities who suffer the daily mutilations of empire's rule, with or without law?

13  This was, after all, explicitly recognized by the 'international community'. A return to the concerns behind the eventual jamboree that was the UN World Summit for Social Development, held in Copenhagen, 1995, might remind us so; see generally the documents of the Summit, at http://www.un.org/esa/socdev/wssd/agreements/. A more recent indictment is contained in the UN Report on globalization, where the 'order' created and maintained by the World Trade Organization was described as a 'veritable nightmare' for perpetuating conditions of impoverishment and dispossession; see J. Oloka-Onyango and Deepika Udagama, 'The Realization of Economic, Social and Cultural Rights: Globalization and its Impact on the Full Enjoyment of Human Rights', *U.N. Commission on Human Rights*, 52nd Sess., Provisional Agenda Item 4, P15, U N Doc.E/CN.4/Sub.2/2000/13 (2000).

14  Issa Shivji, 'Law's empire and empire's lawlessness: Beyond the Anglo-American Law', *Law, Social Justice & Global Development Journal (LGD)*, 1 (2003), at http://www2.warwick.ac.uk/fac/soc/law/elj/lgd/2003_1/shivji2/.

15  Personal communication from the Anjuman Mazarain Punjab, 30 June 2003. The Anjuman Mazarain Punjab is a million strong tenant farmer's movement in Pakistan demanding the rights of ownership to their lands.

16  See, for example, The Universal Declaration of the Rights of Peoples (The Algiers Declaration) 1976, which has served as a powerful articulation of the philosophical-ideological positioning that signals a peoples' law perspective. For discussions on the Algiers Declaration, see Issa Shivji, *The Concept of Human Rights in Africa* (London: CODESRIA, 1989), especially Chapter 4; and Richard Falk, 'The Algiers Declaration of the Rights of People', in Richard Falk, *Human Rights and State Sovereignty* (New York: Holmes & Meier, 1981).

17  This is, as Baxi sees it, a critical role of the 'contemporary' human rights movements:

> In contrast, [to the 'modern' human rights paradigm], the 'contemporary' human rights paradigm is based on the premise of radical self-determination ... Self-determination insists that every person has the right to a voice, the right to bear witness to violation, and a right to immunity against 'disarticulation' by concentrations of economic, social and political formations.

Upendra Baxi, 'Voices of Suffering and the Future of Human Rights', *Transnational Law and Contemporary Problems* (Fall 1998): 125, at 126. See also, Shadrack B. O. Gutto, *Human and Peoples' Rights for the*

*Oppressed: Critical Essays on Theory and Practice from Sociology of Law Perspectives* (Lund: Lund University Press, 1993).

18 The World Social Forum 'Charter of Principles', for example, is a clear statement of reclaiming political space; see http://www.forumsocialmundial.org.br/main.asp?id_menu=4&cd_language=2. For a collective reflection on the WSF imagination and practice, see, Jai Sen et al. (eds.), *World Social Forum: Challenging empires* (New Delhi: The Viveka Foundation, 2004). For voices of disaffection with the World Social Forum, the criticism being that it represents a site appropriated by elite and professional sectors of institutionalized 'movements', see http://www.mumbairesistance.org.

19 See Gustavo Esteva and Madhu Suri Prakash, *Grassroots Post-Modernism: Remaking the Soil of Cultures* (London: Zed Books, 1998), Chapter 5.

20 Thus the recent upsurge in peoples' tribunals initiatives that follows from the tradition of the Bertrand Russell War Crimes Tribunals. See the 'verdicts' of the numerous peoples' tribunals that have become part of peoples' political action. Of these, the Permanent Peoples' Tribunal, based in Rome, has had the longest experience of invoking a peoples' justice; see http://www.internazionaleleliobasso.it/tribu%20eng.html. For a discussion of the politics of 'doing law' and peoples' tribunals as an alternative site for political-legal judgment, see Jayan Nayar, 'A People's Tribunal against the Crime of Silence? The Politics of Judgement and an Agenda for People's Law', *Law, Social Justice & Global Development* (*LGD*), 5 (2) (2001), http://elj.warwick.ac.uk/global/issue/2001-2/nayar.html.

21 See, Istanbul Platform Text, at http://www.worldtribunal.org/main/?b=15.

22 See Nayar, 'A Peoples' Tribunal against the Crime of Silence?'.

23 Jean-Paul Sartre, 'Inaugural Statement', in Peter Limqueco and Peter Weiss (eds.), *Prevent the Crime of Silence: Reports from the Sessions of the International War Crimes Tribunal Founded by Bertrand Russell* (London, Stockholm, Roskilde) Bertrand Russell Peace Foundation (1971), at http://www.homeusers.prestel.co.uk/littleton/v1101sar.htm.

24 http://www.worldtribunal.org/main/?b=16.

25 See http://www.worldtribunal.org/main/?b=21.

26 For a discussion of the respective roles of 'expert' communities to a peoples' tribunal doing, see Nayar, 'A Peoples' Tribunal against the Crime of Silence?'.

27 An important step towards enabling a peoples' tribunals network would be to bring together various peoples' groups and other related organizations who have already engaged, or are presently involved, in tribunals initiatives as a coalition of forces. For this, the first task would be the identification of as many tribunals initiatives as possible and the establishment of a facility for a centralized 'secretariat' to serve as a common link and channel for communication. From this may be developed a capacity for coordination, the sharing of experiences, strategies and outcomes, and a network for future coordinated action, communication and dissemination. This creation of a peoples' tribunals community/network would be a significant contribution to social movements in two ways: first, it would enable greater visibility and profile for peoples' tribunal doings through enhanced capacities for the dissemination of

information; and second, and importantly, it would enable a more confident assertion of the power and vitality of peoples' tribunals as legitimate peoples' law doing against injustice and violation. This effort was attempted with the Peoples' Law Programme of the Lelio Basso International Foundation, to link the Permanent Peoples' Tribunal of the Foundation with a broader tribunals community. A lack of resources, and a degree of ambivalence within the Foundation for such an undertaking has meant that a postponement has been required. It is expected that this work will continue upon my return to the School of Law, University of Warwick.

# 17
# Whither the United Nations?

*Samir Amin*

Translated by Stuart Anthony Stilitz

It is fashionable nowadays to claim that the UN is bankrupt and that it is up to the G7 or G8 – even NATO – to ensure that the international community is 'secure' and 'democratic'. I will argue against this view by demonstrating that while the UN has fallen prey to forces that seek to destroy it, there are other strategies that may be capable of transforming it, although this will of necessity be a very long-term project of the Left and associated social movements. To this end, I discuss the role of the UN, both historically and in its present crisis, the political strategies of the world's leading powers, and the challenges and opportunities of the twenty-first century.

## AN ASSESSMENT OF THE UNITED NATIONS (1945–1980)

Capitalism first triumphed in a particular region of the Old World: a small corner of north-western Europe. This is not to say that it had no roots elsewhere, but it was there that it would adopt its 'definitive' historical form, which it would impose elsewhere. It involved the modern nation-state, a form required to surmount the chaos, a political form that is presently in its final phase of disintegration, excluding any possibility of returning to the *status quo ante*, as we shall see. We are experiencing a return to chaos and a new challenge: to transcend capitalism, which has become obsolete.

The UN was created during the long phase of harmony between market and state (between economic management and political management). In fact, it constitutes this phase's crowning, although belated, achievement. The world-system philosophy on which it is premised, and which it expresses, is based on two principles: (1) the equal sovereignty of states (considered almost always to be 'nation-states'), and (2) polycentrism, that is, the principle of negotiation between states aimed, in part, at protecting their political, economic and cultural autonomy. Below, I will assess the progress made by the world-system. It will be a positive assessment; the constant negative assessments we hear these days are too rash. In doing so, I do not, however, wish to underestimate the UN's limits and contradictions, both of which have intensified, causing its contemporary crisis.

The Treaty of Westphalia (1648) was the first accord based on a system recognizing both the sovereignty of states and polycentrism. When the treaty was signed, this system applied only to the old world of Catholicism. With the Treaty of Vienna (1815), this recognition spread across Europe, becoming quasi-universal with the creation of the League of Nations (1920). I use the term 'quasi-universal' since the League of Nations did not challenge the colonial status of Asia and Africa, which were therefore excluded. The League of Nations remained a world-system organization composed of 'centres' (Europe and Japan), cut off from the United States (which refrained from joining, although it was initially its principal supporter) and flanked by the 'independent' Latin American countries of the periphery. The United Nations, by contrast, was founded on genuinely universalistic principles, which would quickly be actualized when the countries of Asia and the Arab world, and later Africa, regained their independence. Consequently, we should not be surprised that the apogee of UN history occurred precisely at this time of decolonization. It would be a brief period, lasting from the early 1960s to 1975–80, and coinciding with the 'development decades'.

The questioning and crisis that followed were not just of the UN but of the world-system with which the organization was associated. For, as we shall see, conflict among the various authorities in charge of managing the world (particularly the conflict between its economic sectors – the 'market', to use the more common term – and its political sectors) reappeared following two or three centuries of harmony, even though this harmony was limited to the system's centre. However, the discord did not resemble the chaos that had characterized the origins of capitalism. The new chaos was that of a system that had become obsolete;[1] it could not be transcended using models of harmony that belonged to another era. Rather, a complete review of all facets of the problem was required, not only at the local level (that is, nation), but also at the world-system level and future regional sub-system level.

Just as the solution to these local (i.e. national) problems cannot be found by returning to practices institutionalized by the capitalism of a previous era, so too the UN crisis (a major factor in the crisis of global management, and the one that concerns me here) cannot be resolved by preserving the old UN's role. The old UN had many successes, but it met the needs of another era – the post-World War II period.

World War II resulted in two victories, which provided the context for the creation of the UN: the victory of democracy over fascism, and the victory of the peoples of Asia and Africa over colonialism. These two victories provided a beacon for the economic, social and political forms for managing systems at the national and international levels. They provided a footing for the three fundamental 'socio-historic compromises' of the period: that of the welfare state in the West composed as a compromise between labour and capital which made it possible for the working classes who had defeated fascism to attain a dignity unparalleled in previous stages of capitalism; that of actually existing socialism; and national populism in the liberated countries of Asia and Africa.[2]

These compromises paved the way for the negotiated political management of international relations, and thus promoted the role of the United Nations. Today it is common to hear that the bipolarity of the Cold War and the veto power wielded by the five major powers (especially the US and Russia) have paralyzed the UN in this era. However, the opposite is true: the bipolarity, reinforced by the veto, gave the countries of the periphery (Asia, Africa and Latin America) a degree of manoeuvrability they have since lost. For a time, the imperialist centres were forced to adapt: they had to respect the sovereignty of these countries and to accept (or at least put up with) their national and social development projects.

It is impossible to grasp the significance of this encouraging development without comprehending that every stage of global capitalist expansion since its origins (the mercantilist period of 1500 to 1800) has been imperialistic in character. Stated differently, the dominant, immanent, internal logic of capitalist expansion gave rise to a polarization in global power and wealth unlike anything experienced in previous millennia. This tendency has been a dominant and permanent feature of 'actually existing capitalism'. However, it was radically questioned, and tempered, during what I have called the 'Bandung' period (1955–75). It was no accident that this period was one of growth and glory for the United Nations.

It is not difficult to identify the period's positive achievements. Economic growth rates were among the highest in modern times.

There was immense social progress, not only in the system's centres and in the countries of 'actually existing socialism', but also in the vast majority of countries of the liberated periphery. Lastly, there was a burgeoning of proud, modern, national identities.

The United Nations was party to these important changes and facilitated their implementation. The dual principles of national sovereignty and polycentrism proved to be an appropriate instrument for progressive change. On the political level, it prevented the violent intervention that had been common practice in the imperialism of earlier years and that has arisen once again ever since NATO – led, of course, by the US – began imposing its will on the world. On the economic management level, it introduced the principle of negotiation, with nation-states remaining free – on their own territory – to organize their systems of production and distribution of wealth as they thought best. 'Pessimists' will, of course, say that the resulting negotiations (such as those conducted by UNCTAD) rarely resulted in anything other than ineffectual declarations. The fact remains, however, that the sovereignty of states was upheld – at least within national borders. As a result, states had real negotiating power, which their ruling classes used as they saw fit.

While the successes of this period need to be appreciated, its limitations are not difficult to identify. First, the system's references to democracy were purely rhetorical. That said, the peoples of the world are now (although to varying degrees) more demanding in this regard than they were during the post-World War II era. I certainly view this as a positive development, even though the imperialist powers are easily able to manipulate pleas for greater democracy. In the era under discussion, however, sovereignty belonged to states, which were viewed as the exclusive representatives of their populations. This gave rise to another limitation of this period: local ruling classes often used the need for national construction as a justification for abandoning democracy. Second, the concepts of economic and social development themselves were based on premises that were specific to the paradigm of the period. This paradigm was predicated on a harmonious relationship between market and state, that is, between the management of the economy and the exercise of political power. The concept of economic development, which belongs to the capitalist logic of expansion, meant 'catching up'. It assumed that technology was neutral and that capitalism's hierarchical organization would be reproduced. The fact that this model always included an active role for the regulatory state, which sometimes replaced the absentee (or *comprador*) capitalist class, and that it occasionally had a somewhat 'social' orientation, does not mean it was socialist. Some observers incorrectly called this model socialist (I call it national populist).

This approach to development aligned itself with the capitalist globalization of the period, although the terms of this alignment were subject to negotiation. The 'development decades' – the triumph of the United Nations in this period – actively supported this strategy. But, the development projects of this period rapidly met their limitations because they aligned themselves with capitalism. As more projects were implemented, their contradictions accumulated, eroding their effectiveness and leading to an imperialist offensive and an economic slump.

The United Nations made a positive contribution to these experimental projects: its political activities protected national sovereignty and supported polycentrism. Although the political regimes responsible for the projects were not democratic (or, at best, had extremely weak democracies), overall they were not as 'odious' as many today claim. They were often progressive and open to secularization, and they provided support (albeit qualified) for improvements in the status of women; these autocracies often resembled 'enlightened despotism'. In fact, it was the imperialist powers that set up or supported the most odious regimes of the period as the regimes of Mobutu in Zaire, Suharto in Indonesia and the dictatorships in South America all attest.

Today, most criticisms of the United Nations during this period do not accurately account for the realities of the day. An objective comparison between the UN apparatus and other national or multinational institutional systems (such as the European system) would provide a more enlightened view.[3] In addition, a more meaningful and perfectly legitimate assessment of the period would focus on the illusions nurtured by its development successes. However, it is unacceptable for neoliberals to manipulate the 'failure' of the UN in this regard for their own purposes, for they subsequently imposed an even more devastating illusion, namely, the idea that deregulated capitalism would provide a superior form of development. This illusion, propagated through dogmatic rhetoric, has been refuted by the entire history of 'actually existing capitalism'. It has also been cruelly refuted by changes that have occurred over the last two decades: stagnation (development has been brushed aside and replaced by the discourse of the 'war on poverty', i.e. ineffective charity) and a scandalous increase in social inequality.

Despite these limitations and contradictions, the world has entrusted the United Nations with an historically unique and supremely important mission: securing peace and condemning recourse to war (and preventing it to the greatest possible extent). The UN Charter was designed to advance a polycentric approach to globalization. By this, I mean structuring globalization on the principle of negotiation, which is the sole guarantor of genuine respect for diversity in all its forms – cultural and linguistic, of course, but also diversity deriving from inequalities in economic development. Polycentrism respects all nations, big and small. It also accepts that each is, in a sense, its own 'centre'. Consequently, globalized interdependence must also be able to deal with the legitimate demands set out in the inward-looking policies of all parties. Polycentric globalization is 'negotiated', and while it may not provide anything like perfect equality, at least it aims to reduce inequalities rather than exacerbate them.

The UN Charter actually took polycentrism much further than this by condemning war itself, tolerating it only in cases of self-defence, and by condemning the aggressor at the outset. The UN only approves military intervention that it has ordered itself and that is carried out under its own operational and political command. Even if an intervention fulfils these criteria, it must also be an interim and measured response.

My assessment of the way the United Nations implemented these principles until the first Gulf War (1991) is for the most part positive. The United Nations endorsed the wars of liberation against the colonial powers (Britain, The Netherlands, France, Belgium and Portugal), thereby supporting polycentrism in a concrete way. Compared to what was to come later, this period had few 'civil wars'. While certain powers fanned the flames of disputes or exploited them to their own advantage – there are examples of this throughout history – the United Nations for its part did not lend support to these manoeuvrings (as in the case of the war in Biafra). Of course, the United Nations may have been manipulated occasionally (as in the Korean War), or neutralized (as in America's war in Vietnam or the Soviet invasion of Afghanistan). Admittedly, too, with regard to the Palestinian issue, it legitimized the creation of Israel on highly questionable grounds (allowing the Zionists to avoid implementation of the partition plan), although it later tried to halt the expansionist designs of the Israeli government, condemning the tripartite aggression of 1956 and, through Resolution 242, the occupation of Palestinian territories since 1967.

In sum, the United Nations held promise and did not enter into crisis through a natural process of decline. The United States, supported by its allies of the triad (the US, Western Europe and Japan) *undermined* the UN in 1990–91 by its decision no longer to carry out its responsibilities in managing polycentrism and guaranteeing peace through multilateral institutions. Washington's decision to carry out its plan to extend the Monroe Doctrine throughout the world threatened to ruin the United Nations.

George W. Bush did not formulate this outrageous and criminal plan. The American ruling class has nurtured it since 1945. The US came up with the plan following the Potsdam conference, which was based on nuclear monopoly. Indeed, the plan always gave a pivotal role to its military component. The US promptly established a global military strategy, divided up the world into regions, and assigned responsibility for the control of each region to a US Military Command.[4] The objective here was not only to encircle the USSR (and China), but also to make Washington the power with the final say in every region of the world. In other words, the aim of the US was to extend the Monroe Doctrine, which effectively gave it the exclusive 'right' to manage the New World Order, based on what it defined as its national interests, over the entire planet. This strategy implied that the 'supremacy of US national interest' should prevail over all other principles informing political behaviour. It developed a systematic mistrust of all supranational law.

However, many people wanted to see an end to imperialism and began working towards this goal in 1945. The UN was founded on a new principle, the illegality of war, because imperialistic rivalry and the fascists' disregard for human rights and international law had produced the horrors of World War II. At that time, the United States did not merely support this principle, but was one of its early proponents. Just after World War I, Woodrow Wilson advocated reorganizing international politics according to principles that were different from those that had been in effect since the Treaty of Westphalia (1648). This treaty had given absolute sovereignty (the same sovereignty that would later be challenged because it had led modern civilization to disaster) to monarchical states and, later on, to the more or less democratic ones. It matters little that the vicissitudes of American internal politics delayed implementation of these principles. Franklin Delano Roosevelt, and even his successor, Harry Truman, played a decisive role in advancing the new concept of multilateralism, which, accompanied by condemnation of war, is the foundation of the UN Charter.

This fine initiative received universal support at the time. In effect, it represented a quantum leap, setting the stage for the further evolution of civilization. Nevertheless, it never won support from the ruling classes of the United States. Consequently, American leaders always felt uncomfortable about allying themselves with the UN, and today they unabashedly proclaim what until now they have been obliged to conceal: that they do not accept the concept of a law of nations having precedence over what they consider to be the requirements of their national interest. It is, however, inexcusable for these leaders to adopt the same stance as the Nazis in their era, when the latter demanded the destruction of the League of Nations. When in 2003 Dominique de Villepin, then the French Foreign Minister, made a brilliant and impassioned plea to the UN Security Council to uphold the law of nations, the United States defended a past that others had openly proclaimed out of date. But De Villepin's statement should not be regarded as nostalgia for a bygone period, but rather as a reminder of what the future can and must hold.

The US is not the only country responsible for the drift away from a law of nations. Europe, too, played a role by fanning the flames in Yugoslavia (through its hasty recognition of Croatian and Slovenian independence), then by rallying to the positions taken by the United States on 'terrorism' and the war waged against Afghanistan. It remains to be seen if Europe will review its position as may be suggested by its ambivalence over the war waged against Iraq by the US and its imperial subordinates. At any rate, a return to the principle of polycentrism and the restoration and transformation of the role of the United Nations will not figure on the agenda as long as Europe accepts NATO as a substitute for UN management of globalization.

## CONFLICT AND HARMONY BETWEEN STATE AND MARKET: THE NEW CHALLENGE

The contemporary chaos we are witnessing bears no resemblance to the type that existed during the rise of capitalism. It follows that any response to the contemporary challenge cannot be based on the model of harmony that existed during that period. Today, capitalism has exhausted its progressive historical role and has nothing to offer us, except a drift towards barbarism. The challenge is to think 'beyond capitalism' and, consequently, to focus our enquiry on the conflict between the economy (the 'market', that is, capitalism) and society. This conflict affects all aspects of contemporary reality, both national and global. Thus, we cannot make proposals on the role we wish to assign to the United Nations without first clarifying the nature of the challenge humanity is facing.

To accomplish this, we first need to examine, even if briefly, two sets of questions: (1) the nature of the chaos fostered by neoliberalism and the illusions it fosters; and (2) what I call the clash between political cultures confronting this chaos.

We must now face the fact that the dominant powers (serving dominant global capital) have one plan for the future and that they are imposing it through systematic violence, including military violence. Now that 'actually existing capitalism' has reached its present stage of development, and in keeping with its own immanent logic, this is the only plan it can possibly have. This is very different from the 'liberal' plan, whose discourse promises (a) a competitive and transparent market, and (b) democracy that substitutes civil society for the 'bureaucratic' or even 'autocratic' state. While this has been a hollow discourse, the plan of dominant global capital (the 'transnationals' of the imperialist triad) is even more draconian. I have elsewhere termed the future they foresee for the majority of humanity as *'apartheid on a global scale'*.[5] Permanent war waged against the peoples of Asia, Africa and Latin America will play an essential role in ensuring the success of the plan. Obviously, in this scenario the United Nations would no longer have a role of its own to play; it would either become a docile instrument of the forces waging permanent war against the South or disappear altogether.

The question then becomes: Who will take the lead in this barbaric plan and for the benefit of whom? The facts speak for themselves. Through its unilateral decision to invade Iraq, the US has already catapulted itself into the position of leader. We must be aware of both the power and the vulnerability on which its leadership is based. On the one hand, the US has enormous destructive military capability. On the other, its military is vulnerable, due to its limited military combat capability. The US is also economically vulnerable due to deficits, which, for lack of 'spontaneous' financial support from the rest of the world, it will have to reduce through severe policies. For all of these reasons, the decision does not belong exclusively to the American Far Right united behind George W. Bush, but also to its Democratic rivals. The latter would be more inclined to redefine the methods for implementing this plan and to make a number of concessions (how far would they go?) in order to bring their triad allies on board (as ever, in a subordinate position). But it would still, in essence, follow a similar course.

Is there a possibility that the plan will be deployed under the banner of 'genuine economic liberalism'? Given the current climate, we cannot ignore that many, especially in Europe, are of the opinion that this is the proper course of action. An even greater number – among the ruling classes of Southern nations – have accepted economic liberalism on its own terms, considering it the only realistic option. China's membership in the World Trade Organization (WTO), and the positions taken by Third World countries in Cancun (September 2003), reflect this trend.[6] Time will dispel these illusions – but will it then be too late?

Faced with the reality of the plan advanced by capitalism and 'actually existing imperialism', there is only one real alternative: thinking 'beyond capitalism'. In other words, we must take a long-term approach to planning the desired transformations, both nationally and in terms of negotiated globalization. The United Nations has an important role to play in this new approach.

Washington's propaganda machine placed the supposed clash of 'civilizations' (read: religions) squarely on the agenda. It maintained that the clash was unavoidable and that it would play a decisive role for the future of the planet. The US systematically set about making the clash seem real. Its methods included encouraging various kinds of communitarianism (or identity politics), under the pretext of respect for the right to be different; an offensive against secularism (supposedly outdated); praise for religious obscurantism that post-modernism considered just as valid as any other 'ideology'; systematic support for nauseating ethnocracies in Yugoslavia and elsewhere; cynical manipulation (CIA support for terrorist groups mobilized against its adversaries in Afghanistan, Chechnya, Algeria and elsewhere); and a war of lies as well as of bullets and bombs against purported 'terrorism' (whenever terrorism did not serve the purposes of Washington). The idea of a clash of civilizations is an integral part of capitalism's drift towards barbarism, and does not impede the implementation of its plan in any way.

By undermining the fundamental values of universalism, capitalism reveals its weakness. In previous phases of its development, capitalism had been universalistic, though this universalism had remained truncated due to the immanent imperialism of capitalist globalization. In contrast to the political culture of capitalism, in which the past is always present (this culture invariably dominates in contemporary societies), the political culture of the alternative (socialism) can avoid truncation. A socialist culture of the future is not a clever theoretical formulation: it has already penetrated public consciousness. Thus, the real ideologico-cultural conflict of the twenty-first century is not a clash of civilizations, as Samuel Huntington claims, but a conflict in which the political culture of capitalism, drifting towards barbarism, is confronted by that of socialism.

The political culture of capitalism developed its own approach to rights, law and democracy. To understand its contours, it is useful to analyse the thinking that still dominates in America, since capitalist political culture in that country has remained relatively unaffected by the culture of its victims and opponents.

This is a political culture based on the rigorous separation between economic and political life where economic life is dominated by private property and the rights of owners; it ignores the social dimensions of economic life, thereby debasing its concept of 'equality'. Political life is here limited to representative democracy, that is, to the multi-party system and elections. It excludes more developed forms of democracy involving greater participation. The American concept of civil society rounds out our description of American political culture: It is reduced to an amorphous collection of non-governmental organizations that, along with the private sector, are viewed as 'apolitical' (particularly when the organizations are based – as they are most of the time – on 'community', religious, para-religious, ethnic or neighbourhood affiliation). The fact that their methods might sometimes increase inequality is not considered embarrassing in the least, since many of these NGOs do not consider equality to be an important ethical value.

Since the French Revolution, the political cultures of France and continental Europe have differed somewhat from the American pattern, although they have remained wholly within the capitalist camp. Here the values of liberty and equality were on an equal footing from the very start. This meant that the state had to impose forms of 'social management' whenever these values came into conflict. Consequently, it had to regulate capitalistic practices according to the objectives of this social management. The uniqueness of this situation was immediately apparent, since it opened up possibilities (via social struggles) for more participatory democracy. A characteristic of participatory democracy is that it makes public its conflict with the logic of capital accumulation. It proclaims that the 'majority' of citizens can oppose the minority of 'owners' who, in the exclusionary logic of capitalism, are alone recognized as real, active citizens. This cleared the way for recognition of social rights (ignored, on principle, by the American model). These rights involved active legislative and executive intervention by the state, unlike political and civic freedoms, which, considered in isolation, required only that the state refrain from interfering in their implementation. Thus, the concept of a government managing collective services (education, health) to ensure the greatest possible equality plays a major role in social management. The political culture described here paves the way for transcending the limits imposed by the logic of capitalist expansion. The potential for a socialist future already exists in the capitalism of today.

## THE CONFLICT BETWEEN 'MARKET' (CAPITALISM) AND SOCIETY

Contemporary capitalism has entered a phase of genuine and profound transformation with long-term effects. Underlying this transformation is a scientific and technological revolution unlike any of its predecessors. To release this revolution's creative potential it is necessary to transcend the social relationships of capitalism (the private appropriation and domination of capital) and build a 'cognitive economy', as Carlo Vercelone would put it. My analysis, like that of Vercelone, stresses the obsolete character of social relationships under capitalism.[7] However, capitalism is still entrenched, and is going to great lengths to control this revolution and make it comply with the requirements of capitalist reproduction.

Thus, there is a new contradiction – between the potentially liberating effect of developing productive capability and the use of every possible means to maintain the relationships of capitalist social domination. This contradiction highlights more than ever the conflict between the logic of capitalist expansion and the affirmation of social interests. Dominant capital's strategies are tremendously destructive (barbaric), both at the local (i.e. 'national') level and at the global level.

The real alternative with which we are confronted today is between allowing 'market' values alone to control socialization at every level (from the national to the global) and creating forms of socialization based on democracy (in its most profound sense) and introducing them in stages over a long period. All the peoples of the world aspire to social progress, more democratic control over their lives and respect for their national identities. However, the ability of capitalism to satisfy these aspirations in any effective way is declining, both nationally and globally.

To manage this crisis, capitalism needs a political force capable of imposing its barbaric requirements. Without a world state, which is unattainable, the 'American state' will fill this role, as it purportedly wants and is able to do. Since Europe is not 'one nation – one state', but merely an association of nations and states, it does not have the means to contest American leadership of the imperialist triad. Any supposed sharing of responsibility would go no further than substituting NATO (under Washington's control) for the American military; meanwhile, this would not significantly change things for the rest of the world. In this kind of crisis management, the US (or, if need be, triad management under US leadership) would act outside the framework of all international or other law. In sum, the US would turn (is turning?) into a 'rogue' state *par excellence*.

'Global liberalism', the prevailing strategy for managing the crisis, has no future. Consequently, there are two possible scenarios: First, that all nations agree to submit to the supposed dictates of the market. There can be no doubt that in this scenario the future would be very different from what we have known up to now (much worse, and much more barbaric) and maintaining the UN would no longer make sense. The second scenario is not only more desirable but also more likely. Here, states would demand the creation, over a long transitional period, of local social systems and a global system. These systems would demand that the 'market' (and the economy more generally) gradually comply with the needs of socialization based on democracy. In this scenario, the UN would have an important role to play.

Implementation of the second alternative, 'socialization through democratization', requires urgent action on several fronts. First, we need to defeat the current plan – especially that of the US and/or NATO – to control the world militarily. Next, we must (a) re-establish a 'Southern front', but without copying the Bandung Conference model (1955–75); (b) rebuild the European commonwealth project on a solid foundation that would facilitate the development of socialization through democracy; and (c) create a genuine form of 'market socialism' in China that would constitute the first stage in the long transition towards socialism itself. As this suggests, a politicized and structured convergence of social struggles waged at both the national and global levels by the system's victims may and should result in a united front of workers and peasants. The latter constitute half of humankind.[8]

The above framework may be used as a point of departure for identifying the UN's role in managing the proposed alternative 'globalization', which must be consistent with the requirements of socialization through democracy.

## PROPOSALS FOR A UN RENAISSANCE

The proposals in this section are broken down into four sections, each of which describes a role for which the UN should assume major responsibility.

### Proposals for the Political Role of the United Nations

1. Fully restore to the United Nations its apposite and substantial responsibilities: ensuring the security of peoples (and states), guaranteeing the peace and preventing aggression regardless of the motive (the pretext for the war in Iraq proved to be false). This principle must be restated forcefully.

In this vein, it is imperative to condemn the US, NATO and G7 declarations exploited by the powers involved to appropriate 'responsibilities' that are not rightfully theirs. These condemnations must be followed by political strategies to resolve issues affecting the future of countries (such as Yugoslavia, Afghanistan and Iraq) victimized by the intervention of imperialist powers. These strategies must make explicit provision for the withdrawal of foreign armed forces. It is unacceptable to bring the UN in through the back door to justify the *fait accompli* of a condemned intervention. The only role for the UN following this kind of illegal and aggressive intervention would be to facilitate the withdrawal of the aggressors and eventually to enforce the payment of reparations.

2. Restoring this major role to the UN should involve reforming its institutional structure. However, we must remain vigilant. Certain criticisms of the UN can lead to ill-considered proposals that, rather than reinforcing the proper role of the UN, effectively buttress the plan of the imperialist triad to downgrade it. Other criticisms, ostensibly inspired by democracy and realism, may no longer

be valid, particularly attacks on the right to veto. It is quite conceivable, for example, that if France had not wielded this power in the run-up to the war on Iraq, the US would have succeeded in justifying its aggression. Eventual reforms of the Security Council (such as expanding it to include India and Brazil, or increasing the representation of other regions of the world) should be examined meticulously before being proposed. Upgrading the role of the General Assembly and improving the clarity of resolutions (with or without the force of law, depending on the assumptions made) regarding Security Council action could provide a good starting point for these deliberations.

3. Upgrading the role of the UN does not mean returning to a position of support for the absolute sovereignty of the state (as sole representative of the people). In the next section, I develop proposals that seek to replace the exclusive sovereignty of states with the sovereignty of peoples.

4. Restoring the UN's role must lead to real progress in solving the major crises of our time. A few powers, chiefly the United States, bear the primary responsibility for these crises, which they have fomented (or facilitated) by creating turmoil and unrest. Consequently, the UN needs to establish:

(1) An interposition force between Palestine and Israel (based on the pre-1967 Green Line borders). Israel would not defy severe economic sanctions like those imposed on other nations.

(2) The introduction of peacekeeping forces in regions of occupied former Yugoslavia (Bosnia and Kosovo), as was done in African nations that were victims of so-called 'civil' wars.

If necessary, the UN could plan these actions in close collaboration with regional organizations (the European Union, greater Europe and the African Union).

5. The UN must take an active role in developing a comprehensive disarmament plan. This plan must entail much more than the Non-Proliferation Treaty which, in its current form, strengthens the monopoly on the production of weapons of mass destruction held by those who have proved to be the most frequent users of these weapons! Disarmament must begin with the *major* powers and be subject to UN control, which would replace the previous bipolar control of the two superpowers. General disarmament must include evacuation of all military bases set up beyond national borders,

especially those the United States plans to use in extending its military control over the planet.

6. The UN must take an active role in defining the framework and procedures for future humanitarian interventions. There can be no question that this kind of intervention is needed once it is understood that society can, unfortunately, degenerate into savagery (ethnocide, 'religious' or 'ethnic' cleansing and apartheid). But neither the decision nor the implementation of intervention must be left to the imperialist powers, since they can manipulate it for their own purposes, apply double standards and so on as we have seen only too clearly of late.

7. In a similar vein, the UN will have to assume principal collective responsibility in defining 'terrorism'. It must also decide when to take action to eliminate terrorist activity and monitor this action. It must not entrust the 'war on terror' to the major powers, least of all the United States.

8. Finally, proposals for a 'World Parliament' made up of representatives of national parliaments (sometimes non-existent and only rarely representative of the people in any meaningful way) do not have to be bland or unrealistic. Progress in this area is possible even when the global democracy these parliaments uphold is not as mature as its national counterparts.

## Proposals Concerning Peoples' Rights and the Development of International Law

1. The present proposals start from the assumption that the concept of state sovereignty must be redefined. Current public opinion generally holds that all human beings are responsible not only for what occurs locally, that is, within the states of which they are citizens, but also globally. This clearly constitutes a step forward in collective consciousness and puts to the test the older concept (found in numerous accords from the Treaty of Westphalia to the UN Charter) that the sovereignty of states is absolute and exclusive.

The contradiction between this form of sovereignty and peoples' rights is very real. However, it cannot be resolved by eliminating either of its two underlying conditions, that is, either (a) peoples' rights (which can be undermined by upholding the old absolutist concept of sovereignty), or (b) sovereignty (which can be undermined for the purposes of intervention and manipulation by the imperialist powers).

The contradiction can only be transcended if real progress is made in democratizing all societies. Admittedly, in affirming the need for democracy, each society must proceed at its own pace. This is where an international organization could play an important role: it could champion the progress made and accelerate its concrete impact on the exercise of power. The UN is the ideal forum for thrashing out these issues; it should be debating them unflaggingly.

2. Certain declarations, pacts and conventions are already making progress in broadening definitions of human rights. In fact, two pacts eventually complemented the Universal Declaration of Human Rights of 1948. Their joint adoption clearly confirmed a shift from a restricted concept of human rights, limited to civil and political rights, to a broader concept encompassing social and collective rights. The two pacts in question are the International Covenant on Economic, Social and Cultural Rights and the International Covenant on Civil and Political Rights, both adopted in Teheran in 1968. In 1986, the UN General Assembly validated this change by officially proclaiming the Declaration on the Right to Development to be an integral part of the corpus of human rights. However, the United Nations must not let up in this undertaking since these texts are inadequate in their present form, especially since they are constantly being challenged and, for the most part, have not been enforced. In fact, some parties, notably the triad powers, claim that they cannot be implemented; they are uneasy about the economic, social and collective aspects of these texts. Development rights have become the focus of extensive analysis in 'private' circles (such as the International Lelio Basso Foundation for the Rights and Liberation of Peoples in Rome); they also receive enthusiastic support from partial, quasi-state alliances, like the non-aligned nations. In practice, however, development rights are not recognized as prior and universal rights of individuals and peoples. Likewise, the right of access to land of all the world's peasants (half of humanity), and to human and sustainable conditions in which to cultivate this land (irrefutably part of the same logic), has not yet received even minimal recognition.

The UN's universal framework should be used to clarify rights that have not yet been fully recognized, some of which are still in embryonic form. In this category are rights that affirm the principle of equality between women and men, and make provision for their implementation in practice. In addition, 'collective' rights protecting cultural, linguistic, religious and other 'identities' must be extensively debated to define their meaning and determine their areas of application. Stated differently, these rights should not be able to challenge the principle of secularism or of the protection of the individual.

Many so-called realists attach little importance to charters of rights, which are useful only if measures are taken to implement them effectively. It is a mistake to underestimate the importance of law, however, which can become an effective weapon in ensuring compliance with these charters. A system of international tribunals could be set up for this purpose (I will return to the question of courts and tribunals later).

3. The UN must exercise great care in formulating international business and commercial law.

The expansion of global economic relations of every kind makes it increasingly important to improve international business law. However, this area of law should not override national strategies or the basic rights of individuals and peoples. It follows that accords such as the Multilateral Agreement on Investment would be unacceptable.

Furthermore, we must not entrust formulation of this law exclusively to the party representing the interests of dominant capital (the 'transnational club'), as is done in WTO projects. I cannot overestimate this point, given that the party in question sets itself up as legislator, judge and beneficiary in its plan for a business court, over which it has sole control. Rarely have the fundamental principles of law and justice been so brazenly trampled underfoot. Nor is it more acceptable for US courts (whose impartiality is, to say the least, questionable) and US law (particularly primitive) to dominate commercial regulation practices, though this is in fact occurring with greater frequency.

International commercial law should be formulated through transparent discussions that bring together all interested parties. Discussions would include not only business groups, but also workers (not only from the industries involved but also from nations that are affected by the legislation) and states. There is currently no forum for conducting this debate except the UN (including the International Labour Organization (ILO), which is a UN agency).

4. The UN cannot be transformed overnight into a 'world state', 'world government' or even a supranational authority with vast powers in a number of fields. Recognizing this fact, however, does not preclude the possibility of embarking upon a process that in the longer term will lead to desired transformations.

We must, however, exercise caution in reviewing proposals to transform the United Nations. There is currently an outpouring of proposals to ally 'civil society' (in Washington's understanding of the term) with the life of the United Nations. Some of them would like to give the 'corporate world' a pivotal role in this alliance. The defenders of this UN 'reform' consistently ignore the working class – the majority of human beings who must contend with the tiny minority of billionaires.

## Proposals for the Economic Management of Globalization

1. The supposedly deregulated globalization currently in force is in fact just one form of globalization among several. Currently, dominant global capital (comprised chiefly of the transnationals) and the G7 political leaders who are beholden to it have virtually complete and exclusive responsibility for regulation. It will be necessary to replace this form of globalization – which is not inevitable, irreplaceable or acceptable – with institutionalized global regulation premised on the requirements of socialization through democracy. In the future, institutionalized global regulation will support and complement national and regional regulation, which will eventually be used everywhere. Challenges and conflicts among the various levels of modern economic management will be commonplace.

The task ahead is complicated. We can expect that, for a long time, successes will be modest, at best, even if the UN lends its support. The challenge should not be spurned; it can provide positive benefits for both nations and workers.

2. Given its devastating impact, international debt may provide a good starting point for debates on the role of the United Nations in managing the world economy.

The dominant discourse assigns sole responsibility for the debt to borrowing nations, whose actions, it maintains, are indefensible (corruption, complacency and irrationality of policy-makers, extreme nationalism, etc.). The truth, however, is quite different. The World Bank, in particular, but also many major private banks in the United States, Europe and Japan, as well as a number of transnationals, bear a major share of the responsibility, although this is seldom discussed.

Corruption has piggybacked on these policies, once again aided and abetted by the lenders of capital (the World Bank, the private banks and the transnationals) and the heads of affected nations from the Southern Hemisphere and the (former) Eastern bloc. A systematic audit of these debts is urgently required. It would demonstrate that a major portion of these debts is illegal.

The debt service burden is utterly intolerable, not only for the poorest countries of the South, but even for those who are better off. When, following World War I, Germany was ordered to pay reparations amounting to 7 per cent of its exports, liberal economists of the period concluded that the burden was unendurable and that the country's production system could not adjust to the new requirements. Today, economists of the same liberal school have no compunctions about suggesting that Third World economies bend to debt servicing requirements that are five or even six times more onerous. In reality, debt servicing today amounts to plundering the wealth and labour of populations in the Southern Hemisphere (and the (former) Eastern bloc). The plunder is especially lucrative since it has managed to turn the planet's poorest countries into net exporters of capital to the North. It is also brutal, as it frees dominant capital from the management of production. The debt is due, that's all. It is the responsibility of the states involved (rather than the lenders of capital) to extract the necessary work from their populations. Thus, dominant capitalism is freed from all responsibility and worry.

There are various categories of debt that require different responses: debts arising from loans used for odious or immoral purposes should be repudiated unilaterally (following audit). In addition, the creditors should reimburse the payments made on these debts at the same rates of interest the debtors had to pay. We would then see that, in fact, the North is indebted to the South, its victims. There are also debts arising from loans of questionable origin such as those provided by the financial powers of the North (including the World Bank). Most of these loans were not invested in projects and payments were concealed (the lenders were well aware of this). Any court worthy of its name would consider such debts illegal. In such cases, the bank should be put on trial. Finally, there are, of course, debts arising from acceptable loans. In such cases, acknowledgement of the debt cannot be questioned.

The debt management proposed for Heavily Indebted Poor Countries (HIPC) belongs to a very different type of logic. Their entire debt is considered perfectly 'legitimate', even though it is not subject to any kind of review or audit. This is because the debt management proposal is regarded as charity. This stance is unacceptable. On the one hand, the proposal purportedly lightens the burden for the very poor; on the other hand, it imposes additional draconian conditions on them. In so doing, it places them permanently in a situation closely resembling that of colonies administered directly from abroad.

In addition to the suggested audit and the adoption of measures to facilitate regularization of accounts, we must continue developing an international law on debt to ensure that these kinds of situations do not recur. For now, this type of law exists only in embryonic form. In addition, we need to set up genuine tribunals (much more useful than arbitration boards) to enforce the law in this matter.

3. Restoring full responsibility for organizing the world economic system to the United Nations would involve redefining the roles of (a) its major internal institutions, particularly the United Nations Conference on Trade and Development (UNCTAD) and the International Labour Organization (ILO), and (b) its external institutions: the World Trade Organization (WTO), the International Monetary Fund (IMF) and the World Bank (WB).

The main priorities in this exercise should be as follows:

(1) To breathe new life into UNCTAD and identify its new (or revised) functions, including: (i) developing a global framework for a foreign investment code to regulate delocalization and protect the workers of all concerned parties; (ii) negotiating market access for the various negotiating parties at the national and regional levels. These proposals should seek to reverse the total marginalization of UNCTAD that has occurred with the transfer of its powers to the WTO. UNCTAD's role must be rethought, however, from top to bottom, if it is to break away from the strict control of a clique of transnational corporations.

(2) To revitalize the ILO, not in the way suggested by this organization's current management, but by strengthening workers' rights.

(3) To renegotiate the global monetary system and institutionalize regional arrangements to manage exchange rate stability. This would be the responsibility of a new 'IMF' in charge of interlinking regional systems. (It would have nothing in common with the current organization of the same name.) In the current system, the IMF, which is not in charge of the dominant currency system (which includes the dollar, euro, yen, pound sterling and

Swiss franc), operates as if it were a joint colonial monetary authority (for the triad) managing the finances of dependent nations. It subjects these nations to 'structural adjustment' so that it can (i) plunder their resources for the benefit of floating capital, and (ii) bleed them dry financially through debt servicing.

(4) To build a global capital market worthy of the name that would (i) direct funds towards productive investments (in the North and South), and (ii) discourage the so-called speculative flow of funds (the Tobin tax[9] might fall within its agenda). This would challenge the role of the World Bank (Ministry of Propaganda to the G7) and the WTO (executing agency for the transnationals).

Global natural resource management provides the best introduction to the possibilities for global economic management. Theoretically, access to natural resources is a matter of national sovereignty. Nevertheless, sovereignty is not always respected: colonialism destroys it; 'geopolitical' or 'geostrategic' power undermines it. The North's disproportionate access to the planet's resources is the root cause of its squandering of these resources. It also suggests the impossibility of extending the North's consumption patterns to the South, which, subjected to the prevailing form of globalization, becomes the victim of 'global apartheid'. Environmental movements have increased public awareness of the problem's tragic dimensions. However, they have not really managed to get the global power system (epitomized by the Rio and Kyoto conferences, which were evaluated by the Johannesburg conference of August 2002) to accept effective and efficient democratic management of resources at the global level. There is also a link between the militarization of globalization and the hegemonic power's objective of controlling the planet's natural resources.

In theory, the resources being developed are those of 'actually existing capitalism'. The latter practises short-term thinking (financial profitability), since the transnationals, who are making the decisions, understand no other approach. The way capitalism develops resources is a perfect illustration of the alleged rationality of market management. It reveals that, from the standpoint of people's long-term interests, it is, in fact, irrational. Debate on sustainable development originates with an awareness of the contradiction between market interests and the interests of humanity. However, this discourse often fails to draw concrete and practical conclusions from this contradiction.

The alternative to market rationality is rational (sustainable) and democratic management (at the local and world system levels) of natural resources. There are several practical proposals available, but until now they have only been put forward indirectly. Examples include a global tax on rent associated with access to and development of these resources. The proceeds from this tax would be redistributed to the affected populations in such a way as to promote the development of poor countries and regions and to discourage waste. This could be the beginning of a global tax regime.

The topic encompasses a large number of resources – minerals, oil, water and the atmosphere. To start, however, the debate should focus on two areas – oil and water. To take the case of water: We must demand UN management of water, the common property of all humanity without which there is no life. Water has numerous uses, but I will restrict my discussion here to its uses in the field of agriculture, which consumes most of it.

Nature distributes water among the planet's rural societies in an extremely uneven way. In some regions of the world, there is plentiful fresh water within reach. However, in arid and semi-arid regions, people must draw water from rivers or deep wells and distribute it by irrigation over the entire surface of their farmland. In these regions, the cost of water is high. Is assigning a price to resources such as water the only way of dealing with their scarcity?

Locking into the logic of conventional economics and market alienation (on which this economics is based) and bowing to an ethic of competition aligned with unbridled globalization leaves only two choices: accepting systematically lower pay for some workers or ceasing to produce. The liberal approach to globalization condemns vast agricultural regions of the planet to extinction.

We must face the fact that the world consists of persons, peoples, nations and states. They occupy their own territories, though the natural conditions in each locality are not identical. Conventional economics ignores this reality, replacing it with an imaginary globalized world in which all aspects of social life and the human environment are commoditized at the planetary level. This allows it to justify the unilateral objectives of capitalism without worrying about social reality. If the liberals who defended this fundamentalist capitalism were consistent, they would conclude that the optimum sustainable utilization of natural resources (in this case water) requires massive relocation of the world's populations. The contours of this relocation would be determined by the unequal worldwide distribution of this resource. Were this to occur, water would become a 'commons', i.e. a common good or property of all humanity.

For the time being, water is a common good only to the extent that it is common to one nation or one territory. In a given territory, when water is relatively scarce, it must be rationed. Market regulation and an acceptable system of subsidies and taxes can ensure that all inhabitants share the cost of access. The system adopted will depend on compromises related to internal social conditions and the way the country is integrated into the world economy. Thus, there are compromises between peasants and consumers of food products; between development strategies based on a particular vision of society and the export requirements eventually needed to implement this vision (for example, exports that are 'naturally' uncompetitive could be subsidized). The compromises will vary with time and place.

A 'law of peoples and humanity' will aim to provide solutions to these problems. However, a law of this type dealing with water does not yet exist since, within its borders, every country is in principle free to use (and to sell) ground and surface water as it sees fit. Agreements on water management, when they do exist, deal only with the particularities of international treaties. Making rapid progress in developing a genuine law of peoples and humanity is of paramount importance. International business law was designed to serve the interests of capital, and is currently controlled exclusively by the international institutions (especially the WTO) designed for this purpose. Consequently, it cannot possibly serve as a substitute for a genuine peoples' law that would manage water as a 'common good' (humanity's common heritage). On the contrary, the *raison-d'être* of international business law is antithetical to the spirit of such a law.

### Proposals on the Institutionalization of International Justice

International courts of justice already exist. Some even existed before the creation of the United Nations; others came into being recently, in conjunction with war crimes and crimes against humanity. However, the effectiveness of these institutions of international justice is extremely limited: they have limited jurisdiction and certain powers (spearheaded by the US) refuse to recognize their legitimacy. Our first task is, therefore, to carry out a comprehensive review of existing institutions in the area of international justice, critically analysing their shortcomings and identifying any legal gaps that must gradually be closed.

There are also 'courts of global public opinion'. They do not have legal status, yet fulfil a very useful role in informing the public about important issues (good examples are the Russell Tribunal, which sought to expose war crimes during the Vietnam War, and the World Tribunal on Iraq). We should follow their example, support their actions and give them wider coverage, although they should not interfere with campaigns to create recognized international courts responsible for enforcing the law.[10]

We must also develop a system of international courts of justice to implement proposals on UN responsibilities. Ideally, proposals aiming to strengthen the legal aspects of UN actions would involve three groups of courts.

The first group would deal with the political aspects of globalization.

If the United Nations is to judge the transborder actions or interventions of states, whatever the motives, then a UN authority should determine if these actions are justified or should be condemned. Of course, the International Court of Justice in The Hague exercises jurisdiction in this area, although it does not have any power of enforcement as we have seen in the Nicaragua case in which, despite the fact the ICJ found in favour of Nicaragua against the US's intervention, nothing came of this ruling since only the Security Council, on which the US has a veto, had the power to enforce it.[11] Similarly, a recent and unequivocal ruling by the ICJ concerning the Wall of Shame in occupied Palestine led to nothing more than a non-binding declaration of the UN General Assembly, whose role was limited to making recommendations. Consequently, the jurisdiction of the ICJ must be reviewed and its powers broadened. The victimized state and the UN General Assembly should have the right not only to appeal the decision of the Court but also to be satisfied that a decision in its favour – even if contested by the state responsible for the intervention – would have consequences.

Failing this, the imperialist powers (with the US in the lead) will never be held accountable for their violations of international law, even when these violations are irrefutable. Even if they are held accountable, they might never have to face any punishment – except that exacted by mobilized publics.

The second group would strengthen the rights of individuals and nations recognized by the UN.

Such courts could draw their inspiration from the European Court of Justice, to which victimized individuals or groups can appeal directly, as long as their claims fall within the court's jurisdiction. As with the European Court, these victims would not have to get prior approval from their country. It might be advisable to broaden the jurisdiction of international justice (so as to include, among other things, social rights) and, to this end, plan two distinct divisions – one for individual rights and another for the rights of nations.

The third group would manage commercial law disputes.

The court of commercial law could also have various divisions, each with a specific area of competence. A criminal division would try indictable economic crimes. The case of Bhopal demonstrates the outrageous impunity the transnationals currently enjoy, an impunity that any plan aimed at socialization through democratization must contest.

Finally, another division could be empowered to deal with litigation over external debt.

The present proposals are to be sure ambitious, and accomplishing even a few of them will take time and even more effort. However, the future begins today, so there is no reason to postpone implementing an action plan if we want things to improve.

I do not think anything can be gained by asking governments immediately to embark upon a 'Reform of the United Nations'. For the moment, prevailing power relationships are such that their reforms would probably achieve few positive results. In fact, there is every reason to fear that their reforms would be incorporated into the dominant imperialist strategies, since the aim of the leading imperialist power is to further marginalize this international body and control it for its own ends.

Consequently, it is necessary to tackle the problem in a different way – by setting our sights on public opinion. We should set up *ad hoc* international commissions (one for each of our concerns) that will provide reports and proposals to the vast nebula of social movements that work with the national, regional and global 'Social Forums'. The *Forum Mondial des Alternatives* (World Forum for Alternatives) could employ the network of correspondents and associates in its critical think tanks to help coordinate the undertaking. Once it has made sufficient progress, the commissions' work must be used by vast, worldwide campaigns with precisely defined goals for each commission. This would help to rectify the inequitable power relationships that define today's world.

## ACKNOWLEDGEMENT

The translator wishes to thank Jim Best for his assistance.

## NOTES

1  See Samir Amin, *Obsolescent Capitalism* (New York: Zed Books, 2003).
2  Ibid., chapter 1.
3  Interview with Samir Amin: Yves Berthelot, 'UN Intellectual History', United Nations, New York, April 2002.
4  I wrote on this topic even before the collapse of the USSR, noting that the Middle East was high on the agenda in this global policy strategy. See Amin, *Obsolescent Capitalism*, pp. 95ff.
5  Samir Amin, 'Globalism or Apartheid on a Global Scale?' in Immanuel Wallerstein (ed.), *The Modern World System in the Longue Durée* (New York: Paradigm Publishers, 2004), chapter 1.
6  Samir Amin, 'WTO Recipe for World Hunger', *Ahram Weekly* No. 657 (September 2003).
7  Amin, *Obsolescent Capitalism*, chapter 3.
8  Samir Amin, *The Liberal Virus* (New York: Pluto Press, 2004), 29–42.
9  The Tobin tax, initially proposed by James Tobin (an economic adviser in the Kennedy Administration), refers to taxes on financial transactions, currency trading and speculation across borders. While a subsidiary goal of the tax could be to produce revenue to support (domestic or international) social initiatives, its primary aim is to reduce short-term currency speculation with the goal of enhancing national autonomy and limiting financial meltdowns.
10  On the World Tribunal on Iraq see Jayan Nayar's chapter in this volume.
11  On 27 June 1986, the Court ordered the United States to pay reparations amounting to $17 billion (US) to Nicaragua, but the latter never received a cent.

# Notes on Contributors

**Samir Amin** is Egyptian-born and trained in Paris. He is the director of the Third World Forum, Dakar, Senegal, and co-founder of the World Forum for Alternatives. Amin is the author of numerous books including, recently: *The Liberal Virus: Permanent War and the Americanization of the World; Eurocentrism; The Empire of Chaos;* and *Spectres of Capitalism.* He was the director of IDEP (African Institute for Economic Development and Planning) from 1970 to 1980.

**Andrew Arato** is The Dorothy Hart Hirshon Professor of Political and Social Theory and a professor in Sociology at New School University. Author and editor of numerous articles and books including: 'The Occupation of Iraq and the Difficult Transition from Dictatorship' *(Constellations 2003); Civil Society, Constitution and Legitimacy; Habermas on Law, Democracy and Legitimacy; From Neo-Marxism to Democratic Theory; Civil Society and Political Theory* (with Jean L. Cohen); and *The Essential Frankfurt School Reader.* Arato is a member of the USIP/UNDP Workshop on Constitution Making, Conflict Resolution and Peace Building. He is currently working on developing a theory of 'post sovereign' constitution making, as well as a volume on the theory and the history of dictatorship.

**Amy Bartholomew** is an Associate Professor of Law at Carleton University, Ottawa, Canada. She was an expert witness at the BRussells Tribunal in April 2004, part of the World Tribunal on Iraq, and on the panel of advocates at its culminating session in Istanbul in June 2005. She is a member of the Advisory Board of the BRussells Tribunal. She has published on human rights and legal and political theory including (with Jennifer Breakspear) 'Human Rights as Swords of Empire' *(Socialist Register* 2004) and is currently completing a manuscript on 'justice without guarantees'.

**Nehal Bhuta** is the Arthur C. Helton Fellow in the International Justice Program of Human Rights Watch. He is currently observing the trial of Saddam Hussein. In 2003, he was a consultant to the International Centre for Transitional Justice, during which he co-led a field mission to Iraq to interview hundreds of Iraqis to assess their interests in transitional justice. In 2001–02, he advised Oxfam Australia and two East Timor human rights non-governmental organizations about international justice mechanisms for East Timor. Bhuta has published numerous articles in the area of human rights including 'A Global State of Exception? The United States and World Order' (*Constellations* 2003).

**Doris E. Buss** is an Assistant Professor of Law, Carleton University. She teaches and researches in the areas of international law and human rights, international criminal law, women's rights, feminist theory, and social movements, and is the author (with Didi Herman) of *Globalizing Family Values: The International Politics of the Christian Right* and co-editor (with Ambreena Manji) of *International Law: Modern Feminist Approaches*.

**David Coates** is the Worrell Professor of Anglo-American Studies at Wake Forest University in North Carolina. He previously held personal chairs at the Universities of Leeds and Manchester in the UK. He has written extensively on labour politics and comparative political economy, including most recently *Blair's War* (with Joel Krieger) and *Prolonged Labour: The Slow Birth of New Labour Britain*.

**Sam Gindin** is the Packer Visiting Professor in Social Justice at York University, Toronto and is former Chief Economist and Research Director of the Canadian Auto Workers, and author of *The Birth and Transformation of a Union*. His essay entitled 'Capitalism and the Terrain of Social Justice' (*Monthly Review* 2001) won the Daniel Singer Prize in 2001. He is author of many articles, including, recently, articles with Leo Panitch on the new imperialism and the making of global capitalism, including 'Finance and American Empire' (*Socialist Register* 2005) and 'Superintending Global Capital' (*New Left Review* 2005).

**Jürgen Habermas** is Professor Emeritus of Philosophy at the University of Frankfurt and Permanent Visiting Professor of Philosophy at Northwestern University. The author of such classic texts as *The Structural Transformation of the Public Sphere, The Theory of Communicative Action and Between Facts and Norms*, he was named one of the world's 100 most influential people in 2004 by *Time* magazine. Professor Habermas was awarded the Kyoto Prize for Arts and Philosophy (2004), Spain's Prince of Asturias Prize, considered to be the Spanish speaking world's Nobel Prize (2003), and the Peace Prize of the German Book Retailers' Society (2001).

**Denis Halliday** served between 1994 and 1998 as Assistant Secretary-General of the United Nations, and was appointed by Secretary-General Kofi Annan to the post of UN Humanitarian Coordinator in Iraq and administrator of the Oil-for-Food programme as of 1 September 1997. He resigned from his post in Iraq and from the United Nations as a whole in September 1998, protesting the economic sanctions and the inefficiency of the programme.

**Fuyuki Kurasawa** is an Assistant Professor of Sociology at York University and a Faculty Fellow of the Center for Cultural Sociology at Yale University. In 2003–04, he was a Fulbright Scholar and Visiting Fellow at New York University and Yale University, and was named a 'Young Canadian Leader' by *The Globe and Mail* in 2000. Kurasawa is the author of *The Ethnological Imagination: A Cross-Cultural Critique of Modernity*, and is currently completing a book on practices of global justice.

**Jayan Nayar** is a lecturer of law at the University of Warwick, England. His primary area of interest is in developing grassroots peoples' perspectives on, and praxes of, law. He has been involved in peoples' tribunal initiatives since 2000 when he coordinated the organization of a Permanent Peoples' Tribunal on Corporate Wrongs at the University of Warwick. In 2002, he founded the Peoples' Law Programme at the Lelio Basso International Foundation for which he acted as Coordinator until July 2005. He has been a member of the International Coordinating Committee of the World Tribunal on Iraq since January 2004, and was the Coordinator of the Rome Session on Media Wrongs Against Truth and Humanity, February 2005. He is currently working on a series of books on peoples' law, and on peoples' texts and tribunals.

**Leo Panitch** is Canada Research Chair in Comparative Political Economy and Distinguished Research Professor of Political Science at York University, Toronto. He is co-editor of the *Socialist Register* and author of numerous articles on the politics of labour, corporatism, and the state in *Studies in Political Economy, Labour/Le Travail, Comparative Political Studies, Political Studies, Politics and Society,*

*British Journal of Sociology, Monthly Review, New Left Review* and *Historical Materialism*. His recent books include *The End of Parliamentary Socialism and Renewing Socialism: Democracy, Strategy and Imagination*. His recent work on globalization and the state, including 'The New Imperial State' (*New Left Review* 2000) and 'Global Capitalism and American Empire (*Socialist Register* 2004) have been widely translated, and he is currently working with Sam Gindin on a book on the making of global capitalism.

**Ulrich K. Preuss** is Professor of Law and Politics at the Free University Berlin and a Judge at the Constitutional Court of the *Land Bremen*. He has worked on constitutional transition in the post-communist states, the development of a European constitution, in particular on the concept of European citizenship, and on the relations between liberal constitutionalism and multiculturalism. Preuss's books include *Constitutional Revolution: The Link Between Constitutionalism and Progress, Instititutional Design in Post Communist Societies* (with Claus Offe and Jon Elster) and *Kreig, Verbrechen, Blasphemie: Zum den Wandel bewaffneter Gewalt* (2002, 2nd ed. 2003), which addresses the legal and moral questions of 11 September 2001 and the role of the US in international politics and law. He is also the author of works on human rights, including 'The Force, Frailty, and Future of Human Rights under Globalization' (*Theoretical Inquiries in Law*).

**Trevor Purvis** is an Assistant Professor in the Department of Law and the Institute of Political Economy at Carleton University, Ottawa, where he teaches courses related to international law and legal theory, race and ethnicity, recognition/identity/citizenship, and transformations of the regulatory state. He has published articles related to theories of citizenship, governance and state transformation, nationalism, and ideology. His present research focuses on the nature of the international rule of law and the foundations of legal legitimacy in international affairs.

**Hans von Sponeck** is a former United Nations Assistant Secretary-General. He joined the UN Development Programme in 1968, and worked in Ghana, Turkey, Botswana, Pakistan and India, before becoming Director of the European Office of UNDP in Geneva. Serving 32 years with the organization, his last post succeeded Denis Halliday as UN Humanitarian Coordinator for Iraq and administrator of the Oil-for-Food programme in October 1998. Sponeck resigned in February 2000, in protest of the international policy toward Iraq, including sanctions. His book, *Iraq Autopsy* was presented at the October 2005 Frankfurt Book Fair and will be available in English, Arabic and German.

**Peter Swan** is an Associate Professor and Chair of the Department of Law at Carleton University, Ottawa, Canada. His research interests include legal and political theory, environmental law and politics, and the relationship between law and democratic politics. His current research looks at critical legal theory as a response to social crises in modernity. He is co-editor of *Law, Regulation and Governance* (with Michael MacNeil and Neil Sargent).

**Reg Whitaker** is Distinguished Research Professor (Emeritus) at York University, and Adjunct Professor of Political Science at the University of Victoria. Among his recent books are: *The End of Privacy: How Total Surveillance Is Becoming a Reality; Canada and the Cold War* (with Steve Hewitt); and *Cold War Canada: The Making of a National Insecurity State* (with Gary Marcuse). He is presently acting as an adviser to the Canadian Commission of Inquiry into the matter of Maher Arar.

**Haifa Zangana**, a painter and a writer, was born in Baghdad and graduated from University of Baghdad, School of Pharmacy. She joined the Communist party – Central Command – in 1968. She was imprisoned by the Ba'ath regime during 1971–72. Haifa then left Iraq to work with the PLO in 1975, moving between Syria and Lebanon, and moved to London at the onset of the civil war in Lebanon, in 1976. She is a frequent contributor to newspapers, including the *Guardian*, and co-founder of Act Together (a campaigning group for UK based Iraqi and non-Iraqi women) and a founding member of International Association for Contemporary Iraqi Studies (IACIS).

# Index

*Compiled by Sue Carlton*